THE CAMBRIDGE COMPANION TO
GREEK AND ROMAN THEATRE

This series of essays by prominent academics and practitioners investigates in detail the history of performance in the classical Greek and Roman world. Beginning with the earliest examples of 'dramatic' presentation in the epic cycles and reaching through to the latter days of the Roman Empire and beyond, the Companion covers many aspects of these broad presentational societies. Dramatic performances that are text-based form only one part of cultures where presentation is a major element of all social and political life. Individual chapters range across a two-thousand-year timescale, and include specific chapters on acting traditions, masks, properties, playing places, festivals, religion and drama, comedy and society, and commodity, concluding with the dramatic legacy of myth and the modern media. The book addresses the needs of students of drama and classics, as well as anyone with an interest in the theatre's history and practice.

A complete list of books in the series is at the back of the book

Funerary vase of an actor contemplating a mask, 360–350 BC.

THE CAMBRIDGE
COMPANION TO
GREEK AND ROMAN
THEATRE

THE CAMBRIDGE
COMPANION TO
GREEK AND ROMAN
THEATRE

EDITED BY
MARIANNE McDONALD AND
J. MICHAEL WALTON

CAMBRIDGE
UNIVERSITY PRESS

CAMBRIDGE UNIVERSITY PRESS
Cambridge, New York, Melbourne, Madrid, Cape Town, Singapore, São Paulo

Cambridge University Press
The Edinburgh Building, Cambridge CB2 8RU, UK

Published in the United States of America by Cambridge University Press, New York

www.cambridge.org
Information on this title: www.cambridge.org/9780521542340

© Cambridge University Press 2007

First published 2007

Printed in the United Kingdom at the University Press, Cambridge

A catalogue record for this publication is available from the British Library

ISBN 978-0-521-83456-8 hardback
ISBN 978-0-521-54234-0 paperback

CONTENTS

CONTENTS

ILLUSTRATIONS

NOTES ON CONTRIBUTORS

RICHARD BEACHAM is Professor at King's College London. A native of Virginia, he earned his BA and doctorate at Yale University. He is the author of numerous theatre-historical books and articles and of a series of both videos and digital publications about ancient theatre and its legacy; he is also a translator of Roman comedy. He has directed many international research initiatives including THEATRON, a virtual-reality-based teaching and research module in European theatre history, and, together with Prof. James Packer, the Pompey Project, a documentation and excavation of Rome's first permanent theatre. He has worked as visiting professor at Yale, and Museum Scholar at the Getty Museum, where his translation of a Roman comedy was presented on a replica stage based upon his research. His current work includes a book with Hugh Denard on Roman domestic decor and the theatre, and a documentary history of Roman theatre (Cambridge University Press). He directs the 3D Visualisation Group at King's College Centre for Computing in the Humanities.

HUGH DENARD earned his BA in Theatre and Classical Civilizations at Trinity College, Dublin and his MA and PhD in the Classics and Drama Departments of the University of Exeter. He was lecturer at the School of Theatre Studies at the University of Warwick until 2005, before moving to King's College London, where he continues to publish within the areas of ancient drama in performance, the reception of ancient drama since antiquity, and the application of advanced visualization technologies to research in the arts and humanities. He is editor of *Didaskalia: Ancient Theatre Today*, directs a number of grant-funded research projects and is Associate Director of the 3D Visualisation Group. A book on Roman theatricalism, domestic art and architecture, co-authored with Richard Beacham, will be published by Yale University Press in 2007.

SANDER M. GOLDBERG studied Classics and Theatre at Indiana University and University College London. As Professor of Classics at UCLA, he teaches a wide range of courses in Greek and Roman literature and culture, as well as the reception of ancient theatre in the modern world. His publications include *The Making of Menander's Comedy* (1980), *Understanding Terence* (1986) and, most recently,

Constructing Literature in the Roman Republic (2005). From 1991 to 1995 he was editor of the *Transactions of the American Philological Association*.

FRITZ GRAF is Professor of Greek and Latin and Director of Epigraphy at the Ohio State University. His publications include *Nordionische Kulte* (1985), *Greek Mythology* (1985, Engl. 1993), *Magic in the Ancient World* (1997), and *Der Lauf des rollenden Jahres. Zeit und Kalender in Rom* (1997); he has also completed a book on Apollo. His current research concerns show a growing interest in the religions of the Imperial epoch.

RICHARD GREEN is Emeritus Professor of Classical Archaeology at the University of Sydney. He is the author of a number of books and articles on the archaeological evidence for performance in Greek theatre, including *Theatre in Ancient Greek Society* (1994) and *Images of the Greek Theatre* with E. W. Handley, with whom he is currently working on a book called *The Theatre of the Greeks*. He is Director of the excavations at the site of the ancient theatre in Paphos, Cyprus.

MARK GRIFFITH was educated in Classics at Cambridge University. He is the author of commentaries on Aeschylus' *Prometheus Bound* and Sophocles' *Antigone*, as well as numerous articles on Greek drama, poetry, and performance. He has taught at Harvard and Berkeley, and is Professor of Classics, and of Theater, Dance, and Performance Studies, at the University of California, Berkeley. He is currently working on a book on Aristophanes' *Frogs*.

JON HESK is Senior Lecturer in Greek and Classical Studies at the University of St Andrews. He is the author of *Deception and Democracy in Classical Athens* (2000) and *Sophocles' Ajax* (2003). He is currently working on the significance of abusive verbal exchanges in Greek drama and Athenian culture. He is also thinking about the Greek dramatists' representation of class identity and the uses and abuses of Greek and Roman political thought in more recent times.

GRAHAM LEY is the author of *A Short Introduction to the Ancient Greek Theater* (1991; revised edition, 2007), and of *The Theatricality of Greek Tragedy: Playing Space and Chorus* (2007). He has directed Greek tragedies, translated Sophocles' *Women of Trachis* and *Philoctetes* for the Everyman series, and worked as a dramaturge, notably for John Barton's *Tantalus*. His interests lie in the original conditions of performance for ancient drama, on which he has published many essays and studies, most recently 'The Nameless and the Named: *Techne* and Technology in Ancient Athenian Performance' (2005). He is Professor of Drama and Theory at the University of Exeter, where he currently leads a research project on the history of British Asian theatre.

GREGORY McCART held a personal Chair in Theatre Arts at the University of Southern Queensland, Australia. His translations of ancient Greek tragedy have been both published and performed. Productions include Sophocles' *Oedipus the King* and *Oedipus at Colonus*, Euripides' *The Bacchae* and *Medea*, and Aristophanes' comedy, *Women at the Thesmophoria*. He is a playwright and director of over fifty plays for the stage. He has brought the disciplines of theatre practice to the study of ancient Greek drama. In particular, he has worked with mask in performance for many years, both as an actor and director. A record of the objectives, methodology and outcomes of these research projects can be found at www.playingwithtragedy.usq.edu.au

MARIANNE McDONALD is Professor of Theatre and Classics at the University of California, San Diego, and a member of the Royal Irish Academy. Publications include: *Euripides in Cinema: The Heart Made Visible* (1983), *Ancient Sun, Modern Light: Greek Drama on the Modern Stage* (1992), *Sing Sorrow: Classics, History and Heroines in Opera* (2001), *The Living Art of Greek Tragedy* (2003) and, co-edited with Michael Walton, *Amid Our Troubles: Irish Versions of Greek Tragedies*, 2002. Performances of her translations include: Sophocles' *Antigone* (1999, 2003, 2005); Euripides' *Children of Heracles* (2003); Sophocles' *Oedipus Tyrannus* and *Oedipus at Colonus* (2003–2004); Euripides' *Hecuba* (2004); versions: *The Trojan Women* (2000); *Medea, Queen of Colchester* (2003); *The Ally Way* (political satire, based on *Alcestis*, 2004); other plays: *FireStormFlower* (2004); *. . . and then he met a woodcutter* (2005). Awards include: Italy's Golden Aeschylus Award (*Eschilo d'oro*), Greece's Order of the Phoenix, the KPBS Patté Award for theatre excellence; and San Diego Playbill "Billie" Award Artist of the Year. http://homepage.mac.com/mariannemcdonald

RICHARD MARTIN is the Antony and Isabelle Raubitschek Professor of Classics at Stanford University. His primary interests are oral traditions, ethnopoetics, ritual, and performance studies, as they relate to archaic Greek literature, especially Homer. Within drama, his primary work is on Aristophanes. He has also worked on the medieval and modern literature of Greece and Ireland and done fieldwork in both countries. His publications include *Healing, Sacrifice, and Battle* (1983); *The Language of Heroes: Speech and Performance in the Iliad* (1989); and *Myths of the Ancient Greeks* (2003). In addition, he has published articles on Hesiod, Greek lyric poetry, Horace, the ancient novel, wisdom traditions, and the iconography of musical performance.

RUSH REHM is Professor of Drama and Classics at Stanford University and is the author of *Aeschylus' Oresteia: A Theatre Version* (1978), *Greek Tragic Theatre* (1992), *Marriage to Death: The Conflation of Wedding and Funeral Rituals in Greek Tragedy* (1994), *The Play of Space: Spatial Transformation in Greek Tragedy* (2002), and most recently *Radical Theatre: Greek Tragedy and the Modern World* (2003). He also directs and acts professionally, serving as Artistic Director of Stanford Summer Theater. A political activist, he is involved in anti-war and anti-imperialist actions, and in solidarity campaigns with Palestine, Cuba, East Timor and Nicaragua.

GONDA VAN STEEN earned a BA degree in Classics in her native Belgium and a PhD in Classics and Hellenic Studies from Princeton University. As an Associate Professor in Classics and Modern Greek at the University of Arizona, she teaches courses in ancient and modern Greek language and literature. Her first book, *Venom in Verse: Aristophanes in Modern Greece*, was published by Princeton University Press in 2000 and was awarded the John D. Criticos Prize from the London Hellenic Society. She has also published articles on ancient Greek and late antique literature, on the reception of Greek tragedy, on Greek coinage, and on post-war Greek feminism. She is currently researching a book on theatre and censorship under the Greek military dictatorship of 1967–74.

J. MICHAEL WALTON was a professional actor and director before joining the Drama Department at the University of Hull where he was Director of The Performance Translation Centre and is now Emeritus Professor of Drama. He has lectured widely in Europe and America and was a Visiting Getty Scholar in 2002. His books on Greek Theatre include *Greek Theatre Practice*, (1980, 1991), *The Greek Sense of Theatre: Tragedy Reviewed* (1984, 1996), *Living Greek Theatre: A Handbook of Classical Performance and Modern Production* (1987), *Menander and the Making of Comedy* (with Peter Arnott, 1996) and *Found in Translation: Greek Drama in English* for Cambridge (2006). He was Editor for Methuen of *Craig on Theatre* and of the thirteen volumes of Methuen *Classical Greek Dramatists*, the whole of Greek drama in translation, and three collections of Greek and Roman plays. He has translated some dozen Greek and Latin plays, several of them with Marianne McDonald, with whom he has collaborated on a number of other publications including *Amid Our Troubles: Irish Versions of Greek Tragedy* (2002).

DAVID WILES is Professor of Theatre at Royal Holloway, University of London. His publications on Greek Theatre include *The Masks of Menander: Sign and Meaning in Greek and Roman Performance* (1991), *Tragedy in Athens: Performance Space and Theatrical Meaning* (1997) and *Greek Theatre Performance: An Introduction* (2000) – all published by Cambridge University Press. He also writes on Elizabethan theatre, and on aspects of performance space. His *A Short History of Western Performance Space* was published by CUP in 2003. He has also translated and directed a number of Greek plays. His current research project is to explore the masks of Greek tragedy, both in antiquity and in modern performance.

YANA ZARIFI is Artistic Director of Thiasos Theatre Company and Honorary Research Associate at Royal Holloway, University of London. She has directed Greek tragedies and comedies in London, Paris, Cyprus and in the US, including a version of Euripides' *Hippolytos* adapted as Indonesian dance drama. Thiasos arose from her dedication to the re-performance of Greek drama through the use of Eastern theatrical traditions and her desire to reinstate the dancing and singing chorus to the central place it once occupied in Greek theatre.

A NOTE ON TRANSLITERATION

Transliteration from ancient Greek into English is always imprecise, Greek having an alphabet of twenty-four letters, some of which have no single English equivalent. In Greek there is a 'k' (*kappa*), but no 'c'; there are long and short 'o's (*ômega* and *omicron*) and 'e's (*êta* and *epsilon*); as well as single letters for 'th' (*thêta*), 'ph' (*phi*), and 'ch' (*chi*), pronounced as in the Scottish 'loch'. There is no letter 'h' but the sound 'h' is represented by an aspirated 'breathing' mark on an initial vowel.

In the Companion the practice has been adopted of using what is most familiar to the general reader, while acknowledging that the mixture of anglicization and latinization may not always be consistent: hence 'Homer', 'Aeschylus', 'Aristotle', where many classical scholars would prefer 'Homêros', 'Aiskhylos', 'Aristotelês'.

INTRODUCTION

MARIANNE McDONALD AND J. MICHAEL WALTON

Most books on drama are about plays and playwrights. This is a book about theatre and, though the words 'drama' (from the Greek *drama*, 'something done') and 'theatre' (from *theatron*, 'a seeing-place' and *theama*, 'a show') both imply a performance dimension, it is the circumstances of presentation rather than the material that was presented that serve as its focus. Tragedy and comedy are part of a big-city art, their history defined for the most part by what happened in the capitals to which major artists have always tended to gravitate; in the sixteenth and seventeenth centuries, Marlowe from Canterbury, Shakespeare from Stratford, Beaumont from Leicestershire, Fletcher from Sussex and Wycherley from Shrewsbury, all naturally heading for London; Lully from Florence to Paris; Monteverdi from Cremona to Venice; modern American playwrights to New York or Los Angeles.

Aeschylus, Sophocles, Euripides, Aristophanes and Menander were all Athenian bred, but of the Latin playwrights whose work has survived, Plautus was a native of Umbria, Terence born in Africa and Seneca in Spain. They all ended up living in Rome. Herodas, the writer of Greek 'mimes', a few of which have survived in written form, is the exception, living and working in Alexandria, but in the third century BC, when Herodas flourished, Alexandria was as much a cultural centre as was Athens or Rome.

The justification for this second Companion, following the earlier *Cambridge Companion to Greek Tragedy*, edited by Patricia Easterling (1997), is only in part that this new one looks at comedy as well as tragedy, the Roman world as well as the Greek. More important is an acknowledgment that, however much the surviving written playtexts became the foundation of the western repertoire, they form only one element of a broad theatrical tradition. The emphasis here is less on texts than on occasion, on the nature of a performance culture, on the religious thought underpinning every aspect of life from the rules of warfare to the governance and order of society; all of this reflected through the theatre of the times. This is the unifying theme for the first eight essays under the subheading 'Text in Context'.

Complementary is 'The Nature of Performance', eight further essays that look at the detail and organization of ancient performances, from playing-places to properties, costume to costs, ending with what happened to the theatrical repertoire when confronted with newer performance media. Running throughout the book is an awareness that, alongside the recorded and recordable history, there thrived a consistent but variable tradition of presentation: of storytelling, mockery and subversion; of dance, music and mask; of religious, secular and political expression; and, eventually, mechanical ingenuity, the arena and gladiatorial combat.

Much of this was so ingrained in society as to be barely noticed in its own time; some was of the humblest nature, entertainment that happened on street-corners or in tiny villages. It might be amateur or professional but was, for the most part, both and neither, being tied into communities of all sizes in which the sense of holiday or carnival found its expression and where those with some presentational skill might demonstrate it for anybody who turned up to watch or listen.

This, then, is a book that draws attention more to the circumstances of performance than to the substance of its most lasting monument, the classical plays. The nature of the occasion stands alongside the organization that sustained that occasion. The expectations of audiences are balanced against the motives of those who promoted them. There is very little on translation or on modern stage revival, except to enlighten the nature of the original experience and the difference that modern technology has imposed on performance and on historical research. However, attention may be drawn to the various translations in the Bibliography, most of which show an awareness of staging in introductions or through stage directions, including, in the case of Seneca, whether or not his plays were created with a staged performance in mind.

The biggest difficulty in deciding what should or should not be included was the sheer timescale involved. At a conservative estimate the history of ancient Greek and Roman theatre goes back a thousand years before Aeschylus was born, to the Minoan cultures of Crete and Thera. The further terminus, or at least a convenient staging post, is identified with the banning of all forms of theatrical performance in the late seventh century of the Christian era. Such is the range covered by **Mark Griffith** in his synoptic opening essay where he searches for the origins of tragedy and comedy, alongside recitation, dance and music, and traces their development through to Roman pantomime and beyond.

Richard P. Martin looks at the way in which a sense of 'theatre' was a persistent feature of so many aspects of Greek and Roman society, from sport to rhetoric, political systems to the *Ludi*, the Roman games where the emperors consolidated power by giving the people the increasingly savage diversion they demanded. **Fritz Graf** investigates the relationship between mortals and immortals in polytheistic societies, and shows how religious observance formed a framework of dramatic presentation, with gods as characters in dramatic performance as they had been in the Homeric epics. **Jon Hesk** also makes comparisons between the theatres of Greece and Italy, investigating the social and political aspects of both, and the way in which civic responsibilities in Athens impinged on the stage world of Rome as well as of Athens. **David Wiles** revisits Aristotle to look anew at the intentions of the *Poetics*, the most influential document from classical times on the form of later tragedy.

While these five concentrate mainly on tragedy from Aeschylus to Seneca, Old Comedy in Athens is looked at in detail by **Gonda Van Steen,** who dissects the mixture of fantasy and real life in Aristophanes, identifying how some of the same production issues fed into revivals in the Athens of the twentieth century. **Sander Goldberg** picks up where Van Steen leaves off and investigates the nature of New Comedy; the similarities and differences between the work of the Greek playwright Menander and the Roman adapters of Greek Middle and New Comedy, Plautus and Terence. **Hugh Denard** completes the first section by showing how the centre of attention moved outside the cities to the vast range of miscellaneous 'popular' entertainment, virtually none of which survives in any scripted form, but which was a prominent feature of small-town and country life.

The second half opens with **Richard Green** assessing the place of theatre within a visual culture and evaluating the evidence of decoration and artefacts in deciphering what ancient performances might actually have looked like. **Rush Rehm** deciphers what is known about the conduct and organization of festivals and how they differed as a background for play production in Athens and Rome. **Richard Beacham** tackles theatre architecture, making a strong case for his reconstruction of the temporary theatres in wood which have not survived, as well as the magnificent stone monuments which can still be found in varying states of preservation throughout the Greek and Roman worlds. Choreographer and director **Yana Zarifi** reflects on the importance of dance and the significance of the Chorus in modes of presentation, from references within the Homeric epics, via Greek tragedy and comedy, to the Roman pantomime. **Gregory McCart's** essay follows naturally from here, investigating, again with a practitioner's perspective, the use of masks in ancient theatre and how, in an area that is much disputed, working with them today may throw light on ancient conventions. Stage mechanics and external effects, including costume, are scrutinized by **Graham Ley** in his chapter on the 'nuts and bolts' of ancient performance, where he notes how many of those involved with the theatre process were 'makers' of some kind. J. Michael Walton looks at 'commodity', the questions of costs and management, patronage and sponsorship which lie behind any theatrical enterprise. The book concludes with **Marianne McDonald** elaborating on how performance priorities have been refined and redefined when a story from classical myth is dramatized in a new medium, opera, radio, television or film.

Many of these essays manage to cover a greater span of time than that between the birth of Christ and the date of this publication. The total period of more than two thousand years begins and ends in what used to be thought of as 'dark ages', but on which historians are shedding more and more light. With the best will in the world, confining two thousand years of social history within a single book is less like squeezing a quart into a pint pot than pouring a barrel into a thimble. The temptation is to impose a pattern where there is none, or to assume continuity or evolution amongst a mass of activity which is both geographically and historically pure accident. As untenable is to treat the theatre of fifth-century BC Athens as the golden age from which whatever happened in the next millennium was a decline. Though many a classicist might agree, the theatre historian cannot afford to be so judgemental.

One factor that makes the task both easier and more difficult is that 'theatre' under our broad definition is both under-recorded and underestimated. There was apparently a history of the theatre, probably the first such, written in Greek by King Juba of Mauritania some time during the reign of Augustus, the first Emperor of Rome. Unfortunately, like all the rest of Juba's historical work, that book failed to survive. The study of the theatre of Greece and Italy has always been hampered, less by the small selection of surviving playtexts than by the fact that the circumstances of performance survive in haphazard fashion via a mixture of anecdote, reminiscence and incidental reference. The remains of many Roman and some Greek theatres are there to be seen and walked around; there are pictures on vases which appear to reflect theatrical performance; there are incidental comments from lawyers, architects, poets, grammarians and even scholiasts, those shadowy figures who at some time in the transmission of manuscripts added their own comments on what they thought was happening in a scene or how it was originally staged. There are precious few eyewitness accounts from the perspective of an audience member, still fewer from that of a player. There is one treatise on dance by Lucian (second century AD), but no 'dances'; there is virtually no music, though music seems to be one of the few elements that links the performances from earliest Greece to latest Rome.

What we are left with is a vast amount of miscellaneous information, anything from the contradictory and implausible 'Lives' of the playwrights to unlikely anecdotes written up hundreds of years after the time they claim to illuminate: but gossip has its uses. The value of much of this information resides not in its historical accuracy but in its incidental detail. There is a story recorded in the 'Life of Aeschylus' that, when the playwright introduced the Chorus of Furies, pell-mell, in his *Eumenides*, women had miscarriages and children collapsed from shock. This carries no more conviction than any other urban myth exaggerated over time by constant embellishment. As an indication of how *Eumenides* was first staged it is negligible. On the other hand, it is a story that makes little sense of any kind were not some women and children permitted at some time to see plays by Aeschylus.

Julius Pollux, who tells the same story about the impact of the Furies, includes in his *Onomasticon*, an Encyclopedia written in the second century AD, a description of the Greek theatre building giving special significance to various pieces of stage machinery, including *periaktoi*, prismatic scenic units which could revolve to give different indications of stage location. He also writes that:

> There could also be in a theatre a wheeled platform (*ekkuklêma*), crane (*mêchanê*), reveal (*exôstra*), lookout post (*skopê*) . . . lightning-machine (*keraunoskopeion*), thunder-machine (*bronteion*), god-platform (*theologeion*), lift (*geranos*), backdrops (*katablêmata*), semicircle (*hêmikuklion*), revolve (*stropheion*), semi-revolve (*hêmistropheion*), Charon's steps (*charônioi klimakes*) and trapdoors (*anapiesmata*). (Pollux, 4.127)

He goes into some detail of how thunder- and lightning- machines worked, the one involving pebbles being rolled into a copper pot, the other a rapidly swivelling *periaktos*.

Some of the stage devices to be found described in Pollux are simple enough means of offering reveals and tableaux, theatrical devices involving space, dimension or basic semiotics which were to become part of the vocabulary of the stage from the Renaissance onwards.

There are few scholars who believe that many of these scenic units and machines would have been available to Aeschylus or Sophocles. That is not the point. The point is that, at some time during the period covered here, there *were* such devices, in some sort of theatre, somewhere, which Pollux identifies as 'the Greek theatre'. Those ancient 'machines' were to prove a major influence on the elaborate staging for the court masque and for baroque opera. Pollux lived and wrote at the end of the second century AD. There had already been some sort of 'Greek theatre' in existence for seven hundred years. Seven hundred years is a vast period of time during which every aspect of theatre may have altered to reflect major changes in society.

Vitruvius, in his *De Architectura*, written about 16–13 BC, included a whole section (Book V) on Greek and Roman theatres, complete with figure drawings and details over acoustics. Again, Vitruvius is vague about when or what he means by 'a Greek theatre'. But the man was an architect. At some time there were what he identifies as typical 'Greek theatres', and of the dimensions he identifies. New research projects based on 3D imaging are demonstrating how modern technology can offer insights into issues of space and sightline, and transforming long-held suppositions about theatre buildings.

Aristotle was the nearest thing to a theatre historian in Athens, probably still alive (just) when one of the Greek comedians (Menander) was writing. Much of what has been gleaned about the theatre of the fifth century BC, and earlier, is filtered through Aristotle's *Poetics*. The *Poetics* is a philosopher's treatise, which incidentally includes some information about Aristotle's understanding of the development of tragedy. Intriguing document though the *Poetics* may be, it is frustratingly vague about what actually happened in the theatre of his own time, when so much of the classical repertoire was still being performed in revival. Nothing that Aristotle says, in fact, suggests that he ever attended the theatre. If he did, he saw no reason to give an impression of the experience, or much detail of how a play was presented. A much better impression comes from within the plays, especially those of the comic writer Aristophanes.

Though many of the texts, comedy and tragedy, that have come down to us look to have undergone alteration at various points in their transmission, they still offer much of the best evidence for how the plays were actually performed in their original productions. In the passage quoted earlier, Julius Pollux talks about the *mêchanê*, the stage-crane, the means of transporting a character, usually a god, from stage level to the *theologeion*, the 'god-platform'. If the evidence for the stage machine were none other than Pollux there might have been real doubt over whether the fifth-century Athenian audience knew of, or would have tolerated, such an artificial contraption. But when Trygaeus, the farmer frustrated by war in Aristophanes' *Peace* (421 BC), has fattened up a dung-beetle so that he can fly to heaven to discover what has happened to the goddess of Peace, Aristophanes provides us with the nearest we will get to proof. Trygaeus climbs aboard his 'beetle' and takes off, admiring the view of the Piraeus from his aerial perspective before calling out:

> ô mêchanopoie, proseche ton noun, hôs eme
> êdê strephei ti pneuma peri ton omphalon,
> kei mê phulaxei, chortasô ton kantharon.

Oy, you working the crane [*mêchanopoie*], keep your mind on the job.
The wind's already whistling round my navel.
If you're not careful I'm going to give the dung-beetle a meal.

(*Peace* 173–5)

The *mêchanopoios* was clearly the 'flyman', or stage-manager. We have to
be wary of using the language of plays as a means of defining stage action
but, especially in comedy, Aristophanes' sense of metatheatre assumes an
audience who are thoroughly familiar, and comfortable, with having their
attention drawn to the stage-world where the action takes place. The term
theos ex mêchanês, 'god from the machine', came to be used figuratively for
any form of divine (or unexpected but authoritative) intervention to resolve
an awkward situation; it is known better in its Latin translation as *deus ex
machina*.

The *mêchanê* may have been a peculiarly unreal stage machine, but it
helps to confirm that nobody in ancient Greece or Rome was expecting
'naturalism'. The term 'realistic' has to be used guardedly when discussing the
plays of Euripides, Menander, Plautus or Terence. Realism is relative. It also
applies differently to the mechanics of performance and the 'truthfulness'
of situation or character. Another Aristophanes play, *Frogs*, first performed
in Athens at the Lenaea of 405 BC, soon after the deaths of first Euripides,
then Sophocles, features Dionysus, the god of the theatre, so upset about the
consequences for the city that he decides to go down to Hades to try and
bring back Euripides.

When he finally gets down there he discovers that Aeschylus (who had
died in 456 BC, all of sixty years by the time of *Frogs*) is also in contention.
A competition is set up to decide which is the better playwright. The two
dead tragedians compete over language, morality, prologues, and finally over
whose lines are the weightier, judged by their speaking of them onto a pair
of scales.

They also argue over the virtues of 'realism', Aeschylus accusing Euripides of lowering the tone of tragedy by introducing realistic characters. The
wonderful thing about this farrago of nonsense is that Aristophanes offers
the nearest, indeed the only, example we have of contemporary dramatic
criticism, albeit strained through the mesh of comic invention. Eventually
Aeschylus is declared the winner by Dionysus, not because he is the better
playwright, but because he offers the better advice over helping the city of
Athens to survive. He returns to earth with Dionysus to 'save the city and
educate the fools'. The danger was real enough. The Peloponnesian War,
which had dragged on for twenty-five years since 431, was entering its final
stage. Only a year later the Spartans forced the Athenians into submission.

That this 'stage' Aeschylus, in a comedy written by Aristophanes, should condemn a 'stage' Euripides for his 'realism' merely confirms the impression given by the plays that Euripides' approach to drama was comparatively realistic. Indeed there are at least two sequences in Euripides' plays (the recognition scene in *Electra* and the allocation of defenders in *Phoenician Women*) where the younger playwright appears to draw attention to equivalent scenes in Aeschylus (*Libation-Bearers* and *Seven Against Thebes*) in which he parodies Aeschylus' dramatic method as old-fashioned and 'unrealistic'.

In a similar but different way, the ordinary Athenians who inhabit the Athens of Menander's plays, and from there the mix-and-match world of Plautus and Terence, are still recognizable as the everyday characters in Aristophanes. The difference is that the cast of an Aristophanes comedy also includes real Athenians (the politician Cleon, the philosopher Socrates, the playwright Euripides three times in the only eleven plays to have survived), animals, personifications, demigods and Olympian deities.

The 'realistic' characters of Euripides, Menander or Terence still acted in masks, a form that requires presentational acting and a physical body-language of gesture (*cheironomia*). There is still little direct evidence on the nature of masked acting in the ancient world and about the restriction on the number of actors, likely in tragedy, but much less plausible, if not impossible, in Old and New Comedy. Audiences for later tragedy and comedy may have been more able to recognize characters with whom they could directly empathize or even identify. They were still looking at an art of the unreal. Realism did come to the classical theatre, but to the theatre of the Roman arena, where criminals might be publicly tortured or executed. In the theatres of imperial Rome, differently armed gladiators fought to the death; men and women, many for their faith or for minor misdemeanours, sometimes under the guise of a contrived dramatic situation, were tortured and killed in all manner of hideous ways. It was all theatre, the real theatre of life and death, albeit decorated with the trappings of an artificial entertainment.

Formal Greek and Roman drama has an intrinsic value as part of a body of literature from the past revealing, as other forms do not, how people lived and what they thought. It has an equally important function as a stimulus to modern practitioners to renew the plays in modern productions; or to modern writers to return to the world of myth for its flexibility and its power of parable.

This is a vast topic and some readers will inevitably be disappointed by what has been omitted through lack of space. Hopefully, what is included contributes to a kaleidoscopic picture of the importance of the 'performative' as a central element within the two great European cultures of the ancient world.

Members of the Hellenistic guilds, actors who plied their trade as professionals in a Greek-speaking world that stretched from the Black Sea to the Middle East, to North Africa and Sicily, performed from a repertoire that originated in fifth-century Athens. One such made a series of dedications in his home town of Tegea, a little to the south of Argos. He gives thanks for victories in the City Dionysia at Athens (where he played in Euripides' *Orestes*); at Delphi (where he played in Euripides' *Heracles* and the *Antaeus* of Archestratus); also at Argos (in *Heracles* and the *Archelaus* of Euripides); Dodona (*Archelaus* and the *Achilles* of Chaerephon): eighty-eight prizes in various Greek cities; and a prize for boxing at the Ptolemaia in Alexandria. That was the career profile of a Hellenistic entertainer. Eventually, in the third century AD, the Artists' Guilds and the Guild of Athletes joined up to form a single trade union in what Pickard-Cambridge described as 'a fusion of the Old Vic and the Football League'.[1]

It is the history of all these players that we celebrate here, the host of supplementary figures from mimes to mask-makers, alongside the famous names. They all had a part to play in the cultures in which they lived and died. They all added, in however minor a manner, to the sum of theatrical understanding on which our modern entertainment industries are based.

NOTE

1. A. Pickard-Cambridge, *The Dramatic Festivals of Athens*, second ed., rev. J. Gould and D. M. Lewis (Oxford: Clarendon, 1968), p. 301.

PART ONE

Text in context

I

MARK GRIFFITH

'Telling the tale': a performing tradition from Homer to pantomime

Greek and Latin literature and drama have been central and formative components of the Western cultural tradition ever since the Middle Ages; and modern conceptions of theatre in general, as of 'tragedy' and 'comedy' as particular dramatic forms, are indelibly shaped by the specific performance modes that evolved during the sixth to the fourth centuries BC in Athens and during the third to the first centuries BC in Rome. The surviving Greek texts of Aeschylus, Sophocles, Euripides, Aristophanes and Menander, and the Latin texts of Seneca, Plautus and Terence, comprise a body of 'classical' drama that has long been recognized as canonical and that sometimes feels almost inevitable. (As Aristotle put it, with Sophocles and Euripides 'tragedy attained its nature [*phusis*]', *Poetics* ch. 4. 1449a15.) But as one follows the developments in Greek and Roman culture that led to the evolution of these forms of drama, one quickly comes to see what a large and diverse body of performance traditions had preceded them, and how many options were available to those theatrical pioneers as they set about shaping the plays that we have come to know so well.

Of course the Greeks were not the first to perform stories, or act out social and religious rituals, using words, music, dance, costume and impersonation in some combination or other. 'Theatrical' performances, in the sense of solo or group activities formally presented to an audience in a designated space and for a conventionally recognized purpose or occasion, can be found in almost all societies, ancient or modern, Eastern and Western, and the line between ritual and theatre, ceremony and 'play', may not always be easy – or necessary – to draw.

Our story should probably begin (if we must begin somewhere) with the 'Minoans', a non-Greek people whose civilization on the islands of Crete and Thera (Santorini) during the mid-second millennium BC is conspicuous for its large public ceremonies, often involving hundreds of performers. Their wall-paintings depict in brilliant detail performances of dances, bull-leapings and priestly rituals held in wide, paved spaces full of crowds of well-dressed spectators. Unfortunately, no decipherable texts survive from that society, so we can only guess about the content of these performances. Later, the 'Mycenaean' Greeks who took over the Minoan palaces and administered them for themselves also borrowed many of the same architectural and iconographical styles to adorn their mainland palaces (at Mycenae, Pylos, Thebes, etc.). In general, these Mycenaeans appear to have been less interested in peaceful play and performance than the Minoans; in any case no narratives or literary texts of any kind have survived among the Greek (Linear B) documents from this palace era (*c.*1500–1200). But the material remains make it clear that they were in contact with Egyptians, Phoenicians, Syrians and Canaanites, Hittites and several Luvian-speaking peoples (probably including the inhabitants of Wilusa/Ilion, i.e. Troy, in North-West Anatolia). So there can be no doubt that already during this period, as again later during the archaic period, Greek society was absorbing a number of Near Eastern stories and artistic forms. As for the Greeks' long-term cultural debt to the Minoans, it is notable that even in much later generations (the epics of Homer, for example) the Cretans – now 'Greeks' – were famed for their dance-floors and musical performances (e.g. Homer *Iliad* 16.617, 18.590–2, etc.).

With the demise of the Bronze Age palace culture in the twelfth century BC, not only on Crete and the Greek mainland, but also throughout the Near East, the level of artistic activity of all kinds dropped precipitously for the next three to four hundred years. But oral traditions certainly persisted, and archaeological finds of recent years have confirmed that the iron-using communities that gradually re-emerged into a mode of expansion and experimentation during the late ninth and eighth centuries had preserved much that was originally derived from those Mycenaean ancestors and their Anatolian and Mediterranean neighbours. The rich and extensive mythology for which archaic Greece is so renowned abounds with stories of gods and heroes, genealogies and adventures, that link Greeks with the nearer or more distant East. Many leading Greek families and cities of the classical period liked to trace their ancestry and foundation back to immigrants from the East: e.g. Phoenician Cadmus as founder of Thebes, Phrygian Pelops as founder of the Olympic Games and of the 'Peloponnese', and Cretan Daedalus as imagined inventor of technology and sculpture for the Athenians.

Greek, Hellenic, Athenian

I have been writing so far of 'Greek' and 'non-Greek'. But defining who the 'Greeks' were, let alone how their various cultural institutions – including theatrical performances – came to evolve by the sixth and fifth centuries BC into such distinctive and influential forms, is a complicated matter. This is not the place to try to provide a detailed account of all the political, economic and social developments within the Greek-speaking communities of the Archaic period (c.750–500 BC) through which they were transformed into the innovative and culturally accomplished city-state society that we find represented in their classical architecture, sculpture, painting, music, literature – and in that unique synthesis of them all, drama. But it is important to bear in mind two contradictory facts about the Greeks of this period: on the one hand, this was a people united by a common language (despite considerable dialectal variation from one region to another), and united too by shared participation in a complex mass of traditional stories (mythoi), customs (nomoi) and genealogies (real or imagined); yet on the other hand, the different Greek communities that were sprinkled all over the Mediterranean and beyond, from Marseilles and Cadiz to Syria and Byzantium, and from Egypt and Libya to the Black Sea, lived under a wide variety of political systems (monarchies, more or less narrow oligarchies, loose federations of feudal aristocrats, and democracies), and they consequently experienced very disparate relationships to their environments and surroundings. There were many different ways of being 'Greek'.

Amidst such socio-political diversity, indeed, it may be said that it was primarily through their cultural productions (epics, hymns, cosmogonies and other widely circulated poems; temple architecture and dedications; athletic and musical festivals, etc.) that the Greeks of the Archaic period first developed a sense of Panhellenic identity. The Olympic and Pythian Games (both established in the eighth or early seventh centuries), the Delphic oracle of Apollo, the crystallization and public recitation of a standard 'theogony' (Hesiod's) establishing the names and titles of the common gods and goddesses, along with 'Homer's' monumental epics about the Trojan War and the Theban saga, all helped to mark out a common Hellenic heritage (real or fictitious) and a shared set of cultural institutions.[1] The stories (mythoi) of Agamemnon, Menelaus and Helen, of Jason and Medea, of Cadmus, Agave and Pentheus, and scores of others were regarded by all Greeks as being about 'their' collective past – even though particular local versions of these stories might tie those events and personages to the present in quite different ways. Such mythological variation continued always to be present – and the Athenian dramatists in due course made the most of it, as such figures as Orestes (of Argos), Hippolytus (of Troezen) and Medea (of Colchis) were reimagined and represented as forming a part of the distant Athenian past.

Genres of literature and rival performance modes

In the classical period, the Greeks came to make quite formal distinctions between separate 'kinds, families' of poetry (*genê*, whence Latin *genera*, whence French/English *genres*), each with its appropriate metre, level of diction and subject-matter – *epos* (epic narrative), *iambos* (invective, satire) and *drama* (both tragic and comic), as well as a number of choral and solo 'lyric' types named after the occasions for which they were performed. Whether or not such distinct categories were observed before the fifth century BC, it is clear that a wide variety of different but overlapping modes of performance existed in the Archaic period, many of which contributed to the development of the forms we recognize as Athenian tragedy (*tragôidia*) and comedy (*kômôidia*). And while we are accustomed to thinking of these as genres of 'literature' (epic, lyric, satire, etc.), originally they were delivered orally (aurally), as songs or chants, often accompanied by instrumental music and dance, and generally performed by a group rather than read by an individual.

The oldest surviving poetic texts are probably the Homeric epics, along with the Hesiodic *Theogony* and *Works and Days* (all perhaps from the late eighth century, but each representing the final stage of a long performance tradition). But it is evident that other forms of solo and group musical-poetical performance coexisted with them. So, for example, the *Iliad*, as well as describing hymns of thanks or propitiation sung by groups of young men or women (1.472–4, 6.286–311), and a 'wedding-song' (*hymenaios*) danced to the accompaniment of pipes and kithara (18.491–6), includes also an elaborate antiphonal dirge (*thrênos*) conducted at a warrior's funeral, following a format for ritual lamentation that has continued in Greece until the present day – and that is found repeatedly in Athenian tragedies (e.g., Aeschylus *Libation-Bearers* 306–508, Euripides *Suppliants* 778–836).[2]

Two scenes from the Homeric epic describe groups of dancers performing publicly to the sung accompaniment of a narrative of some kind. The first is the 'Linos-song' depicted by the divine craftsman Hephaestus for the Shield of Achilles (*Iliad* 18.567–72; see Zarifi in this volume, ch. 12, p. 229).[3] The second comes from the *Odyssey*, as the blind singer Demodocus, who has previously sung solo about the events of the Trojan War, entertains the assembled Phaeacian community (8.104–369):

> The herald . . . taking Demodocus by the hand, led him from the hall . . . and they came to the assembly-place (*agorê*), and a large crowd followed, huge numbers of them (*murioi*) . . .

> [*A little later*] Nine chosen judges stood up, public officials, who were to prepare everything properly for the contests (*agônas*); They made smooth the

dance-floor (*choron*) and cleared a fine contest-space (*agôna*), And the herald came close, bringing the clear-sounding *phorminx* for Demodocus. Then he took his place in the middle; and around him the adolescent youths took their places, skilled in the dance (*orchêthmoio*), and struck the splendid dance-floor (*choron*) with their feet. And Odysseus was watching (*thêeito*) the flashing of feet, and admiring it with all his heart. So, playing his *phorminx*, Demodocus began a beautiful song about the love-affair between Ares and Aphrodite. . .

This passage presents us with several key terms concerning dance (*choros*, *orchêthmos*), contest (*agôn*), spectators (*theâtai*) and performance-space (*agorê*), that will recur in any account of the 'origins' of Greek theatre; and it is clear that the bard's amusing narrative of divine misadventure involves a highly theatrical combination of sung poetry, instrumental accompaniment and choral dance.

It is impossible, unfortunately, to determine how closely this performance is modelled on actual contemporary practice. But the picture it presents is confirmed by the material and literary remains of the seventh and sixth centuries: visual images of *phorminx*-players and of dancing groups (usually same-sex, whether young men or young women) are matched by (fragmentary) textual remains of songs composed by individual poets – usually male (e.g., Alcman, Stesichorus) but occasionally female (e.g., Sappho, Praxilla) for choral performance. Sometimes the chorus sings by itself, but in other contexts the solo singer takes the lead, or they may alternate.[4] The usual accompaniment of such performances was the *phorminx* or *kithara*, a multi-stringed instrument with a deeply resonant sounding-box capable of filling a large area and supporting multiple voices. (By contrast the *lura* ['lyre'] was a smaller instrument usually employed indoors for less formal solo singing.) For certain types of song, however, especially those connected with the celebration of Dionysus or the Great Mother (Cybele), the *aulos* ('double-pipe') was preferred: its penetrating tone and breathy 'beat' (something between the bagpipes and alto saxophone in timbre) gave it a more exotic flavour, which the Greeks associated with the far North (Thrace) or East (Phrygia). Occasionally too percussion was employed: *tympana* ('drums'), *krotala* ('clappers'), etc.

In the case of both strings and pipes, certain musical modes, melodies and scales were traditional and fixed, but tunings might vary from one locality or performer to another. Between 700 and 400 BC, numerous innovations in the construction and performance technique of all these instruments took place – some of them highly controversial and associated with (real or imaginary) changes in the social and psychological 'make-up' (*harmonia, hexis*) of both performers and audience. For the Greeks saw a close connection between musical modes (tunings, scales, melodies) and social-political-physiological institutions and modes of behaviour, and several of the same terms were applied to both. Thus *nomos* means both 'law, custom, norm' and 'melody'; *harmonia* both 'arrangement' and 'tuning, harmony'; *tonos* both '(physical/moral) training' and '(musical) pitch'; etc. And since 'musical' performances were also songs, and often dances too (for purely instrumental music played a relatively small role in Greek public performance), the verbal content of a lyric narrative was generally felt to be inextricably bound up with its melody, metres and choreography (or, in the case of a solo performer, her/his style of delivery). Choral performance, along with athletics and military training, both of which likewise involved much disciplined bodily training and movement to musical accompaniment, was thus felt to be integral both to 'good bodily formation/melodies' and to 'good order/discipline/laws' (*eutaxia/eukosmia/euexia/eunomia*). Indeed, such public performances constituted the most visible and prestigious forms of group solidarity and self-definition.[5]

By no means all forms of poetical and narrative expression involved choruses, however. Individual poets like Archilochus, Alcaeus and Sappho composed chants of praise or invective, political commentary, accusation or self-promotion, as well as invitations to erotic or comradely intercourse. Much of this poetry was delivered in the context of the symposium, where the visual and musical components of the entertainment were provided in part by the elite participants themselves (often in more or less friendly competition with one another), in part by professional or slave performers.

In the case of the solo narrative poetry of Homer and Hesiod, which, though originally sung to a *phorminx*, had come by the sixth century or so to be merely chanted or spoken, a professional reciter (*rhapsode*), travelling from city to city and competing against others or presenting chosen scenes to assembled audiences, was expected to deliver the lines quite dramatically and to stir his audience through his effective impersonation of individual characters:

> 'So tell me this, Ion' [says Socrates]: 'When you are dressed up in your elaborate finery and gold crown, and recite well and most amaze your audience – say when you sing Odysseus' leaping on the threshold, revealing himself to the suitors . . . or some pathetic passage about Andromache or Hecuba or Priam – are you at that time in your right mind, or beside (*exô*) yourself? Does your mind imagine itself, in its state of enthusiasm (*enthousiazousa*), present at the actual events you describe – in Ithaca or at Troy or whatever the poem requires?' 'I'll tell you, Socrates' [replies the rhapsode Ion], 'when I recite a pathetic passage, my eyes fill with tears; when it is something alarming

or terrifying, my hair stands on end in terror and my heart jumps . . .' 'Yes, and you people have the same effect on many of the spectators (*theatôn*) . . . !'

(Plato *Ion* 535 b–d).

Both the performer of epic scenes and his audience are felt to be 'beside, outside' (*exô*) themselves and 'possessed by god' (*en-theos*, whence *enthousiasmos*), as a result of the vividness and emotionality of the narrative, and it should be borne in mind that almost one third of Homeric poetry is presented as direct speech. Thus the differences between 'epic' and 'drama' could be less sharp than they came to be in later generations of western culture and criticism.

The range of 'stories, myths' (*mythoi*) available to a Greek poet and chorus as they set about developing and performing the narrative most appropriate to a particular festive occasion was in fact almost immeasurably extensive and extendable. While certain elements might be fixed and unalterable (such as the identity of the particular deity or human object of praise, and the location of the celebration), even these might allow room for considerable variation and poetic embellishment, while other details of the narrative could be quite freely invented. This principle of mythological innovation, encouraged by the conditions of pervasive competition for individual prizes assessed according to the poets' individual skill and originality, was continued by the fifth-century Athenian dramatists, as traditional stories of kings and heroes were adapted for performance in a new democratic context. The ancient commentators on the surviving tragedies often remark, in fact, that this or that genealogical detail or unexpected twist in the plot was derived from an earlier poetic version, e.g. of the 'Cyclic' epics about Troy (now lost), or the choral lyrics of Stesichorus (also now largely lost, though a few have been recovered in papyrus finds). Thus every audience was alert to the ways in which a poet was adapting and improving on the 'standard' versions of a particular story. One familiar – and unendingly controversial – example will suffice here: To what extent (if at all) should Helen be blamed for the Trojan War? Was she forced, or did she follow Paris willingly? Did she even go to Troy at all? Homer in his two epics, Sappho and Stesichorus in their sixth-century lyric poems, Herodotus in his fifth-century prose *Histories*, the sophist Gorgias in his playful showpiece *Helen's Defence* and Aeschylus and Euripides in their various tragedies (*Agamemnon, Trojan Women, Helen, Orestes* – also Aeschylus' satyr play *Proteus*, set in Egypt, which concluded the *Oresteia*), all provide different answers, none of them definitive or conclusive. In each case, the prize might be awarded not to the version that is proven to be correct (for who could ever demonstrate that?), but to the one that is most suitable to the occasion, most ingenious or most surprising.[6]

Each type of poetry (epic narrative, lyric hymn, invective, etc.) was generally restricted by convention to a particular metre and formal structure. As for the music and choreography, the evidence is thin; but it appears that certain regions were renowned for their specialized harmonies ('Dorian', 'Aeolian', 'Lydian', etc.) and performance styles, especially in the context of the *dithyramb*, or 'circular chorus' (*kuklios choros*), performed in honour of Dionysus.

As early as the seventh century, the poet Archilochus from the island of Paros boasts (fr. 120 West):

> I know how to lead-off (*exarxai*) the fine song of Dionysus, the dithyramb, when I am blasted in my wits by wine!

And in the next century the city of Corinth witnessed developments to the dithyramb that were associated with the name of Arion. Some later traditions even credited him with the composition of the first 'tragedies'; but none of his poetry survives and we have no way of judging what these choral performances were like. Nonetheless, Aristotle does state (*Poetics* 4.1449a11) that 'tragedy came from those leading-off (*exarchontôn*) the dithyramb', and it is striking that in the neighbouring city of Sicyon during the early sixth century, Cleisthenes (grandfather of the Athenian proto-democrat), when he was recently elevated to power as *turannos* and still engaged in a struggle with rival families supported by Argos, is said by Herodotus (5.67–8) to have first abolished the rhapsodists' competitions in reciting from Homer's poems, because they were full of praise of Argos and the Argives'. Then Herodotus continues:

> One of the most important tributes [previously] paid to Adrastus [a mythological Argive hero] was the tragic choruses (*tragikois chorois*), which the Sicyonians celebrated in his honour. Normally the tragic chorus belongs to the worship of Dionysus, but in Sicyon it was not so – it was performed in honour of Adrastus, treating his life-story and sufferings (*pathê*). Cleisthenes however changed this: he transferred the choruses to Dionysus and the rest of the ceremonial to Melanippus [a Theban hero, mythologically hostile to Adrastus and Argos] . . .

This account is important for at least two reasons: not only does it mention an institution of 'tragic choruses' fifty years or so earlier than the first attestation of 'tragedy' in Athens, but it also makes clear that choral performances (especially those connected with Dionysus) could be charged with intense local and political significance, and the choice of hero or divinity to be dramatized could be quite controversial.

Various kinds of choral performance involving men dressed as animals or satyrs, or wearing fat-suits, dancing and sometimes carrying huge phalluses, are attested in different cities during the sixth century. To what extent any of them were 'dramatic' is impossible to judge; the majority were doubtless improvised and involved no written text, nor perhaps even any fixed plot. Out of such traditions, and drawing too on the tradition of epic recitations and solo poetic narratives and invectives, Athenian tragedy and comedy eventually evolved, with a story-line, masks, impersonated characters and rehearsed dialogue.

But as we have seen, neither tragedy nor comedy seems in fact to have been originally an Athenian invention – for they were preceded not only by the sixth-century 'tragic choruses' at Sicyon but also by comic dramas that were performed in Dorian communities in the Peloponnese and Sicily several decades before the earliest attested Attic comedies.[7] As for the peculiar Athenian institution of the satyr play (i.e. dramas with heroic plots, and choruses of men costumed as satyrs or silenes), it appears that these were not brought into Athens until the very end of the sixth century, apparently introduced specifically in 505 BC by the distinguished playwright Pratinas from Phleious (a small town near Argos).

The development of Athenian tragedy and comedy

When Pisistratus, tyrant of Athens, sought in the mid-sixth century to develop more centralized civic ceremonies and institutions (legal, artistic, political), with a view to bolstering the sense of collective 'Athenian' identity, one of his first major innovations was the Panathenaic festival, at which athletic and musical events were held that soon became a major draw for competitors all over Greece; and subsequently he and his sons presided over the inauguration of the City Dionysia (probably in 535 BC), at which 'tragedy' was first performed to a mass Athenian audience. (See Graf, ch. 3 and Rehm, ch. 10 in this volume.)

This distinctive new art-form, reputedly first developed by Thespis in the Attic deme of Icarion, employing masked chorus and actors, musical accompaniment from the *aulos*, and alternations between choral song and spoken dialogue between one or two individual 'responder(s)' (*hupokritai*), combined many elements taken from other traditional performance traditions – though it is unclear where the distinctive notion of the mask may have originated, allowing the performers to abandon more completely their mundane identities in order to 'represent' or even 'become' the mythological characters they were impersonating: possibly this was an Athenian (Thespian?) innovation. In any case, it was this Athenian amalgam of previous traditions that was destined to become henceforth the central and 'classic' form of serious Western drama.

The details of the performance spaces and buildings, festival procedures, and rules of competition employed for the various tragic and comic dramas presented around Attica, above all in the central area near the Acropolis (in the *Agora* or the Theatre of Dionysus), but also further afield in the rural demes, are described more fully in other chapters of this volume (Beacham, ch. 11 and Denard, ch. 8). From small-scale, locally based improvisations and choral dances, first tragedy and then comedy evolved into the elaborate formal productions some of whose texts survive today, with their complex plots, actors playing multiple roles, intricate choral lyrics and sophisticated dialogue, all designed for performance before a city-wide, seated audience. The key figures in this evolution, apart from Thespis (a semi-mythical figure, perhaps datable to the 550s–530s), were Phrynichus (active *c.*510–470), renowned for his innovative dances and choral melodies, and Aeschylus, an aristocrat from the deme of Eleusis, who came to dominate the competitive scene of tragic and satyric performance from the 490s until his death in 456. His sons and nephews were also in due course prizewinning dramatists, as is also true for Sophocles, Euripides and Aristophanes; for it seems that playwriting, like most other occupations in ancient Greece, tended to run in families. In the early years of the annual competitions, the playwright was his own lead actor. But before the end of Aeschylus' career, he and the young Sophocles had introduced a second actor; in due course, a third was added; and by the later fifth century the playwrights had apparently ceased to act in their own productions.

The *chorêgos* and chorus members were always Athenian citizens: the playwright, *aulos*-player and actors not necessarily so. By the 440s, the growing importance of the actors' contribution was recognized by the introduction of an acting prize; and in the years ahead the focus gradually shifted from the *chorêgos*, poet and chorus to the actors. Towards the end of the fifth century, more complicated techniques of *aulos*-playing and singing evolved, requiring a professional level of expertise; and increasingly it became customary for the aulete to be a non-Athenian (often a Theban), while the lead actor and his team of subsidiary actors would be expected to be able to deliver ornate arias as well as exquisitely pathetic scenes of suffering and/or madness. In awarding the prizes to the competing tragedies and comedies each year, audiences and judges thus had a wide range of dramatic components and techniques to evaluate and respond to: the visual aspects of costume, masking, blocking, gesture, tableau and scenic design; choral and solo songs and dances that might employ a variety of musical idioms; vivid narratives and descriptions delivered in messenger-speeches and other actor-monologues; agonistic pairs of speeches modelled on the latest techniques of argumentation from the law-courts or assembly; rapid-fire dialogues of questioning, supplication, persuasion or mockery; and (in comedy) ribald slapstick, invective and political satire.

The surviving plays of Sophocles and Euripides, spanning the period from the 450s to 405 BC, display a remarkable consistency of structure and style, and it appears that this was also true of the competing plays by their main rivals, including Ion of Chios, Plato's friend Agathon, and Aeschylus' and Sophocles' own sons, Euphorion and Iophon.[8] In any case, by the mid-fifth century, tragedy and comedy were firmly established as the most prestigious and popular performance mode in Athens – which was itself the cultural hub of the Greek world.

The reasons for this enduring and universal popularity (for both tragedy and comedy clearly appealed both to elites and to the lower citizen classes) are not hard to understand. The Theatre of Dionysus had become a site at which Athenian citizens of all levels and backgrounds, and visitors from all over Greece, could watch, agonize, laugh, weep, vicariously suffer, survive and finally judge some of the most extreme and disturbing issues of their own personal (psychological) and political existence. As the masked actors and chorus-members played out new and surprising versions of the familiar stories involving heroic elites from long ago and their humdrum dependants (guards, messengers, nurses, advisers, attendants, etc.), each member of the theatre audience was brought to confront and experience the most extreme issues of class and gender conflict, family violence and incest, political ambition and treachery, loyalty and self-sacrifice – in short, their wildest fantasies or ghastliest nightmares. There was almost no corner of the human imagination that the masked, exotically costumed actors and dancing choreuts might not explore and expose, all under the reassuring pretext that this was the domain of Dionysus, and therefore only 'play', a 'pretence, imitation' (*mimêsis*) of a serious or shameful action. The pleasurably 'mind-bending' experience (*psuchagôgia*) of allowing the god to enter 'inside' oneself (*en-thousiasmos*, i.e. being *en-theos*) – as Ion and Socrates described it (above, pp. 18–19) – and thus moving 'outside' (*exô*) one's normal state of consciousness was recognized by audiences and critics alike as being brought about more powerfully by tragedy and comedy than by any other art-form. No wonder Plato regarded Athenian drama as the most dangerous and corrupting of all forms of entertainment. No wonder too that Aristotle praised it as the most complete and satisfying. And no wonder, therefore, that Athenian

tragedy and comedy quickly spread to become the most universal and popular of all the performing arts throughout Greece.

From Athens to Rome

In addition to the main Athenian festivals of the City Dionysia and Lenaea,
there were local re-performances of plays during the fifth century and later
in the Attic demes (theatres are known from Icarion, Eleusis, Thoricus and
several other locations). It is not known whether the personnel, style and
conditions of performance for these were the same as at the first production:
they may well have been scaled down or adapted. But even though tragedy –
and even more so, comedy – was in many respects extremely 'Athenian' in
its focus and mentality, visitors from other parts of Greece soon began to
show an interest in staging plays by the Athenian champion dramatists. Sicily
in particular was a hotbed of literary and musical invention and Syracuse
already boasted a large stone theatre by the mid-fifth century – perhaps even
earlier than the first one built in Athens itself. Aeschylus staged performances
of his *Persians* for Hieron there; and he also composed a play entitled *The
Women of Aetna* for a Sicilian audience. Later in the fifth century, both
Euripides and Agathon were invited by the King of Macedonia to stage plays
there, and by the early fourth century, South Italian cities such as Tarentum
were likewise staging plays, both Aristophanic-style comedies and tragedies
old and new.[9]

After Aeschylus' death in 456 BC, the Athenians passed a resolution allowing his plays to be restaged instead of newly composed tragedies. By the
fourth century a category of 'Old Plays' was a regular part of the annual
competition – with Euripides by now the favourite source. By the time the
Macedonian kings (Philip and his son Alexander) came to dominate the rest
of Greece (from the 330s BC onwards) and in due course to extend 'Hellenic'
culture throughout what had been the Persian Empire, tragedy and comedy
(and possibly the satyr play too, though the evidence is spotty) had ceased
to be specifically Attic commodities and were now part of the Greek mainstream. More and more cities were building their own *theatron*, in some
cases on a huge scale (e.g. Epidaurus, Selinus, Ephesus); and soon this would
become as much a standard feature of Hellenization as a gymnasium or
stadium. These theatres were the site not only of full-scale dramatic productions but also of solo musical competitions, and even political rallies and
meetings. As the centuries passed, architects, engineers and painters came up
with increasingly elaborate buildings, stage-designs, perspective-techniques
and other visual innovations, which made possible a greater variety of theatrical effects and displays, while the actor's art was made both grander

and more static, it appears, through innovations in masks and costuming (built-up hairpieces, exaggerated facial expressions, platform shoes). At the same time, alternative forms of spectacle and performance drew even larger audiences to other venues, especially athletics, chariot-racing and (from the first century BC onwards) various kinds of games and gladiatorial combats in the amphitheatre.

The process of dissemination of plays and Athenian-style dramatic perfor-mance around the Mediterranean world was facilitated by the emergence of a strong 'guild' of actors and musicians, the Artists of Dionysus (*Dionysou technitai*), with members drawn from many different cities. Travelling groups of actors could thus find support for festival performances and collaborations of various kinds. On a more domestic scale, well-educated elites would read plays at home and their children would read the classics in school (mainly Euripides and Menander), dinner parties might be the occasion for readings or enactments of selected scenes, performed by hired professionals, highly trained slaves or the guests themselves, and budding orators would train their voices and gestural techniques by studying with actors.[10] Athenian tragedy and comedy had become mainstream Greek art-forms.

New plays were still being composed and produced in Athens through-out the fourth century and later. Some of these tragic poets were highly regarded (e.g. Theodectes, admired by Aristotle); but their works have not survived and it is hard to tell how much tragedy changed – declined? – after the death of Sophocles and Euripides. Nor can we assess whether the per-formance style for restaged 'old tragedies' remained close to that of their original production or was adapted by the actors and musicians to reflect changing tastes and conditions. The small scraps of musical notation that survive on papyrus from *c.*300 BC, containing a few lines from Euripides' *Orestes* (and another containing part of *Iphigenia at Aulis*) may or may not accurately transmit the actual melodies composed by Euripides – perhaps not. Certainly it seems highly unlikely that the lengthy choral segments of the *Oresteia*, for example, were any longer sung or danced in Aeschylean style if performed two hundred or more years later. Musical idioms had changed radically even between the time of Aeschylus and that of Euripi-des (as Aristophanes' *Frogs* makes clear), and no system of choreographical notation existed in antiquity. Theatre audiences were now in any case more interested in brilliant individual acting than in collective choral performance. Often – then as now – plays were cut, rewritten, interpolated and otherwise 'updated' by the actors, to ensure audience comprehension and appreciation. (Evidence for some of these interpolations and adaptations can be found in the existing medieval manuscripts of some of the plays.) In the case of com-edy, once the intensely topical and Athens-focused invective and political commentary characteristic of Aristophanes and his Old Comedy rivals had given way to the character-focused and romance-driven (and chorus-less) New Comedy, the plays were easily transferable to almost any corner of the Hellenistic world – including Italy and Rome, as we shall see.

The annual competitions in Athens were still taking place, however; and although the surviving inscriptions informing us of the victorious poets, actors and producers of dithyramb, tragedy and comedy at the City Dionysia do not continue past the late fourth century BC, the festival was still going strong in the second century AD. But after the fourth century BC, Athens was no longer the leader in cultural innovation or opulence of production. Indeed, poetical/musical competitions (*mousikoi agônes*) were held widely throughout the Hellenistic world (e.g. at Delphi, Delos, Ephesus), providing multiple – and sometimes lucrative – venues for leading musicians and actors to ply their craft. Hellenistic monarchs too, like the Ptolemys in Egypt or Seleucids in Pergamum, and subsequently the wealthy senatorial and imperial patrons of Rome, could afford to stage far more lavish productions than the citizens of Athens.

And so to Rome

Just as the first great Athenian playwrights had drawn from a number of pre-existing performance traditions in forging an art-form that became known universally as 'Greek' tragedy and comedy, so did Roman theatre owe many of what came to be its most characteristic elements to other indigenous Italian peoples – as well as to the Greeks themselves. During the centuries in which Rome was still no more than a small to medium-sized city competing with others for power and prestige within Italy and its immediate surroundings (the eighth to the fourth centuries), the different regions of the peninsula contained several kinds of theatrical performance. It was only after Rome had come to dominate all of Italy (by the third century BC) and then to spread its power more widely still, embracing all of Greece, eliminating Rome's arch-rival Carthage and gaining control of the whole Hellenistic East, that a distinctively 'Roman' theatre tradition emerged – one that combined elements borrowed from all of those conquered neighbours, even as these elements continued to flourish side by side and in some cases even to eclipse it in popularity and longevity.

During the period in which Greek choral and theatrical forms were evolving along the lines we have sketched above (*c.*750–350 BC), the different regions of Italy were experiencing major cultural evolutions of their own. Rome, located in the central region of Latium (hence 'Latin'), was surrounded by neighbours who seem in many respects to have presented more distinguished and interesting musical and theatre traditions than those of Rome itself. To the north, the Etruscans, whose culture included several Greek and Phoenician elements, were renowned for their troupes of travelling players. Wall-paintings show masked performers, dancers, musicians playing double-pipes (*auloi*) and *kitharas*, and acrobats, as well as seated spectators; but no written texts survive and it is unlikely that any were ever published, though the distinguished Roman antiquarian Varro (first century BC) does tantalizingly mention 'Etruscan tragedies' (*De Ling. Lat.* 5.55). The fact that Etruscan art of this early period also often represents satyrs, together with a brief and confusing phrase from the Roman historian Livy (first century AD) about *satura* (a word that usually in Latin seems to mean 'hodge-podge, mixture', but was sometimes confused with the Greek term *saturoi*, meaning 'satyrs'), has led some modern scholars to suggest that the Etruscan performances were in fact a kind of satyr drama. But the evidence for this is thin, and the Etruscan performers depicted in paintings and described by Livy and others seem to be dancing more gracefully and solemnly, less energetically and animalistically, than did the Greek satyr choruses. In any case, some later Roman authors claimed that the Roman term for 'actor' (*histrio*) was derived from the Etruscan word for 'player' (Livy 7.2.4–8); and while this etymology is not in itself convincing, the suggestion that Roman theatre owed a large originary debt to the Etruscans is probable enough.

Much less is known about the performances of the Umbrians to the northeast (birthplace of Ennius, one of the true founders of 'Roman' drama, about whom we shall have more to say shortly), or of the Campanians directly to the south, with one important exception: the Oscan-speaking inhabitants of the town of Atella, near the border between Campania and Latium, had developed a widely popular – and eventually much-imitated – form of improvised farce (*fabulae Atellanae*, 'Atellan stories/plays'), employing masks, stock characters and conventional plots, which also allowed room for some audience involvement too. These stock figures (Pappus the father/old geezer, Bucco the braggart, Dossen(n)us the trickster, Maccus the clown and Manducus the ogre) show up in more or less recognized form in many Plautine comedies, and an ancient (and not incredible) biographical tradition asserted that T. Maccius Plautus was so named because of his early success as a professional Atellan 'clown' before he came to Rome.

Further south still, the largely Hellenized cities of Lucania, Apulia and Sicily existed quite independently of Rome and its small range of local concerns. This was the area of Italy known as Magna Graecia ('Larger Greece'); and many of its inhabitants, especially the urban elites, were completely Greek in language and culture. During the fourth and third centuries BC, as the performance of Athenian-style tragedy and comedy came to be exported far and wide throughout the Greek world, many of these South Italian and Sicilian cities built substantial theatres on the Greek model. Even earlier, the Sicilian tyrants, just like Pisistratus and his sons in sixth-century Athens (or even earlier, Cleisthenes of Sicyon), liked to entertain their citizens with lavish choral and dramatic performances, and Aeschylus, as we noted above, was invited more than once to bring his plays to be performed in Sicily. Euripides' tragedies – already classics – were widely performed from the fourth century BC onwards both by travelling and by local acting troupes, though we do not know what kind of choral and musical components were involved. We may assume too – though evidence is almost entirely lacking – that 'new' plays from the leading Hellenistic tragedians were also being produced.[11] One rare and remarkable surviving example of the range of possibilities available for new tragedies is the 'Exodus' drama (*Exagôgê*) by Ezekiel, a Hellenized Jew probably writing in Alexandria during the third century BC: the play (of which over three hundred lines survive in quotation by early Christian authors) is competently composed in the same style and metre as Euripides (iambic trimeters), and presents key moments in the life of Moses and the escape of the Hebrews from Egypt. There is no trace of a chorus in what survives, and it is not certain that the play was written to be staged (how, for example, would the burning bush and voice of God have been performed?); but it is an effective recitation-piece, and appears to show signs of the influence of Aeschylus' *Persians* as well as of Euripides and the Septuagint (Greek) Bible.[12]

As for comedy, the 'Old' Comedy of Aristophanes and his contemporaries was no longer performed (too topical, too wild and crazy, too scurrilous and gross), though some of those plays were still read in schools as examples of fifth-century Attic conversational style. In the theatres, it was the more allegorized and mythological dramas of Middle Comedy (including Aristophanes' late *Wealth*), or the intricate social-romantic comedies of Menander and the other 'New' Comedians that were chiefly performed. But a separate tradition of 'Doric' comedies had also long flourished in Sicily, of which the most famous representative was Epicharmus; the mimes of Sophron (much admired by Plato) may also have been staged there, unless these were intended purely for a reading public.

In Apulia (notably Tarentum and other towns nearby) another comic theatrical form came to enjoy great popularity in the early fourth century, the so-called *phlyax* farces, perhaps derived originally from Laconian tradition in the Peloponnese. Several scenes from these plays are preserved on vase-paintings (see Green, ch. 9, in this volume). With padded, phallus-wearing actors wearing grotesque masks, as well as some straight heroic-looking characters too, these plays were performed on temporary wooden stages which could be set up quickly and transported from one town to another. Some of the productions represented in these illustrations may even be Old or Middle Comedies, brought over from Athens.[13] In any case, it is clear that the language in which these plays were performed was Greek; and from *c*.300 Rhinthon and others produced written versions of some *phlyax*-plays, as the genre adopted a slightly more highbrow tone, combining farce with more serious mythological themes (*Orestes*, *Heracles*, etc.), in what came to be known as *hilarotragôdiai*.

Rome itself did possess indigenous performance traditions of its own, though in the early centuries they do not seem to have amounted to full-blown dramas. Among these were the ribald Fescennine verses (yet another form of ritual invective and mockery), the exotic dance of the Salii ('Leaping Priests') and the eerie aristocratic funeral ceremonies at which masks of the ancestors (*imagines*) were paraded around on sticks as the glorious achievements of the family were narrated. As we noted earlier, Etruscan and Atellan performances also came to be well established in Rome from at least the fourth century onwards, and Livy mentions that young Roman aristocrats liked to experiment with their own kinds of Atellan farces, presumably performed in Latin rather than Oscan (Livy 7.2).

At first a single annual festival, the *Ludi Romani* ('Roman Games'), sufficed for all the public theatrical entertainments (which might also include acrobats, jugglers and dancers). As the popularity of these occasions grew, before the end of the third century BC a second festival (*Ludi Florales*) was added. It was these and other additional festivals that were in due course to provide the occasion for Rome's earliest comedies and tragedies. (See further Rehm, ch. 10 in this volume.) By the third century BC, the city had expanded enormously both in its range of cultural contacts and in the size and diversity of its population, and henceforth it was to serve (even more than Athens had done for the Greek world of the fifth century) as a magnet for enterprising artists in all genres from all over the Mediterranean and as the prime market for the latest and most sophisticated cultural forms (though one should not ignore the cultural life of other Italian cities, such as Naples and Tarentum). Educated and widely travelled Roman elites were by now becoming more and more fixated on Greek culture as the acme of sophistication, and were attempting to acquire or emulate it in every way possible. It is during this period that the first examples of a distinctive 'Roman' theatre (plays written and performed in Latin) are attested, and from the first these comprised an adventurous blend of indigenous (Italian) and imported (mainly Greek) elements. In 240 BC, a Tarentine immigrant to Rome (perhaps an ex-slave), Livius Andronicus, already the author of an epoch-making translation into

Latin of Homer's *Odyssey*, produced the first written Latin comedy – itself a 'translation' of a Greek comedy whose title is unknown to us – and some tragedies too, on mythological Greek themes. Several more were to follow; and when he was joined in Rome by the prolific Campanian author Gn. Naevius (*c*.270–200 BC), whose comedies and tragedies alike were to enjoy many centuries of popularity,[14] the future in Rome of tragedy and comedy on the Greek (Athenian) model was assured. The array of Greek texts available to be translated or adapted into *fabulae* (*comoediae*) *palliatae* ('plays in Greek dress') was enormous, both in the form of acting scripts from travelling companies and as more formal, even 'published' texts on papyrus or parchment, based on the editions collected, annotated and further disseminated by the scholars at Alexandria, Pergamum and elsewhere. The Roman theatre public was acquiring a taste for such Greek-based theatre – though the prologues of Plautus and Terence make clear that conflicting tastes were still in evidence. Naevius also wrote a few plays at least based on early Roman legend and history (*fabulae praetextae* or *praetextatae*), 'plays dressed in the [purple]-border', i.e. the toga), one of which is reputed to have landed him in trouble with the distinguished family of the Metelli.

By at least the second century BC, the Roman Senate recognized a *collegium* of poets and playwrights. This 'trade-union' was perhaps modelled on the Greek institution of the 'Artists of Dionysus' (above, p. 25), though it was not possessed of quite the same political-social prestige – mainly because Roman theatre practitioners, unlike Greek, were not citizens. Nonetheless it did reflect the growing prominence of actors, musicians and writers within Roman society, even as it also recognized the fact that many of these were immigrants and therefore in need of institutional protection and representation.

One conspicuous specimen of this cluster of professional theatre practitioners was Plautus (254–185 BC), who was credited by some with over two hundred comedies adapted from Greek originals, though eventually the grammarian Varro (first century BC) narrowed this number down to the twenty that survive today. During this early boom period of Roman theatre, new plays were constantly being composed and adapted, and the temporary stages erected for each festival could be expected to present new plays more often than not.

Not all the major playwrights owed their social position and upkeep to the *collegium*, however; some enjoyed their own aristocratic connections and individual elite patrons. This was certainly the case for the distinguished multi-lingual Oscan writer Q. Ennius (239–168 BC), later known as the 'father' of Latin poetry, and likewise his nephew Pacuvius (220–130 BC), who became the foremost tragedian of Republican Rome;[15] likewise the North African ex-slave M. Terentius Afer (Terence, c.185–159 BC), who would never have had the opportunity to see his refined and sophisticated comedies performed but for the patronage of P. Cornelius Scipio Aemilianus. The difference between the sources of support enjoyed by Plautus and Terence may have much to do with the very different flavour and dramatic thrust of their respective comedies.

In adapting the tragedies of Euripides and Sophocles (and also presumably of various now lost Hellenistic tragedians), or the comedies of Menander and Diphilus and the other masters of New Comedy, the Roman playwrights of this early period felt themselves free to make considerable changes both in substance and in manner of presentation. In general, use of a chorus seems to have been rare (there was in any case no space for a large group of performers to dance on a Roman stage, unlike the Greek *orchêstra*), but the musical elements of early Roman drama were nonetheless more prominent and pervasive than their Greek counterparts: dialogue scenes were rewritten to become *cantica* or recitatives, and more than half the lines of most of these plays appear to have been sung or chanted to the accompaniment of the *tibia* (double-pipe, similar to the Greek *aulos*). In later years, however, Roman playwrights and actors became more rhetorical and less musical (as far as can be judged from the scanty remains). Terence's plays are markedly less musical than those of Plautus, and in the tragedies of Seneca (first century AD), even though these are often based quite closely on Sophoclean or Euripidean originals, there are virtually no sung parts for actors, while the neat, self-contained lyrics assigned to 'chorus' may have been spoken by a single voice and never intended to be sung or danced by a group at all.[16]

Up until the very last years of the Republic (mid to late first century BC), dramatic performances of all kinds at Rome seem always to have taken place on temporary stages. The first permanent stone theatre was built by Pompey the Great (c.60 BC); others quickly followed and proliferated throughout the Roman world. Likewise festival occasions for the production of plays (along with other events, musical, spectacular or sporting) became more and more common, and their audiences bigger and bigger. Paradoxically, this expansion of theatrical spaces and opportunities came at a time when the composition of new plays had almost dried up – instead it was the classic comedies of Plautus, Caecilius and Terence, or the tragedies of Ennius, Naevius, Pacuvius and Accius, that were being re-performed by star actors under the sponsorship of wealthy aediles and populist politicians. It was actors, rather than playwrights, who dominated the theatrical scene throughout the later Roman period. As for the plays of Seneca, so influential for the later history of European theatre, we have no record of the circumstances of their composition or performance – if indeed they were performed at all, and not merely recited.

Even in Cicero's day, the actor Roscius was renowned throughout the city for (mainly) his comic roles from Plautus; and by the early Principate (under Augustus, Tiberius, Nero and others) professional actors were pin-ups equivalent in popular appeal to modern film-stars or sporting icons. The result in elite circles was a curious ambivalence about the value of theatrical performance: on the one hand, every well-educated Roman knew intimately the plays of Euripides and Pacuvius, Menander, Plautus and Terence, both from reading and from seeing them performed; yet at the same time there was a strong prejudice among moralists and snobs that the sensational and over-emotional nature of tragic performance, and the scurrilous and unrestrained behaviour characteristic of comic slaves and parasites, appealed to 'lower' human instincts that were better suppressed.[17]

A number of other theatrical forms continued to compete with tragedy and comedy for popular appeal, if not for elite approval: Atellan farces, public musical and/or rhetorical competitions, mimes, recitations of poetry or declamatory rhetoric (usually non-commercial performances for an invited audience), private after-dinner dance-shows, instrumental music and of course numerous more violent acts presented in the arena. The visual arts too reflect an ongoing fascination with the theatre, as wall-paintings, vases and mosaics all frequently depicted scenes or stage-settings drawn from the theatre.

The most popular, and perhaps the most interesting and aesthetically complex, of all Roman theatrical forms of the Imperial period came to be the pantomime. This was a highly skilled multi-media combination of speech, song, dance, music, gesture and scenic design, in which particular scenes or stories from mythology were performed by one or more professional actor-dancers to the accompaniment of instrumentalists and narrator(s). Thus as the narrator described the experience of Medea or Orestes, and the musicians played evocative melodies and rhythms, the dancer(s)[18] acted out the events and the characters' feelings, thus conveying the mood of the whole drama to the hundreds or thousands in the audience. Pantomime performers were the biggest stars of all (after gladiators and charioteers), and it is a matter for much regret that we possess such scant evidence about the actual performances: no text, musical score or choreography survives, and most of the witnesses whose descriptions are available to us are hostile to the form – mainly, it seems, because of its sheer popularity.[19] (See Denard, ch. 8 in this volume.)

During the later years of the Roman Empire, even as Rome and the western provinces came under increasing pressures both from invaders and from moralistic Christian authorities, theatrical performances of many kinds continued to be subsidized by wealthy citizens and/or emperors. As late as the fifth century AD, the famous old theatre of Pompey was elaborately restored, and Claudian refers to a variety of dramatic performances of quite traditional kinds (*Paneg. Man. Theod.* 323–30). Even Ostrogoth and Vandal rulers were quite willing to encourage the continuation of popular spectacles and performances, and the western (Latin-speaking) half of the Empire appears in general to have been less restrictive than the (Greek-speaking) east in its attitude to the theatre. In the end, it seems to have been as much a matter of general economic and educational collapse as of official policy that led to the demise of all large-scale public entertainments. The closing of the theatres by Justinian in 526 AD may not have been a permanent measure, as performances of one kind or another are attested up until the 540s; but the defeat of the Byzantine administration (based in Ravenna) by the Lombards in 568 seems to have spelled the end of classical drama in the West for the next eight hundred years or more. In 692 AD, the Trullan Council banned all forms of theatrical performance. Thus while Byzantine scholars continued intermittently to copy and study texts of classical Greek plays – and even adapt them occasionally to Christian contexts, with Jesus Christ speaking lines written for Prometheus or Dionysus in the cento known as *Christos Paschôn* ('The Suffering Christ'), or Mary, Mother of Jesus, taking on aspects of Medea – the original plays themselves appear no longer to have been performed at all. Thus in both East and West, the various traditions of theatrical acting, dance, music, masks and mime retreated underground – some to be lost for ever, others to emerge eventually in the Renaissance.

NOTES

1. The question of whether 'Homer' and 'Hesiod' were individual poets who wrote down the long hexameter poems attributed to them, or just names given to the imagined authors of these orally composed and transmitted tales, need not occupy us here. For discussion, see I. Morris and B. Powell (eds.), *A New Companion to Homer* (Leiden: E. J. Brill, 1997).
2. See M. Alexiou, *The Ritual Lament in Greek Tradition* (second ed., Cambridge: Cambridge University Press, 2000).
3. See also D. E. Gerber (ed.), *Greek Iambic Poetry* (Loeb Classical Library), (Cambridge, Mass.: Harvard University Press, 1999).
4. On choral performances, see especially C. J. Herington, *Poetry into Drama* (Berkeley: University of California Press, 1985) and C. Calame, trans. D. Collins and J. Orion, *Choruses of Young Women in Ancient Greece* (Lanham: Rowman and Littlefield, 1997). On Sappho, see the essays collected in E. Greene, *Reading Sappho: Contemporary Approaches* (Berkeley: University of California, 1996). In Greek mythology and the poets' own programmatic accounts of the origins

of poetry and music, both the male Apollo and the female Muses were credited as the chief sources of inspiration and ideal models of performance.

5. On Greek music in general, see M. L. West, *Ancient Greek Music* (Oxford: Oxford University Press, 1992); G. Comotti, *Music in Greek and Roman Culture* (Baltimore: Johns Hopkins University Press, 1989). For the sociology of musical performance in Greece, especially in relation to the theatre, see W. B. Anderson, *Ethos and Education in Greek Music* (Cambridge, Mass.: Harvard University Press, 1966); P. Murray and P. Wilson (eds.), *Music and the Muses* (Oxford: Oxford University Press, 2003), with further references; also P. Bourdieu, *The Logic of Practice* (Stanford: Stanford University Press, 1980), pp. 52–79. In Plato's *Laws* it is suggested that 'one who is unskilled in dancing (*achoreutos*) is uneducated (*apaideutos*)' (*Laws* 673c–d); see further S. H. Lonsdale, *Dance and Ritual Play in Greek Religion* (Baltimore: Johns Hopkins University Press, 1993), pp. 8–9, 21–43.

6. For the range of mythological possibilities available to Archaic and classical writers and painters, see in general T. Gantz, *Early Greek Myth* (Baltimore: Johns Hopkins University Press, 1993); and for the agonistic techniques of contradiction and paradox that were typical of such poetry, see M. Griffith, 'Contest and Contradiction in Early Greek Poetry', in M. Griffith and D. J. Mastronarde (eds.), *The Cabinet of the Muses* (Atlanta: Scholar's Press, 1990), pp. 185–207.

7. The Sicilian playwright Epicharmus was composing mythologically based comedies in Doric dialect by the early years of the fifth century BC. Over forty of his plays were apparently known to later scholars in Alexandria; but none has survived, except in little scraps.

8. This conservatism seems to have persisted into fourth-century BC tragedy as well, though we have precious little evidence to go on. By contrast, the Old Comedy of Aristophanes and his rivals (Eupolis, Cratinus, Pherecrates, etc.) was superseded in the fourth century by new forms, first the mythological comedies of Middle Comedy (Alexis etc.) and eventually the sophisticated New Comedy of Menander, Philemon and Diphilus, with their domestic contexts and intricate romance plots (see Goldberg, ch. 7 in this volume).

9. See P. E. Easterling, 'From Repertoire to Canon', in P. E. Easterling (ed.), *The Cambridge Companion to Greek Tragedy* (Cambridge: Cambridge University Press, 1997), pp. 211–27; C. W. Dearden, 'Plays for Export', *Phoenix* 53 (1999), pp. 222–48.

10. C. P. Jones, 'Dinner Theatre', in W. J. Slater (ed.), *Dining in a Classical Context* (Ann Arbor: University of Michigan Press, 1991), pp. 185–98; Quintilian, *Inst. Orat.* Book 11; M. W. Gleason, *Making Men* (Princeton: Princeton University Press, 1994); E. Fantham, 'Orator and Actor', in P. E. Easterling and E. Hall (eds.), *Greek and Roman Actors* (Cambridge: Cambridge University Press, 2002), pp. 362–76. For Cicero's admiration of the comic actor Roscius, see C. Garton, *Personal Aspects of the Roman Theatre* (Toronto: Toronto University Press, 1972), pp. 170–88.

11. See G. Sifakis, *Studies in the History of Hellenistic Drama* (London: Athlone Press, 1967); Easterling, 1997; H. D. Jocelyn, *The Tragedies of Ennius* (Cambridge: Cambridge University Press, 1969).

12. See H. Jacobson, *The Exagoge of Ezekiel* (Cambridge, Mass.: Harvard University Press, 1983); C. Holladay, *Fragments from Hellenistic Jewish Authors* 2 (Atlanta: 1989).

13. O. Taplin, *Comic Angels and Other Approaches to Greek Drama through Vase-Painting* (Oxford: Oxford University Press, 1993); Dearden, 1999.

14. See E. H. Warmington, *Remains of Old Latin*, Vol. II (London: Heinemann, Loeb Classical Library, 1935). Even for a non-specialist, it is easy to recognize the flamboyant verbal play and sound-effects in Naevius' dialogue, of the kind that Plautus was later to practise with equal relish.

15. See H. D. Jocelyn, *The Tragedies of Ennius* (Cambridge: Cambridge University Press, 1969), pp. 12–47; and for the surviving fragments of Ennius and Pacuvius in English translation, Warmington *ROL* Vol. I, pp. 218–357, Vol. II, pp. 157–323.

16. Unfortunately, nothing remains of the highly regarded tragedy *Medea* by Ovid, nor of Julius Caesar's *Oedipus*. Nor do we know whether such products of elite writers competed in the theatrical marketplace along with the canonical classics by Naevius, Ennius and Pacuvius, or were presented in more exclusive surroundings to a more limited audience.

17. See e.g. Quintilian, *Inst. Or.* Book 11; further Erik Gunderson, *Staging Masculinity: The Rhetoric of Performance in the Roman World* (Ann Arbor: University of Michigan Press, 2000); Fantham, 2002, pp. 362–76.

18. The word *pantomimos* is Greek ('imitator-of-everything'), but oddly it seems to have been a term used only by Romans; Greeks referred to this form of entertainment as 'dance' (*orchêsis*).

19. See Denard, ch. 8 and Zarifi, ch. 12 in this volume.

FURTHER READING

Beacham, R. C., *The Roman Theatre and Its Audience*. London: Routledge, 1991.

Campbell, D. A. (ed.), *Greek Lyric*, Vols. I–III. Cambridge, Mass.: Harvard University Press (Loeb Classical Library), 1982–91 (for Sappho, Alcman, Stesichorus, and ancient testimony as to the nature and social function of choral lyric performance).

Herington, C. J., *Poetry into Drama*. Berkeley: University of California Press, 1986.

Lonsdale, S. H., *Dance and Ritual Play in Greek Religion*. Baltimore: Johns Hopkins University Press, 1993.

Murray, P. and Wilson, P. (eds.), *Music and the Muses: The Culture of mousike in the Classical Athenian City*. Oxford: Oxford University Press, 2004.

Warmington, C. H. (ed.), *Remains of Old Latin*, Vols. I–IV. Cambridge, Mass.: Harvard University Press (Loeb Classical Library), 1935 (for the fragments of Naevius, Ennius, Pacuvius and the other early Roman dramatists).

2

RICHARD P. MARTIN

Ancient theatre and performance culture

Definitions and methods

Aristotle's definition of tragedy may seem odd to modern viewers for whom psychological drama is the norm:

> 'Tragedy is a representation (*mimêsis*), not of people, but of an action (*praxis*) . . . They do not act so as to represent character (*êthê*) but they include character on account of the actions' (*Poetics* 1450a20–23).[1]

Yet the formulation deserves renewed attention in light of the advances made by critics and theorists in the last few decades. Tragedy – and, we might say, drama as a whole – is primarily about *action*. Aristotle's own reference to the etymology of the Greek word *drama* (from the verb *dran*, 'act, do') asserts this in another way, although he simply includes the suggestion in his report on possible non-Athenian origins for theatrical activity (*Poetics* 1448a30–38).

To say that tragedy, comedy and satyr play are actions is not to deny that they are also masterpieces of verbal artistry. For readers since late antiquity, it is as texts that these dramas have most often been encountered. Well into the twentieth century, the fascination and power of Greek plays have been found in their textual qualities, whether imagery, rhetoric, sound or structure. (The comparative undervaluation of Roman drama in the twentieth century stems from this fixation, abetted by New Criticism and related interpretive modes.) At the same time, however, the increasingly fruitful rediscovery of classical drama as live performance, starting in the late nineteenth century, has generated a body of valuable work, by scholars and producers, on stagecraft, spectacle, the actor's body, masking, the meaning and use of space and other features of theatre beyond the purely verbal. In part, this trend has led to a renewed interest in Aristotle's wider view of drama: he, too, was well aware that spectacle (*opsis*) and song and dance (*melopoiia*) were components of live Greek theatre (*Poetics* 1449b31–36), although he thought them ultimately dispensable. In another way, the trend has made room for, if not encouraged, a different way of treating 'action' in ancient drama, which we can call the anthropological – while acknowledging that linguistics, sociology, folkloristics and studies of cognition also support it. Aristotle might be thought the progenitor of this approach, as well, if we feel the need to find ancient authority – but the Aristotle of the *Rhetoric* and *Politics*, the philosopher concerned with the effect of actions on daily life. Using such an approach, this essay will pursue the inter-relationship between staged plays and other forms of social action, in order to show how an appreciation of 'actions' outside the theatre enriches the understanding of the action (*drama*) which constituted ancient theatre.

Right away, two problems confront us. First, how do we recover a 'native' sense (the anthropologists' 'emic' definition) of the category of social action? Can we simply inventory all the phenomena connected with the Greek verbs *dran* or *poiein* ('to make', root of 'poetry'), or *telein* ('make complete; perform a rite'), or the Latin *facere* and *agere* (which give us 'fact' and 'act')? Or are we forced to fall back on an 'etic' sense, imposing our own common-sense ideas about significant acts? An awareness of cultural differences is crucial.

We might, for instance, believe that washing one's hands is a trivial, private matter, of social concern only when involving doctors or restaurant workers. Yet one of our earliest Greek texts specifically surrounds this ordinary act with ritual prohibitions regarding its performance:

> Do not at dawning pour the shining wine with unwashed hands to Zeus and other immortals . . .

> Who ever crosses a river with unwashed hands and wickedness angers the gods, and they give him pains thereafter. (Hesiod *Works and Days*, 724–5, 740–1)

One can easily find in Greek tragedy occurrences of hand washing in a marked or implicitly ritual context. Such acts within the stylized medium of drama pose interpretative questions. In the *Persians* of Aeschylus (472), the barbarian queen tells the chorus how she 'touched the fair-watered stream' before sacrificing to ward off the bad omens of her dreams (lines 201–2). Knowing that this action is significant within the traditions of Greek religious practice might lead an audience to see Atossa as a more sympathetic character, or the Persian royal use of a familiar custom as ironic (unless this is simply a projection of the playwright's own environment onto the erstwhile enemy of his city-state). What counts is that an action, known to be culturally significant, has been cited and embedded in another, larger cultural act: the drama itself. The semantics and conventions attached to the smaller gesture have an impact, beyond words, when reproduced in the larger space of the theatre, given the sensitivity of the viewers about such actions. The practical result of studying these smaller gestures and actions should be that our translations and re-stagings of ancient drama focus attention on such moments and relate them (in the actor's words and movements, and in staging) to other significant moments and images (e.g. washing of the corpse, or aspersion of a sacred space, as in Ion's cleansing of Apollo's temple at the opening of Euripides' *Ion*). We should no longer treat them as ordinary but put virtual quotation marks around them. The search for natively 'significant' action inevitably draws one into the study of history, archaeology and semantics, the academic specialties that seek to visualize precise social contours of an ancient culture through identifying its primary signifiers and their force-fields.

The second problem haunts two of the terms just mentioned: 'ritual' and 'performance', words notoriously over-extended in current parlance. 'Performance' can apply to anything from automobiles to athletes. 'Ritual' crops up in descriptions of religious occasions, New Age happenings and obsessive-compulsive disorders. Critics of ancient drama need definitions that retain some of this broad flexibility of usage while focusing more on occasions for social enactment. In this connection, the summary by the folklorist Richard Bauman proves useful: 'performance usually suggests an aesthetically marked and heightened mode of communication, framed in a special way and put on display for an audience'.[2]

The anthropologist Stanley Tambiah, meanwhile, provides a workable definition of 'ritual' that can clarify dramatic contexts:

> Ritual is a culturally constructed system of symbolic communication. It is constituted of patterned and ordered sequences of words and acts, often expressed in multiple media, whose content and arrangement are characterized in varying degree by formality (conventionality), stereotypy (rigidity), condensation (fusion), and redundancy (repetition).[3]

In this light, ritual is a more tightly bounded subset of the larger area of 'performance'. Both depend on the notion of communicative acts directed toward an audience of one or more onlookers, and both are marked out in some way from ordinary processes of communication. We might want to contrast the two in terms of relative emphasis on aesthetic enjoyment versus functional power (the difference between a poem and a magic spell); but a striking feature of Greek and Roman cultures is the way these aspects are often merged. More beautiful, aesthetically appealing prayer or sacrifice is thought to be more effective; for this reason song and dance accompany offerings, and the horns of the sacrificial bull are wrapped in gold. With these definitions in mind, we can narrow slightly the range of phenomena that one must keep in mind when interpreting such alien art forms as Greek tragedy. Yet we are also made immediately conscious that, alongside theatre, Greek and Roman societies, at various times, contained many more opportunities for highly visible 'performances' than do highly privatized modern industrial societies. In a Mediterranean climate, with a high proportion of life lived outdoors and at close quarters, what might seem to us histrionic becomes the norm for social behaviour. It is not inaccurate to refer to fifth-century Athens and second to first-century BC Rome as 'performance' cultures, if by that we mean groupings where being seen to *act* – whether in assembly, senate, military, the forum or the agora – was a key component of social identity for members of certain classes. The 'performance' rubric enables us to combine the analysis of theatre, on the one hand, and oratory, civic spectacles or many related acting formats, on the other. The universe of discourse expands, multiplying the possibilities for interpretation.

Another way to put this would be to see performance itself as a subset within an even wider area, that of social interaction. But then how do we keep the study of ancient drama from spreading out indefinitely into analyses of entire cultures? Or, is that not the goal? Greek and Roman plays offer a crystallization of those cultures, enabling us to investigate many other facets. To study them as performances means to enter deeply into all the performance realms that surround them. But then what practical methods and categorizations can produce interpretative results from the insight that theatrical art and social life form a seamless web? The following examples are an attempt to stake out a few areas and suggest modes of investigation.

Personal performances

The sociologist Erving Goffman, using dramaturgy as a model, called attention to the 'presentation of self' in everyday life.[4] When we meet others, we stage ourselves. But if one's interactions with others can be read as theatrical – as requiring rehearsal, arrangement, selection of details, attention to audience, expressive stylization and so forth – then theatre in a sort of geometrical progression is a drama of self-dramatizations. This means that it would be conceivable to study any given ancient play by segmenting the drama into its constituent social interactions, and to treat each of these as a mini-drama in itself, with a successful or failed outcome. Such a fine-grained observational technique might single out charged interactions such as first encounters, or attempts at persuasion. A famous scene involving both types marks the triumphal return of Agamemnon after the destruction of Troy. Clytemnestra addresses her husband, but plays at the same time to an internal audience, the chorus of Argive elders (Aeschylus, *Agamemnon* 855–913).

The speech in which she dramatizes her years of loneliness and anxiety shifts at the end to become a torrent of praise for the hero (897–8: 'saving forestay of a ship, roof-pillar, a father's only son'). The skill and force of her rhetorical self-presentation up to this point prepares the audience for the next stage, when she persuades Agamemnon, despite his religious caution, to enter his palace by treading a luxurious purple carpet (914–74). His willingness to do so is a symptom, not a cause, of his downfall, a sign of his malleability. The poet explicitly frames it as a defeat for him and victory for his wife (940–3). Ironically, Clytemnestra's victory is itself a poetic *tour de force*, an enactment of vivid imagination and striking imagery (e.g. 958–74: the sea of purple dye; the tree that wards off heat; the vintage). In terms of personal performance, she is at this moment more like an Aeschylus, and her audience (persuaded, by words, of the reality of a fiction) more like the crowd in the theatre itself. The playwright immediately undercuts this riveting individual self-performance with a communal performance, marking a less than successful act of persuasion, as the chorus dance and sing of their abiding anxieties (975–1033). But the impression of Clytemnestra's outsized character remains uppermost. It is worth noting that typically for Greek drama – and unlike the indirection found in realistic or psychological theatre – characterization here is a matter of *personae* speaking out in an agonistic setting, attempting to convince an interlocutor in front of an audience (the chorus). Almost every major figure in Greek tragedy and comedy has such encounters. This configuration can be seen as archetypal, not only for theatre, but for the presentation of heroes in epic (a forerunner of Greek drama). It also structures the related performances of self in symposium, court and assembly, which we will examine below.

Persons and traditions

A slightly more complex form of social interaction triangulates the actor, the audience and a shared body of knowledge about how one should speak and act. In this configuration, the performer not only does or says something; his performance is judged in relation to many previous such acts. Greek athletics and the related phenomenon of hero tales encourage the urge to *compare* performances: is a Theseus up to the level of a Heracles, or this year's pankration winner as good as the victor at the previous Olympic games? On a practical level, ancient playwrights, often by overt reference to earlier or contemporary plays, exploit the possibilities inherent in audience awareness of other performances. A well-known example comes in Euripides' *Electra*, which alludes, in its recognition scene, to the *Libation-Bearers* of Aeschylus. The multiple repeated titles in lists of dramas no longer extant show the effect of the competitive atmosphere in which Greek theatre operated. Every new *Philoctetes* or *Lemnian Women* was an opportunity to parody, subvert or outshine another's version. That comedy and the satyr play could also offer refractions of tragic plots made the audience all the more attuned to pointed allusion.

On a smaller scale, within the dramas rather than in the dramatic production milieu, a personal relationship to verbal tradition could be represented and used for characterization. Again, recognizing this aspect requires us to think more broadly about performance. Recent work by folklorists has drawn attention to the 'performance' in everyday life of certain communicative genres (tales, gossip, personal history narratives, proverbs, etc.). This work has predecessors in linguistics and semiotics, which in turn bring it closer to the study of drama. The Czech literary theorist Jan Mukarovsky referred to the dialogization of texts in which proverbs, representing anonymous voices from outside the present space and time, have intervened. In his memorable phrase, 'proverbial allusions are equivalent to the theatricalization of an utterance'.[5]

While personal performances (as Clytemnestra's) might rely on a number of devices, the decision to have a dramatic figure utter a proverb raises the stakes for characterization because, by definition, the audience is already ahead of the performer; it knows the proper use and intent of the utterances, and its knowledge adjusts the asymmetry between a persuasive rhetorician and passive auditors.

Aristotle indicates an awareness that proverbs are good for displaying opinion and character. In the *Rhetoric* he defines the term *gnômê* as 'A showing forth (*apophansis*) not of particular things such as what sort of a man a certain Iphicrates is – but in general; and not about everything – such as straight is opposite to curved – but about all that has to do with actions (*praxeis*) and what is to be chosen or avoided with regard to action'. Given his comments on action in the *Poetics*, we might say that the *gnômê* is a kernel form of drama, a verbal directive that might blossom into a plot. Aristotle (*Rhet.* 2.21.2) even cites an example from Euripides' *Medea*. In the passage Jason has already informed his wife of his new alliance with the daughter of Creon. When the new father-in-law comes to order Medea out of Corinth he calls her *sophê* – 'clever' or 'wise'.

She replies (lines 292–3): 'This is not the first time, Creon; often my reputation has harmed me and done great evils.' A proverbial expression now comes into play as a transition from her recollection of previous experiences. 'No sound-minded man should ever have his children well taught to be overly clever' (*sophous*, 295). The full elaboration of Medea's gnomic utterance continues (298–9): 'If you put new, smart things before the eyes of fools, you'll appear useless and not wise' (*ou sophos* – the masculine adjective at this point is ambiguous and can also refer to her interlocutor, Creon). She herself must endure this fate, 'for being wise, to some, I am an object of jealousy, to others I am irksome. But I am not so very wise' (*sophê*, 305). In fact, her ironic repetitions and variations of this small theme persuade us by the end of the scene that she *is* much wiser than anyone else in the drama, and that they will suffer for it. Ironically, too, if Medea performs proverbs so proficiently, the audience for this play has to view her as an *expert* in Greek discourse, contrary to her self-presentation as helpless foreigner. In short, such performances of familiar non-dramatic genres within drama provide an audience with a measure to judge the ethos of a staged figure.

Game, play, contest, education

As we have seen, from a performance perspective the landscape of everyday life outside the theatre is never flatly undramatic. Contours and prominences emerge from the activities of social 'actors' in a variety of settings. Thus it pays to take account of other activities involving heightened communication and display, all of which may have shaped stage drama, its performers and audiences.

A story was told in antiquity that Solon, the Athenian lawmaker of the sixth century BC, as an old man attended the first performances of Thespis, the legendary inventor of tragedy, in the days before drama competitions. After seeing the playwright acting in his own production, Solon angrily asked whether he was not ashamed to tell lies in front of audiences. When Thespis replied that it was all done in play, Solon responded that honouring this sort of play would lead to the breakdown of contracts (Plutarch, *Solon* 29). The lawmaker's fears about the negative effects of dramatic fiction foreshadow Plato's rejection of tragic mimesis generations later (*Rep.* 388–94). But the basic acknowledgement that drama is a type of 'play' (*paidia*) has a positive legacy, as well. Aristotle considered play an essential for relaxation and a good means of educating the young (*Politics* 1336a28–35; 1339b16–20), for whom it provided a way to imitate more serious adult pursuits – a view that may not be surprising, given his generally favourable attitude toward mimesis. Even Plato, who denigrated imitation, finds a place for orderly play in the ideal city of the *Republic*, where it serves as children's earliest education in rules (425a). By his last work, the *Laws*, play has become a model for existence: 'Each should live out life', says the Athenian in the dialogue, 'playing at certain forms of play (*paidias*) – sacrificing and singing and dancing – so as to be able to render the gods favourable to him and to defend himself against enemies and defeat them when he fights' (803e). It is striking that three of the most important Greek aesthetic and ritual actions are thus regarded as forms of creative pleasure. It is likely that drama was implicitly regarded as another.

A broad spectrum analysis of 'play' would range from children's imitative role-playing, through games for all ages, to competitive sports and performance contests. The last two categories, often occurring together, are fairly well documented, unlike the less formal and occasional activities. Yet an audience raised on children's games like 'king and donkeys' (Plato *Theaetetus* 146a), or 'night and day' (Plato comicus fr. 152K), might well have detected the stylized patterns of these choose-and-chase games in dramatic stagings of royal power and its pitfalls, whether *Agamemnon, Bacchae, Oedipus Tyrannus* or *Antigone*. Group games not only initiated children into the basic theatrical format of individual responding to chorus; some (such as 'tortoise') also were accompanied by iambic verses (the dominant metre of dramatic speeches) alluding to gender roles and disaster:

Q. Torty-tortoise, what are you doing in the middle?
A. I am weaving wool and Milesian cloth.
Q. What was your son doing when he died?
A. Jumping from white horses into the sea.[6]

Playwrights were associated with other amusements. The tragedian Sophocles was known as an expert ball-player, a skill he exhibited when playing the role of the maiden Nausicaa in his *Pluntriai*. A lucky throw of the knucklebones was called 'Euripides' – apparently from a pun on his name ('Goodtoss-son'), not from gambling skills.[7] More seriously, it has been argued that adult board games, such as *pessoi*, helped to structure the archaic Greek imagination concerning space and power and mould a social consciousness of symbolic action – again, an important preparation for interpreting drama. The symposium, the ubiquitous male drinking party, and its accompanying *kômos* (often inebriated informal procession) provided opportunity for further fun. The frequent use of riddles as a sympotic pastime (Athenaeus 452) meant that many Athenians naturally had a keen interest in interpreting such puzzles as the Sphinx enigma underlying *Oedipus Tyrannus* and the *Phoenician Women*, and ambiguous Delphic oracles (cf. *Ion, Medea*). All these forms of play enriched the metaphorical texture of ancient drama.[8] At the same time they reinforced awareness of the 'zero-sum' nature of social life, an attitude that must have nourished the theatre audience's appreciation of the 'play' of fate and chance.

The historian Thucydides reports Pericles' praise of the Athenian lifestyle: 'We celebrate contests (*agônes*) and sacrifices (*thusiai*) all through the year' (Thuc. 2.38.1). This coordination of activities that Plato later called 'play' is significant, as is their marked frequency in the birthplace of drama, which was from at least the mid-sixth century BC organized as a competition.

The City Dionysia held yearly in early spring featured contests among three playwrights, each producing three tragedies and one satyr play, as well as a comic competition (with three or five dramatists involved).[9] Prizes for first-, second- and third-place productions were awarded; the lead tragic actors (later, in the fourth century BC, the comic as well) also competed for honours. In the fifth century, the larger role of the non-professional chorusmen in all forms of drama made such contests more like team events. The same festival saw even larger numbers competing in a non-theatrical medium, the choral dithyramb. This event (from which no whole text survives) seems to have overshadowed drama in creating crowd passion, as two choruses (one of fifty men, the other fifty boys) represented each of ten Athenian tribes. With a thousand participants annually in the dithyrambs and another hundred or so in the plays, the state-sponsored drama competitions enjoyed an audience that was at once huge (perhaps fifteen thousand persons) and full of performance connoisseurs.

An analogy might be made with athletics, ancient and modern. Staged in crowded stadiums, like drama, the ancient variety were deeply embedded in ritual contexts. *Agônes* were a part of many local festivals that commemorated mythic heroes by projecting the spirit of conquest into the sphere of non-lethal sport. Events with a martial usefulness (running, javelin throwing, combat sports) appeared alongside *agônes* in lyre-playing, singing and even painting. As in the Dionysia, contest and religious worship coincided: the four major Panhellenic ('all-Greek') athletic festivals were dedicated to Zeus (Olympian and Nemean), Poseidon (Isthmian, at Corinth), and Apollo (Pythian, at Delphi). A fifth festival, the Greater Panathenaea, developed by Pisistratus at Athens about the same period as the organization of the Dionysia, included competitive recitation of Homer, but not dramas. Like the heroes whom they commemorated, winning athletes and musicians gained at these games a nearly religious aura and celebrity throughout Greece. Inscriptions, statues and poetry celebrated the gleam of victory. Euripides wrote the victory song for Alcibiades (Plutarch *Alc.* 11) – a reminder that the tropes of hero-cult, athletics and politics often converged.

Athletic 'performance' thus converges with Greek drama in heroic presentation. If athletes, in celebratory odes of Pindar and others, are figured as heroes, so mythic heroes can be staged as athletes, winning or losing. Herakles takes pride of place. He reports his struggle with Death, in the Euripidean *Alcestis*, in terms of *agônes*, with the recovered bride described as the victory prize (*Alc.* 1025–8). The spectacle of a powerful man struggling against crushing forces energizes and adds suspense to such plays as

Philoctetes, *Ajax*, *Hippolytus* and *Women of Trachis*; 'agony' not acciden-
tally comes from the word for 'competition', and playwrights presented it
with the gusto of sportscasters.

Performance skill was vital to the upbringing of young Greeks, especially
males. *Gymnastikê* (physical training) and *mousikê* (poetry, song and dance)
were the two components of traditional education. The *Clouds* of Aristophanes (423 BC) revolves around their contested relative valuation (see
esp. lines 962ff.). His *Frogs*, perhaps in answer to the loss of tradition in
a changing culture, asserted that drama itself educates state and citizens (cf.
Frogs 1039–44, 1419–77). It is clear that older forms of song and dance,
which were associated with group education, rituals and non-dramatic performance, provide the ultimate origin for choral and solo performance in
tragedy, comedy and satyr play. The older forms are 'sociopoetic' inasmuch
as their pre-dramatic usage played a key role in the operation of city-state
institutions. Choruses, especially of young women, are attested in poetry and
visual art from the very beginnings of Greek culture. One of the earliest lyric
poetic texts (seventh century BC) represents a chorus of Spartan maidens
engaged in a ritual to Artemis.[10] Euripides alludes to similar ritual choruses
at the Panathenaea (*Heracles* 781–3), ceremonies of the Great Mother (*Helen*
1338–68) and cult to Aphrodite and Hippolytus (*Hipp.* 1423–30), among
others. For interpreting drama, the existence of such forms goes beyond speculation about genre origins to questions of audience reaction. To what extent
did theatregoers treat choruses on stage, such as the women of Trachis, the
Bacchants worshipping Dionysus, or women celebrating the Thesmophoria,
as 'natural'? How were their reactions affected by their expectations about
such groups in everyday life? The further complication that male chorusmen
played such female choral roles must have foregrounded the stylized nature
of the dramatic versions. Winkler's suggestion that such male choruses were
composed of young men serving as ephebes (aged between eighteen and
twenty) links the educational function of actual non-dramatic groups with
the broader civic role of fictionalized drama as it evolved in Athens.[11]

Religious ritual

The performances of self mentioned in the first two sections above might be
categorized, in terms from cognitive studies, as 'routines', predictable ways
for handling events, that are 'scripted' only to the extent that they match
broad expectations. A greeting, for example, does not employ the word
'goodbye', nor does hand-washing involve pouring of dirt (although Greek
chaire can mean both hail and farewell, and certain encounter rituals, like
supplications, *do* employ the symbolism of soiling the body). The communal

actions named in the third section (above) involve a different level of scripting and evaluation: how well did the body of social actors, whether in dance, procession, symposium or funeral lament, 'perform'? Essentially, this is an aesthetic judgment. Similar critique could frame religious ritual (cf. Socrates' aesthetic judgment about the Bendis celebration at Piraeus, *Rep.* 327a).

It would be heretical to claim that a more aesthetically pleasing Mass (to take an example) is also more effective as ritual action, despite the variety of liturgical styles. Ancient Greek rites, by contrast, pivot on the notion that a performance filled with charm, offering the best combination of song, music and dance, attracts divine favour all the more. Religious acts from the singing of hymns to the dedication of statues can be thought of as containing 'grace' or *charis*, which is then echoed in the gods' reaction to them. This inherently reciprocal notion covers the semantic range of 'grace' and 'charm' but also 'pleasure' and 'thanks'. One way of pinpointing the appearances of the notoriously slippery concept of 'ritual', it seems, would be to trace the usage of this crucial term, in extant dramas. The salient point is that such a concept blurs the line (largely a modern construct) between drama and ritual, aesthetic and effective actions.

Whatever drama's genetic ties to ritual, the two are contiguous in Athens because the primary theatrical event, the Dionysia, was a religious festival.[12] Was every staged action therefore somehow dedicated to the god of theatre? Even if we had explicit evidence to suggest this, the gains for interpretation would still be questionable. More fruitful investigations examine the relationships among dramatic festivals and other large-scale ritualized performance events (like the Panathenaea); the logic of ritual actions within a single play or trilogy (for instance the movement from sacrifice to lament to procession in the *Oresteia*); or the associative resonances set up through allusions to ritual gestures and vocabulary.

If ritualized behaviour implies actions in which formality and proper sequence are heightened, to counteract social breakdown, then perhaps the most important way in which ritual occurs in drama is as foil and fantasy. Stylized theatrical versions of rites complement the actual forms, as a tool for making thematic parallels, for compressing time-frames and for suggesting change, through an apparently unchanging medium. The comedies of Aristophanes provide numerous examples. The *Acharnians* (425), produced in the midst of the Peloponnesian War, plays on the ambiguity of ritual *spondai* (meaning 'libations' and by metonymy 'treaty') to imagine its protagonist as possessing the liquid essence of a separate peace. When Dicaeopolis celebrates with his own private Dionysus procession at home, he further transgresses, since the Rural Dionysia was a communal rite – not just a matter of a single household. Yet scholars have regularly taken the scene in which Dicaeopolis tells his slave how to hold up the model phallus, and instructs his daughter on the niceties of basket-bearing (*Ach.* 241–79), as a snapshot of actual ritual. Subsequent 'rituals' in the *Acharnians* should make one less positive, especially as they are jammed together in theatrical time. The Rural Dionysia (occurring throughout Attica in December) is presented in a play actually produced at the Lenaea festival (early January), while the main struggle between Dicaeopolis and the *miles gloriosus* figure of Lamachus plays out as the distinctive drinking contest associated with the citywide ritual of the Anthesteria, which took place during three days each February. As it collapses three of the four Dionysus theatre festivals, so too the *Acharnians* elides the location of its performances, the theatre of Dionysus on the slope of the Acropolis, with the place for drinking on the festival day *Choes* ('cups'), probably near the river Ilissus, a mile or so to the south. Dramatically, the misplaced rituals provide a substructure that induces a no doubt familiar mood in the theatre audience: the modern equivalent of putting on stage such celebrations as New Orleans Carnival or New Year's Eve parties.

We might contrast this with the technique of alluding to or borrowing from a particular pre-existing script. The first lines of the *Persians* of Aeschylus (472) modify slightly the opening of an earlier play by Phrynichus (as the ancient scholarly tradition noted) and for Aeschylus' audience, it seems this was made meaningful by the subsequent *change* in dramatic handling (Phrynichus' play revealed the Persians' loss right away, while the news is suspensefully delayed in the version by Aeschylus). But the familiar 'text' of the Choes drinking ritual is more amorphous, less scripted than a dramatic rendition; to allude to it involves a different sort of technique and a different cognitive process on the part of the audience. Yet both 'scriptural' and ritual borrowings are resources for enhancing the emotional impact of theatre, and it may well be that the former grew out of the community's long experience with the latter.

Performing in the *polis*

Gender and ethnicity depend on incremental, interactive display: how one dresses, walks, speaks, gestures, builds or decorates. Staged drama partakes of such self-dramatization at the level of the individual, but also of the Athenian *polis*, the city-state of approximately forty thousand citizen males and 150,000 others (slaves, women, children, resident foreigners).[13] Drama provided the space for interpreting and disseminating a version of the history of Athens (as in the *Persians*), but more importantly, its ideology. Plays such as *Ion*, *Erechtheus*, *Oedipus at Colonus* and *Women in Assembly* and

Euripides' *Suppliants* presented an image of an autochthonous, exclusive society that was also a divinely protected, hospitable and democratic state.

The delicate political negotiation enacted by tragedy and comedy in Athens was framed by the city-state's contemporary institutions – especially the assembly (*ekklêsia*), council (*boulê*) and courts – all of which both borrowed from and contributed to theatrical performance. Not only comedy (*Acharnians*, *Women in Assembly*) but also tragedy, more subtly, regularly acknowledges the existence of a parallel space, the Pnyx (a few hundred yards south-west of the Athenian theatre) in which impassioned debate and audience judgement also took place. As with ritual, what matters is the complementarity of these performance arenas. Actual decisions (such as the enslavement of Melos, or the expedition to Sicily of 415) can be explored in theatrical form (in e.g. *Trojan Women*, *Birds*) behind the scrim of myth. The fictional curses and blessings of a Hecuba or Athena might express broader political feeling, even though they do not directly bring it to bear on events.

At the heart of democracy was rhetoric, the art of persuasive speech. The scenario of one figure speaking persuasively to a group structures not just drama (actor to chorus) and the assembly (politician or *rhêtor* to citizens) but also the Athenian courts (plaintiff or defendant to jurymen). An ordinary Athenian male could theoretically participate in all three groups in the space of the same month. Any citizen could speak his mind at the *ekklêsia* or act as prosecutor. Like dramas, trials were 'contests' (*agônes*): they, too, dealt with evidence and detection, innocence or guilt, passions and characters. Court speeches were often scripted by professional rhetoricians to be 'performed' by the litigant – another theatrical element. From the *Wasps* of Aristophanes and other sources, it is clear that Athenians came to expect entertainment in court.[14] By the same token, even our earliest plays contain extended arguments coloured by the language of court and assembly. The *agôn* of words is a regular feature of Old Comedy and frequent in tragedy. The *Oedipus Tyrannus* centres on investigation and prosecution, while the *Eumenides* is pure courtroom drama. Good examples of the structural device of paired opposing speeches occur in *Medea* (465–575), *Philoctetes* (1004–62), and in comedy, *Clouds* (961–1104) and – most prominently – *Frogs* (907–1073). Audience appetite for competitive speech was further heightened by the intellectual climate of fifth-century Athens, which encouraged rhetorical display. Philosophers for hire – Protagoras, Gorgias, Hippias and other sophists – taught success through public speaking, offering as sample wares their own often highly wrought epideictic speeches. The effects were bemoaned by at least one politician, Cleon, who accused his fellow citizens of treating vital deliberations like contests, and becoming 'spectators of speeches' (Thuc. 3.38). Given their similarities, Plato could label tragedy a flattering form of 'rhetorical public speaking' (*Gorgias* 502b–d). In this energetic cross-fertilizing of genres, Euripidean drama, in particular, shows the signs of acquaintance with sophistic style and strategies. At the same time Athenian oratory, especially that of Lycurgus and Antiphon, used tragic language and quotations to add drama to courtroom narrations.

The Athenian state and its citizens dramatized their status, finally, through the medium of civic spectacles that interwove the institutions discussed so far. In the fourth century BC, and perhaps earlier, young men of the age for military service assembled yearly in the theatre, where they drilled before the people and received a shield and spear at state expense (Aristotle, *Ath. Pol.* 42.4). At least once a year, the Assembly met in the Theatre of Dionysus. This was the focal point, of course, for the City Dionysia. But the procession preceding the yearly drama contests marked the bounds of Athenian territory, accompanying the rough wooden cult image of the god from Eleutherae, on the Boeotian border, to be installed at the altar of his sanctuary near the Academy, whence, on the eve of the feast, it processed to the god's shrine near the theatre, site of a bull sacrifice. Amid the bearers of offering trays, wineskins, ritual water and the sacrificial pig (whose blood would cleanse the theatre periphery), the drama producers walked in their ornate costumes. Models of phalluses (some large enough to require carts) were paraded, a relic of fertility functions of the local Dionysus cult. In a typically Athenian melding, this too was political: in the fifth century BC, each colony of the expanding empire sent a phallus for the procession. The announcement of honours to citizens and foreigners, the recognition of children of fallen warriors, the parading of subject states' monetary contributions – all made the festival into civic theatre, a spectacle of optimism and celebration counterbalanced by the darker tragedies on view.

Rome

All the categories above might be applied to the culture of Rome as it developed over several centuries, but with changes of scale, emphasis and linkage. Drama was tied intimately to sanctioned games (*ludi*) of various types, but (unlike at Athens) not exclusively to festivals in celebration of one particular god. *Ludi scaenici*, in which plays figured, honoured Apollo, Flora, the Great Mother and Jupiter Optimus Maximus, among others. While many were instituted during the period of the Punic Wars, according to Roman tradition the very first *ludi scaenici* originated in the form of pantomime dances to flute accompaniment, performed by Etruscan actors, in a ritual seeking divine help during a pestilence in 364 BC (Livy 7.2). Thus, the functional, almost magical nature of drama is foregrounded, its role as a 'performative utterance' (to use the terms of speech-act theory) as well as a performance.

Such a practical function seems an odd match for the high artistic heritage of surviving early Roman dramas. The polished New Comedy of Menander, Diphilus and other Greek playwrights is, after all, the explicit forerunner of the plays of Plautus and Terence, and Athenian tragedy was the model for works by Ennius, Accius and Pacuvius. But we should not let the modern polarization of aesthetics and ritual obscure the picture. Furthermore, Roman drama, like its Greek counterparts, seems to have evolved rapidly in constant dialogue with other para-dramatic or non-fictive forms of impromptu entertainment (cf. Greek *iambos* and *dithyramb*, above). In Livy's account of origins, the foreign *ludiones* with their graceful wordless dances were soon imitated by Roman youths, who introduced exchanges of jocular verses, with gestures to match. A mixed genre, called *saturae* (apparently, musical skits), next evolved. After further experimentation, Livius Andronicus, a Greek captured from Tarentum, in 240 BC at the *Ludi Romani* staged plays that featured plots. Livy's sketch fails to mention the Greek literary learning of this innovator (who was also the translator of the *Odyssey* into Latin), but makes clear that native traditions like informal verse contests and the farces associated with the town of Atella continued to develop, even after theatrical art had become professionalized. This contrasts with Athens, where the pre-eminence of stage drama seems to have eclipsed other entertainments.

A Roman of the first century AD could see plays at least forty-three days a year, much more often than a citizen of classical Athens. But until the general Pompey built his theatre complex adjoining a temple of Venus in 55 BC, no permanent structure existed for productions.[15] The fear that a successful producer of plays in the republican period could establish a dangerous political power, even more than Roman ambivalence about the moral effects of theatre, had confined earlier audiences to temporary wooden seating. In contrast to Athens, where wealthy citizens undertook to finance drama for their own prestige, Rome encouraged young politicians to lavishly supplement at their own expense the state funding of *ludi* as a way of gaining the edge in local elections. Themistocles, Pericles or Sophocles – all of whom served as play producers (*chorêgoi*) – may also have won popularity, but vote-buying had no place in the Athenian system. They stood to obtain more prominence through the political messages of the plays they funded, and the visibility of the expensive choregic monuments they erected upon winning. Although the plays of Plautus and Terence, Naevius and Ennius dealt with war, slavery, education and money, their half-Greek heritage (and frequent revivals) must have muted their value as immediate political propaganda. Making up for this as a way of getting personal attention were the total entertainment packages devised by ambitious sponsors. *Ludi circenses* (races on foot and in chariots, boxing, wrestling) accompanied drama, not always harmoniously, at such festivals as the *Ludi Romani* or *Megalenses*. At the latter, in April 165 BC, the first performance of Terence's *The Mother-in-Law* was halted when an unruly crowd burst in, expecting to see a tightrope walker and a boxing match. A second attempt (at funeral games for L. Aemilius Paullus, 160 BC) got as far as the first act before the rumour of gladiatorial games at the spot attracted a mob interested in rougher performances.

As the Republic neared its end, games, drama and political spectacle increasingly merged. At the inauguration of Pompey's huge new theatre complex, a production of the *Clytemestra* of Accius boasted a procession with six hundred mules carrying the booty of Troy – an evocative touch, since Pompey several years before had stage-managed a two-day triumph featuring himself in a gem-studded chariot, a parade of plunder, painted depictions of his famous battles and hundreds of chained captives. Athenian spectacles such as the Panathenaic procession or the parades at the Dionysia required broad participation by citizens, whereas Rome's celebration of successful generals sharply separated the triumphal 'performer' from adoring audience. A similar dynamic – massed crowds and single performers – marked the most famous non-theatrical events with which Roman drama had to compete: gladiatorial games. In the eastern Empire, these were often held in reconstituted theatres, while in Rome itself and the west, purpose-built amphitheatres housed the wildly popular contests of man against man or animals. (Hunts and mock naval battles were also hosted.) The Colosseum (dedicated AD 80, with a hundred days of games) held fifty thousand spectators. They enjoyed blood-sport with the trappings of stage shows, as when gladiatorial production of a mime (a popular Roman genre) featured a real criminal, actually killed when the fiction called for it. An 'Orpheus' character might be surrounded by real beasts and done in by the bear. Attendants at the shows dressed as Pluto, Mercury and other gods. And the gladiators themselves often took on 'dramatic' roles: the fish-helmeted *murmillo* tried to dodge the net-carrying *retiarius*, slaves or prisoners of war played exotic tribal warriors in combat against courageous Romans. As larger-than life characters – some of whom had superstar status – gladiators in turn became figures in Atellan farces.

The first recorded gladiatorial show (264 BC) was part of a funeral commemoration, like athletic events in the archaic Greek world. As a performance, Roman aristocratic burial rites offered a potent mixture of entertainment, public spectacle and mimetic theatre. The historian Polybius (6.53) describes funeral processions featuring actors wearing lifelike masks (*imagines*) that represented the deceased's illustrious ancestors (six hundred of them at the funeral of M. Claudius Marcellus, 208 BC). The formal laudations, in the presence of the corpse and the elaborately dressed mummers, at the speaker's platform in the Forum, thus resembled monologues delivered to an audience of the famous dead. In this and other respects, the social dramas to be found in Rome's public spaces could command far more attention than the work of her playwrights.

Forum, courts and Senate provided arenas for oratory, the personal performances that could sway the state. Even more than in Athens, the study of persuasive speaking dominated education, occupied the leisured class, and seeped into the composition and reception of poetry (by way of staged public reading, the *recitatio*). Performances with a fictional colouring involved hypothetical, often bizarre, legal cases (*controversiae*) or imagined admonitions (*suasoriae*). The first century BC, in particular, saw tense interminglings of criminal prosecutions and political speech-making. The career of Cicero (106–43 BC) affords some glimpses of the cross-connection of genres, performers and audiences in his time. The orator was not unusual in his acquaintance with actors; a good friend was Quintus Roscius Gallus, known for excelling in the role of the pimp Ballio in Plautus' *Pseudolus*. A tragic actor, Clodius Aesopus, is said to have instructed the young man in elocution. In a defence speech (*Rosc. Am.*), Cicero makes easy allusions to a comedy of Caecilius Statius to support his assertions about rural Italian life (even though the play was set in Greece), presuming that his audience knew such dramas of the previous century.

The tie between oratory and drama was longstanding. Cicero records (*Brutus* 167) that the playwright Afranius (second century BC) imitated the style of Gaius Titius, an urbane orator and tragedian. It was at a revival of an historical drama by Afranius, reports Cicero, that the troupe of actors looked directly at his political nemesis in the audience, Publius Clodius, and spoke with dramatic intensity words about a profligate: 'The continued course and end of your wicked life'. To Cicero's delight, 'He sat frightened out of his wits; and he, who formerly used to pack the assemblies which he summoned with bands of noisy buffoons, was now driven away by the voices of these same players' (*Sest.* 118).[16] Public figures in Rome were acutely sensitive to applause in the theatre, games or assemblies; for some, as Cicero says, 'it is inevitable that applause must appear immortality and hissing death' (*Sest.* 115). And crowds were just as sensitive to the political possibilities of dramatic performance: 'amid the great variety of sentences and apophthegms which occur in that play,' said Cicero of Afranius' drama, 'there was not one passage in which any expression of the poet had any bearing on our times, which either escaped the notice of the main body of the people, or on which particular emphasis was not laid by the actor' (*Sest.* 118). His own exile (Cicero claims) had been alluded to this way on stage by a tearful actor, to the groans and applause of the audience. After his assassination by the henchmen of Antony in 43 BC, the orator's head and right hand, with which he wrote and gestured, were cut off and displayed in the Forum – a final theatrical counterthrust. Such histrionics, set against a long history of drama (theatrical and social), worked effectively throughout the long reign of performance culture in Greece and Rome.

NOTES

1. This and following translations are mine unless otherwise noted.
2. R. Bauman (ed.), 'Performance', in R. Bauman (ed.), *Folklore, Cultural Performances, and Popular Entertainments: A Communications-Centered Handbook* (New York: Oxford University Press, 1994), pp. 41–9.
3. S. Tambiah, *Culture, Thought, and Social Action: An Anthropological Perspective* (Cambridge, Mass.: Harvard University Press, 1985), p. 128.
4. E. Goffman, *The Presentation of Self in Everyday Life* (New York: Doubleday, 1956; rpt. Garden City, New York: Anchor, 1959).
5. J. Mukarovsky, *The Word and Verbal Art: Selected Essays by Jan Mukarovsky*, trans. and ed. J. Burbank and P. Steiner (New Haven: Yale University Press, 1977).
6. D. L. Page, *PMG* 876 in *Poetae Melici Graeci* (Oxford: Clarendon Press, 1967), p. 464.
7. Suetonius, *On Games*, 2.2.
8. E.g. the image of the dice-toss at Sophocles fr. 895, in Stefan Radt (ed.), *Tragicorum Graecorum Fragmenta* 4 (Göttingen: Vandenhoeck & Ruprecht, 1977), p. 574.
9. See further Denard, ch. 8 and Rehm, ch. 10 in this volume.
10. Alcman fr. 1 *PMG* (see note 6).
11. J. Winkler, 'The Ephebes' Song: *Tragôidia* and *Polis*', in J. Winkler and F. Zeitlin (eds.), *Nothing to Do with Dionysos? Athenian Drama in Its Social Context* (Princeton: Princeton University Press, 1990), pp. 20–62.
12. On the possible ritual origins of drama, see Graf, ch. 3 in this volume.
13. See Walton, ch. 16 in this volume. Estimates of the number of citizens range from 60,000 for the mid-fifth century BC to 30,000 for the fourth century.
14. See E. Hall, 'Lawcourt Dramas: The Power of Performance in Greek Forensic Oratory', *Bulletin of the Institute of Classical Studies* 40 (1995), pp. 39–58.
15. See Beacham, ch.12 in this volume.
16. This and following translations from the oration are by C. D. Yonge, *The Orations of Marcus Tullius Cicero* (London: George Bell and Sons, 1891).

FURTHER READING

Connor, W. R., 'Tribes, Festivals and Processions; Civic Ceremonial and Political Manipulation in Archaic Greece', *Journal of Hellenic Studies* 107 (1987), 40–50.

Easterling, P. E., 'Tragedy and Ritual', *Metis* 3(1988), 87–109.

Goldhill, S., 'The Great Dionysia and Civic Ideology', in Winkler and Zeitlin, 1990, pp. 97–130.

Kurke, L., *Coins, Bodies, Games, and Gold: The Politics of Meaning in Archaic Greece*. Princeton: Princeton University Press, 1999.

Neils, J. (ed.), *Worshipping Athena: Panathenaia and Parthenon*, Madison, Wis.: University of Wisconsin Press, 1996.

Phillips, D. and Pritchard, D., *Sport and Festival in the Ancient Greek World*. Swansea: Classical Press of Wales, 2003.

Scullion, S., '"Nothing to Do with Dionysus": Tragedy Misconceived as Ritual', *Classical Quarterly* 52 (2002), 102–37.

Wiedemann, T., *Emperors and Gladiators*. London: Routledge, 1992.

Winkler, J., and Zeitlin, F. (eds.). *Nothing to Do with Dionysos? Athenian Drama in Its Social Context*. Princeton: Princeton University Press, 1990.

3

FRITZ GRAF

Religion and drama

Introduction: ancient religion

Ancient religion, as the modern mantra goes, is ritual-based, polytheistic and embedded; its gods are anthropomorphic, its rituals sociomorphic; belief and its higher form, theology, are incidental only. As far as it goes, this is correct. Ancient religion pervaded every aspect of collective and individual life. It expressed itself in rituals that treated the gods in human shape as social partners: they received gifts through offerings, praise and promises from prayers, and were invited to common meals through sacrifices. It was not what one believed that counted, but participation in the collective rituals of one's group. This did not preclude personal piety or personal scepticism, even agnosticism, nor did it exclude public debate on the character of the divine powers and their role in the life of the city, the family and each individual.

Drama, as representation of human life, reflects the importance of ritual in the lives of Greeks and Romans. But it also reflects their complex and often contradictory thinking and speaking about the gods and heroes who were honoured in the rituals, all the more contradictory in the absence of any process for creating binding dogmas about what humans were to think about their gods.

Drama and festival

Drama is ritual, literally: dramatic performances were part of city festivals. In Athens, where tragedy and comedy originated, they were part of the complex programme of athletic and musical contests that characterized more than half of the city festivals.[1] Other Greek cities quickly adopted dramatic performances during their festivals of Dionysus, including Rome in 240 BC (Cicero. *Brut.* 72). Over time, the theatre became the main architectural expression of Greek urban life, together with the agora and, in the Imperial epoch, public baths; in many cities, it was also the place where the citizens assembled, and where the city publicly honoured its benefactors.[2] As in Athens, Dionysiac ritual, stage performance and the expression of civic identity were inextricably linked, although dithyrambs and dramas were very often performed by itinerant professionals, the Dionysiac *technitai*, rather than by citizen groups.

Athens

In fifth-century BC Athens, three of the four main festivals of Dionysus included dramatic performances: the City Dionysia, the Lenaea, and to a lesser degree the Rural Dionysia. These performances were an integral part of the overall ritual programme of the respective festivals.

The best documented among these festivals is the City Dionysia. This festival was constructed as a complex ritual sequence of which the musical and dramatic contests were only a part. The introductory rites of the festival – the introduction of the image and the procession to the theatre – expressed the alterity that entered the city with Dionysus: the god arrived from the margins of the Athenian territory. Drunken revelry was another expression of alterity, as was the presentation of unrestrained male sexuality in the phallic procession; the phallus-song that Dicaeopolis sings during his private celebration of the Rural Dionysia in Aristophanes' *Acharnians* (262–79) revels in what to him is highly gratifying sexual violence. The space of the ritual itself, the theatre of Dionysus on the slope of the Acropolis, was a liminal space inside the city. Thus, the City Dionysia appears as a liminal festival in which the ordinary social structures have been replaced by the unstructured unity of *communitas* which, according to Victor Turner, opens up a space of reflection.

The other ritual theme was Athenian civic ideology.[3] It is not alien to alterity: the *polis* is the focus of dramatic reflection. The rituals, furthermore, concentrated not on the city ordered by Athena and Zeus but on the exploits of its males: Dionysus himself was a military leader whose maenads and satyrs conquered the east. Thus, the rituals of the City Dionysia opened a liminal ritual space that allowed reflection on civic ideology, on Athens, its values and its destiny. And that is exactly what both tragedies and comedies offer, from Aeschylus' *Seven Against Thebes* to Euripides' *Bacchae* or the comedies of Aristophanes.

In the Lenaea, civic ideology seems to be less prominent or altogether absent; the same is true for the Rural Dionysia. The dominant themes of the Lenaea are ecstasy and role change. According to one etymology, its main actors were the *lênai*, the ecstatic women (maenads) who gave the festival its name. (Another etymology derives the festival's name from *lênos*, the 'wine-vat' in which the grapes were pressed: although Dionysus is a god of wine, the pressing of the grapes was long over by the midwinter date of this festival, and the etymology is unconvincing.)

Rome

Rome, the city at the margins of the Greek world, was somewhat different. Roman festivals existed for centuries without dramatic performances. The innovation of Livius Andronicus, who in 240 BC introduced dramatic performances, was part of the hellenizing process that characterized most of Rome's Republican history. (See also in this volume, Griffith, ch. 1 and Rehm, ch. 10.) But the festivals that featured them were not those of Liber, Rome's Dionysus. The two main festivals of Rome's political groups, the *ludi Romani*, for which Livius Andronicus staged the first dramatic performances, and the *ludi plebeii*, adopted this innovation; and also the two main festivals for gods of Greek origin, Apollo and the Mother of the Gods.

Drama in Rome, that is, did not have the very close connection with religion it had in Athens; it was moving towards becoming popular entertainment. In 160 BC, the playwright Terence complained that his comic actors had to compete with boxers, tightrope walkers, and gladiators (*The Mother-in-Law*, 25–40). It remained entertainment when Augustus had a tragedy, Varius Rufus' *Thyestes*, staged for the victory celebration after Actium in 29 BC, although it must have had a strong political function as well, given that Augustus paid the poet a million sesterces. Nevertheless, the public performance of drama in Republican Rome never moved away from the state festivals and their religious institutions. When the public wanted a popular piece repeated, the only way to do so was to repeat the entire festival through the mechanism of *instauratio*, the repetition of a ritual because of a formal flaw. It cannot be a coincidence that during Plautus' lifetime the *ludi Romani* were repeated more often than at any time before or after. The most memorable *instauratio* happened in the year 205 BC, when Plautus staged his wildly successful *Miles Gloriosus* (*The Swaggering Soldier*): the *ludi* had to be performed seven times, more because of the poet's genius than the incompetence of Rome's sacred officials. In about 200 AD, the Christian writer Tertullian still remembered the religious context of drama well enough to ban public spectacles for the very reason that they were part of pagan ritual: 'It is agreed that every performance of spectacles is based on idolatry' (*On Spectacles* 4.3). Beyond antiquarianism and rhetorical stance, Tertullian's argument retained a basic insight into the religious role that dramatic performances played in pagan culture.

Ritual and drama

General theories

Dramatic performances during a festival are not exclusive to Greece and Rome or other ancient societies, as is demonstrated by initiatory masquerading, medieval Passion plays and the *Festspiel* of nineteenth-century political festivals. This intimate connection between festival and drama stirred scholarly interest in the nineteenth century, when folklore studies, ethnology and religious studies were about to turn into academic disciplines; according to their prevalent explanatory paradigm, these early scholars focused on origins to explain the connection. Hermann Usener, one of the founding fathers of the study of religion, analysed rituals in European folklore traditions and in antiquity, understanding them as dramatizations of the battle between Winter and Summer.[4] Inspired by Usener, James G. Frazer frequently used the term 'ritual drama' for a specific type of ritual that staged a myth, such as the Sacred Marriage Rite, or the *Passion of Tammuz* in the Persian *Saccaea* festival. Ritual dramas were not performed 'simply to stir the emotions of the spectators and to while away the languor and tedium of idle hours': in their roles as mythical figures, the players incorporated the forces that these figures represented, and thus they magically influenced nature.[5]

Although these paradigms have long been discarded, their basic insight is correct: ritual and drama are closely connected.[6] On a very elementary level, both consist of action. In both cases, it is action performed by specialized actors; the actors have well-defined roles that, in the case of ritual, might also be their social roles – the head of the group as sacrificer or the priest who prays, the assisting servants, the wailing women; the tragic or comic actor with their often somewhat stereotyped roles, the chorus. It is action that has been isolated in space and in time from daily life and from pragmatic function, and that is often make-believe. Although I know of no pagan ritual that is so blatantly make-believe as the Christian transubstantiation of wine and bread into blood and flesh, there is no need to assume that, for example, the sacrificial animal really agreed to being killed, or that the ritual marriage between an Athenian priestess named the Queen and the god Dionysus involved actual sexual intercourse. Ritual and drama have their own space that is separated off from other public or private space and often gives rise to specialized architectural forms, the sacred precinct, the sanctuary, the theatre. This spatial arrangement goes together with the differentiation of the participants into two groups, agents and audience; often, the audience's space has been specially shaped in order to give them the best possible view – the initiation hall in Eleusis contained steps along the four walls where the spectators could sit or stand, and some sanctuaries in

Roman times even contained a theatre constructed around their cultic space. Ritual and dramatic time is different from empirical time. Both turn past into present by staging what performers and audience understand as a past event.

Tragedy represents the heroic past, or in a few cases such as Aeschylus' *Persians*, a historical past; in Greek thought, there was no essential difference between mythical and historical past anyway, the heroes of myth were simply living much earlier. Drama also manipulates time: its action can concentrate a much longer time-span into the duration of a play. And finally, both ritual and drama have a simple and clear structure, articulating a beginning, a middle and an end. Rites of passage or sacrificial rites are organized in a sequence of separation – liminality – reintegration; almost every drama progresses from a prologue through several scenes that are separated by choral songs to a clearly marked end. This structure is easily remembered and reproduced, and it helps actors and audience to orientate themselves in a similar way as empirical time helps us to orientate ourselves in ordinary life.

Thus, ritual and drama share very basic characteristics. In itself, this does not force us to derive the latter from the former; they might well be parallel forms of collective expression, and the similarities could result from a common function. In a very general sense, collective rituals such as festivals create, structure and legitimate collectivities: Emile Durkheim postulated this as the primary function of religion, Victor Turner specified how rituals create the feeling of 'being together', *communitas*.[7] One begins to understand why it is that fifth-century tragedy and comedy in Athens thought so much about communal life and about the conditions, history and institutions of Athens. And even after participatory democracy had lost some of its appeal and much of its function, the comedy of Menander still thought about communal life, but narrowed community down to family and neighbourhood. Roman comedy continued this exploration, Plautus sometimes in an only gradually less serious way than Terence. Senecan tragedy in turn explored human life in a way that made some interpreters wonder whether the philosopher used tragedy as a vehicle for philosophical teaching; in the same epoch, emperors turned against tragic poets. The inheritance of fifth-century Athens still made drama into a literary genre that was far from being harmless.

Greece and Rome

Already ancient theories of how tragedy and comedy evolved insist on the connection with ritual, without however agreeing on one origin; their disagreement suggests that not even Aristotle could tap into actual memories of how drama evolved in Greece. But whatever the derivation of tragedy and comedy, no one ever doubted the ritual roots that language seemed to guarantee. The terms *tragôidoi* and *kômôidoi* referred to groups of singers, to choruses employed in ritual. Modern explanations followed suit. From Welcker to Nietzsche, Wilamowitz and beyond, it was the derivation from the satyr play that was accepted as true. Against this general consensus, Walter Burkert introduced the derivation from the goat sacrifice that rapidly became common knowledge. More recently, however, Jack Winkler turned the 'billy-goat singers' into Athenian adolescents whom their society allegedly called goats – there is no real evidence for this, and the solution follows the fashionable initiation pattern as neatly as an earlier generation followed the now defunct vegetation pattern.[8]

Drama in Rome had similar ritual connections, at least in Roman eyes. According to Livy, who reproduces an earlier account, when Rome was ravaged by the plague in 364 BC, the Romans first performed a *lectisternium*, a banquet for the gods, and when this did not help, they called on Etruscan dancers, *ludiones*, to pacify them (Livy 7.2.3f.; see also Horace, *Epistle* 2.1.139–55). *Ludi scaenici*, as Livy calls them, thus had the same religious functions as feeding the gods. Roman youngsters quickly imitated these dancers: thus developed Rome's indigenous tradition of stage play, and the introduction of Greek tragedy and comedy – in themselves part of religious festivals – was grafted upon this indigenous tradition. It is even more difficult than in the Greek case to gauge how much historical memory this and similar stories preserve; I suspect not much in either case. It is clear, however, that there were 'theatrical' traditions indigenous to Italy, such as the *Fabulae Atellanae* or the South Italian *phlyax* dramas; but we know nothing about their background and social setting before they arrived in Rome.[9]

Rituals on the stage

In the same way as they were an important part of daily life, rituals were part of the ancient stage. Characters invoke the gods in prayers and oaths, pour libations on graves and altars, sacrifice animals, incense or fruit; and although Roman comedy is set in Greece, its rituals are not manifestly Greek. The heroic ancestors of tragedy perform more or less the same rituals as the contemporary common man of comedy. Every Greek theatre housed an altar of Dionysus somewhere in the orchestra; it was used for the libations and sacrifices that were part of the festival and preceded the theatrical performances, but it could also be used as a prop in the play. Complex rituals such as animal sacrifice were usually reported by a messenger or some other observer; prayers, libations, smaller offerings could be performed as part of the stage action; this difference has as much to do with the constraints of the stage as with the convention not to show killings on stage. Characters and choruses could be characterized by their ritual activities, and sometimes a play got its title from them. Among the lost plays of Aeschylus, there is the *Conjurors of the Dead* (*Psychagôgoi*), and the founder of Athenian tragedy, Thespis, performed a piece called *The Priests*. Among Menander's comedies is *The Possessed Woman* (*Theophoroumenê*); the Roman Naevius wrote a *Soothsayer* (*Ariolus*). Outside the Athenian tradition, we hear that the Syracusan Epicharmus staged *The Victory Celebration*, his contemporary Sophron *The Women Who Promise to Ban the Goddess*. Aeschylus' *Suppliants* has the daughters of Danaus implore the gods of Argos for help against their cousins, his *Libation-Bearers* featured a female chorus offering libations at Agamemnon's grave. In Euripides' *Suppliants* the chorus is identified as a group of Argive women who supplicate the Athenians to help them obtain the bodies of their sons killed in Thebes; his *Bacchae* are the ecstatic female worshippers of Dionysus and the same title is preserved for four other lost tragedies by fifth-century writers; Aristophanes' *Women at the Thesmophoria* features Athenian matrons performing the Thesmophoria festival.

Plays could be set entirely or in part in a sanctuary. Euripides' *Ion* is set in the Delphic sanctuary; Aeschylus' *Eumenides* opens in Delphi, then shifts its action to Athens. Sophocles' *Oedipus at Colonus* is staged in front of the local sanctuary of the Eumenides, Euripides' *Iphigenia among the Taurians* in front of the sanctuary of a barbarian Artemis; Menander's *The Bad-Tempered Man* (*Dyskolos*) is set in the countryside with a grotto of Pan and the Nymphs, Plautus' *The Rope* (*Rudens*) in front of a sanctuary of Venus at the shore of Cyrene. Some plays even open on an impressive ritual scene that sets the tone for much that is to come. Sophocles' *Oedipus Tyrannus* opens on a chorus of old Theban men imploring the gods for help against the plague that is ravaging their city; Aeschylus' *Eumenides* begins with the Delphic priestess in the morning opening the doors of Apollo's temple.

Sacrifice and drama

But the representation of ritual on stage is not simply a reflection of daily life in a society with an embedded religion. Sometimes, the poets stage rituals that were never performed, such as the necromantic rites in Aeschylus' *Persians* or in Seneca's *Oedipus*. Usually, however, even regular ritual is not simply reproduced, but used as a tool to shape the audience's expectations and perceptions. Changes sometimes seem minute, but the audience, steeped in rituals, was perfectly capable of spotting even these.

It has been argued that the influence of ritual went deeper than this. Given the ritual character of tragedy and comedy and their embeddedness in Dionysiac festivals, the very plot structure could be understood on the background of a ritual pattern, be it initiation or sacrificial ritual.[10] This sometimes comes dangerously close to older evolutionary paradigms, and caution is advisable. Heroic myth regularly ends with the death of the hero whose grave then becomes the focus of a cult, and the narrative structure of heroic myth is often enough identical with the tripartite structure of passage rites,[11] insofar as tragic narration and ritual share a common structure. The observation that tragedy often uses sacrificial language for the death of its heroes confirms such a view, but should not be pressed; even if tragic language uses the vocabulary of sacrifice more often than choral lyrics do, there are counter-instances as well, and details matter.

Animal sacrifice was the main ritual of Greek religion, on the stage as well as in real life.[12] Its controlled violence ordinarily led to a common meal, and the otherwise rare commodity of meat established communication between humans and gods and affirmed social roles and cohesion in the sacrificing group. Ordinary sacrifice is often alluded to in drama; but detailed descriptions of sacrifices serve their special ends. In Aeschylus' *Agamemnon*, the imagery of sacrifice that the chorus uses several times helps to establish a mood of foreboding and of a world gone wrong.[13] After the nightwatchman's prologue and the first song of the chorus of Argive old men, Clytemnestra enters in order to perform a thanksgiving sacrifice: Troy has fallen to the Greeks. But the first choral ode has alerted the audience to the problems of sacrifice. Very early, after narrating the reasons for the war that make Paris and the Trojans look very guilty, the old men summarize: 'The matter is where it is, and it will be fulfilled to its destined end, and neither by burning nor by libation of fireless sacrifices will he [the guilty man] charm away the relentless wrath' (67–71). Sacrifice does not work automatically; whatever sacrifice one offers to the angry gods, the guilty will not be able to escape divine retribution. At least for the audience, this influences the interpretation of the lavish sacrifices that then catch the chorus's attention and that Clytemnestra has ordered to be performed: 'Of all gods that rule in the city, of those above and those under the earth, those outside the walls and those on the market-place, the altars are laden with gifts' (88–92). The chorus then moves on to recalling the beginning of the war: the assembly of the army, the portent of the two eagles devouring a pregnant hare (characterized as a sacrifice, 136) and the seer's fear that Artemis will claim 'yet another sacrifice, one without precedent and law, without a feast, a worker of quarrels' (151f.). That very sacrifice is demanded, Agamemnon agrees to offer his daughter, and the chorus describes the violent and unusual human sacrifice: how, after his prayer, the father gives order to grab the girl 'like a kid', 'by force' to muffle her mouth lest her cries disturb the sacrifice 'as a curse to the house';

and how she shed her robe and begged with her eyes for pity. This sacrifice, in which the victim is a nubile girl and has to be manhandled instead of willingly submitting to the act, announces evil to come:[14] the curse that Agamemnon wanted to avoid falls back on him. The returning victor in turn makes clear his intention to perform a thanksgiving sacrifice, as does Clytemnestra who invites Cassandra to participate 'among the slaves at the altar of Zeus Ktesios'. Her killing of Agamemnon responds to the human sacrifice at the outset of the war and, in the same way as that sacrifice did not open the path to victory, the victory sacrifice does not end the dark time, but leads to further evil instead.[15]

In his *Electra*, Euripides makes a very different sacrifice the occasion of Orestes' killing of Aegisthus. A messenger relates the events (773–858). Orestes and Pylades have found Electra; they set out to find Aegisthus. They meet him in a grove preparing a sacrifice to the Nymphs; he graciously invites the foreigners to participate. They accept so eagerly that Orestes refuses the invitation to bathe first in the palace, under the pretext that they had purified themselves that very morning in a river. The sacrifice proceeds as it should. Aegisthus prays for the death of his enemies (Orestes silently sets his prayer against this, to retake his father's house), then offers the knife to Orestes: he should slaughter the calf. Orestes obeys, kills, skins and opens the animal; Aegisthus scrutinizes the entrails: they are deformed and predict disaster. And while Aegisthus is bent over them, Orestes strikes a second time, breaking his back: 'His entire body convulsed, he gasped and shrieked and died badly by murder' (843f.). The killing of a human is opposed to the ritual killing of an animal: Orestes the sacrificer proceeds according to rule, kills the animal quietly and efficiently, and its entrails even yield the expected negative oracular sign (Euripides uses technical vocabulary all the way); Orestes the murderer attacks from behind and kills messily and cruelly (*phonos*, the killing of a human). Throughout the entire scene, Aegisthus has appeared as a friendly, generous and pious man, easily duped by an Orestes who lacks even the respect for ritual that would have made him take a bath. The gods, however, are not with Aegisthus but with his murderer; they fulfil not the prayer of Aegisthus, but Orestes' silent prayer, although silent prayers are highly unusual in ancient ritual.[16] It fits a play where the other murder victim, Clytemnestra, is lured to her daughter's house under the pretext of another ritual, the sacrifice after the birth of a healthy child, and where the blame for all this is firmly put on fate and 'the wisdomless words of Apollo's tongue' (1302). In such a world, even reverence for rites counts as nothing.

Seneca stages a similarly unsuccessful sacrifice on stage. In his *Oedipus*, the Theban king has his seer Tiresias and his daughter Manto perform a mantic sacrifice (298–402); Manto relates the action, which is supposed to take place off stage, to her blind father. The signs are as bad as they can be: the fire on the altar does not burn right and hides Oedipus' head in smoke, wine turns to blood, the animals are afraid, and one has to be hit twice and still dies only slowly; blood runs out of the victims' mouths and eyes; and the entrails look absolutely wrong. These signs are too bizarre and convoluted to be realistic, but they very efficiently convey the very dark atmosphere of the play and the world that has gone terribly wrong.

The gods on stage

Prologues and endings

Gods speaking the prologue were becoming a standard feature in New Comedy, after some experiments of Euripides: in *Alcestis* and *The Trojan Women*, a dialogue between two gods (Apollo and Death, Athena and Poseidon) gives the exposition and at the beginning of *Hippolytus* Aphrodite addresses the audience. But these Euripidean prologue gods are much more involved in the plot than Menandrian ones or the few gods that act as *prologi* in Plautus: Aphrodite's wrath causes Hippolytus' death; Apollo's intervention with Death reveals that he intends to save Alcestis as well as Admetus; Poseidon and Athena decide against the Greek victors who are enjoying their victory. Seneca, in the one divine prologue, follows the Euripidean model: his Juno in the *Hercules* moves the very plot with her deep hatred of Hercules.

The gods that cut the knot at the end of several Euripidean plays (and of Sophocles' *Philoctetes*) are similarly involved in the story. They are the famous *dei ex machina*, the 'gods from the crane', swept in over the stage in a masterful scenic move that expresses both their sudden appearance and their position high above the hopelessly entangled humans. But they too have a stake in the action, be it only as the tutelary goddess of Athens who foretells the glorious history of Ion's offspring in the *Ion*, where the audience must have noticed the non-appearance of Apollo; or who saves Orestes and Iphigenia in the nick of time and foretells their ritual roles in Brauron and Halae (*Iphigenia among the Taurians*).

Greek comedy does not need a *deus ex machina* and the prologue gods are minor only: Pan in *The Bad-Tempered Man*, the Lar Familiaris in Plautus' *The Pot of Gold*, Arcturus in *The Rope*. But again these gods are not chosen randomly. The *Bad-Tempered Man* is staged in the countryside which Pan protects; *The Pot of Gold* has to do with the family fortune, which the Lar defends; Arcturus, who is a sort of guardian angel, was responsible for the storm that triggered the entire action of the play. More often, the prologue is spoken by a deified abstraction, such as Fortune (Menander's *The Shield*), Ignorance (his *The Shorn Girl*), or the pair Luxury and Poverty (Plautus' *The Threepenny Day*); it is these very powers that pull the strings of the plot. Deified abstractions had appeared already in Aristophanes, as participants in the action – such as Demos, 'Lord People', in the *Knights*, or Polemos, 'Lord War' and Eirene, 'Lady Peace', in *Peace*. Such abstractions are a constant feature of ancient myth and cult; in an indigenous perspective, they are minor gods no less than Pan or the Lar. Over time, they became more numerous in real cult as well as on the stage: instead of addressing a major, but somewhat distant Olympian god, humans turned directly to the forces that so manifestly governed their lives.

The gods in the play

Few tragedies are played by gods alone. In Aeschylus' *Prometheus Bound*, the Olympians, Zeus and his henchman Hephaestus, are violent and cruel: the just rule of Zeus in our own world has rather brutal and unjust antecedents, and the trilogy must have explained this evolution. In his *Eumenides*, divine laws and prerogatives – the right of the Eumenides to persecute murderers, or of Apollo to protect the *lex talionis* – are replaced by the laws of Athenian democracy, not without divine help: when an Athenian jury tries the murderer Orestes against the opposing claims of Apollo and the Eumenides, the result is a hung jury and it is Athena's decision that solves the issue.

In other tragedies, gods appear more episodically, but their appearance is theologically just as momentous. In Euripides' *Heracles*, the sudden appearance of Iris and Lyssa, 'Lady Madness', marks the savage turning point of the play and sheds a terrible light on Hera who has sent them: they will make Heracles kill his wife and sons. In *Hippolytus*, Artemis appears in the penultimate scene, mirroring Aphrodite in the prologue and showing the unbridgeable gap between gods and humans: Artemis is unable to save the dying Hippolytus and even has to leave him before he dies. Olympians cannot be polluted by death. In Sophocles' *Ajax*, a similar incongruence is perceived by an almost wise Odysseus when addressed by an Athena who is set on pursuing her very personal revenge: against her triumphalism ('Do you now see how great is the power of the gods, Odysseus?'), he sets human pity and the insight into our essential weakness. Unlike with their more neutral appearances in prologue and finale, it is usually rather sinister when a god breaks into the tragic action.

Then there is Dionysus, the god of drama. He deserves special attention not only because his stage presence belies the proverbial saying that drama has

'Nothing to do with Dionysus'; in his case, the difference between tragedy and comedy becomes crucial.[17] He is the main character of a preserved tragedy (Euripides' *Bacchae*) and a preserved comedy (Aristophanes' *Frogs*). In both dramas, the god is disguised as a mortal – a young missionary in Euripides, Heracles in Aristophanes: it is as if Dionysus could become the main hero only in human disguise (Cratinus' lost *Dionusosalexandros*, where Dionysus disguises himself as Paris, confirms this impression). The disguise, however, is incongruous and throws the god's nature into even sharper relief. The comic Dionysus visibly cannot live up to his models: he lacks Heracles' strength and courage, and Paris' seductiveness; he is thus an easy target of humour. In a clear disjunction, in tragedy Dionysus' human disguise makes the absolute gap between divine and human all the clearer: he plays his cruel games with Pentheus, Agave and her sisters who refuse to look beyond his disguise.

Theological issues

Staging theology

The gods on stage cannot but provoke theological issues, both for the native spectator and the modern reader. This is as true for comedy as it is for tragedy. But whereas the gods in tragedy have never scandalized modern readers, their seemingly irreverent treatment on the comic stage often did so. Not all scholars went as far as Nilsson, who decreed that 'nobody who believes in gods can treat them as Aristophanes treats them'; this projects Protestant notions of belief onto fifth-century comedy. 'The gods, like the Greeks, were sensible and not easily shocked,' as A. D. Nock remarked. To make fun of one's own gods has a longstanding tradition in the societies of the ancient Mediterranean[18] and the irreverent treatment of figures of authority is also part of carnivalesque inversion, in Greece as elsewhere.

Although Euripidean tragedy has some traces of such irreverence, in the drunken Heracles of *Alcestis* or the cowardly Apollo of *Ion*, it is mostly Old Comedy that can indulge in slapstick with the gods. The 'bourgeois' comedy of Menander, Plautus and Terence has no need for them outside the prologue, with the exception of the *Amphitruo*: once comedy unfolds the web of ordinary lives, gods disappear in the background. Not so in the *Amphitruo*: although Mercurius as the slave Sosias leads to delightful slapstick only, Jupiter's assumption of Amphitruo's role complicates things between husband and wife so much that Jupiter has to step in in his own guise. Old Comedy, on the other hand, happily mixes mortals and immortals, from the chorus of Socrates' newfangled goddesses, the Clouds, to Plutus, 'Wealth', the title-character of Aristophanes' last comedy. When they encounter gods on stage, Aristophanes' humans lack any respect. In the *Birds*, the Athenian Pisthetaerus establishes a bird-state in the sky and effectively blocks the sacrificial smoke from reaching the gods. The gods send a peace delegation – Poseidon, Heracles, and a strange god called Triballus – but Prometheus, sneaking down from Olympus, has already warned the humans. The gods are caricatures: the clumsy and foreign Triballus is utterly useless and does not even speak Greek, Heracles oscillates between violence and hunger, Poseidon is as pompous as a senior ambassador can get. They are no match for the clever Athenian who is helped by a Prometheus who is at his most conniving and sleazy. This is slapstick, not theology, and should bother no one: it highlights the distance between the seriousness of cult and the playfulness of myth.

Still, some perceptive ancient spectators might have felt tensions between dramatic representation and cultic worship. People who were aware of the philosophical criticism of myth could have been tempted slowly to dissociate theological reality and stage make-believe. The full break surfaced with Varro (whose theological model had Hellenistic antecedents). He posited three types of *theologiae*, 'discourses on the gods': the cultic discourse of the state, the allegorical discourse of philosophy, and the entertaining narrations of myth – *civile, physicon, mythicon* (*Antiquitates rerum divinarum*, frg. 7 Cardauns). This last is entirely fictional, but 'most apt for the stage'. There is no need to take staged gods seriously any more, and Senecan tragedy drastically reduces their importance. While Euripides' *Hippolytus* frames the human tragedy between Aphrodite's prologue and Artemis' heartwrenching appearance immediately before Hippolytus' death and thus proposes a theological reading of the myth, Seneca's *Phaedra* dramatizes the same story without either goddess, focusing on the destruction wrought by human passions. In early modern Europe, Racine will follow Seneca, not Euripides.

Debating the gods

But theology is not just involved when gods appear on stage: in a world where religion is embedded in life, the imitation of life cannot do without the gods. 'No one is happy without the gods,' claims an unknown Euripidean character (Frg. 684 *Tr.Gr.F.*). 'Nothing of this has not been Zeus' sings the Chorus at the end of the *Women of Trachis*, after Deianira has stabbed herself and Heracles burnt himself on the pyre. It could be said at the end of every tragedy: after all, Zeus was the god who was presiding over the order of things as the Greeks knew it. But in this respect, Sophocles differs not that much from Aeschylus or Euripides, only that their theology is sometimes more explicit. In the famous ode early in Aeschylus' *Agamemnon*, the chorus invokes Zeus in a manner that resonates with traditional prayer formulae, but turns them into instruments of theology: 'Zeus, whoever he be, if to be called thus is pleasing to him: thus I do address him' (160–2). Divine names are a tenuous bridge only over the abyss that separates the divine from the human world. If we are lucky, the names will please the god they invoke and we will profit from divine help: Athena, in the *Eumenides*, casts the decisive vote for Orestes. Sophocles, in his outlook as severe as Aeschylus, is usually less outspoken. But the stage play of *The Women of Trachis*, *Antigone* or, of course, *Oedipus Tyrannus*, makes his theology very clear: human life is determined by the gods, even if it turns out terrible; the gods might be following their own selfish agenda, as does Athena in *Ajax*. Human resistance only makes things worse; to submit to the gods and to pity the victims is the better course.

The most obvious, and the most controversial, theologian is Euripides, although he is less isolated than scholars tend to think. His characters are most outspoken in their distrust of the gods, and they are willing to draw radical conclusions. 'Who should pray to such gods?', asks Heracles, after Hera made him kill his wife and sons (*Heracles* 1307). 'If gods do evil, they are not gods,' states an unknown character (Frg. 286b *Tr.Gr.F.*). The belief in divine justice is ambivalent at best: in *Iphigenia in Aulis*, Clytemnestra admonishes herself: 'If there are gods, they act nobly towards just humans' (1034); but she will lose her daughter. Already in Sophocles' *Oedipus Tyrannus*, however, the Chorus complains that wrong is done with impunity and 'no reverence exists for the seats of the gods': in such a world, 'why should I dance?' If the gods do not punish transgressions, why should humans continue to worship them? In the case of Oedipus, who killed his father and married his mother, in the end theodicy is preserved, although in an unexpected and humanly terrible manner; in other cases, the issue is left unsolved and theodicy is questioned; and not only in tragedy. In Aristophanes' *Wealth*, the title hero, the god 'Wealth', is represented as a dirty and blind old man: Zeus blinded him to prevent him from helping only good and just humans. He regains his sight in Asclepius' shrine and turns into Athens' new protector. But the consequences that are so positive for humans are bad for the gods. Hermes describes their plight: 'Since Wealth began to see, no incense, laurel, cake, nor animal has any man on any altar burned to the gods'; he himself is out of work, unless the Athenians hire him. And although the play ends happily, the underlying message is disturbing: traditional worship depends on the grossly unjust *status quo* of social life; the justice claimed by traditional theodicy would make cult superfluous. After the upheavals of Athenian history following the Peloponnesian Wars (the *Wealth* was staged in *c*.388 BC), such a dark theological view is not implausible. Comical irreverence can turn into scathing social and theological criticism.

Rarely, however, went a dramatic figure as far as Sisyphus does, in a famous fragment that is ascribed either to Euripides or to Plato's uncle, the sophist Critias, and which turns theodicy on its head (*Tr.Gr.F.* 43 F 19).[19] Sisyphus, whose disdain for the gods was well known, proposes nothing less than a theory of how religion was invented. The first humans lived without law and order; the invention of laws with their punishment provided some order, but did not prevent secret evildoing. To remedy this, 'a wily and clever man' invented the gods who would notice and punish even secret transgressions. The gods are nothing but an instrument of social control.

Much later, in Seneca, things are more opaque. Seneca the Stoic philosopher knows that the gods of myth are metaphors for the powers that drive human life; his nephew Lucan tried to get rid of them when narrating his epic versions of Caesar's 'Civil Wars'. Seneca's characters, however, still talk about the gods, and sometimes are driven by them; if his *Phaedra* can do without them, his *Hercules Furens* begins with a Juno who wages war against a hero whose merits she has to acknowledge. It seems too simplistic to read this Hercules as the Stoic sage only, unbent even in the worst adversities. Although the other Senecan Hercules, *Hercules on Oeta*, ends with a triumphalist choral ode – 'Glorious virtue never descends to the shadows of Hades' – too much suffering, too much collateral damage is done on the way to philosophical virtue to turn the tragedy into a facile allegory.

What ancient drama teaches us is the widely divergent public debate about the role gods played in human life. Gods are good to think with, from Aeschylus to Seneca (or, for that matter, from Homer to Nonnus). But as long as these same gods received prayers and sacrifices, what one thought with them was relevant for how one perceived the interaction between the humans and the forces beyond human control. To separate myth and cult, as Varro did and as some modern scholars do, sanitizes what should not be sanitized. And when everything is counted, the sceptical or outright negative opinions on life and the gods prevail both on the comic and the tragic stage. I take this as a sign of maturity rather than of despair.

NOTES

1. R. Osborne, 'Competitive Festivals and the Polis. A Context for Dramatic Festivals at Athens', in A. H. Sommerstein (ed.), *Tragedy, Comedy, and the Polis* (Bari: Levante, 1993), pp. 11–37.
2. O. Longo, 'Teatri e *theatra*. Spazi teatrali e luoghi politici nella città greca', *Dioniso* 58 (1988), 7–33.

3. See S. Goldhill, 'The Great Dionysia and Civic Ideology', in J. Winkler and F. Zeitlin (eds.), *Nothing to Do with Dionysos? Athenian Drama in Its Social Context* (Princeton: Princeton University Press, 1990), pp. 97–129.

4. H. Usener, 'Heilige Handlung', *Archiv für Religionswissenschaft* 7 (1904), 261–339.

5. James G. Frazer, *The Golden Bough: A Study in Comparative Religion*, 2 vols. (London: Macmillan, 1890).

6. Victor Turner, *From Ritual to Theatre: The Human Seriousness of Play* (New York: Performing Arts Journal Publications, 1990); R. Schechner and Willa Appel (eds.), *By Means of Performance: Intercultural Studies of Theatre and Ritual* (New York: Cambridge University Press, 1990).

7. Emile Durkheim, *Les formes élémentaires de la vie religieuse: Le système totémique en Australie* (Paris: Quadrige/Presses Universitaires de France, 1912); Turner, see previous note.

8. Walter Burkert, 'Greek Tragedy and Sacrificial Ritual', *Greek, Roman, and Byzantine Studies* 7 (1966), 87–121; John J. Winkler, 'The Ephebe's Song: *Tragôidia* and *Polis*', *Representations* 11 (1985), 26–62; rpt. in Winkler and Zeitlin, 1990, pp. 20–62.

9. O. Taplin, 'Do the "Phlyax Vases" Have Bearings on Athenian Comedy and the *Polis*?', in Sommerstein, 1993, pp. 527–44.

10. Besides Easterling's essay cited at the end, see the debate between E. Krummen, 'Ritual und Katastrophe: Rituelle Handlung und Bildersprache bei Sophokles und Euripides', in Fritz Graf (ed.), *Ansichten griechischer Rituale. Geburtstagssymposium für Walter Burkert* (Stuttgart and Leipzig: B. G. Teubner, 1998), pp. 296–325, and Hugh Lloyd-Jones, 'Ritual and Tragedy', *ibid.* pp. 271–95.

11. The starting point was a remark of Walter Burkert; see especially H. P. Foley, *Ritual Irony: Poetry and Sacrifice in Euripides* (Ithaca: Cornell University Press, 1985) and R. Seaford, *Reciprocity and Ritual: Homer and Tragedy in the Developing City State* (Oxford: Oxford University Press, 1994).

12. Angelo Brelich, *Gli eroi greci: Un problema storico-religioso* (Rome: Ateneo, 1958).

13. For contemporary theories of sacrifice, see R. G. Hamerton-Kelly (ed.), *Violent Origins. Walter Burkert, René Girard and Jonathan Z. Smith on Ritual Killing and Cultural Formation* (Stanford: Stanford University Press, 1987), and J.-P. Vernant, 'A General Theory of Sacrifice and the Slaying of the Victim in the Greek *Thusia*', in F. Zeitlin (ed.), *Mortals and Immortals: Collected Essays by Jean-Pierre Vernant* (Princeton: Princeton University Press, 1991), pp. 290–302.

14. See Froma Zeitlin, 'The Motif of the Corrupted Sacrifice in Aeschylus' *Oresteia* (Ag. 1235–1237)', *Transactions of the American Philological Association* 96 (1965), 463–508.

15. On this and other virgin sacrifices, see Ruth Scodel, '*Domôn Agalma*: Virgin Sacrifice and Aesthetic Object', *Transactions of the American Philological Association* 126 (1996), 111–28.

16. P. W. Van der Horst, 'Silent Prayer in Antiquity', *Numen* 41 (1994), 1–25; S. Pulleyn, *Prayer in Greek Religion* (Oxford: Oxford University Press, 1997), pp. 184–8.

17. O. Taplin, 'Comedy and the Tragic', in M. S. Silk (ed.), *Tragedy and the Tragic. Greek Theatre and Beyond* (Oxford: Oxford University Press, 1996), pp. 188–202, esp. pp. 194–6.
18. Martin P. Nilsson, *A History of Greek Religion*, trans. F. J. Fielden (New York: Norton, 1964); Walter Burkert, *Greek Religion*, trans. John Raffan (Cambridge, Mass.: Harvard University Press, 1985).
19. C. S. Kahn, 'Greek Religion and Philosophy in the Sisyphus Fragment', *Phronesis* 42 (1997), 247–62.

FURTHER READING

Easterling, P. E., 'Tragedy and Ritual', in Ruth Scodel (ed.), *Theatre and Society in the Classical World*. Ann Arbor: University of Michigan, 1993, pp. 7–24.
Mikalson, J. D., *Honor Thy Gods. Popular Religion in Greek Tragedy*. Chapel Hill: University of North Carolina Press, 1991.
Rainer, F., 'Everything to Do with Dionysos? Ritualism, the Dionysiac, and Tragedy', in M. S. Silk (ed.), *Tragedy and the Tragic: Greek Theatre and Beyond*. Oxford: Oxford University Press, 1996, pp. 257–83.
Seaford, R., *Reciprocity and Ritual. Homer and Tragedy in the Developing City State*. Oxford: Oxford University Press, 1994.

4

JON HESK

The socio-political dimension
of ancient tragedy

In this chapter I will argue that the 'socio-political dimension' of fifth-century Greek tragedy amounts to its engagement with the collective ideology and competitive ethos of the democratized classical *polis* on the one hand, and more traditional Homeric and mythic conceptions of religion and heroic self-assertion on the other. In addition, I will consider the Greek tragedians' interest in framing dilemmas of action with debates over the merits and meanings of certain key fifth-century socio-political concepts. I will address the pressing question of how far Greek tragedy's 'socio-politics' speak to watching Athenians and their guests from other Greek states as *polis*-dwellers in general as opposed to singling out the *democratic* aspects of the Athenian civic experience. We will see that while Greek tragedy sometimes used tales of monstrous royal goings-on and heroic extremism to highlight the civilized values of Athens, this city's democratic citizenry rarely watched a play which would not have unsettled their senses of social and political well-being. However, any claim to the effect that Greek tragedy had real socio-political 'bite' for its audience has to be tempered with a recognition that Greek tragedy's overarching mythical idiom should preclude any reading of it as a vehicle for specific messages or manifestos.

Having dealt with the case of classical Athens, I will briefly argue that the social and political force of tragedy did not diminish after the classical period. Neither the facts of Hellenistic or Roman 'appropriation' nor the paucity of available evidence should prevent us from realizing that Roman Republican tragedy spoke provocatively and productively to its audience's specific socio-political milieu. The politics of writing tragedy under the Roman emperors were a different matter again. I will show briefly that Seneca's distinctively baroque, bloody and highly rhetorical mode of tragic presentation reflects the socio-politics of Nero's Rome through its very eschewal of direct political 'comment' or allusion.

The 'tragic moment'

Nearly all of the extant Greek tragedies were first performed at an Athenian festival (The City Dionysia) before a huge citizen-audience who constituted a significant proportion of the city's direct democracy. As Rush Rehm shows in chapter 10 of this volume, this annual event's ceremonial and competitive features were thoroughly civic in character. And, following Cleisthenes' reforms of 508/7 BC, this civic dimension was bolstered by the city's specifically democratic modes of organization and ideology.

This means that Greek tragedies have a 'socio-political' context of performance and original reception which is completely different to the modern western experience of theatre. The Dionysia's pre-play ceremonies – for example, the onstage parade of war-orphans in hoplite armour provided by the state, or the proclamation of citizens whose benefactions to the city had been voted the award of a crown – were a very graphic (re)performance of the Athenian democracy's civic ideology. These ceremonies showed that a citizen's self-sacrifice – the donation of one's life or one's money to the city – would be met with state-sponsored recognition and compensation. Then there were the Dionysia's funding and seating arrangements, its blend of intra-choral cooperation and tribe-based inter-choral rivalry; its democratically controlled auditing and regulation, and its manipulation by elite impresarios (*chorêgoi*) as an arena for conspicuous and highly competitive euergetism before the masses.[1]

All these elements of the Dionysia are crucial for understanding the socio-political impact of the tragedies on their audience. For the ceremonial and organizational frame of the festival constituted a celebration of collective will and its melding with the competitive, honour-seeking behaviour of individuals. Athenians called this behaviour *philotimia* ('ambitious striving' or 'love of honour'). By contrast, the plays themselves present a more troubled picture of the relationship between honour-loving heroic individuals and their communities. Thus the tragedies take on enhanced socio-political resonances when set within the frames of civic festival and democratic ideology through which spectating citizens would have viewed them.

A good example of the socio-political frisson generated by this specific context of performance is our one trilogy which survives in complete form. Aeschylus' *Oresteia* (458 BC) climaxes in Athens with the establishment of a homicide court on the Areopagus. This was a very real and controversial socio-political institution at the time of the trilogy's first performance. The ending of the final play, *Eumenides*, is undoubtedly a form of political aetiology which – despite uncertainty over the extent of its positive thrust – grounds Athens' current legal and political structures in a momentous past event where Athena must conjure up a jury of Athenian citizens to offer a non-violent settlement to a cycle of vengeance in the Argive House of Atreus. Thus Aeschylus happily stages a confrontation between old-fashioned 'heroic' and aristocratic ways of seeking honour and redress and the new, developing mode of peaceful juridical dispute-settlement sanctioned by state authority and democracy. We may want to argue that Orestes' acquittal is a problem for any 'triumphalist' democratic reading and we will have to return to the fact that the Areopagus was a controversial institution in 458. Nevertheless, this trilogy's key socio-political meanings are generated from a dialectic between its Homeric-heroic setting and the political culture of its original audience.

Sophocles' *Ajax* (perhaps performed in the 440s BC) offers a very different example of this dialectic at work. When the arms of Achilles are awarded to Odysseus, Ajax's slighted honour and feelings of betrayal are so profound that he attempts to do violence to his own comrades. And when Athena ensures that the attack fails, he kills himself rather than rejoin the ranks or go home in disgrace. His delusions and suicide are set up by Athena as punishments for this hero's arrogant self-regard. He believes that real heroes like himself do not need the gods to help them win glory in battle. After his death, Agamemnon and Menelaus argue that Ajax should have submitted to the collective will and discipline of the army. Their version of collective ideology – and they explicitly use words like *polis* (city-state) and *nomos* (law) – is tainted by excessively authoritarian overtones. These overtones problematize the civic ideals of military discipline, empire and service to the state, a message identified in the Dionysia's pre-play parade of war-orphans in armour, its proclamation of state-benefactors and its display of imperial tribute gathered from subject-states.[2]

Tragedy's characters frequently use political language which is culled from the milieu of their fifth-century audiences: there is talk of the *dêmos* (the 'people'), *turannoi* (tyrants), *stratêgoi* (generals) and *poleis* (city-states). These and other terms often act as 'zooming devices' which give the language of mythical characters a contemporary, fifth-century edge.[3] For example, in Euripides' *Andromache* (possibly 425 BC) the protagonist rails against the mendacious Spartan king Menelaus and mocks his martial abilities by recalling the way in which Hector easily routed him at Troy. She sarcastically dubs Menelaus a 'fearsome *hoplitês*' (458). Andromache's use of the word 'hoplite' underlines the fact that Spartan mendacity is incompatible with the values of the ideal citizen-soldier as understood by any fifth-century audience participating in the war between Athens and Sparta. The evidence of Herodotus, Thucydides, Xenophon, Aristophanes and other tragedies shows that the Athenians liked to stereotype their Spartan enemy as duplicitous.[4]

Andromache invites the audience to map that pervasive fifth-century Athenian represention of deception as typically Spartan, un-Athenian and anti-hoplitic onto the mythical past. Andromache styles Menelaus as the prototype of Spartan duplicity and contrasts that prototype with an image of what contemporary military manhood should look like.

So Greek tragedy's uses of contemporary language sometimes 'zoom' an audience towards making significant connections between the mythical world of the tragedy and their own socio-political contexts and discourses. However, Greek tragedy deploys a mixture of artificial, archaic poetic and heroic language on the one hand, and elements of contemporary discourse on the other. This fact, coupled with Greek tragedy's aristocratic, mythical and heroic settings, should deter us from thinking that Greek tragedy was straightforwardly didactic, persuasive or politically transformative for its intended audiences.

The idea that a tragedy can only be 'social' or 'political' if enough of its scenes and speeches can be shown to resemble a political tract or direct social commentary gains much of its force from the unwitting application of a Brechtian theatrical manifesto – what Lorna Hardwick has recently called the 'interventionist' tradition – to ancient tragedy.[5] This tradition – in which Sophocles and Shakespeare are made to speak very directly to, and of, political and social struggles of the twentieth and twenty-first century – has made us think that drama can only be 'political' if it can be shown to contain explicit and crude messages which clearly aim to be politically transformative. In modern adaptations and performances of ancient tragedy, the Brechtian approach can be very fruitful: when Robert Auletta and Peter Sellars turned the *Ajax* into an allegory of Reaganite neo-imperialism or when Seamus Heaney made the *Philoctetes'* chorus speak of political violence in Northern Ireland, the resulting theatrical experiences were wonderful and powerful. But such performances highlight the fact that Greek and Roman tragedy were not, or at least not exclusively, forged according to Brechtian principles.[6] If you want your Greek tragedy to be politically didactic for the modern age, you have to do a lot of work with staging, costuming and adaptation to make it so. And if you want your Greek tragedy to be politically didactic for its original Athenian audience, you have to accept that its 'lessons' – if indeed they can be so simplistically described – took the form of open-ended social and ethical problems rather than pat solutions. This is to accept a more complex model in which tragedy confronts, questions (and only very occasionally affirms) the social, moral, political and ideological discourses of its audience.

Fortunately, this more complex model can already be found in the work of the so-called 'Paris School' classicists: J. P. Vernant, P. Vidal-Naquet,

N. Loraux and M. Detienne.[7] And in the last twenty years or so, the 'Paris School' model has been refined and critiqued by a range of scholars whose work is concerned with the 'socio-politics' of Greek tragedy. Vernant's understanding of the specific historical moment that generates Greek tragedy's socio-political complexity is still a very useful starting point for approaching Greek tragedy's 'socio-politics'. Vernant argues that the 'tragic moment' occurs when 'a gap develops at the heart of social experience in fifth-century Athens'. This gap, caused by the rapidly developing social entity that was late sixth- and fifth-century Athens, had the new legal and political system of Athenian democracy on the one side, and the archaic religious system on the other. For Vernant, this gap is wide enough for the opposition between 'legal and political thought' and 'mythical and heroic traditions' to be clearly visible. But the gap is narrow enough for 'the conflict in values still to be a painful one and for the clash to continue to take place'. Thus, tragedy stages the clash between the two systems and their very different conceptions of human agency and authority. The individualistic and excessive actions of aristocratic heroes are subjected to divine will on one plane and collective or domestic constraints on another. Thus the heroes and heroines of Greek tragedy are problems rather than models for watching Athenians and their 'problematic' status derives from their conflicted position between competing worlds (the heroic and the contemporary) and claims (self-assertion and personal honour versus family and/or friends and/or community). Even the basic form of tragedy (hero in dialogue with chorus, and an *agôn* between opposed viewpoints) betokens a confrontation between the monolithic authority of gods and kings and the new claims of collective authority, attended as they are by questioning, contest and debate.

Tragedy and the Athenian *polis*

The Vernantian 'tragic moment' is itself complicated by the fact that Attic tragedy and Athenian democracy may not have come into being at the same time. Tragedy of a kind probably already existed when Cleisthenes' reforms heralded the world's first democracy in 508/7 BC and it is by no means certain that it was a specifically Athenian invention. Furthermore, there is some evidence to suggest that the Athenian deployment of tragedy at the City Dionysia was the brainchild of the Pisistratid tyrants. In order to bolster their power, the tyrants of Athens had to forge a heightened identification between individual and state and indeed to create collective cults through which the state could be imagined. Thus the 'tragic moment' has its origins in authoritarian attempts to create a sense of belonging. Only later did it take on the democratic frameworks discussed above.

Despite these origins for Attic tragedy, all the Greek plays we have are post-Cleisthenic and many of them explore the transgressions and flaws of tyranny very explicitly. The protagonist of *Oedipus Tyrannus* (possibly performed around 430 BC) is called a *turannos* and its Chorus famously remark that '*hubris* breeds the tyrant' (872). *Hubris* was a word that either denoted, or else was spun to denote, excessive and uncitizenly self-assertion, grievous bodily harm and the very antithesis of the much-prized virtue of moderate self-control (*sôphrosunê*) in classical Athenian law-courts and other democratic fora. Thus the tragic tyrant's *hubris* is partly an object lesson in uncitizenlike behaviour. Indeed, the Greek tragedians' focus on the errors and arrogance of mythical *Theban* tyrants is part of their construction of this city as a mirror-opposite of Athens, an 'anti-Athens', onto which important questions of self, family and society which were pertinent to Athenian citizens are displaced and more easily explored. It is often the case, then, that tragedy depicts its autocratic heroes and heroines as transgressive, arrogant and prone to errors which are socially and religiously disastrous.[8]

This depiction of autocracy is not in itself evidence that fifth-century Attic tragedy is quintessentially democratic: anti-tyrannical discourse is also a feature of aristocratic poetry emanating from Greek cities in the seventh to fifth centuries BC. However, I find it hard to believe that tragic representations of tyranny would not speak specifically to a watching Athenian's sense of being a democratic citizen when we know that at each meeting of the assembly which he attended, the debates were preceded by a herald loudly proclaiming a curse against anyone plotting a tyrannical overthrow of the state. Anti-tyrannical feeling was so germane to Athenian democratic ideology that Aristophanes was able to mock it as a form of paranoia typical of the older generation who fought at Marathon (*Lysistrata* 614–35).

The tragedians' frequent focus on the mythical ruling families of cities outside Attica shows that tragedians sometimes promoted Athens as opposed to any other state. For tragedy usually represents repressive rule and the perverted behaviour of dynastic families as Argive, Spartan or Theban problems rather than as Athenian ones. And in tragedies such as Aeschylus' *Eumenides*, Sophocles' *Oedipus at Colonus* and Euripides' *Suppliants*, a proto-democratic Athens is often the site of refuge from, or (partial) resolution of, crimes and sacrilegious acts committed in other Greek cities.

But Greek tragedies also often worked to problematize the very oppositions between Athenian or Greek, civic, lawful 'self' and non-Athenian or non-Greek, autocratic, bestial, unjust 'other' which the discourses of the fifth-century *polis* projected for the purposes of defining and policing cultural and political identity. In Euripides' *Trojan Women* of 415 BC we have a reversal of a dominant ideological polarity whereby Greekness and the values of the Greek *polis* (the 'self') were favourably contrasted with the non-Greek 'barbarian' cultures of the past and present (the 'other'). In this tragedy the Trojan women transcend their 'barbarian' traits and look very like noble Greeks by the ideological lights of the late fifth century. And by those same lights, the Greeks who are enslaving and executing the Trojan survivors behave much like barbarians. The widowed Andromache actually points out this paradox as her son Astyanax is earmarked for elimination (764): 'Oh you Greeks (*Hellênes*) who devise barbarian evils (*barbara kaka*)!' This comment would have been particularly disturbing to the play's original *Athenian* audience because it was performed immediately after Athenian forces had massacred the adult males and enslaved the women and children of the small island of Melos. As Thucydides records, this massacre happened because the island had refused to bow to Athenian imperial power. Whatever his actual intentions, Euripides' play must have been seen as a dramatic, provocative and shaming analogy between the cruelty of Agamemnon's army at Troy and the recent Melian atrocity.

Although *Trojan Women* shows how radically questioning of its sociopolitical milieu Greek tragedy could be, there is no 'one-size-fits-all' template that can be applied to the impact of individual tragedies. Some plays are much less questioning of, or indeed much less focused upon, their original audience's ideology, discursive context or recent political decisions. And while some tragedies seem to represent Athens as the place where problems can be solved, it is not *always* the case that 'Athens *qua* democracy' is necessarily implicated in a tragedy. A more general notion of 'Athens *qua* best *polis* in Greece' is sometimes the more plausible formulation. For example, Euripides' *Erechtheus*, which was performed some time between 423 and 421 BC to celebrate the building of the Erechtheion on the Acropolis, is one of several tragedies which seem to have patriotically celebrated the early mythical history of Athens. In this tragedy, of which some substantial fragments survive, it is not so much the Athenians' democratic identity that is at stake; rather, their male-biased and mythological claim to be 'aboriginal' is authorized and celebrated. For, according to the myth attaching to Erechtheus, the first king of Athens, the founding mother of the earliest Athenians was Mother Earth herself. Thus, the Athenians could lay strong political claims to their ownership of Attica because they were 'autochthonous' – that is to say, they claimed to be descended from the very soil which they inhabited and cultivated. The masculinist political culture of Athens was also legitimized by this story of origins in which normal human female reproduction played no part. With its invocations of 'autochthony' and its depiction of Erechtheus' and his daughter's self-sacrifice in a patriotic war against the Poseidon-worshipping Thracians, this tragedy projected the legitimacy and superiority of the male Athenian citizen body *per se* rather than its particular political constitution.

Even when tragedies are not set in Athens, they can sometimes imply this city's autochthonous superiority by invoking other cities' foundation myths as perverted by violence. For example, several extant tragedies set in Thebes – Aeschylus' *Seven Against Thebes*, and Euripides' *Phoenician Women* and *Bacchae* – figure their stories of fratricide, incest and tyrannical *hubris* in relation to the unhappy circumstances of the city's foundation by Cadmus. Cadmus slew the dragon of Ares and sowed the monster's teeth in the ground. From this planting sprung the Spartoi (the 'Sown Men') who in turn slew one another, except for five who survived as the first autochthonous inhabitants of Thebes. Again, the tragic imagination explores its darkest personal, social and political themes by constructing Thebes as an 'anti-Athens'.

The extent to which our extant tragedies spoke to Athens as a model *polis* in general, as opposed to a model *democracy* in particular, may be an issue bound up with varied audience 'reception' rather than the configuration of the tragic texts themselves. For example, an ambassador visiting the City Dionysia from Thebes, Argos or Mytilene was likely to apply many of these tragedies to his own experience as a *polis*-dweller without reference to Athenian democratic discourse: many Greek *poleis* had assemblies and judicial bodies even though they were not democratic (or not *as* democratic as Athens) and thus their explorations of, and allusions to, notions of 'the civic' in relation to heroic myth would still be pertinent. On the other hand, some plays do seem to invite their audience to reflect on the specific dynamics of democracy and I will now look at a few of these more closely.

Tragedy and democracy

Euripides' *Suppliants* was performed some time in the 420s. The play is set in the sanctuary of Demeter in the Attic town of Eleusis. A group of Argive women, together with the general Adrastus, have come as suppliants to ask for the assistance of Theseus, the king of Athens. The Argive Seven have marched on Thebes in support of the claims of Polyneices in his power struggle with his brother Eteocles. But the Argive forces have been defeated and the Theban tyranny is refusing to allow the wives and mothers of the Seven to retrieve the dead warriors for burial. Now Athens is being asked to risk its own men in a conflict with Thebes in order to bring humanitarian relief to an ill-advised expedition of questionable legitimacy. In this tragedy, Theseus is styled as a constitutional monarch who is proud of the way in which his people are free, are equal under the law and rule themselves. Watching Athenians are asked to imagine that their democratic sovereignty essentially goes back as far as Theseus' patronage of their city.

Much of Theseus' praise of Athens' political culture forms part of a striking *agôn* over the relative merits of tyranny and democracy, which he holds with a herald who has been sent from Thebes to warn Athens about the consequences of any intervention. The pro-tyrannical Theban herald scores some powerful points against democracy (410–16):

> The *polis* from which I come is ruled by one man only, not by the mob. Nobody there puffs up the citizens with specious words, or twists them this way or that for his own profit, one moment sweetly flattering them with lavish favours, the next harming everyone. Nobody there hides his former mistakes and escapes punishment by making up slanderous lies against others.

He goes on to point out that even an 'educated' poor farmer does not have the leisure to do politics properly. Hence a system based on the sovereignty of the masses is flawed. The herald even provides an unsettling image of a democracy's fondness for war: 'whenever the city has to vote on the question of war, no man ever takes his own death into account . . . if death were before their eyes when they were giving their votes, Hellas would never rush to her doom in mad desire for battle' (481–5).

This political debate contributes to Euripides' overall presentation of the Athenian military intervention to retrieve the unburied Argives as morally and religiously complex. For at the same time as the Athenian citizen who watches this debate is undoubtedly having his democratic way of life affirmed through a contrast with the corruption and violence of tyranny, the herald's critique underlines certain vulnerabilities and imperfections in popular sovereignty: demagogues and elected generals are manipulative with their speeches; good decision-making can be undermined by the flattery of advisers or poor knowledge and commitment on the part of the people; democracies can fail to imagine the consequences of war as much as any other political system.

We can be sure that *Suppliants* was written and performed during Athens' protracted and costly hostilities with Sparta and her allies. The herald's worries about the masses' susceptibility to manipulation and the lure of war mirror Thucydides' analysis of Athenian assemblies during this war. Indeed, this is just one of several war-era tragedies which are inscribed with intellectual critique of, and popular interest in, the nature and conduct of political, legal and rhetorical discourse in Athens. This is searching material for the Athenian *dêmos* who watched it and is thus one of those plays that provides a good match with the Vernantian model.

There are many other Greek tragedies where both positive and negative reflection upon democratic structures and leadership are woven into the texture of the drama. Most famously, there is the implicit eulogy of Athenian democracy contained in Aeschylus' 'historical' tragedy, the *Persians* (472 BC). This play imagines the scene in the court of the Persian emperor Xerxes as his mother, Queen Atossa and the Chorus (an elderly team of advisers) wait for news of her son's ill-fated attempt to invade Greece. The play focuses on the naval battle of Salamis in 480 BC as the decisive event which destroyed Xerxes' hubristic designs. It plays up the contribution of Athens to this Panhellenic victory and stresses the city's status as a democratic community of hoplites and rowers. As Atossa becomes increasingly concerned that the Persian forces may have been routed despite their superiority of numbers, she asks the Chorus who is the Athenians' despot. The Chorus reply that 'they are called neither the slaves nor subjects of any Athenian man' (242). Given this lack of autocratic leadership, the queen cannot understand how the Athenians can resist invasion. The Chorus respond with the chilling reminder that they destroyed the 'large and excellent army' of Darius (244). Darius was the previous Persian emperor who tried, unsuccessfully, to invade Greece and whose forces were defeated by the Greeks at the battle of Marathon in 490 BC. His ghost later appears to Atossa and laments Xerxes' invasion as an act of *hubris*.

In tragedies that seem to engage with their Athenian audience's political identity, it is not always the case that Athens' political mechanisms are named explicitly. In these plays, the possibilities for audience (dis)engagement are even more varied than for those tragedies where a mythical/quasi-historical Athens is the explicit backdrop. For example, Euripides' *Orestes* (408 BC) is set in Argos rather than Athens and contains a fascinating report of the assembly that decides on the fate of Orestes, Pylades and Electra following their vengeance-killings of Clytemnestra and Aegisthus (866–956). This messenger-speech represents a sovereign people deliberating and voting. But its account of the way in which factional interests and unscrupulous speakers successfully manipulate the crowd makes the process of popular decision-making seem deeply ambiguous. This aspect of *Orestes* undoubtedly offered topicality to its original Athenian audience. Only three years before, their city had been convulsed by factionalism and democracy had been briefly supplanted by an oligarchy. Many of the oligarchic plotters were elected generals or prominent speakers and advisers in Athens' assembly. They had managed to persuade the Athenian assembly to suspend full democracy with the promise of Persian financial aid in the war against Sparta if they did so. The coup was short-lived. Democracy was restored in 410. For the first time in its history, however, radical Athenian democracy had voted itself out of existence through the manipulation of pro-Spartan crypto-oligarchs. It is easy, then, to imagine Athenians reacting very strongly to Orestes' Spartan uncle, Menelaus, when he discusses the best way to deal with a *dêmos* when it is angry (697–701):

> It is like having a raging fire to extinguish. But if one gently slackens oneself and yields to its tension, taking care with one's timing, it may well blow itself out, and when it abates, you may easily get everything you want from it.

After the events of 411, it is difficult to believe that at least *some* of the Athenians watching *Orestes* did not experience the play as a reminder of democracy's vulnerability to internal and external subversion. Tyndareus (Clytemnestra's father) knows how to sway the crowd in favour of stoning Orestes to death and there is a strong sense that popular opinion might otherwise have gone the other way. Tyndareus points out that law (*nomos*) exists to prevent an endless cycle of vengeance-killing: murderers are to be shunned and punished with exile by the community. His persuasive view of the law as a bulwark against the proliferation of violence culminates in a statement which sounds similar to the sorts of civic oath sworn by jurors and newly initiated citizens of Athens: 'the law (*nomos*) I will defend with all my might, to put an end to this brutal spirit of murder, which is always the ruin of countries and cities (*poleis*) alike' (523–5). The Greek for 'brutal spirit' here is *to thêriôdes*, which literally means 'what is beast-like'. Tyndareus is positing the classic ancient Greek ideological polarity between civic culture (*nomos* and *polis*) on the one hand, and uncivilized, animalistic savagery on the other.

And yet, Tyndareus' decision to goad the popular assembly into a public stoning of the matricides – a decision that actually provokes yet more violent behaviour from Orestes – leads an audience to think hard about the boundary between good law and civic law-enforcement on the one hand, and mere state-sponsored savagery and mob rule on the other. Although Orestes' fate is decided in Argos – there is no Aeschylean trial scene in Athens – its dramatization of a city's response to homicide surely shook any Athenian juryman and assembly-goer out of ideological complacency concerning his city's decision-making institutions.

In this section, I have argued that even tragedies which are not set in Athens can still make their audiences think about Athens. But I cannot prove this argument for Athenian 'relevance' conclusively. A number of factors can allow audiences and interpreters to deny tragedy any significant currency for their immediate political and ideological milieu: the decision to set the drama in a place which is emphatically 'other' to the location of the watching audience; the medium of myth; the archaisms of tragic form and language. This conflict between drawing out tragedy's socio-political 'specificity' and insisting on more general ethical universality dogs all discussion of Greek and Roman tragedy. Furthermore, even if we accept the Vernantian argument for 'specificity', it would be hard to draw up a 'model' for discussing tragic socio-politics which adequately encompassed such diverse works as (for example) Aeschylus' *Persians*, the *Oresteia*, Sophocles' *Electra*, Euripides' *Alcestis* and the unattributable *Rhesus*. Again, it is tempting to accept that tragedy's socio-politics are too flexible for a single explanatory template.

Tragedy and 'social comment'

I have argued that we should be wary of seeing Greek tragedy as straightforwardly didactic when it comes to 'socio-politics'. But we have to concede that classical Greek writers themselves had no problem with thinking of their tragedians as creating drama that was directly instructive and relevant to their audience's specific socio-political milieu. One thinks of Plato's extreme formulations, where tragedy 'teaches' audiences to become morally, emotionally and intellectually debased and 'drags' them towards (in Socrates' view) the imperfect political systems of tyranny and democracy. But there is also a 'didactic' assumption behind Aristophanes' comic vision of tragedy's social and political impact. Nothing claimed by an Aristophanic character or chorus should be taken too seriously, but a play like *Frogs* makes no sense unless we accept as genuine the cultural purchase of the assumption that tragic poets are meant to make men 'better citizens' by teaching true and useful things (*Frogs* 1006–72). This contemporary view of the tragedian as a socially engaged 'teacher' fits with Euripides' fondness for making mythical-heroic characters speak in ways which clearly draw on the lived social experience of their fifth-century audience. When the eponymous heroine of *Medea* (431 BC) famously speaks of the unhappy situation of mature married women brought to a foreign land she speaks as a barbarian queen (230–52). And yet, much of what she says shows a remarkable empathy with what must have been the lot of many Athenian wives.

Whether there were women in the tragic audience of the City Dionysia or not, Medea's words speak directly and powerfully to Athenian husbands. Of course, there is also much about Medea that would allow an Athenian male to disassociate her from the real women in his life: there is her self-fashioning as an Homeric warrior seeking respect and revenge, her manifest barbarity and, most strikingly, her divine parentage. But her famous speech on the lot of women connects her extreme response to Jason's faithlessness to recognizable Athenian social reality. This means that Medea oscillates between two positions in relation to 'social comment' and didactics. She is sympathetic in terms that might make Athenian men think carefully about their responsibilities as husbands. But, as the play progresses towards the shocking infanticide she can also be construed as a negative paradigm against which one can contrast Athenian ideals of femininity. Thus, the 'didactic' label fits the tragedians if we gloss that didacticism as the provocation of reflection and questioning about the 'relevance' of the tragedy in question rather than the social message or imperative which must be implied by the play.

We should also be wary of thinking that the staging of debates over class or gender in Greek tragedy provoked the kinds of agitated response that we associate with the socially concerned drama of modern twentieth- and twenty-first-century stage, television and film. This is because tragedy's mythical idiom is very different to the 'realist' idiom of modern serious drama. Let us look at that mythical idiom more closely.

Heroic vagueness

Greek tragedy's intimations of the *polis*, tyranny, democracy, gender politics and mass–elite relations have to be set against a recognition that its overarching idiom is one of linguistic and thematic fuzziness about space, time and historically specific practices. One critic has usefully described this idiom as 'heroic vagueness'.[9] This 'vagueness' is useful to the Greek tragedian because it allows him freedom from distracting socio-legal or socio-political considerations where they might be inappropriate. The 'heroically vague' idiom may also be what ultimately made Greek tragedy a 'unifying' cultural form in sociological terms – just as all social groups in Athens united to worship heroes and gods in cults and festival, so they united around dramatized tales of the sufferings of those same heroes and gods. Many tragedies clearly link a hero's or heroine's suffering to the establishment of a real and particular hero-cult.

Paradoxically, however, I think that tragedy's 'heroic vagueness' may sometimes have had a very defined and historically specific political effect on its less-than-united citizenship. As we have already seen, the last play of the *Oresteia* depicts the origin of an Athenian homicide court. But the text of *Eumenides* does not offer any specific date for this event: all we can say is that its action takes place soon after the Trojan War. The procedures of the court and the trial of Orestes are so vague and the arguments of Athena and Apollo are so peculiar that it is hard to go beyond the general sense that the acquittal of Orestes and the pacification of the Furies represent a very qualified 'thumbs-up' for juridical dispute settlement as a flagship element of the audience's democratic society. Aeschylus' text does not make any specific or unequivocal recommendations concerning Athens' real-time social or political fabric – except, that is, for the pleas from the Furies and Athena that *stasis* (civil war) be avoided at all costs (696–7, 987–9).

Thus critics have been frustrated in their desire to determine the *Eumenides*' relationship to a very important 'real-time' political event. Before 461 BC, the Areopagus council was a bastion of aristocratic power which limited the true extent of Athens' democracy. In 461 an Athenian politician called Ephialtes 'democratized' Athens by convincing the assembly to pass measures limiting the power of the Areopagus. More importantly, his reforms enabled the creation of a judicial system of courts manned by male citizens over thirty years old chosen by lot for each case. The reforms made it virtually impossible to bribe the citizen jurors because trials were concluded in a day, and juries were large (several hundred). There was no judge to instruct the jurors. Jurors made up their own minds after hearing speeches from the plaintiffs and defendants. These reforms were clearly controversial – Ephialtes was assassinated soon afterwards. Between 461 and 456 Athens was beset with political violence and came close to outright *stasis* between conservative and radical political forces.

Performed in the midst of this instability, the *Oresteia*'s climactic deployment of the Areopagus court is neither a conservative endorsement of the pre-Ephialtic set-up nor a radical new charter-myth for the reformed institution. Rather, the playwright uses 'heroic vagueness' to allow *both* conservatives and radicals to see their preferred vision of the court conjured into life by Athens' patron goddess. At the same time, however, it must have been significant for a citizen audience that either of the two historical instantiations of the court could be imaginatively construed as having the same origin, namely a crisis in which privately generated vendetta, fuelled by the chthonic Furies, threatened to destroy the entire city of Athens. To protect Athens, its patron Olympian goddess has to create a human, socio-political institution, and, although the troubling acquittal of Orestes indicates that the Areopagus is not perfect, a factionalized audience in 458 BC can be reminded by the *Eumenides* that this court's status as the juridical and legal bulwark of civic and civilized values transcends any class-based struggles over the extent of that court's political power.

'Heroic vagueness' could thus be a vehicle for eliding faction and promoting civic togetherness. Indeed, it may be tragedy's valuable tendency to offer a much grander perspective on messy socio-political realities which made the genre so attractive to Hellenistic and Roman culture.

Hellenistic and Roman tragedy

We have to distinguish between four chronological phases of post-classical ancient tragedy, each of which had its own distinctive conditions of production and performance. These are the Hellenistic period, Roman Republican period, Roman Imperial period and the so-called 'second sophistic' or 'Late Antique' period. Of course, in the last period the Mediterranean world was still under Roman rule and it is important to stress that Republican tragedy and Hellenistic tragedy overlap chronologically. There are now many good accounts of post-classical tragedy, both in this volume and elsewhere, which can be used further to contextualize and explain my necessarily selective treatment here.[10] My aim is merely to sketch some faint and suggestive outlines for understanding the shifting 'politics' and sociology of post-classical tragedy.

The socio-political significance of ancient tragedy after the fourth century BC is bound up with the appropriation of Greek culture in the early Roman Republic and the enduring appeal of Greek tragic paradigms under the Roman emperors. However, all talk of 'appropriation' needs to be hedged and glossed very carefully with the following two points.

First, although Hellenistic and Roman tragedy 'appropriate' the fifth-century Greek paradigm of tragedy rather than create an entirely new one, it is not fair or accurate to see the decline of the *polis* and the rise of the Hellenistic kingdoms as attended by a concomitant decline in the value and potency of tragedy. Second, and more importantly, scholars of Roman history and literature are now beginning to question a picture of early and middle Roman Republican culture as in some sense so culturally retarded or primitive that its elites needed to 'import' Hellenistic tragedy, epic and historiography to provide them with the means and matter of socio-political self-expression. Instead, it can now be argued that in the mid-third century BC Livius Andronicus' and Naevius' tragedies were performed in a sophisticated and authentically Alexandrian Rome in which it makes little sense to pigeonhole writers and their works as more or less Greek or more or less Roman. Ennius, Pacuvius and Accius were no less sophisticated in their 'appropriations'.

Roman Republican tragedy had a political and ideological vibrancy which seems to have turned a Greek dramatic genre into an art form that spoke directly to, and perhaps questioned or meditated upon, the nature and values of *Romanitas*. The performed tragedy of the five most celebrated Republican Roman playwrights was certainly based on Greek tragedy for the most part. But scholars are only now beginning to understand that the process of 'translating' Greek tragic models into Latin was a creative, selective and inevitably political one where the prestige and value of knowing Greek traditions and literary genres went hand in hand with a need to speak seriously to Roman concerns.

Chief among those concerns, as far as we can tell from the very fragmentary remains, was the aristocratic Roman elite's notion of *virtus* in war and politics. This notion is better translated as 'manliness' rather than 'virtue' but it really encompassed a whole range of ideal and competitive socio-political skills: physical fitness, endurance, bravery, initiative, piety, versatility and eloquence. The Roman Republican aristocrat was supposed to service the community and thereby garner personal honour and renown.

By the 130s BC the writing of tragedy had become more and more an *activity* for leisured gentlemen. Between the period of the Gracchi and the age of Augustus, the writing of tragedy was the typical private occupation for educated men and often illustrious politicians. So we can imagine the Roman elite's conception of *virtus* being transmitted through a dramatic genre which was very much their preserve. We can also use Polybius, Livy and a host of other Roman sources to see that the various *ludi* ('games' or 'festivals') at which tragedies were staged were indeed used by aristocrats as a means of self-promotion and cultural control in the city. The elite control of the writing and performance context of Republican tragedy might make us think that the genre became nothing more than a vehicle for Roman aristocratic self-representation and socio-cultural hegemony. When we look at the actual fragments of the plays, however, it seems preferable to transfer Vernant's model of 'problematization' from the Athenian 'moment' to the Republican Roman situation. This would be to argue that the contextual frame of third- and second-century Roman Republican tragedy – namely the use of festivals to gratify the masses and to express elite values – must not be confused with the content of the plays themselves. For example, here is an Ennian tragic character almost certainly asking or advising Achilles to hand over Hector's corpse (fragment LXXI in H. D. Jocelyn *The Tragedies of Ennius* [Cambridge: Cambridge University Press, 1969]):

> A better thing than *virtus* is justice (*ius*);
> For the wicked often attain *virtus*
> But justice and equity do spurn themselves
> Far from the wicked.[11]

Here, military 'manliness' is seen as an inadequate guide to social and moral behaviour on its own: justice and equity are necessary supplements. And yet, as with Greek tragedy, we should expect and remember that this speech would have been either answered with, or provoked by, an opposing viewpoint. If this is Priam claiming that the act of returning Hector's body is the best thing to do, we can imagine Achilles or one of his followers espousing a very different (and yet equally 'Roman') view in which battlefield ethics are distinguished from those of peacetime.

The history of Roman tragedy rests on a paradox: 'Not a single play performed publicly at Rome survives intact, while those that have survived – the ten plays of the Senecan corpus – lack all traces of production history.'[12] However, political and social-contextual readings of Senecan tragedy can be, and have been, produced. Many critics have been tempted to see Seneca's preparedness to bring dismembered bodies and other gory scenes onto his stage – even if that stage is imagined during a recitation or reading – as an ambiguous response to imperial culture's love of gladiatorial games and other spectacles of savagery. Seneca expresses revulsion for such violent entertainment in his philosophical writings and yet we sense that the baroque descriptions of human suffering and bloody violence in his tragedies are meant to be *enjoyably* disgusting.

The precarious political world depicted in Senecan tragedy, where both rulers and their subjects can be destroyed by sudden and unpredicted disasters and crimes, has strong affinities with the political climate of Seneca's own lifetime. Seneca himself suffered a long exile under the emperor Claudius, but was then recalled in 49 AD to become tutor, speech-writer and political adviser to Nero. In 62 AD, however, he lost influence with the emperor and three years later he was accused of being involved in a conspiracy. He was forced to commit suicide. And so, for example, it is tempting to think that Seneca's closeness to the mechanisms of autocracy led him to represent Atreus (in *Thyestes*) as a larger-than-life Nero and to see this play as a moral statement of resistance to the decadence of Neronian Rome. It is also plausible to see political and social criticism in the highly wrought declamatory rhetoric of the debates, monologues and even choruses that make these plays so distinctive in tone. When Creon threatens to banish Medea, she declaims at him with *sententiae* (maxims) that were the staple of contemporary Roman rhetoric: 'unjust kingdoms never last for ever . . . when someone has grasped a sceptre with arrogant hands, how king-like he thinks it is to stick to the course on which he has embarked' (*Medea* 196, 203–5). But Atreus is as much a 'playwright figure' as he is a 'Nero figure', and the *Thyestes'* political and moral status is complicated by its own prologue's message that to reenact the tragedy of Atreus' revenge is itself an ethically and politically dubious business. Meanwhile, the *Medea*'s Creon is not a wilful tyrant: he simply does his best to protect his city's interests. And again, the *Medea* is self-consciously complicit with its own representations: 'Just as Medea chooses to do evil, so the poet chooses to write a play about evil, rather than not write at all.'[13]

Many would argue that Seneca's self-consciousness and philosophical interests make his tragedies disturbing studies of psychology and emotion rather than being critiques of contemporary autocracy or social mores. It would certainly have been risky for Seneca to have been too critical of the imperial regime in his dramas. A story about the fate of an earlier playwright during the reign of an earlier emperor illustrates the risks:

> Mamercus Aemilius Scaurus . . . was convicted because of a tragedy he had composed and fell victim to a worse fate than that which he had described. *Atreus* was the name of the drama, and in the manner of Euripides it advised one of the subjects of that monarch to endure the folly of the reigning prince. Tiberius, on learning of it, declared that this had been written with reference to him, claiming that he himself was Atreus because of his bloodthirstiness, and remarking, 'I will make him Ajax', he compelled him to commit suicide. The above, however, was not the accusation that was brought against him, but indeed he was charged with adultery.   (Dio Cassius 58.24.3–4)

This anecdote shows us that the slightest perception of 'political' content to a tragedy could get an imperial playwright into serious trouble. But it also reminds us that the surviving tragedies of Seneca speak to the 'socio-politics' of Rome in other ways. For, when Tiberius answers the tragedian's imagined 'political' analogy between himself and Atreus with a blood-curdling equation between Scaurus and Ajax, the emperor signals his rhetorical facility with mytho-tragic examples. And thus, Dio captures perfectly the educational and social context of the early empire where rhetorical skills were still part and parcel of Roman elite self-fashioning. Seneca's highly wrought monologues, debates and even his choruses speak directly to an elite culture which valued the bandying of paradoxes, mythical exempla, allusions and maxims through the format of 'topics for debate' (*controversiae* and *suasoriae*). In the absence of any safe forum in which to do real political oratory, Senecan tragedy transposes general debating topics about morality and leadership into its own 'heroically vague' idiom. Thus the 'socio-politics' of Senecan tragedy looks very different from that of its earlier Greek and Roman ancestors because too much 'specificity' could get an imperial playwright killed. But the question of the extent of any underlying socio-political resonances and relevances is still one which turns, to a great extent, on whether we as readers have a temperamental inclination towards or away from a notion of tragedy as a 'universalizing' genre.

NOTES

1. The ideological significance of the pre-play ceremonies: Simon Goldhill, 'The Great Dionysia and Civic Ideology', in J. Winkler and F. Zeitlin (eds.), *Nothing to*

Do With Dionysos? Athenian Drama in its Social Context (Princeton: Princeton University Press, 1990), pp. 97–129. The *chorêgia*: P. Wilson, *The Athenian Institution of the Khorêgia: the Chorus, the City and the Stage* (Cambridge: Cambridge University Press, 2000).

2. See J. Hesk, *Sophocles: Ajax* (London: Duckworth, 2003).

3. 'Zooming devices': C. Sourvinou-Inwood, 'Assumptions and the Creation of Meaning: Reading Sophocles' *Antigone*', *Journal of Hellenic Studies* 109 (1989), 134–48. Critique of 'zooming': H. P. Foley, 'Tragedy and Democratic Ideology: The Case of Sophocles' *Antigone*', in B. Goff (ed.), *History, Tragedy, Theory: Dialogues in Athenian Drama* (Austin: University of Texas Press, 1995), pp. 131–50.

4. See J. Hesk, *Deception and Democracy in Classical Athens* (Cambridge: Cambridge University Press, 2000).

5. See L. Hardwick, *Translating Worlds, Translating Cultures* (London: Duckworth, 2000), pp. 63–78.

6. I say 'not exclusively' here because, from a much more anti-theatrical perspective, Brechtian assumptions can be found in Plato's writing about tragedy. For tragedy as politically transformative at a constitutional level, see Plato *Republic* 568a–b.

7. Two 'Paris School' studies: J.-P. Vernant and P. Vidal-Naquet, *Myth and Tragedy in Ancient Greece* (Brighton: Zone Books, 1988); N. Loraux, *Tragic Ways of Killing a Woman* (Cambridge, Mass.: Harvard University Press, 1987).

8. On tragic Thebes as an 'anti-Athens' see F. Zeitlin, 'Thebes: Theater of Self and Society in Athenian Drama', in Winkler and Zeitlin, 1990, pp. 130–67.

9. See P. E. Easterling, 'Constructing the Heroic', in C. Pelling (ed.), *Greek Tragedy and the Historian* (Oxford: Oxford University Press, 1997), pp. 21–38.

10. The best overviews of early Republican tragedy and its socio-politics are: A. Gratwick, 'Drama', in E. Kenney and W. Clausen (eds.), *The Cambridge History of Classical Literature*, Volume II, Part 1: 'The Early Republic' (Cambridge: Cambridge University Press, 1982), pp. 77–137; G. B. Conte, *Latin Literature: A History*, J. B. Solodow (trans.), and revised by D. Fowler and G. W. Most (Baltimore and London: Johns Hopkins University Press, 1994), pp. 13–132; E. S. Gruen, *Culture and National Identity in Republican Rome* (London: Duckworth, 1992), pp. 183–223.

11. Translation adapted from E. Warmington, *Remains of Old Latin* Vol. 1 (Cambridge, Mass: Harvard University Press, 1961), p. 291.

12. S. Goldberg, 'The Fall and Rise of Roman Tragedy', *Transactions of the American Philological Association* 126 (1996), 265–86.

13. H. Hine, *Seneca: Medea* (Warminster: Aris and Phillips, 2000), p. 48.

FURTHER READING

Boyle, A. J., *Tragic Seneca: an Essay in the Theatrical Tradition*. London: Routledge, 1997.

— *Roman Drama*. London: Routledge, 2006.

Conte, G. B., *Latin Literature: A History*, J. B. Solodow (trans.) and revised by D. Fowler and G. W. Most. Baltimore and London: Johns Hopkins University Press, 1994.

Easterling, P. E. (ed.), *The Cambridge Companion to Greek Tragedy*. Cambridge: Cambridge University Press, 1997.

Foley, H. P., *Female Acts in Greek Tragedy*. Princeton: Princeton University Press, 2001.

Goldhill, S., *Reading Greek Tragedy*. Cambridge: Cambridge University Press, 1988.

Mendelsohn, D., *Gender and the City in Euripides' Political Plays*. Oxford: Oxford University Press, 2002.

5

DAVID WILES

Aristotle's *Poetics* and ancient dramatic theory

Aristotle (384–322 BC) was the greatest polymath of antiquity, whose aim was to create a systematic science of everything. He wrote about social policy, personal morality, logic and cosmology, but is perhaps most impressive in the field of biology. For two millennia, no one would improve upon his applied research into the different forms of animal life. Amidst this huge intellectual output, we find at the end of his *Collected Works* a set of condensed lecture notes on poetry. Little read in antiquity, these notes would exercise a huge influence upon the Renaissance, and on later generations of playwrights. Known as the *Poetics*, the notes attempt to do two things: firstly, they compare tragedy to epic in order to argue that tragedy is the highest form of literary art, and secondly, they offer a guide to a would-be writer in how to write the best possible tragedy. Aristotle regards tragedy as a biological 'organism' (*Poetics* xxiii.1), and the way to study an organism is to see how its different bodily parts interrelate.

In recent years, film theorists have continued to study and admire the *Poetics*, because of the emphasis which Aristotle gives to narrative, described as the invisible 'soul' of the organism (vi.14). A Hollywood story analyst in 2002 published *Aristotle's Poetics for Screenwriters: Storytelling Secrets from the Greatest Mind in Western Civilization* as a guide for aspirant writers.[1] Theorists of performance, however, have wanted to assert that 'liveness' differentiates theatre from cinema, and have often baulked at Aristotle's uncompromising view that the power of tragedy is the same with or without performance and the actors (vi.19). The importance of good storytelling rates much higher in film theory than it does, for example, in mainstream actor training. Moreover, radical performance theorists have frequently found themselves uncomfortable with what they take to be Aristotle's bourgeois politics. In a celebrated Marxist manifesto, Augusto Boal lambasted Aristotle's 'coercive' system of tragedy, which manipulates the emotions of the passive spectator.[2]

Certainly, many Athenians were suspicious of Aristotle's politics. Aristotle was a northerner who came to Athens to study under the great philosopher

Plato, whose hero Socrates had been put to death by Athenian democrats. After Plato died, Aristotle retreated from Athens to pursue his biological research, until a call came to be tutor to the young Alexander the Great, future King of Macedonia and conqueror of Asia. The Macedonians took control of the whole Greek mainland, and were resented by the mass of Athenians during the period when Aristotle returned to Athens to set up his philosophical school. Alexander died a year before Aristotle's death and, in the ensuing chaos, Aristotle thought it best to retreat from a democratic city that wanted to assert its autonomy.

In his *Politics*, based on extensive research into different systems of government, Aristotle argues for a society governed by a ruling class of landowners, trained in warfare but spared from manual labour or trade. The legitimacy of such a system assumes that the rulers are superior people who deserve their elite status. War is a means to achieving leisure, and leisure must be devoted to self-improvement. This reasoning leads him, in the final book of the *Politics*, to a debate about the arts. What is the function of the arts in shaping character? Should a member of the ruling class merely watch performances, or be a participant and perform? What kind of entertainment should be provided for those who do not belong to the elite? These are some of the questions that lie behind the *Poetics*, and help to explain why a natural and social scientist should think it so important to engage with dramatic literature. It was all to do with the formation of minds.

In order to understand Aristotle's take on theatre, we have to go back to the views of his teacher, Plato. Plato was a well-born Athenian who became deeply disillusioned with democracy after the fall of Athens to Sparta. In his *Republic* he mapped out a utopia in which the ruling class were philosophers – and from this utopia, tragedy was banished. Plato argues that Homer and drama present the gods and heroes in a very poor light, whereas in a good society the young should only be given positive role models, and he finds drama particularly problematic because it involves *mimesis*, 'imitation' or 'performance'. In his ideal society, every member has a single role, with which they should be content, but drama fosters the adoption of multiple roles, which undermines that acceptance of one's lot (*Republic* 394–7). Towards the end of the book Plato returns to the theme again. From a philosophical and religious standpoint, he claims that life itself is a kind of illusion, so representational art is nothing but an illusion of an illusion. And from a moral standpoint, he argues that theatrical experience is about being carried away by one's feelings – towards grief and sentimental pity in tragedy, towards uninhibited laughter in comedy – and surrender to these emotions weakens one's powers of self-control. He ends his discussion with the wry comment that philosophers and artists often disagree; if anyone can demonstrate that drama and poetry do indeed have a place in a model society, he will be only too delighted, for he knows their fascination (607c). Many critics have considered this to be the challenge that Aristotle took up: how to demonstrate that drama, with all its pain and ribaldry, belongs in an ideal society.

What Aristotle developed was a theory of drama-as-literature rather than drama-as-performance. The six ingredients of tragedy are listed as follows (vi.7):

1. story
2. character
3. intellectual argument
4. language
5. song
6. visuals

At the core is the story. Character is a function of storyline, and characters express themselves by developing arguments. All of this has to be rendered by the playwright in a certain poetic idiom. Music and decor are regarded by Aristotle as embellishments, making the play more attractive to an audience but not affecting the substance of the story.

So how did this downgrading of the performance aspect come about? Firstly, Aristotle had no basis on which to construct a satisfactory theory of acting. He remarks elsewhere that acting was late in being considered an art because originally poets acted in their own plays.[3] When playwrights ceased to act the central role in their own plays, they supervised rehearsals and imparted the text orally with the appropriate intonations, so the notion of *interpretation* only arose in the next generation when plays started to be revived as classics. The star actor seemed to Aristotle to be an obstruction, getting in between himself and the play as it was written.[4] Secondly, there was social prejudice. Performance seemed to involve pandering to popular taste. In the *Politics* Aristotle writes of a divide in the theatre audience between the leisured classes, on the one hand, and manual workers and traders on the other; the vulgar tastes of the latter had somehow to be accommodated (viii.7). Plato expressed himself more vigorously on the same issue, contrasting the rowdy and uncontrollable 'theatrocracy' of his own day with the deferential audience behaviour of an earlier generation (*Laws* 700–1). Thirdly, Aristotle inhabited an ever more cosmopolitan world. Alexander used actors as the cultural arm of his invasion force when he moved eastwards, implanting Greek culture alongside Greek soldiers in the regions he conquered. Theatre had become the property of the Greek-speaking world rather than the Athenian city-state. This left Aristotle with a dilemma as to how far the leisured citizen should participate in the arts in the old collective spirit of the city-state, and how far one should simply appreciate what expert touring professionals had to offer. The translation of Athenian performances into texts that could be read, adapted and interpreted across the expanding Greek world meant that the script was the thing for Aristotle to consider, not the performance.

Since Aristotle was not an Athenian, he had no personal investment in the Athenian dimension of tragedy, in terms either of political message, or physical circumstances of performance. The most drastic omission from the *Poetics* is proper consideration of the chorus, which Aristotle declares should be treated like one of the actors (xviii.7). Again we have to look at the conditions of the time. There was no longer the same prestige attached to the Athenian *chorêgia*, the system whereby a rich individual won public acclaim through the magnificence of the chorus that he selected from amongst his fellow citizens and funded for months of training.[5] In Aristotle's day famous actors toured Greece, recruiting choruses locally or taking a small entourage with them, and playwrights were turning choral odes into detached interludes. Aristotle takes for granted a spatial separation of the chorus from 'those on the stage' (xii.2) and recent architectural changes emphasized that separation.[6] When the chorus became marginalized, the meaning of Greek plays shifted. It became impossible any longer to see them as works fundamentally concerned with socio-political problems.

To put Aristotle in perspective, the best text we can look at is Aristophanes' *Frogs*. Old Comedy often reflected upon tragedy. Through its mockery and parody, comedy educated the mass Athenian audience, helping to produce ever more sophisticated viewers of tragedy. *Frogs* was produced in 405 BC, a year before the surrender to Sparta. This defeat could have resulted in the physical destruction of the city, with the slaughter or enslavement of the population, so it is hard to overestimate the urgency of the situation. Aristophanes' comic proposition is that the god Dionysus descends to the underworld to bring back Euripides, whose wisdom will save the city, but then has to make a choice between the merits of Euripides and Aeschylus. Like Plato and Aristotle, the comic playwright assumes that watching plays will shape the minds and moral fibre of the audience. Unlike Aristotle, however, Aristophanes takes the traditionalist view that the role of the poet is to be a 'teacher', directly imparting his wisdom to the city.

Aristophanes' play locates itself on the cusp between a literary and an oral culture. Dionysus is sitting on board a warship reading the text of Euripides' *Andromeda* (which is about rescue at sea) when he develops an insatiable craving for Euripides that sends him on his mission to the underworld (*Frogs*, 52–4). Reading plays for pleasure is a new thing to do and clearly preposterous in the context of a military campaign. Euripides himself is characterized as a man of words who owns a library. The contest in the underworld pits Euripides, who claims to make the Athenian population more clever, against Aeschylus, who claims to instil a martial spirit. Though the chorus urge the contestants to argue with subtlety because all the audience now own books (1113–14), the plays are conceived as performances, not literary artefacts. When Euripides recalls the beginning of Aeschylus' *Niobe*, for example, he evokes the position of the body, the costume and the command of silence. When Dionysus recalls the chorus of *Persians*, he evokes the gestures and sound quality attached to the choral lyric (911–12, 1029). It is the event, not the text, that the dramatist is seen to have created.

For Aristotle, diction and metre are the external form that conceals the invisible core of the play, the story, but for Aristophanes the physical impact of the words is part of the effect and meaning. In a climactic scene, the words of the two playwrights are placed in the scales and weighed. When Euripides condemns Aeschylus for his ungated mouth, his lack of small-talk (838–9), Aeschylus' words are taken to be the expression of a recognizable voice. The tragedy remains an integrated conception, where sound, movement, costume and music are all part of an author's responsibility. The text that Dionysus reads on his warship simply whets his appetite for the real thing, the performance in an Athenian festival.

With this context in mind, we can return to Aristotle and his central proposition that 'a tragedy is a mimesis of an action' (vi.2). The idea that art of whatever kind is a form of *mimêsis*, something pretending to be something else, is entirely foreign to Aristophanes, for whom the reality of the performance event in the here-and-now is paramount. While Plato related 'mimesis' to the idea that true reality belongs to the world of the gods, Aristotle as a materialist gave the word a rather different inflection. He celebrated mimesis on the educational grounds that children learn through imitation. In common with Plato, he saw, not only drama and painting, but also music and dance as mimetic arts, so we must not confuse Greek notions with late nineteenth-century naturalism and the idea that art should exactly reproduce life. While Plato often links the idea of mimesis to impersonation by a performer, Aristotle does his best to move the debate onto a more conceptual level.

Aristotle's greatest stroke of genius was to perceive that good drama is in the first instance an imitation of an action, not an imitation of character. Shaw's playtexts provide the reader with a precise description of each character, so each figure is a recognizable type when the curtain opens. In reaction to this way of working, method actors are trained to comb a script for clues to motivation, then root themselves in a unique characterization that explains why the person behaves as they do. Character is again the thing that comes first. Aristotle, however, was quite clear that the basis of a play lies in *what* happens, not *why* it happens, or who makes it happen. In Aristotelian tragedy, character emerges exclusively from the choices people make in the situation set up by the play. The Greek word for 'character', *êthos*, implies a moral attitude rather than a set of idiosyncrasies. Classical Greek tragedy was a theatre of masks, and no personal traits or distinctive qualities were imprinted onto those masks; all they provided was some limited information about class, age and gender. There was no given character set before the audience at the beginning of a performance. It was up to the audience, on the basis of how the stage figure behaved and made moral choices, to project 'character' onto the blank face of the mask.[7]

In modern productions of *Antigone*, character usually comes first. A military uniform may place Creon as a dictator, whereas the casting of a black actor might place him as an idealist. A southern Irish accent, in certain circumstances and according to the political persuasion of the audience, might signify at the outset that Antigone was a threat to social stability, or a fighter for freedom. Voice, casting and costume, together with facial expressions and vocal inflexions, are likely to tell the audience at the outset who is right and wrong in this struggle. In Greek theatre, mask, verse and formalized costume offered no clues. It was the moral choices made by Creon and Antigone in the course of the action of the play, and those choices alone, which according to Aristotle shaped the audience's perception of character. Roman tragedy, where emotional expression was inscribed on the mask, diverged sharply from Aristotelian principles. Horace writes of how sad words suit a mournful face, threatening words an angry face. Orestes must be full of sorrow in accordance with tradition, Medea must display her ferocity and drive, Achilles his short temper and ruthlessness.[8]

Aristotle's concept of 'action' should not be confused with spectacularity. The Greek taboo upon representing scenes of killing in the theatre relates to this distinction between two sorts of action. A true 'action' is what turns one situation into another. The American playwright David Mamet echoes Aristotle when he explains how working in the movies taught him not to cheat. The budding screenwriter must avoid the temptation of the 'Death of my Kitten' speech, when the action stops so the hero can deliver a sentimental account of how as a child he lost his pet, a speech that pours out emotion and develops character background without advancing the narrative:

> The rule in question here is Aristotle's notion of unity of action: in effect, that the play should be about only one thing, and that that thing should be *what the hero is trying to get.*
>
> Unstinting application of this rule makes great plays because the only thing we, as audience, care about in the theatre is WHAT HAPPENS NEXT?[9]

In Aristotle's list of the six parts of a tragedy, after narrative and character comes not 'emotion' but 'intellectual argument', or more simply 'thought'. This sounds a rather cerebral category and is missing from modern manuals of screen and playwriting. Greek plays are full of oratory, long speeches where pairs of characters develop competing arguments, using the art of public speaking to impress the chorus. Modern playwrights tend to prefer private settings, where characters seem to reveal their true selves, but Greek playwrights liked public settings such as the marketplace, believing that people defined themselves through their contributions to the community. The art of public speaking, which every citizen needed to master, is the subject of Aristotle's *Rhetoric*. A long section of that book is devoted to an analysis of fourteen key emotions, for public speaking was universally recognized to be the art of working on the feelings of an audience. Characters deliver rhetorical speeches in tragedy in order to create a particular emotional response in those who listen. Modern actors often have difficulty in playing these argumentative speeches because they look for the hidden motivations of the speaker, not the public art of creating emotion in listeners. Aristotle's emphasis on 'argument' or 'thought' does much to invalidate Augusto Boal's savage critique, which presumes Aristotle to deal in emotions at the expense of ideas.

Aristotle's analysis of audience response is a subtle one. He assumes that 'the poet must provide the pleasure that derives via mimesis from pity and fear' (xiv.3). Psychology has yet to come up with a compelling analysis of why human beings derive such evident pleasure from watching sentimental melodramas that provoke tears of pity, or from horror movies that make one go pale or shake with fear. Crucial to any explanation is the fact that the viewer knows such experiences belong to make-believe or 'mimesis'. Aristotle analyses pity and fear at some length in the *Rhetoric*. Fear relates to an imminent danger threatening us, whereas pity relates to other people. Fear is more active than despair, for we urgently think how to escape. Pity is felt most strongly for people who are like ourselves in age, class or lifestyle. Whilst fear stems from situation, Aristotle concedes that the performative dimension has much to do with generating pity, because tears, gestures and ragged clothing make the suffering seem closer to us. He illustrates the distinction between pity and fear with the story of an Egyptian king who wept, i.e. experienced pity, when he saw a friend in the rags of a beggar, yet did not weep when he saw his son led off to die; in this case the emotion was fear, since he regarded his son as part of himself (*Rhetoric* ii.5, 8). In Aristotle's subtle account of tragic emotion, pity and fear are opposed physical impulses, one drawing us towards the object of pity, the other pulling us away from the object of fear. In a well-constructed tragedy, both emotions are generated together, keeping us in a state of tension, fixed in our places.

The most famous word to have entered our vocabulary from the *Poetics* is 'catharsis', literally a 'cleansing'. Aristotle defines tragedy as 'through pity and fear effecting the *katharsis* of such emotions' (vi.2). The obvious key to the meaning of 'catharsis' is found at the end of the *Politics*, where he discusses the role of the *aulos*, the emotive double-pipe used in Greek tragedy and banished from Plato's republic in favour of the measured lyre. Aristotle here argues that there is a place for the orgiastic effects of Dionysiac music. Music can be character-forming or action-inducing, or 'enthusing'; 'enthusiasm', the feeling of being possessed, sits alongside pity and fear as part of a spectator's experience, dangerous for a participant, but valuable for one who is merely a spectator. Aristotle goes on to argue that music has several functions: education, or 'catharsis', or entertainment, i.e. relaxation and a pause from stress (*Politics* viii.7.3).

Elaborating on catharsis, Aristotle cites the therapeutic value that sacred music on the *aulos* can have in setting people with a certain malaise on their feet, and explains that pity and fear can work in the same way. He truncates his discussion with the promise that he will explain more fully about catharsis in the *Poetics*, but unfortunately this discussion is missing from our surviving text. The drift of the argument, with its critique of Plato, is very clear. Something else is going on in the experience of tragedy, beyond pleasure and education. The remarks that conclude the *Politics* help to explain what lay behind the debate. In Athens, public performance had to cater for the uneducated classes of society. To justify music in straightforward educational terms, as Plato had done, was incompatible with the realities of the world Aristotle knew. We have to distinguish between how society theoretically ought to be and what is actually possible given human limitations.[10]

Quite what Aristotle meant by catharsis has been much debated. Jacob Bernays in the mid-nineteenth century argued that the metaphor was a medical one. Emotionality is a bad thing, and noxious emotions are purged by the experience of watching tragedy. Bernays' niece married Sigmund Freud, and it was probably by this route that the word catharsis entered the vocabulary of psychoanalysis: a model of the mind premised on the notion of repression was quick to respond to the idea that tragedy released repressed emotions. The medical interpretation accords with Aristotle's biological cast of mind, but obliges us to accept that the Christian virtue of pity is something a Greek may have in excess, something he may have to vomit up in order to restore psycho-physical balance. The main competing theory holds that catharsis is a ritual term, relating to cleansing and purification. Aristotle, for example, refers to a 'cathartic' ritual in Euripides' *Iphigenia among the Taurians* (*Poetics* xvii.4). According to this interpretation, which lays more emphasis on the educative possibilities of catharsis, the experience of emotions in the mimetic environment of the theatre helps us to purify and clarify them so they can arise in the right real-life situations.[11] Back in 1957, when American 'New Criticism' held that a poem was a self-contained work needing no context to give it meaning, Gerald F. Else published an influential book in which he argued that 'catharsis' applied purely to the resolution of the plot and had nothing to do with audience response.[12] Though critics today remain baffled by what goes on in the mind of a theatre audience and the balance that actually exists between surrender to emotion and residual self-awareness, all seem agreed that Aristotle was making a brave attempt to address the intractable problem of audience response.

We find a clear alternative to the theory of catharsis in the writings of the Roman dramatist Seneca. As a Stoic, Seneca was committed to the idea that emotions should be controlled, not released. The good life is not about pleasure, or finding a point of mental equilibrium, but about making an absolute commitment to virtue within the constraints that one has been allotted. Seneca makes a distinction between involuntary emotional impulses, conscious responses and fully fledged emotion, when one acts without rational regard for consequences. Physiological responses – like weeping, shivering, turning pale, one's hair standing on end – belong to this first instinctive phase, and do not reflect on the morality of the spectator. Seneca paints a vivid picture of pseudo-emotion in a crowd that rages at a failed gladiator, then forgives him in response to his tears. Unlike Aristotle, he is alert to the experience of being part of a collective audience and to the fact that one tends to yawn when a neighbour yawns, laugh when others laugh and weep when the crowd weeps.[13] Seneca's tragedies reflect his different understanding of tragic emotion. Plot is no longer the first consideration. After five centuries, the stories of Medea, Oedipus, Andromache and Phaedra are too well known to carry surprises. What is of interest is the way characters deal with their emotions of fear, grief and anger, and so engage with their destinies. His plays ratchet up the horror and explore feeling for its own sake. A Roman theatre audience will never yield to true emotion in the theatre, but it will learn to recognize the initial physical impulses, and thus be better equipped to deal with painful situations in real life.

Aristotle's major focus is storyline. He accepts that some tragedies do in fact turn primarily on character, emotion or visuals, but argues that the best rely on their plotting. He declares that plots should be unified, which is to say single rather than simple. Although a single tragic hero does not suffice to create unity, he expresses disapproval of double plots where different characters have different outcomes. He recognizes that this point is controversial and some disagree with him (xiii.4). One guesses that Aristotle thought *Oedipus Tyrannus* superior to *Antigone*, given the double focus of the latter. And I shall return to the problem of the Aeschylean trilogy.

A well-plotted Aristotelian play is a closed structure with a beginning, middle and end. The complication must be wound up and then unravelled. The incidents follow logically from one to the next, and anything that smacks of randomness or irrationality is part of the back-story, set up before the play begins. Everything that happens must have plausibility. Within these constraints, the question continues to be the same: what will have the greatest impact on the emotions of the audience? On the level of character, it is important that the audience should feel a certain admiration for people in the play whom they judge to be not perfect but nobler than themselves. If such people suffer, emotions of pity and fear are triggered. Mere poetic justice, when the good are rewarded and the bad punished, often accords with public taste, but is not truly tragic. At the other extreme, outrage at a terrible misfortune which befalls someone entirely admirable, and seems to be a random event with no sense of logic in the chain of events, is incompatible with the pleasurable emotions of tragedy. Aristotle does not speak of the audience 'identifying' with the protagonist, for moral evaluations are always being made; but he does assume that the audience will keep relating the characters of the play to themselves.

On the level of plot, Aristotle's two key concepts are *peripeteia* and *anagnôrisis*. *Peripeteia* is a turning around of the situation to its direct opposite, subject always to the logic of the plot. Oedipus the detective becomes Oedipus the criminal, to give an obvious example. *Anagnôrisis* is recognition of the truth, as for example when Orestes is recognized by his sister, or again when Oedipus recognizes that he himself is the source of the plague. *Oedipus Tyrannus* is such a fine play, Aristotle argues, because the *anagnôrisis* and the *peripeteia* are one and the same (xi.2). He cites 'scenes of suffering' as the third aspect of a good plot, but makes no further comment. The close relationship between scenes of suffering and virtuoso singing in Greek tragedy is an aspect of tragic form that he seems reluctant to discuss. However, we should not underestimate the usefulness of Aristotle's two key categories. The playwright Nicholas Wright recently published a set of 'masterclasses' in a Sunday newspaper, with the aim of imparting his skills, and examples of *peripeteia* and *anagnôrisis* from modern plays are offered to the modern playwright as examples of best practice.

It is one of the paradoxes of reading Aristotle's *Poetics* that so much of what he writes has value for the present, yet so little serves to illuminate the Oresteian trilogy of Aeschylus. Today we see the arts as leisure activities uncoupled from religion, and we commonly attribute more aesthetic value to the hundred-minute film than to the multi-episode TV series. Aristotle's emphasis on dramatic unity inspired seventeenth-century French theorists to go much further and rule that plays should observe 'three unities' – being set in one place, during one day, with no subplot. Aristotle's argument in favour of the well-made single play has to do with intensity in the first instance: what, he ponders, would Sophocles' *Oedipus* be like if stretched to the length of the *Iliad* (xxvi.5)? But the reasons why Aristotle was unable to engage with the form of the trilogy run much deeper.

Aristotle sees tragedy as a development from epic poetry, not from religious practices honouring Dionysus. Some of the distinctive qualities that Aristotle admires in Homer, like grandeur, the possibilities of simultaneous action and scope for the irrational apply equally well to Aeschylus (xxiv.4). We infer that Aristotle regards Aeschylus as a halfway house in the evolution of tragedy out of epic. Aristotle has no theory to explicate religious practice within society. His scientific mind does not accommodate anything that smacks of mystification. Plato delighted in creating his own improved myths, but Aristotle stuck to facts. The traditional stories are convenient for the dramatist, he explains, because they help the audience accept the plausibility of extreme events and they help distinguish poetry, concerned with universal truth, from history, concerned with particularities. These ancient stories are not sacred or essential to the purpose of tragedy and can potentially be discarded (ix.3–7). In his historical account, he explains that tragedy emerged from the dithyramb, just as comedy emerged from phallic songs, but shows no further interest in these superseded Dionysiac practices (iv.12). His object is to distinguish epic from tragedy within a genre called 'poetry'. He sticks to facts in order to explain how tragedy generates such powerful emotions, and his taste for Euripides and Sophocles reflected the responses of his generation.

Whilst Plato took a deeply religious view of the world, Aristotle banishes the gods to the extremity of his scientific universe, seeing them merely as forces that first set the universe in motion. In the *Poetics*, he cites the argument of Xenophanes that the form of the gods is a mere projection of the human imagination (xxv.7). He tolerates gods in the back-story of a tragedy, or in the form of a *deus ex machina* foretelling the future in order to tie the play up, but he criticizes the ending of *Medea*, where the heroine makes her escape on a magic solar chariot (xv.7). A certain ambivalence enters the argument when he states that tragedy requires an element of the 'amazing', and things are amazing because they transcend rationality (xxiv.8). It is a matter of what the audience will accept as amazing yet paradoxically also accept as plausible, and he allows that poets may get away with divine interventions on the grounds of 'so they say', i.e. tradition (xxv.7). It is clear that Aristotle would have been uneasy when faced with the decisive roles of Athene, Apollo and the Furies in the *Oresteia*, where Aeschylus was plainly breaking with tradition. The movement of the trilogy from a world of myth to recent political events in Athens confused the categories of myth and history. The form of the trilogy was linked to Dionysiac ritual by virtue of being followed by a satyr play, and within the *Oresteia* elaborate rituals like the pouring of libations to the dead do little to advance the plot.

A materialist view of the world, rejecting any notion of divine intervention, contributes to Aristotle's reluctance to engage with the chorus. Choreography drew heavily upon ritual dances, and the words of the chorus keep taking us back to the power of the gods. The chorus dominates the *Oresteia*, and two of the component plays are named after choruses, but Aristotle is interested only in the behaviour of individual characters. His perspective was that of a Greek who migrated from one city to another, not that of a democratic Athenian, and the collectivist ethos of fifth-century Athens was not something to which he would or could respond. He did not believe in rule by the common people, and was unsympathetic to a dramatic convention that gave collective voice to a ruled or oppressed class. He stressed the universality of tragedy, and the particular reference which the *Eumenides* makes to the evolution of democracy would have seemed to him a failure of art. He wanted tragedy to deal with morally autonomous individuals and, though Orestes certainly makes a moral choice at the turning point of the trilogy (in an exemplary scene of *peripeteia* and *anagnôrisis*), the characters often seem to function as elemental forces, particularly in the *Agamemnon* – where Clytemnestra, for example, is associated with the raging flames of a beacon.

Finally, Aristotle's theory of language makes it very hard for him to deal with Aeschylean poetry. While Plato was a consummate stylist who wrote beautifully crafted dialogues, Aristotle always expresses himself plainly and directly. In his *Rhetoric* he attacks sophists who used verbal pyrotechnics to carry the day and teaches students how to win through the quality of their argument, through content rather than external form. In his *Poetics* he sets up a clear distinction between poetry and verse, since scientific works can be put into verse. The essence of a tragic poem is its story, its content, and that story has then to be rendered in a particular style. He declares that tragic style should always be clear, though raised above the commonplace; a 'brilliant' style will obscure the essential qualities of argument and character. When he mentions that iambic metre is close to everyday speech, and the optimum way of elevating it is through metaphor rather than exotic or compound words (xxii.9), we recall that Aeschylean language is characterized by variety of metre and by exotic and compound words of just this sort. Aristotle distinguishes the dance-based trochaic metre (dum-di . . .) from the action-based iambic metre (di-dum . . .) normal in tragedy (xxiv.5). Aeschylus is plainly a throwback to the past, before tragedy had reached its 'natural' form. The physicality and energy of Aeschylean language, the way it communicates through sound and rhythm at the expense of semantic clarity, the way it suggests rather than explains, all run counter to Aristotelian taste. In Aeschylus form is inseparable from content, something Aristotle could never accept.

So far I have been concerned with Aristotle's theory of tragedy. Umberto Eco's novel *The Name of the Rose* imagines how the final chapters of the *Poetics* dealing with comedy were lost in the flames that consumed a medieval monastery.[14] No one in antiquity, except Socrates in a flight of fancy at the end of Plato's *Symposium*, seems to have questioned the principle that tragedy and comedy are opposites, practised by different playwrights and different actors. Yet tragic actors and playwrights were responsible for satyr plays, and satyr plays were unquestionably funny, so a rather complex theoretical model was needed to deal with the phenomenon of 'comedy'. Aristotle writes off the satyr play as a primitive form, but the Roman poet Horace, advising writers how to work in the Greek style, faced the problem squarely. How is a dramatist to be serious and witty at the same time? How is he to avoid spoiling the effect of the preceding tragedy? How is he to prevent satyrs talking like slaves in comedy? The answer for Horace was not to adopt a different dramatic language, but to create splendour through the skilful ordering of everyday words. He compares the tragedian writing a satyr play to an aristocratic woman who is required to dance in public because it is festival time, and manages to do so without losing rank and joining the 'fried-peas-and-nuts public'.[15] Horace's link between theatre and festival, legitimating what may be described as amoral 'saturnalian' behaviour, offers a distinctively Roman perspective.

Plato argued that just as too much pity makes spectators self-pitying, so too much pleasure in comedy, too much laughter and letting go, will eventually turn someone into a clown in everyday life (*Republic* 606c). Aristotle's counter-argument had to deal as effectively with comedy as it did with tragedy. In the surviving text of the *Poetics* he explains that while tragedy presents superior people, comedy presents inferior people, who are not evil but risible. The risible involves something flawed, something that is ugly, but causes no pain or injury. The comic mask, for example, is shameful and distorted, but painless (v.1). A short essay known as the *Tractatus Coislinianus* appears to preserve the continuation of the core argument. The essay refers to comedy 'through enjoyment and laughter effecting the *catharsis* of such emotions'.[16] The Greek word for enjoyment or pleasure is *hêdonê*, as in our word 'hedonism'. By analogy with pity and fear, one infers that laughter is the defensive impulse, the movement away from the object, whilst *hêdonê* is the sympathetic impulse, the movement towards. Aristotle's argument makes comedy innocuous, but at the same time, plainly, it served to depoliticize. Horace had no equivalent to the Aristotelian theory of catharsis, which allowed theatre to be both pleasurable and beneficial for the human organism. In the moralistic Roman universe, where pleasure and morality were antithetical concepts, the challenge for Horace was to work a combination of opposites, and find a compromise that would satisfy the divergent tastes of rich and poor, young and old. Ribald comedy was not something he could accommodate and admirers of Plautus are dismissed as fools.[17]

The *Tractatus* also preserves a theory of comic character consistent with Aristotle's ethical writings. The 'ironist' is set in opposition to the 'boaster', for the first understates his nature, the second overstates. The ironist out to amuse himself is contrasted with the 'clown' whose concern is to amuse others.[18] In the *Nicomachean Ethics* Aristotle sets the clown in opposition to the boor who makes no effort to please others (ii.7). These are suggestive categories in relation to many of the double-acts that we find in Aristophanes: Dionysus the boaster is undercut by his ironical slave Xanthias in *Frogs*, for example. Old Philocleon triumphantly plays the clown in *Wasps*, while his right-thinking son is a killjoy. However, when we look at some of Aristophanes' comic protagonists who stand alone, like Dicaeopolis in *Acharnians*, we are obliged to see these categories merging in a single figure, if the theory is to hold.

Finally, the *Tractatus* sets up 'middle' comedy as an ideal, poised historically between the origins of the genre in personal satire and the over-serious New Comedy that would soon be associated with the name of Menander.[19] Menander's comedy can be interpreted as a reinvention of the comic genre in accordance with Aristotle's theory of plot, for his plots are meticulously crafted to set up moral choices that reveal character. Someone is said to have asked Menander, shortly before the Dionysia: 'Haven't you finished your comedy yet?' – to which Menander replied: 'Yes indeed, the comedy is finished. I have devised the plot, and simply have to add the accompaniment, the lines.'[20] When Menander's carefully plotted comedy became the norm, the need to justify comedy in terms of laughter receded. Critics focused their attention on mimesis, and the complex relationship of comedy to real life. One of the most famous formulations is attributed to Cicero, who described comedy as 'an imitation of life, a mirror of custom, a reflection of truth'.[21] The staging of Menander's plays on a shallow stage cut off from the audience by the orchestra contributed to the feeling that a play resembled a two-dimensional reflective mirror. An audience could look into the mirror and learn about itself. When the ethical benefits of comedy became self-evident, Aristotle's therapeutic explanations were no longer relevant.

NOTES

1. M. Tierno, *Aristotle's Poetics for Screenwriters: Storytelling Secrets from the Greatest Mind in Western Civilization* (New York: Hyperion, 2002).
2. Augusto Boal, *Theater of the Oppressed*, trans. C. A. and M.-O. Leal McBride (London: Pluto, 1979). Boal's main source appears to be Arnold Hauser's *Social History of Art* 1 (New York: Knopf, 1951).
3. Aristotle *Rhetoric* iii.1.4. For poets as actors see E. Csapo and W. J. Slater, *The Context of Ancient Drama* (Ann Arbor: University of Michigan Press, 1995), pp. 224–5.
4. Cf. Aristotle *Rhetoric* iii.1.4; A. Pickard-Cambridge, *Dramatic Festivals of Athens*, revised by J. Gould and D. Lewis (Oxford: Oxford University Press, 1968), p. 100.
5. See Rehm, ch. 10 and Walton, ch. 15 in this volume.
6. I have addressed this controversy in *Tragedy in Athens: Performance Space and Theatrical Meaning* (Cambridge: Cambridge University Press, 1997), pp. 63ff. See also Beacham, ch. 12 in this volume.
7. J. Jones, *On Aristotle and Greek Tragedy* (London: Chatto and Windus, 1962), pp. 43–6.
8. *Art of Poetry*, 105–25.
9. David Mamet, 'A Playwright in Hollywood', in *Writing in Restaurants* (London: Faber, 1986), p. 76.
10. For a discussion of some of the terms involved in this debate, see for example the translation and commentary by Richard Kraut, *Aristotle, Politics, Books VII and VIII* (Oxford: Oxford University Press, 1997).
11. For a selection of recent views, see A. O. Rorty (ed.), *Essays on Aristotle's Poetics* (Princeton: Princeton University Press, 1992).
12. G. F. Else, *Aristotle's Poetics* (Cambridge, Mass.: Harvard University Press, 1957).
13. *On Anger* ii.2–6, translated and analysed in R. Sorabji, *Emotion and Peace of Mind* (Oxford: Oxford University Press, 2000), pp. 72–5. Cf. *On Anger* i.2.4–5.
14. *The Name of the Rose*, trans. W. Weaver (London: Secker and Warburg, 1983); film version (1986) dir. Jean-Jacques Annaud.
15. *Art of Poetry*, 220–50. I have drawn on D. A. Russell's translation in D. A. Russell and M. Winterbottom, *Ancient Literary Criticism: The Principal Texts in New Translations* (Oxford: Oxford University Press, 1972).
16. See R. Janko, *Aristotle on Comedy* (London: Duckworth, 1984), pp. 24–5.
17. *Art of Poetry*, 333–4, 341–4, 270–3.
18. Janko, 1984, pp. 97, 216.
19. *Ibid.*, p. 99. Cf. *Poetics* v.2–3.
20. Plutarch *Moralia* 347f. See D. Wiles, *The Masks of Menander: Sign and Meaning in Greek and Roman Performance* (Cambridge: Cambridge University Press, 1991), pp. 26ff.
21. Cited by Donatus: see M. S. Silk, *Aristophanes and the Definition of Comedy* (Oxford: Oxford University Press, 2000), p. 85.

FURTHER READING

Else, G. F., *Plato and Aristotle*. Chapel Hill: University of North Carolina Press, 1986.

Halliwell, S., *Aristotle's Poetics*. Bristol: Bristol Classical Press, 1998.

Janko, R., *Aristotle on Comedy: Towards a Reconstruction of Poetics 11*. London: Duckworth, 1984.

Jones, J., *On Aristotle and Greek Tragedy*. London: Chatto and Windus, 1962.

Russell, D. A. and Winterbottom, M., *Ancient Literary Criticism: The Principal Texts in New Translations*. Oxford: Oxford University Press, 1972.

Tierno, M., *Aristotle's Poetics for Screenwriters: Storytelling Secrets from the Greatest Mind in Western Civilization*. New York: Hyperion, 2002.

6

GONDA VAN STEEN

Politics and Aristophanes:
watchword 'Caution!'

'The cultural moment I most regret having missed is the heyday of Aristophanes,' begins Joshua Kosman, music critic for the *San Francisco Chronicle*, in an article from 16 February 2003 entitled 'Ancient Greek Fun'. He explains that Aristophanes' comedies may well be the most 'context-dependent' works of literature of the past three thousand years, because the playwright drew his humour from the multi-layered political and cultural life of fifth- and fourth-century BC Athens. Kosman regrets: '[O]ur level of understanding is pitiable. Even for Greek scholars, huge numbers of in-jokes, topical allusions, *ad hominem* digs and serious satirical points whiz by in silent mystery. The rest of us are nowhere.' Kosman warns that even advanced scholarship may fail to crack many of Aristophanes' barbed stings and jokes. My message, too, will be one of caution, especially where the most problematic aspect of the study of Aristophanes – his relationship to politics – is concerned.

The problem originates in the fact that very little is known about the comic playwright's life and personality. This dearth of biographical data did not stop the later tradition from creating an aura of notoriety around Aristophanes that was based solely on the bold content of his corpus of eleven preserved comedies, or a mere quarter of his total output, which was, in all likelihood, very diverse. Diversity and turbulence, too, characterized his life: he saw democracy at work – or at fault – in Athens and its surrounding territories. He observed the city's imperialist expansion and the political and moral demise of a naval empire that could have lasted much longer. He noticed how many Athenians became fascinated with the political model that Sparta harboured and that appeared to supply the basis of its military strength, of which Attica suffered the damaging consequences during the Peloponnesian Wars. These wars, which ended with Athens' submission to Sparta, formed the background to the bulk of Aristophanes' comedies. Of course, this protracted war was no laughing matter. Its destructive material repercussions and broad psychological impact caused Aristophanes to rethink the public as well as the private role of drama and, in particular, of comedy in responding to the need for release, consolation, political perspective, and ideological guidance. These concerns are reflected in what has traditionally been called Old Comedy, or that first distinct phase of Attic comedy that was very engaged with the public predicament of urban Athens, but also of the countryside of greater Attica. The comedies written by Aristophanes in the earlier part of his career (from the early 420s to the traumatic end of the Peloponnesian Wars in 404 BC) are such homegrown products of the *polis*, or city-state, of Athens. These are the comedies that are key to any investigation into the politics of the playwright himself. They include *Acharnians, Birds, Peace, Knights, Wasps, Clouds, Lysistrata* and *Frogs*. The three remaining comedies, *Women at the Thesmophoria, Women in Assembly* and *Wealth*, have traditionally been called 'less political'. *Women at the Thesmophoria* is of a literary and parodic nature, but still concentrates its attacks on public figures, the tragic playwrights Euripides and Agathon. *Women in Assembly* and *Wealth* operate on a more utopian and domestically orientated plane; these plays also reveal structural features that bring them closer to the later phases in the historical development of Attic comedy that are conventionally called Middle and New Comedy.

This essay briefly outlines a few important trends in the way Aristophanes' politics have been read and understood, but moves away from neat answers and – inevitably – returns to the message of caution. Emphasis on Aristophanes in his own time will be counterbalanced with caveats imposed by insights from the study of the later reception of the classical comedies. The intricacies of the links between the Athenian comic stage and the political processes of its historical reception have not yet been sufficiently emphasized. Here is where a lot of research remains to be done in order to respond with new answers to the old question. I make a start by relating Aristophanes' politics to some of the political purposes that the playwright has served in modern Greece. The avant-gardist Greek stage director Karolos Koun may be credited with making pioneering steps to modernize Aristophanes' politics *and* aesthetics. His production of the *Birds* in 1959, staged at the Herodes Atticus Theatre beneath the Acropolis, remains a milestone in the modern Greek history of breaking political, social, religious, literary and linguistic taboos through the voice of Aristophanes.[1] In this short essay, however, I can only refer to the political row provoked by Koun's student, Alexis Solomos, when he staged a production of Aristophanes' *Peace* in 1964, at the ancient theatre of Epidaurus. In general, it is typical of the later Greek tradition that the search for the playwright's 'own' political intentions becomes less important than the modern goal of rendering one or more perceived political or ideological messages intelligible to the present. The author, Aristophanes, and his political perspectives have had to make room for the *auteur*, in the

French sense of the word, or the modern (re-)creator of the ancient comic play, who sees him/herself as entitled to promulgate personal political views and objectives.

Before we can proceed, however, the all-too-crudely put question of what Aristophanes' own politics were all about calls for at least some refinement. It bears repeating that Aristophanes is the only classical Greek comic poet who left us more than mere fragments and that he represented a genre that emerged quickly and evolved even faster. Classical comedy grew up in an era in which it was still closely tied to its probably humble origins (however problematic the reconstruction of those origins may be). It was a genre in search of identity, repute and prestige, especially vis-à-vis tragedy and the firmly established Dionysiac festivals for competitions in tragedy. Comedy as a genre re-fractured politics through its own lens and cultivated an eye-catching acting and performance style and poetic and lyrical language. It therefore needed to define itself also in relation to oratory and rhetoric, which engaged with politics head-on rather than indirectly. It comes as no surprise then that – at times insecure, slighted or over-confident – comedy used both tragedy and oratory as sounding-boards before a Greek public that was largely one and the same in the theatre, the law-court and the democratic assembly:[2] the majority consisting of Athenian male citizens of age, joined in the theatre only by a minority of social and political outsiders (foreigners, women, and slaves).[3] Aristophanes' transmitted – and, undoubtedly, altered – texts open up unique windows onto a very rich performance context that poses multiple archaeological and material puzzles which are far from resolved. For philologists, the preserved text may be of the utmost significance; it is unlikely, however, that contemporary theatregoers deemed it equally important. Like spectators of all times, the ancients may have been much more intrigued by the action and setting of a play than by its script.

Only about a quarter of Aristophanes' comedies have been preserved, but this fraction does represent the development of a poet during a long lifetime. Therefore, again, caution is needed if we are to try to reconstruct the politics of a man who was extremely creative and versatile and an excellent observer, as his work reveals, and who produced a corpus of plays over decades rather than over a mere few years. Every author has the right to demonstrate his or her own genre and politics as being in flux, especially in an era changing as rapidly as the later fifth and early fourth century BC. Even if we feel that we may be closing in on the politics of Aristophanes, we should not forget that the execution of his plays and, in particular, the intended humour of his verbal, paraverbal and visual gags, was still dependent on many more factors and variables – for one thing, the actors, who were not hand-picked by the playwright but officially assigned to him. Students of classical theatre may need to attach more importance to those variables, which stand out – loud and clear – in the later reception history of Aristophanes' works (as an example below will illustrate), in order to make sense of the political dimensions of fifth- and fourth-century BC comedy. This focus must become part of our thinking, not as much in terms of this and other authors' horizon of intents, but in terms of their situated-ness in practical circumstances in which all sorts of anticipated and unexpected variables can play.

We must, then, distinguish between Aristophanes' politics and our reading of his politics. The first item, Aristophanes' politics, we may never truly know, but we may surmise that, like many personally and publicly held political opinions, they may have changed, matured or sharpened over time. They probably depended on shifting circumstances and on historically and culturally specific data, standards and codes. They were likely to have differed in their private expressions from the many public forms they could take. In the comic theatre they took (semi-)official forms, whether they were conveyed by the leading or minor character(s) of a given play, or embedded in fixed structural parts of (Old) Comedy. At the core of any investigation into Aristophanes' politics have been a few key passages and characters and also the structural element of the comic *parabasis*. They come back to the general discussion with such regularity – almost like soundbites and one-liners – that they here deserve, not repetition, but a brief mention, nonetheless.

The *parabasis*, in which the chorus steps forward and addresses the audience 'directly', has often been regarded as a 'moment of truth' that sheds light on Aristophanes' own political stance. This formal component of Old Comedy, however, is as much of an 'act' as any other part of the play. And yet, Dicaeopolis in Aristophanes' *Acharnians*, for example, has often been identified as an articulate spokesperson for the poet mainly based on his 'moralizing' statements, his speech in self-defence and the words of the *parabasis*.[4] In lines 630–2, for instance, the protagonist – comically – attests to the intertwined nature of civic-political education and normative moral authority when he, in no uncertain terms, rebukes the collective citizenry, or the *dêmos*, for being a whimsical mob, quick to make up its mind and even quicker to change it (*tachyboulois . . . metaboulous*).[5] The identification and the general argument, however, may be grounded more in the effectiveness of the formats chosen for enunciating political opinions on the public stage and may disclose less about the contents of those opinions or their validity in reflecting the poet's thinking. Even Aristophanes' comic complaints and jokes about possible political repercussions against the outspokenness of the protagonist-poet have to be taken with a grain of salt. They may be just that – jokes; and we should not forget that humour was the driving force for all comic poets, regardless of their loudly protested claims to seriousness or moral-didactic authority. The reading of certain plays – or, often, mere passages or lines – as evidence of the poet's personal commitment to any specific policy of fifth- or early fourth-century BC Athens is problematic on many levels. Political outspokenness was a conscious facet of Old Comedy. But does that outspokenness operate on the level of true (personal) politics and does it justify the belief in the inseparability of oeuvre and author – a tenet that underlies many face-value judgements? Do politics on stage ever change existing politics or the views and actions of politicians currently in power? Or would Aristophanes and his audience have been satisfied if the actors just managed to put alternative political viewpoints 'out there', at the risk of diluting a play's, and an entire competition's, aesthetic and cultural dimensions?

Ancient commentators much admired the *parabasis* of Aristophanes' *Frogs* of 405 BC and the play's general emphasis on the teaching and influencing of politics.[6] In the famous *parabasis*, the chorus members, presumably in Aristophanes' own voice, offered political advice and defended a group of right-wing conservatives. The chorus was thought to seek amnesty for the Athenian oligarchs who had been involved in, and later severely punished for, the abortive revolution of the repressive Council of the Four Hundred (which lasted only a few months in 411 BC). Aristophanes' plea resorted to the particularized imagery of recent changes in local coinage and the concomitant economic inflation. To unravel the details of the poet's elaborate economic and financial metaphor and its political implications is to historicize comedy – and comic licence – in more old-fashioned scholarly ways. While these methods may be productive of much detailed knowledge (even of daily life in ancient Greece, a currently fashionable area of study), they continue to take Aristophanes' politically inspired comments, voiced through the 'mouthpiece' of the chorus and the chorus-leader, at face value – an extremely hazardous practice in the notoriously protean realms of comedy and humour that straddle every possible variety.

Many scholars may retort that modern readers and audiences of Aristophanes do not necessarily have to remain in the dark on the subject of the political meaning and intention of the playwright's ancient jokes. Plentiful scholarly literature and editions of later commentaries (*scholia*) allow us to probe at these and other traces of the complex political history and culture of classical Athens.[7] Yet, the later *scholia* tend to be far removed in time from the heyday of ancient comedy and from its location of origin, and they prove to be famously 'creative'. Complex questions remain. Scholars have tried to fit Aristophanes in one of the political 'camps' of antiquity, representing him either as a right-wing conservative, a left-wing reformist, or somewhere in the middle. These solutions, however, reveal more about how our own political mind-set (influenced by the two-party system of the United States and other countries) works and processes political data than about the political and social predicaments and changes of the later fifth and early fourth century BC. The anachronistic terms 'right' and 'left' also evoke polarizations that may be characteristic of the twentieth century, but that fail to capture the differences that set apart, for example, the farmers of the Attic countryside from the landholding aristocracy, the urban busybodies from the powerful demagogues, or the Athenians of obscure or contested citizenship from the progeny of prestigious families. The large body of farmers of Attica, to whom Aristophanes appeals on numerous occasions, is perhaps the most difficult group to identify as either 'right-' or 'left-wing': while they may have formed the socially and religiously more conservative strata, they may also have been more committed to the direct democracy of Athens in its heyday than their wealthy aristocratic neighbours, whose sons studied with the best in the city and vaunted the fashionable tendency of looking favourably upon the oligarchic to despotic regimes of Sparta and Persia.

Different schools of classical scholars have endeavoured to define Aristophanes' relationship to the politics of his time, whether they have mined his plays for historical references or have rejected the possibility of unmasking the poet's personal beliefs. Below follows a brief discussion of merely some of the representative trends in the mode of which Aristophanes' personal and publicly voiced political position(s) have traditionally been read. Arnold W. Gomme's essay of 1938, entitled 'Aristophanes and Politics', was perhaps the earliest and most decisive 'purist' statement to reject the possibility of gauging the poet's personal convictions.[8] His study stressed that comic poets were in it for the comedy, for the art and entertainment, and that they did not maintain any outspoken political agenda. Other scholars have established an overtly democratic programme for Aristophanes. Here, Jeffrey Henderson adopted a very careful approach, especially when compared to Tom Rothfield, who ascribed radical democratic leanings to the playwright. Bakhtinian explorations of Aristophanes' comedy, on the other hand, uncover political meanings and methods that are vested less in explicit content, than in (ritualized) format and societal function. But let me take a closer look at the most recent of these readings.[9]

Henderson has analysed relations between Aristophanes' Old Comedy and democracy, especially with respect to the issue of freedom of speech. He illustrated comedy's democratic role in advocating this principle and demonstrated its kinship with that other, more easily recognizable, pillar of Athenian democratic life: public speaking – in the adoption by comedy and oratory of *isêgoria* and *parrhêsia*, or the equal rights of every citizen to offer advice and frank criticism. According to Henderson, comedy's defence of the principle of free speech and its readiness to voice open criticism and to give often unasked-for or risky counsel transform a stage genre into a useful tool of civic protest and instruction. Henderson's aim was also to point up the differences between ancient and modern comedy as genres and to support 'the classical understanding of comedy as essentially democratic and politically engaged, as against the modern tendency to see comedy as detached, innocuous, and essentially apolitical'.[10] Henderson concluded that ancient comedy had to play by many of the same rules that confined oratory: it could engage in personal abuse and vulgarities, but could not speak or present what could be seen as detrimental to democracy or to the functioning of its democratic processes. Contemporary and later observers, including Plato and other detractors of comedy, already noticed the close connections between comedy and the history and development of Athenian democracy.

This devotion of Old Comedy to democratic procedure may reflect more on the genesis of the genre of comedy, its self-justification and its search for identity traits, than on the individual playwright himself. When Henderson makes the transition to Aristophanes' own political agenda, he sees the playwright leaning toward a 'more conservative practice of democracy' and clinging to an 'idealized past democracy'. For him, Aristophanes, who lampoons contemporary radical leaders, criticizes those who 'mislead' the *dêmos*, and champions country folk over town-dwellers, may be recalling the *dêmos*'s 'past greatness'. Aristophanes has also located and learnt how to exploit what has been a rich vein for comedy in all periods: the resentment of the underdog. Playing out – in all meanings of the words – his understanding of political power, social status and ineradicable oppression, the poet discovered a sure road to popularity with the broad masses, who had become politicized through years of democratic practice of which comedy was a part. For this mass audience, ridicule *per se* carried political importance, especially given the locale and the occasion of the state-sponsored festivals, which were, very likely, the talk of the town – and of the countryside of Attica. Comedy then becomes a privileged site for the underprivileged to engage in protest, contention, subversion, or a show of resilience; the *polis* institution of full-blown comedy must have been a constant cause of anxiety to the upper strata. Yet it would be hard to measure the popular responses of the awakened 'underdogs' in this 'contest of public voices' (to redeploy one of Simon Goldhill's definitions).[11] If historical specificities of classical comedy are hard to come by, this holds true *a priori* for comedy as a forum of broad public interests and of a diverse mass audience.

The temptation to please the crowd is hard to resist. Within the public framework of the dramatic competitions, the comic poets were rivals for popular favour and did well to protect themselves, to the extent possible, from the loss of popularity that resulted from endorsing unpalatable and anti-democratic views. And yet they would frequently court the danger of castigating or alienating their audience. Comic stage practice was a balancing act between, on the one hand, the playwright's attempt to educate his viewers and to shape public opinion and, on the other hand, his response, whether conscious or not, to popular concern and expectation. Bakhtinian studies have explored comedy as a venue for the release of political and other resentment and for the reversal of norms in the mode of carnival. Seen in this light, comedy's role is that of society's controlled safety valve, its outlet for impulsive or dysfunctional behaviour and for a settling of scores: the genre makes a mockery of the high and mighty and counters the inclination to conform and obey. Comedy then becomes an important link in the precarious system of checks and balances that a well-organized democracy would strive to maintain.

Yet how much of Aristophanes' own political viewpoint overlaps with this rebellious sense of otherness that encourages underdog activism or the search for a viable outlet of frustration? How much of it would, rather, be determined by the historical contingencies of a genre in the making that continues to face tough competition from tragedy and oratory? Comedy might try to assert itself or to (over)compensate by tapping the broader popular strata to boost a feeling of collective superiority. Why would Aristophanes not make a show of his levelling stance that politicizes his lampooning and (temporarily) triumphs over the class of mismanaging politicians, upstart leaders and urban mongers of wealth and power? The poet withholds public support from target politicians and vilifies them much more often than politics in general or even specific policies. Cleon, the 'political arch rival', becomes, through Aristophanes' target practice, one of the most representative specimens of the class of detested politicians. In the *Acharnians* (381–2), the hero Dicaeopolis bitterly complains that he nearly 'perished' because of the relentless legal persecution inflicted on him by Cleon.[12] For the sake of instant, unambiguous, comic and other reactions from the audience, even big issues such as war and peace, amnesty and retribution are embodied in the political personalities of the day and are only loosely tied to abiding socio-political crises of long duration. Aristophanic comedy as a genre plays on the micro-level of personality politics more often than on the macro-level of coherent political programmes or long-term developments. It registers dissatisfaction and resentment more intensely than approval, but it does so in a controlled manner, as if it were taking a straw-poll on small aspects of big issues – an informal procedure essential to the smooth working of the demo-cratic system. Aristophanes deliberately reduces big issues to the scope and size of what his folksy protagonists (with whom his spectators may identify) can grasp. The daily setbacks of Dicaeopolis (*Acharnians*), Trygaeus (*Peace*), Strepsiades (*Clouds*) and Peisetaerus (*Birds*) make up that portion of the bar-rage of relentless ills which threaten to wipe out the *polis* at war or in distress, but can be managed by one man – or one woman (Lysistrata and Praxagora in the *Lysistrata* and *Women in Assembly* respectively). Solutions, too, are presented as the clever individual's overcoming of – and instant gain from – a relatively small shift in the bigger, more general burden. Any improvement is, inspiringly, depicted as feasible and manageable, one person and one step at a time.

In this manner, Old Comedy is far from politically detached and remains welded to Athenian democracy, both thematically and functionally. Ideally, Aristophanes would be a playwright who attacked the pitfalls of fifth-century BC democracy rather than the institution of democracy itself, who distin-guished demagoguery from democracy when he mingled civic subjects with literary and aesthetic ones, and who probed the boundaries of rivalry, rib-aldry, justice, peace and war. A poet of an unusual intelligence, he knew how to test and steer the impact of each comic component to the full, but he also insisted that he was seeking spectators who, in turn, possessed sufficient *sophia* to realise the genius of his plays (as in *Clouds*, 518–48).

We may still want to refrain from transforming Aristophanes into the exceptional champion of an idealized radical democracy or of a grass-roots activism. A recent example of how, for some, the playwright must be unconditionally wedded to a radical type of democracy is the analysis by Tom Rothfield. In a 1999 book entitled *Armoury of Laughter, Democracy's Bastion of Defence*, the author celebrated democracy, free speech and an 'uncompromising spirit' in Aristophanes-the-political-reformer.[13] A typical quotation from his introduction reads:

> Aristophanes' comedies embody this intensely felt feeling for Athenian democracy: for the City and the *polis*; for justice and the rule of law; for the issues that affect all classes from top to bottom – female as well as male; young and old, rich and poor alike, and in this respect differing from tragedy little concerned with ordinary citizens . . . , usually helpless or hapless victims embodied in a grieving Chorus, incapable of doing very much for themselves but implore, weep, or watch *powerless as events unfold* . . . How differently comedy spoke out on matters affecting ordinary people's lives! From his first comedy until his last, Aristophanes struck out in every direction where he saw a threat, dangerous atrophy, or an attack on democracy's values and standards; bringing the subject to light, airing what was at stake on the stage. No subject,

even at the highest level in the State's affairs, being regarded as sacred or spared his scrutiny and highly intelligent mocking probing and scarifying wit. Comedy and democracy. in Aristophanes, as in no other playwright, are the two inseparable. (italics in original; pp. xx–xxi)

Rothfield places the perceived effects of comedy as a genre, and of Aristophanes as its brilliant representative, in the widest of contexts. His study also exemplifies the danger of reading the politics of comedy at the expense of ancient tragedy. One could easily place a twist on his argument for Aristophanes as the spokesperson for a radical Athenian democracy. If, as in the late fifth century BC, the far 'left' has become the political establishment, then our playwright could be subversive for positioning himself to the right in politics. Some would concur by pointing out that the stance of the cultural traditionalist is the one that lends itself best to the comic poet or comedian who assumes the role of a public critic. Acting as a detractor is simply the better pose for the job. Political criticism can then substitute for more hazardous political self-positioning; it encourages the 'older-is-better' advocate to single out novelties and weaknesses – and the persons embodying these – for effective public ridicule. Again, we see emerge an Aristophanes capitalizing on the support from the underdog in Greek society in meeting his essential needs of the stage. The underdog class, which saw innovations move in and move through at too rapid a pace, found instant satisfaction and generous comfort in the publicly aired nostalgia for the past and its certainties, even if that past, too, had failed to lend this class power, prestige, prosperity, full freedom, or recognition.

Obviously, Greek comic poetry, the ultimate primer of comic versatility, was never so monolithic as to be characterized by a single mode of political thinking, and neither was its author. The problem of Aristophanes' politics is constantly confounded by the undeniable fact that his plays are delightfully unpredictable comedies, based on absurd plots, wild fantasies, laughable mythological figures, frequent and inconsistent changes of locations, multiple reversals, 'chance' encounters, impossible missions, exaggerated sexual exploits and much more. Precisely because we are dealing with the genre of Aristophanic comedy, our focus may justifiably be more on the ancient and modern vibrancy of his plays than on their – often presumed – static politics. A creative genius like Aristophanes, who did not put any limits to his language or humour, is unlikely to have accepted any limits imposed upon his political thinking. In fact, his may have been the self-styled duty of probing the boundaries and pitfalls of any restrictive political thinking – much in line with the creative and elusive fantasies of his own characters. This is the man who showed that he liked to play with all the possibilities, that a play could be politics, and that even dry politics could be play. 'Behind the mask of Aristophanes one finds many masks,' Thomas K. Hubbard concluded, 'but this is not to say there is not at the same time also a real man there with real views and with all the complex contradictions which thoughtful and genuinely funny human beings possess.'[14] The above assertions and positionings of our comic poet, then, may speak volumes about authors' own scholarly preoccupations (including my own), while the validity of projecting modern concerns onto classical comedies and personalities remains highly questionable. All of the above would hold at least some validity if Aristophanes were the only one in charge of the execution and performance of his works. But he was not. He was, instead, dependent on actors, chorus-members, musicians, technicians as well as thousands of spectators, who all brought their own cultural and socio-political assumptions to the theatre. They could take charge of certain lines, songs, or scenes, even against the will of the dramatist.

The problem of Aristophanes' political views left in the hands of others is an urgent one, in particular in modern revival productions of his comedies. The nineteenth- and twentieth-century reception history of the playwright (as far as we can reconstruct it) points up no single consistent line of political interpretation but, instead, many diverging and even diametrically opposed readings. The modern performance practice again urges us to exercise caution and to steer away from facile partisanship on the poet's behalf. The very same preserved lines of a play may mean different things to different spectators or groups of spectators at different times, even in the course of the same performance. Let me now turn to a notorious example from the modern Greek reception history of Aristophanes to clarify some of the points made above.

In 1964 director Alexis Solomos of the National Theatre of Greece was busily preparing a production of Aristophanes' *Peace*. The show was scheduled to open on 18 July at the ancient theatre of Epidaurus, before thousands of spectators, Greeks and foreigners, as part of the Epidaurus Festival of Ancient Greek Drama. The National Theatre had been slow to accept Aristophanes, but by the time of this production, the Athens and Epidaurus Festivals had seen nearly ten years of regular outdoor revival productions of classical comedy performed in modern Greek translations – enough for nobody to expect any unpleasant surprises. In his production of Aristophanes' *Peace*, Solomos had assigned the role of Hermes to Theodoros Moridis, who provoked a scandal on stage. In a particular dialogue of the original comedy, Hermes, on behalf of Peace, makes enquiries of the farmer Trygaeus about the state of contemporary political affairs in Athens:

Hermes: Now listen, [Trygaeus,] what else Peace just asked me:
          Who is currently holding sway over the speaker's rock on the
          Pnyx?
Trygaeus: Hyperbolus . . .
          (*To Peace, who makes a movement of averting her face.*)
          Hey, what are you doing? Why do you turn your head away?
Hermes: She is turning away from the people, because it pains her that they
          have chosen such a villain as their leader (*ponêron prostatên*).

                                                                    (679–84)

Director Solomos wanted to turn this exchange into a political stab at the then Greek Prime Minister, Georgios Papandreou (father of the better known Andreas Papandreou), the leader of the liberal Centre Union Party, which had won the elections of February 1964. The eloquent Papandreou had gained an unprecedented but legitimate position of power after years of right-wing government under his rival Konstantinos Karamanlis (1955–63). Solomos made Moridis/Hermes update his enquiry on Peace's behalf by changing it from 'Who is currently holding sway over the speaker's rock on the Pnyx?' into 'Who rules the fatherland now?' The director planned then to skip Trygaeus' answer and to leave a brief pause instead, allowing the spectators time to insert – silently or out loud – the name of Greece's most powerful politician at the time, Georgios Papandreou. Next, while the mute Peace again averted her face, Hermes was to rejoin with his original answer: 'She is turning away from the people, because it pains her that they have chosen such a villain as their leader.' In this way, Solomos planned an immediate public assault on Papandreou. The director had his actors practise the modern political 'dig' many times before the scheduled opening performance and all seemed set.

But Solomos had not counted on the personal initiative that Moridis would and could take even at the very last moment, despite the numerous rehearsals of his line of attack. Moridis was a supporter of Papandreou and had been planning his own sweet revenge on the political right and on his director. For all to hear at the play's opening performance, Moridis changed Hermes' enquiry into: 'Who ruled the fatherland *then*?' This question, turned in the past tense, made the audience fill out the name of Karamanlis, who had led a repressive regime, but who, by July 1964, had left Greece for a prolonged self-exile in Paris. Still in charge of the scene, Moridis then continued with the contemptuous denunciation that Solomos had originally targeted at Papandreou, but that now vilified Karamanlis: 'She is turning away from the people, because it pains her that they chose such a villain as their leader.' The audience burst out in rapturous applause and clearly enjoyed its own, unscripted and unexpected, part in the performance.

Solomos was furious and demanded that at the following day's performance, Moridis stick to the original plan. But Moridis again altered the cue question as he had done on the night of the premiere: 'Who ruled the fatherland *then*?' He even went one step further in his attack on Karamanlis: 'She is turning away from the people, because it pains her that they chose that embezzler [literally: 'eater'] of building-plots (*oikopedophagos*) as their leader.' In the summer of 1964, Karamanlis stood accused *in absentia* of involvement in an irregular land deal. After this more blatant provocation, all hell broke loose, both onstage and offstage. The newspapers had a field day with this double slur against Karamanlis. The president of the National Theatre's board demanded that Moridis offer up a written apology for his 'arbitrary' interventions in the text. Moridis complied, but was still forced to pay a hefty fine. Matters did not end there. Upon further investigation, Solomos, too, was fined by the National Theatre's board for interfering with the text of the modern Greek translation made by the well-respected Thrasyvoulos Stavrou. He resigned in protest. This incident of tampering with the text and distorting its 'established' meaning and political intent deeply perturbed the board. Many sensitive text-bound readers, who saw Greek national identity vested in their country's classical literature, were upset, too. The scandal left, in the end, no winners at all, except for the political enthusiasts among the theatre audience and broader public. It is still fondly remembered by the older generation of Greeks.

Different modern Greek political views determined the reception of a slightly altered passage. The director's interpretation would have resonated with the opposite end of the ideological spectrum. The actor pre-empted the director's plan and concentrated his personal political attack in his own lines, which functioned as a circuit of stage dialectics between ancient and modern times, between literary fiction and tangible reality. As contemporary producers, actors and audience members received the lines, the illusion of the ancient play and the modern revival shattered under the impact of reverberating Greek actuality. Enriched by additional layers of meaning, whether anecdotal or historical, the 1964 *Peace* became transgressive on a larger socio-political and metatheatrical scale. In the eyes of its supporters, this revival celebrated freedom of speech and democratic political action for encouraging the actor and his public to shape their own ideological world on stage. This incident allows us to deduce a set of variables that affect play production: the director, the actor and fellow-actors, the audience and its setting, and the theatre management. Issues of translation, adaptation and censorship play important roles as well. A modern performance-based approach, more than a textual or formal analysis of the original ancient Greek play, allows us to articulate caveats that should prevent the student of comedy from over-interpreting Aristophanes' political intention or position – if either one of those was ever singular. Warning signals need to go up, too, wherever attempts are made to ground contemporary Greek personalities, political ideologies and official institutions in ancient parallels – as if the issues, and the city of Athens itself, would never change. Attic comedy has often displayed its capacity for meaning in ways relevant and particular to contemporary audiences. At any time, flashes of modern historical specificity can (re-)occur in the form of any actor or spectator's reaction even to a conservative translation. Actors and theatregoers frisk Aristophanes, as it were, for the metaphorical weapons of words, passages and short scenes, whether rendered verbatim or in modified, anachronistic versions. Those lines that the Greek actor or public pillage do not so much appeal to universal themes as give meaning to their collective modern experience. Severed from the original, they privilege political and ideological interpretations easily perceptible in the fabric of the drama of contemporary Greek life.

Aristophanes has remained a living paradox, and his oeuvre has meant to modern readers (in the broadest sense) precisely what they wanted it to mean. Even when contemporary assumptions are made 'consciously', they are never fully transparent. How the texts or, more commonly, the productions have been read has been a function of the interpreter – an effect of his or her receptive background, both diachronic and synchronic. Though sometimes defined as acts of apprehending without presuppositions, the modern literary and theatrical interpretations have unambiguously mirrored socio-political and broad cultural needs of the present time. The supposedly objective, historicizing results of those readings have often reflected modern conditions more than they have the 'real' ancient context of Attic comedy. The poet speaks through a number of different characters and these characters, in their turn, are interpreted by actors. Thus, when an audience receives a play, it should be in no doubt about its mediated quality. If we transplant this model to the modern platform that is the contemporary production of the ancient play, the level of mediation only intensifies. It seems, therefore, superfluous for us to go and reclaim for the playwright the privilege of speaking with his own voice.

In sum, the student of Aristophanes will want to keep in mind that the question of the precise evaluation of the poet's politics will remain a lively one. Here, we have concentrated on difficulties and complications rather than on ready-made or often repeated solutions. Politics of the late fifth century and early fourth century BC were characterized by fast, tumultuous and at times destructive changes. Aristophanes, too, must have needed time to sit back, rethink, and readjust. That his plays felt the pulse of that rapidly transforming society may certainly be true. That they would speak the last word on that society's democracy, imperialism, war policy, literature and art, class friction or gender could not be further from the truth. Comedy may have captured the fast and the fleeting developments as it ever so quickly tried to adapt to the newest circumstances. Such a process, however, again jeopardizes any certainties regarding Aristophanes' more long-lasting political views. Given the multiple and contradictory conclusions reached thus far by modern scholars, translators and theatre practitioners, I posit the impossibility of reading singular intention and of determining final meaning – even of assuming that we can equate the author's intention and the meaning of his or her text. The narrow search for ancient political allusions, in particular, loses much of its justification when one takes into account the unpredictability of the plays' impact on their public. As different revival productions and later traditions show, the same line or scene may unexpectedly generate contrasting meanings, depending on altered historical conditions or horizons of reception and on the varying psychological colorations that actors, artists and audiences may add to any given work. Yet all readings derive from the same original text and the same playwright, who always prioritized the comic and the poetic 'reality' of any political meaning. In modern Greece, the iconography of Aristophanes, more than of any other classical author, has brought out a shifting, diffuse set of meanings, taking shape when the original texts, or segments of them as small as individual words, find translations relevant to the circumstances and micropolitics of the present day. The Aristophanic sense with which contemporary events become invested discloses as much about the cognitive domain of the modern world as it does about ancient society.

NOTES

1. For a broader introduction to the reception history of Aristophanes in Greece of the nineteenth and twentieth centuries, see G. Van Steen, *Venom in Verse: Aristophanes in Modern Greece* (Princeton: Princeton University Press, 2000). The scandal provoked by Koun's *Birds* in 1959 is discussed in ch. 4 of this study.
2. Aristophanes makes this identification explicit in a passage of the *Knights* (163–5), in which the sausage-seller is promised political power over the Athenians in the audience, who are the same as the Athenians of the market, the harbour and the *ekklêsia* (assembly).
3. Jeffrey Henderson argued persuasively that ordinary women would have been present in the audience in classical times. Jeffrey J. Henderson, 'Women and the Athenian Dramatic Festivals', *Transactions of the American Philological Association* 121 (1991), 133–47. Some scholars still disagree.
4. See, for example, H. P. Foley, 'Tragedy and Politics in Aristophanes' *Acharnians*', *Journal of Hellenic Studies* 108 (1988), 33–47.
5. For further examples, see *Acharnians*, 317, 366–84, 497–506, 515–17, 560–2, 595, 628–64. See also G. Van Steen, 'Aspects of Public Performance in

Aristophanes' *Acharnians'*, *L'Antiquité Classique* 63 (1994), 212 n. 6 and 220 n. 41.

6. For key passages, see *Frogs* 686–7, 954–5, 1019, 1026, 1035, 1054–7.

7. For a recent return to the topical political treatment based on *scholia*, see Vickers, *Pericles on Stage: Political Comedy in Aristophanes' Early Plays* (Austin: University of Texas Press, 1997).

8. A. W. Gomme, 'Aristophanes and Politics', in D. A. Campbell (ed.), *More Essays in Greek History and Literature* (Oxford: Blackwell, 1962), pp. 70–91.

9. Plenty of other studies exist that have dealt with the problem of Aristophanes' politics. Among the book-length studies are: Ephraim David, *Aristophanes and Athenian Society of the Early Fourth Century B.C.* (Leiden: Brill, 1984); Geoffrey E. M. de Ste Croix, *Origins of the Peloponnesian War* (Ithaca, NY: Cornell University Press, 1972); Malcolm Heath, *Political Comedy in Aristophanes* (Göttingen: Vandenhoeck and Ruprecht, 1987); and Gilbert Murray, *Aristophanes* (Oxford: Oxford University Press, 1933).

10. Jeffrey J. Henderson, 'Attic Old Comedy, Frank Speech, and Democracy', in Deborah Boedeker and Kurt A. Raaflaub (eds.), *Democracy, Empire, and the Arts in Fifth-Century Athens* (Cambridge, Mass., and London, England: Harvard University Press, 1998), p. 255. In the same comprehensive study, Henderson further discussed restrictions on free speech in detail and placed them in their cultural and political context.

11. Simon Goldhill, 'Comic Inversion and Inverted Commas: Aristophanes and Parody', in *The Poet's Voice: Essays on Poetics and Greek Literature* (Cambridge: Cambridge University Press, 1991), p. 167.

12. See further *Acharnians*, 300–1, 377–82, 502–3, 631; *Wasps*, 1284–91; *Clouds* 581–94; and *Knights*. On Cleon's alleged legal suits against Aristophanes, see also Gonda Van Steen, 1994, 213 and nn. 8, 9; 219–21 and nn. 42–7.

13. Tom Rothfield, *Armour of Laughter, Democracy's Bastion of Defence: Introducing a Law of Opposites* (Lanham/New York/Oxford: University Press of America, 1999).

14. T. K. Hubbard, *The Mask of Comedy: Aristophanes and the Intertextual Parabasis* (Ithaca, NY: Cornell University Press, 1991), p. 225.

FURTHER READING

Cartledge, P., *Aristophanes and His Theatre of the Absurd*. Bristol: Bristol Classical Press, 1990.

Dover, K. J., *Aristophanic Comedy*. Berkeley: University of California Press, 1972.

Gomme, A. W., 'Aristophanes and Politics', in *More Essays in Greek History and Literature*, ed. D. A. Campbell, pp. 70–91. Oxford: Blackwell, 1962.

Henderson, J. J., 'Attic Old Comedy, Frank Speech, and Democracy', in *Democracy, Empire, and the Arts in Fifth-Century Athens*, ed. D. Boedeker and Kurt A. Raaflaub, pp. 255–73. Cambridge, Mass. and London: Harvard University Press, 1998.

MacDowell, D. M., *Aristophanes and Athens: An Introduction to the Plays*. Oxford: Oxford University Press, 1995.

Van Steen, G. A. H., *Venom in Verse: Aristophanes in Modern Greece*. Princeton: Princeton University Press, 2000.

7

SANDER M. GOLDBERG

Comedy and society from Menander to Terence

'Menander and Life! Which of you imitated which?'
Aristophanes of Byzantium

The third-century scholar Aristophanes of Byzantium, one of Alexandria's greatest figures, certainly knew Greek literature and how to read it, but his oft-quoted epigram has not been especially helpful to Menander's reputation. Finding in the conventional (some have said 'hackneyed') plots and characters of Menandrean comedy, where citizen boy will get citizen girl even if he is a rapist or she a foundling, an adequate reflection of 'life' as commonly lived on this planet, requires powers of generalization that not every critic is willing to apply.[1] His genre may itself be partly to blame: New Comedy's canvas is said to be too small, its vision too narrow, its artificiality too apparent. When comedy lost its active engagement in the loud and vigorous life of the fifth-century *polis*, the assumption goes, it embraced all too thoroughly an effete and superficial, perhaps even decadent, dream of bourgeois life in the backwater that was post-classical Athens.

Literary critics had little incentive to question this view. New Comedy's limitation was also seen as its salvation. Aristophanes may have been brilliant, but Old Comedy's persistent focus on the political, social and cultural concerns of fifth-century Athens rooted the genre so deeply in its own society that any appeal beyond Attica was decidedly limited. A play like *Women at the Thesmophoria* (*Thesmophoriazousae*), spun from the peculiarities of an Attic festival and the mannerisms of an Athenian playwright, could hardly interest audiences beyond the boundaries of its time and· place. Comedy became exportable only in the course of the fourth century as it gradually unmoored from the specific preoccupations of Athenian society and generalized its themes. The process already discernible in the 380s, when Aristophanes created the ageist, sexist fantasy of *Women in Assembly* (*Ecclesiazousae*) by draining *Lysistrata* of politics before moving to the wry allegory of *Wealth* (*Plutus*), culminated in the domestic plots of New Comedy that brought problems of family rather than community life to centre stage. Attic comedy survived in this form by focusing on what Athenians shared with other people, not on the institutions and preoccupations that set them apart. The plot of Menander's *The Woman from Samos* (*Samia*) may turn on distinctly Athenian ideas of legitimate birth and domestic responsibility, but when old Demeas begs his son not to let a momentary fault erase the kindness of a lifetime (*Samia* 694–712), the appeal resonates far beyond the confines of fourth-century Athens. Moments like this would inspire later comedy from third-century Rome to the situation comedies of today as Aristophanic comedy never could, because New Comedy's themes of anger and forgiveness, communication and miscommunication within and between families transcend time and place and will move any audience composed – as audiences inevitably are – of parents and children.

Comedy's evolution from the specific to the general was most easily demonstrated by privileging the evidence of texts. There was not much choice in the matter so long as New Comedy was known largely from the Roman adaptations of Plautus and Terence, but even after whole plays and extensive fragments of Greek originals were recovered from ancient papyrus books, the focus on literary analysis remained comparatively narrow. Material evidence of potential relevance tended either to be relegated to the sidelines (like the Lipari figurines) or dismissed as irrelevant (like the so-called *phlyax*-vases), and the social history of the 'decadent' fourth century attracted very little scholarly interest. This is no longer the case, and the new attention being paid to the material culture and social history of the fourth century has presented formidable challenges to many conventional literary opinions. The recognition, for example, that an Apulian bell-crater of the 370s not only illustrates the Telephus-scene of *Women at the Thesmophoria* (**Fig. 1**), but almost certainly reflects memory of a contemporary stage performance has destroyed forever the idea that Old Comedy's stage life was comparatively short and confined to Attica.[2] We must instead consider Old Comedy against a broader background. New Comedy is in turn being read more specifically as critics recognize in its conventions the working out of significant fourth-century concerns. Thus even a stock figure like the cook (*mageiros*), boastful, sly, vain and abusive, is now regarded not simply as a device for regulating the comic tempo of a scene by introducing dependable comic routines, but as a way to introduce themes of ritual sacrifice, luxury and thrift, indulgence and abstinence that gave New Comedy a topical edge. As a result, features of New Comedy that have long been interpreted along literary lines must now also be measured against fourth-century realities.

Menander, for example, has a habit of slipping into tragic rhythms and tragic language to enrich the tone and signal the importance of a dramatic moment, and ancient scholars sometimes claimed that characteristic plot devices like the recognition of lost children were actually borrowed from

Figure 1. Parody of Euripides' *Telephus* as in Aristophanes' *Women at the Thesmophoria*, *c.*370 BC.

Euripides. It is thus hardly surprising that a messenger's speech in his *The Man from Sicyon* (*Sicyonios*), which reports the debate of an impromptu assembly that judged a young woman's claim to citizenship and determined the best way to protect her interests (176ff.), is modelled on the speech in Euripides' *Orestes*, which reported how an Argive assembly condemned the matricides Orestes and Electra to death (866–88). The conventional reading of this echo notes the similarity of plot function in the two speeches, as well as the reversal of the assembly's outcome: there is thought to be relief in the tacit observation that contemporary problems lack the magnitude of tragic situations. The one literary form then seems to smile at the other.

Recent discussions of *Orestes*, however, stress that Euripides' play, immensely popular throughout antiquity, does not evoke the tragic grandeur that characterizes Aeschylus' version of the story. Euripides explores the consequences of Orestes' matricide against a social background that is distressingly and disconcertingly like the real world of human affairs. Orestes is denounced less for what he did than for what he did not do, namely prosecute his mother in court, as if there were a legal mechanism available to resolve the conflict that in Aeschylus brought Olympian and chthonian powers to the brink of conflict. The Argive assembly of *Orestes* is all too contemporary, the human players acting out its melodrama are all too human, and the only thing mythic about the story Euripides tells is that Apollo finally appears on the machine to extricate these flawed humans from the trouble they create for themselves. What saves Menander's echo of that scene for comedy is that his assembly reaches what the world of comedy deems a correct decision: protection for the girl Philumena, discomfiture for the sinister Moschion, and an opportunity for the hero Stratophanes to reclaim his patrimony. The difference between comedy and tragedy thus seems to rest on faith in the mechanisms of democratic justice.

Yet the debate that Menander's messenger brings so vividly to life is hardly innocent in its manner or its method. The mechanisms of democracy recalled by this play were always problematic. There was nothing trivial about the process of establishing citizenship at Athens and nothing comic about the power of its assemblies. We might think not just of Euripides' Argives but of Menander's own Athenians, who in 318 met in an impromptu and illegal assembly to judge the aged statesman Phocion, a hero of the Lamian War and a man elected general forty-five times. They condemned him to death without permitting him even to speak in his own defence (Plutarch, *Phocion* 34–5). Phocion fell victim to a democratic revival that did not itself last a year – it was replaced, with Macedonian support, by the tyranny of Demetrius of Phalerum – but the memory of what an assembly could do did not quickly fade, and that memory, working in conjunction with the Euripidean allusion, gives Menander's scene a very sharp edge if, as seems likely, the play was performed sometime after 316 BC. The ostensibly literary conceit of *The Man from Sicyon* takes on a different, more anxious aspect when read against the social tensions of the late fourth century.

Characters too may reflect attitudes and behaviours set more deeply in fourth-century ideology than was once apparent to critics. In the second act of *The Bad-Tempered Man* (*Dyskolos*), for example, the young farmer Gorgias learns from his slave that a rich youth has been lurking about the neighbourhood and was actually seen in conversation with Gorgias' half-sister, the reclusive Cnemon's daughter. Conversing with an unescorted, unrelated young woman is suspicious under the best of circumstances, and fearing the worst, Gorgias accosts and harangues the urbane Sostratos at the first opportunity.

> You seem to me to be intent on perpetrating
> a vile deed. You're hoping to lead astray
> An innocent free girl, or are looking for a chance
> To commit a crime worth many deaths.
>
> (289–93)

Gorgias alludes here to the two great motivators of comic plots in this tradition, seduction and rape, though he cannot bring himself to speak their names, and before Sostratos can get a serious word in edgeways, he moves quickly from denunciation to threat.[3] A poor man, he says, may at first sight appear helpless, but he will not remain passive once aroused by such injustice.

> At first, he's just pathetic; later, he takes all he
> has suffered not just as injustice but as *hubris*.
>
> (297–8)

He has entirely misunderstood the situation, as Sostratos' bewilderment soon makes clear, but this is not simply the empty rant of an indignant, fearful, and slightly boorish rustic. Gorgias' choice of words suggests a very specific kind of threat. *Hubris* has become for us the 'destructive pride' that modern critics often identify with a certain kind of tragic heroism, but *hubris* in Athenian parlance had broader connotations of 'swagger' and could be applied in Athenian law to various kinds of overbearing and abusive conduct. Gorgias here is in fact threatening such a suit for *hubris*, which was one of the legal remedies available to an Athenian citizen in the face of sexual aggression, and the social implications of his threat are essential to the dynamics of the scene.

On one level, Athenian practice confirms what the comedy of the moment would suggest: Gorgias' threat is out of proportion to even his worst imaginings of Sostratos' intentions. At Athens, the rape or seduction of a free girl was not generally treated as what Gorgias has just called a capital offence. Although Dracon's law on justifiable homicide apparently permitted the killing of a rapist or seducer caught in the act, what the law allowed was not necessarily what people did. There were too many risks. An avenger could himself face a charge of murder, as a real Athenian named Euphiletus discovered to his dismay after killing his wife's seducer, while public prosecution of the offender could bring shame and embarrassment to the injured party and his household. Private settlement was therefore a much more likely recourse, either an arranged marriage between the victim and her assailant or a cash payment to indemnify the injured party and provide a dowry attractive to a husband from outside the family's usual circle.[4] Gorgias is thus grotesquely and even laughably hyperbolic, which is dramatically satisfactory since we know that Sostratos is no sexual predator but just a hapless, helpless suitor trapped into love by the god Pan and by his own good nature. Gorgias, like his slave Daos, has rushed to the wrong conclusion on the basis of class prejudice and his own limited experience of the world. The misunderstanding is set straight with an alacrity that is itself comically improbable (315–19), but not before touching on an Athenian preoccupation considerably less than comic.

That preoccupation, however, has less to do with sex than with social class. Beneath Gorgias' threat of a suit for *hubris* lies the discourse of poverty and wealth. *Hubris* is a term of the Athenian moral rather than legal vocabulary, and it entered the legal picture to provide redress for moral rather than purely physical outrage. The technical distinction between 'an action for violence' and 'an indictment for *hubris*' lay not in the alleged deed, but in the state of mind of the alleged offender. An act of *hubris* was not just a wrongful act but an act done with wanton or wilful disregard for the rights of another. As Demosthenes says in his prosecution of Meidias, who had slapped his face in public, 'serious though it is for a free man to be struck, it is not as terrible a thing as to be struck out of *hubris*' (Demosthenes 21.72, cf. Aristotle, *Rhetoric* 1374a13). Such insolence was, at least in theory, the particular vice of the rich and powerful against the poor and weak. Aristotle says that the rich are hubristic (i.e. 'insolent') and arrogant as a consequence of their wealth: *hubris* was their way of demonstrating their superiority. The privileged class identified itself as the group that threw its weight around.

Yet actions for *hubris* were rare at Athens. This was no doubt in part because motive is much harder to prove than mere fact,[5] but Athens also appears to have been relatively free of serious class antagonism in the fifth and fourth centuries. The very rich were perennial objects of suspicion and envy, but there were not many of them. The kind of wealth that allowed a young man like Sostratos to don a fine cloak and take his entourage hunting in the shadow of Mount Parnes was never enjoyed by more than a few thousand Athenians, perhaps five to ten per cent of the population. Those few were not prone to flaunt their fortunes: ostentatious display could invite additional taxes or an extortionate lawsuit. The Athenian system instead encouraged discretion in the rich by giving them the means to cultivate prestige and gratitude through a civic largesse that benefited donors and recipients alike. While the people (*dêmos*) ruled at Athens, the elite knew how to flourish within its rules. Gorgias' readiness to accept Sostratos' unaffected affability at face value can thus claim a basis in reality as well as in comic necessity. Their confrontation, like the assembly in *The Man from Sicyon*, ends well because comedy trusts not just in its own conventions but in those of its society. The cooperation that secures Sostratos' goal, rewarded at the end by the corresponding willingness of Sostratos' father to accept Gorgias as a son-in-law, reflects the good social relations to which Athenian society aspired. Tension between rich and poor has a long history as a comic topos, but its manifestations in Menander must be read against the record of real classes functioning in the real society that he knew.

Social historians increasingly take Menander as a source for, not just a reflection of Athenian social history since issues of gender, family and private law are so well represented in his plays.[6] Their success has invigorated the study of New Comedy in recent years, but using drama as a source for history raises further issues of great interest. How, for example, might dramatic context distort a play's evidence for social attitudes? Chrysis, the Samian woman of Menander's title, had clearly entered into a long-term, monogamous relationship with Demeas. She appears to be what Athenians called not a courtesan (*hetaira*) but a *pallakê*, and a person of some status, though her character is hard to judge since key scenes are missing in the papyrus. When a furious Demeas later threatens her with a whore's life (390–8), however, and his neighbour Niceratos, even more laughably angry, suggests selling her as a slave (even though she is clearly free), the evidence most plausibly suggests not that a *pallakê* had only servile status at Athens, but that angry old men in comedy easily lose their moral way and may defame even the innocent. Still more difficult to control is the balance between the social attitudes reflected in characters and plots and the actual centre of dramatic interest. *The Bad-Tempered Man* seems far more concerned with the misanthropic Cnemon and what he does and does not learn about social responsibility than with the romance that so taxes his equanimity. As for *The Woman from Samos* (*Samia*), the fact that Moschion has raped Niceratus' daughter and that Chrysis may have overstepped her position in Demeas' household, however significant for the study of gender relations at Athens, are less important to Menander than the challenge those actions pose to relations between Moschion and his father. Neither play is 'about' sex, love, or even marriage except as means to a somewhat different end. Menander's plays have much to say about the making of legitimate marriages in fourth-century Athens, but, plot summaries aside, that is not *all* they have to say.

This disjunction between reading texts as social documents and as dramatic scripts recalls the problem with which we began, the relative appeal of the general and the specific in the reception of ancient comedy. There is, after all, some truth to the old clichés about New Comedy. Plays of Menander survive today precisely because his style of comedy could be lifted from its original time and place and remain meaningful in worlds far removed from fourth-century Athens. Those Greek-speaking readers of the third, fourth, and even fifth centuries AD, whose worn-out books preserved

Menander's plays in the trash heaps, storerooms and mummy wrappings of Roman Egypt, not to mention the rich burgher of Mytilene on the island of Lesbos, who decorated his dining room with Menandrean scenes, knew little (and probably cared less) about the Athenian law of *hubris* or the difference between *pallakê* and *hetaira* in a Greece already half a millennium or more behind them. Yet they still read – and in some cases perhaps even saw – Menander's plays. So, of course, did the Romans, though in their own way and for their own purposes, and the evident appeal of the New Comedy tradition in Italy demands still another way to think about comedy and society.

This part of the story takes us back to the Hellenistic world as the Greek kingdoms of Alexander's successors were on the wane and Rome was on the rise. And it mixes politics and literature from the beginning. The kind of comedy we associate with Plautus and Terence – at least eight other poets are known to have written plays in the same style over a period of nearly 150 years – began with an official action. In 240 BC, following their success in the first war with Carthage, the Romans expanded their annual festival in honour of Jupiter, the *ludi Romani*, in something like the Greek fashion by adding a set of plays to the programme. A man known to history as Livius Andronicus, in origin probably a native Greek-speaker from Tarentum, adapted a Greek comedy and tragedy for the occasion. Unfortunately, not even their titles survive. Andronicus' work failed to hold the interest of later generations: Cicero, with a significant choice of words, says that his plays were not worth a second reading (*Brutus* 71). The number of plays and the number of opportunities to perform them nevertheless expanded considerably in later years, and Andronicus' basic decisions lived on, establishing the parameters of Roman comedy for generations.

Andronicus translated rather freely into Latin with a greater musical component than he found in his models, but he retained their Greek settings and costumes. The resulting *fabula* (*comoedia*) *palliata*, 'comedy in Greek dress', thus reversed a central presumption of New Comedy: the 'reality' of actors who dressed and spoke like their audience and moved in a world that mirrored their own became at a stroke a fantasy land of make-believe Greeks cavorting in a manner quite alien to common experience. Plautus would joke frequently about the result:

> Don't be surprised that little old slaves like us
> can drink, make love, and ask our friends to dinner.
> Stuff like that's okay for us at Athens.
>
> (*Stichus* 446–8)

Licence like this might be expected among Greeks, for whom most Romans reserved a special mixture of awe and contempt, but it also entailed the renegotiation of comedy's relationship to the society that now produced it.

What, for example, would the move from Athens to Rome do to the topical elements that informed the Greek originals? If left intact, Athenian realities might become exotic oddities, like citing prices in minae and talents, or they might lose their resonance entirely, which is how the socially fraught rapes of New Comedy acquired the callousness so embarrassing to Latin studies.[7] If tweaked and cajoled into a semblance of Roman realities, the result might clash with the Greek aura that the genre at other times affects. Thus the joke of 'Greek' slaves entering into Roman contracts with their 'Greek' masters or preparing for Roman-style weddings. If simply removed, a play might lose the specificity its plot required. Roman comedy experimented with all these responses to the challenge of topicality.

The comic soldier, whose history of braggadocio and cowardice stretched back to Aristophanes' Lamachus, provides a good example of the possibilities. Soldiers were familiar on the ancient stage because they were familiar in life, whether marching with citizen-armies in classical times or with mercenary ones in the Hellenistic world. Menander apparently created a fairly typical soldier in a lost play called *The Flatterer* (*Colax*), but he sometimes turned the existing stereotype on its head by creating young men who enter service abroad (or threaten to do so) in hope of solving a problem at home or return from service to find to their confusion and dismay that the brutality of combat makes a poor introduction to civilian life. Thus Cleostratos (*The Shield*) seeks his fortune abroad and Moschion (*Samia*) feigns such service to shame Demeas, while Thrasonides (*The Hated Man*), and Polemon (*The Shorn Girl*) learn to their cost that boorishness and brutality find no reward at home.[8]

Plautus instead burnished the old stereotype to a special brilliance, but even his most outré embellishments were never complete fantasies. Though he cannot resist stretching the boundaries of Greek nomenclature with a name like Pyrgopolinices ('Habitual Tower-Sacker'), a real Greek general was indeed styled Poliorcetes ('Besieger of Cities'), and contemporary Romans were beginning to assume honorific titles like Africanus, Macedonicus and Asiagenes, which in the conventions of Roman nomenclature had the connotation 'conqueror of . . .'. Similarly, though it was only a stage figure who earned a commemorative statue,

> because the Persians, Paphlagonians
> Sinopians, Arabs, Carians, Cretans, Syrians,
> Rhodes and Lycia, Devouria and Drinkupia,
> Centaurfightia and the Singlebreasted Fleet,

Libya, the whole coast, and all of Dethundria,
and half of just about every tribe in the world
he overcame alone within twenty days. (*Curculio* 442–8)

a real Roman erected the following inscription to honour his relative Lucius
Aemilius Regillus:

> Under his auspices, command, good fortune, and leadership near Ephesus,
> Samos, and Chios, while Antiochus himself watched them, the entire army,
> cavalry, and elephants, the fleet of King Antiochus though previously unde-
> feated was routed, shattered, and put to flight, and on that same day forty-two
> warships with all their crews were captured.[9]

Plautus clearly found the line between pride and vainglory at Rome easy
to erase. Almost every prominent Roman of the day was a potential
gloriosus.

A generation or so later, Terence created an equally memorable, though
rather more complex, soldier in Thraso of *The Eunuch*. He too can sound
like a contemporary Roman, an *imperator* prepared to send his centuries and
maniples against a courtesan's house as he once sent them against Pyrrhus
(776–83), though he will, like the Duke of Plaza Toro (and for the same
reason), lead them from behind. Yet 'Thraso' was a real Greek name, not
a joke like Pyrgopolinices and Therapontigonus Platigidorus, and Terence's
soldier has delusions of wit (419ff.) and an endearing awareness of his own
flaws (e.g. 446). Thraso has only some of the bluster and little of the brutality
that so often lurks just beneath the surface of Plautine soldiers. His eventual
acceptance into Thais' ménage in order to pay the bills is both the penalty
and reward for his simplicity (1072ff.). He is so easily domesticated because
he is essentially a literary creation – his attempt at wit explicitly echoes an
old stage joke – and his particular kind of swagger recalls the long literary
tradition behind him more vividly than the reality that surrounds him. His
world is the stage world.

Terence's retreat from specificity also reveals itself on the level of plot.
Athenian law, for example, required her nearest male relative to provide an
unmarried heiress (the *epiklêros*) with a satisfactory husband. This characteristically Athenian mechanism protected the interests of a household bereft of
its male head. It also proved useful to a comic tradition eager to manufacture
plots about marriage. About a dozen Greek plays are known to have worked
from this idea, including Menander's *The Shield* and Apollodorus' *The Victorious Claimant (Epidicazomenos)*, which both involved claims made on
a putative *epiklêros*.[10] This was too specifically Greek a notion for Plautus, but not for Terence. He successfully turned Apollodorus' play into his

Phormio by simply paraphrasing the law in his exposition and then taking it for granted:

> The law is that orphaned girls marry their closest male relatives,
> and the same law commands the relatives to marry them.
>
> (*Phormio* 125–6)

What was a law at Athens eventually becomes simply a comic device at Rome.[11]

Social institutions also demanded choices between generality and specificity. Slavery, ubiquitous throughout Greco-Roman antiquity, is represented differently in Greek and Roman comedy. Menander's slaves are often little more than their masters' agents, recalling Aristotle's definition of slaves as 'living tools'. Daos of *The Shield*, so instrumental in launching the play's initial scheme, is a partial exception, though later events eventually turn the plot in a different direction. His earnest, respectful instruction of his masters (299ff.) makes a significant contrast in this respect with Palaestrio's imperiousness at a comparable moment in *The Swaggering Soldier* (599ff.). The music-girl Habrotonon, whose actions reunite the estranged couple in *The Arbitrants* (*Epitrepontes*), is even more interesting an exception. She is a slave – the role could have been written otherwise – and her servile status clearly helps to motivate her behaviour. Freedom may be the reward of her intervention (538ff.), and her striking combination of selfishness and generosity recalls the perils of real women in that social position.

Plautine slaves, like Plautine soldiers, are broader and bolder comic figures. Not only do consummate schemers like Pseudolus and Chrysalus act well beyond the limits of their Greek predecessors, but Plautus calls proud attention to the difference. As Chrysalus boasts:

> I'm not impressed by those Parmenos and Syruses,
> who lift two or three minae from their masters.
>
> (*Two Sisters Named Bacchis* 649–50)

The joke is all the keener since the slave in Plautus' Greek model was himself called 'Syrus'. This licentious fantasy, however, also licenses a particular kind of fantasy. It becomes possible for Plautine comedy to invert, convert, subvert and even pervert prevailing definitions of dominance and submission and the social roles they entail, an especially pointed exercise in a society as hierarchical as Rome's, where almost everyone stood simultaneously in positions of dominance over and submission to others. Comedy wreaked havoc with Roman hierarchies not simply by juxtaposing the perspectives of free and slave, rich and poor, quick and slow but by confusing the behaviour associated with those distinctions. Slaves may thus assume the authority of masters and masters the dependence of slaves. It is all still a fiction, of course. Comedy's heroes are not life's heroes. Everyone admires Chrysalus, but once the curtain falls, no free man (or even woman) would willingly take his place. The artificiality is part of the fun, though it does not make the slaves' machinations any less true to the realities of authority and obligation in Roman society. Recent scholarship is right to consider not just the slaves of Plautus as characters, but the place of slavery itself in the Plautine imagination.[12]

Terence, who was himself once a slave at Rome, remains marginal to this discussion. His slaves struggle to stay ahead of their masters (e.g. Davus of *The Girl from Andros*) or fail to seize the limelight (e.g. Syrus of *Brothers*). By restoring the proportions of Menandrean comedy, Terence created a deeply ironic, morally searching kind of *palliata* that skirted the edges of that Roman reality Plautus embraced with such enthusiasm. The difference between them is traditionally explained by appeals to the growing Hellenism of second-century Rome, which encouraged flight from the crass, often farcical materialism of Plautus to a more gentle, even sentimental view of humanity. Terence was identified with the enlightened circle surrounding the younger Scipio, and the struggle between the urbane Micio and rustic Demea of *Brothers* (*Adelphoe*) was thought to reflect the second-century culture war waged so bitterly between Scipio and Cato. Unfortunately, none of this is very true. There was no 'Scipionic Circle' as literary scholars have sometimes imagined it. There was no simple divide in the second century between phil- and anti-Hellenists. Scipio and Cato are not easily typecast, nor is either Micio's discomfiture at the end of *Brothers* or Demea's ostensible conversion a clear victory for one set of values or a repudiation of the other. The truth, as so often in matters concerning Terence, is much more complex.

His own acknowledgment of aristocratic support in the prologue to *Brothers* has long been problematic:

> As for what those spiteful critics say, that distinguished men
> help this poet and constantly share the writing,
> what they so vigorously judge to be a slander
> he deems the greatest honour, since he pleases those
> who please you all and the entire population,
> men whose deeds in war, in peace, in business
> benefit all in time of need without a hint of arrogance.
>
> (*Brothers* 15–21)

Later tradition identified these benefactors as the younger Scipio and his friend Laelius, but this is unlikely. Laelius had earned no special distinction by 160, and Scipio, who commissioned *Brothers* for his father's funeral games in 160, had barely begun the distinguished career that eventually made him 'Africanus' in his own right. Terence, who died in 159, was long gone before this Scipio became a cultural force at Rome. No specific cultural agenda lurks in the Terentian scripts, nor are the obvious differences in comic style between Plautus and Terence adequately explained by reference to the changing cultural climate at Rome in the second century. Plautine plays never left the repertoire, even as Terentian plays won favour in and beyond their original productions in the 160s.[13] The scripts of both dramatists remained the prized possession of professional acting companies for generations. When those scripts did finally become part of a cultural agenda, it was to do different work for the Romans of a different time.

One of the great ironies of drama's history at Rome is that theatres there became more permanent as theatrical entertainments became more occasional. By the time Rome had its first permanent stone theatre, dedicated by Pompey the Great in 55 BC, the *comoedia palliata* had been all but eclipsed in performance by mime, and the verbal art of tragedy was increasingly supplanted by the attractions of pageantry and spectacle. The plays of Plautus and Terence, however, were by then secure in a new role as Roman classics. Their scripts, collected and edited by the gentlemen-scholars of the late Republic, turned into books that were studied in schools, mined for linguistic oddities and literary tags, probably still read (and sometimes seen) for fun, but were most assuredly prized commodities in that store of cultural capital with which Romans of privilege came increasingly to secure and to assert positions of educational and social authority in their ever-expanding world.

That process of reading and acculturation is quite different from the process that brought Menander's *The Bad-Tempered Man* to the stage in fourth-century Athens, and that is just the point. The relationship of comedy to society changed fundamentally and in almost every conceivable way in the centuries between Menander and Terence. Comedy changed. Society changed. And, of necessity, the relationship between them changed. The famous 'mirror of life' created by a comedy rooted in the look, the feel and the preoccupations of fourth-century Athenians became in time the fun-house mirror that Roman dramatists held up to their own Roman audiences. In the course of this evolution, the very idea of theatrical entertainment changed, too, as the great civic festivals of Athens generalized and professionalized as they spread throughout the Greek world and then inspired the *ludi scaenici* of the Roman one. That evolution did not cease with the death of Terence. Comedy continued to develop throughout antiquity, though what went on in ancient theatres came increasingly to distance itself from what went on in the schoolrooms and the libraries of the Mediterranean world. That further development might itself claim a place in a study of ancient comedy and society, but it would require a new chapter in a new history well beyond the boundaries of the ancient stage.

NOTES

1. Sander M. Goldberg, *The Making of Menander's Comedy* (Berkeley: University of California Press, 1980), pp. 109–21.
2. Oliver Taplin, *Comic Angels and Other Approaches to Greek Drama through Vase-Painting* (Oxford: Clarendon Press, 1993), pp. 36–40.
3. R. Just, *Women in Athenian Law and Life* (London: Routledge, 1989), pp. 105–25; R. Omitomoju, *Rape and the Politics of Consent in Classical Athens* (Cambridge: Cambridge University Press, 2002), pp. 72–115; S. Lape, *Reproducing Athens: Menander's Comedy, Democratic Culture, and the Hellenistic City* (Princeton: Princeton University Press, 2004), pp. 115–19.
4. A. C. Scafuro, *The Forensic Stage: Settling Disputes in Greco-Roman New Comedy* (Cambridge: Cambridge University Press, 1997), pp. 211–16 (private remedies), pp. 331–4 (Euphiletus); C. B. Patterson, *The Family in Greek History* (Cambridge, Mass.: Harvard University Press, 1998), pp. 166–74.
5. Thus the young man prosecuting the rich Conon and his sons for assault in Dem. 54 explicitly considers but rejects a charge of *hubris*. The thousand-drachma fine for failing to secure a fifth of the votes might also discourage a prosecutor, especially one of limited means.
6. E.g. Scafuro, 1997, pp. 14–19; Patterson, 1998, pp. 191–205; Omitomoju, 2002, pp. 141–54; and most fully Lape, 2004.
7. Z. M. Packman, 'Call it Rape: A Motif in Roman Comedy and its Suppression in English-Speaking Countries', *Helios* 20 (1993), 42–55.
8. N. Zagagi, *The Comedy of Menander* (Bloomington: Indiana, 1995), pp. 29–36. Contrast on the Roman side J. A. Hanson, 'The Glorious Military', in T. A. Dorey and D. R. Dudley (eds.), *Roman Drama* (London: Routledge, 1965), pp. 51–85, and more generally, Erich S. Gruen, *Studies in Greek Culture and Roman Policy* (Leiden/New York: E. J. Brill, 1990), pp. 124–57.
9. The exploits of Plautus' Therapontigonus Platigidorus (Comradeson Blowbestower) are recorded at *Curc.* 442–8. Livy 40.52.5–7 preserves most of the inscription placed by the censor M. Aemilius Lepidus on the temple he dedicated to the Lares Permarini, with a copy set for good measure in the temple of Capitoline Jupiter. Menander's soldiers have appropriate, but not overtly comic, names.
10. Scafuro, 1997, pp. 293–305.
11. Cf. Ter. *Brothers*, 650–2, paraphrasing the same requirement. Both Terence's predecessor Caecilius and his successor Turpilius wrote plays called *Epiclerus*.
12. K. McCarthy, *Slaves, Masters, and the Art of Authority in Plautine Comedy* (Princeton: Princeton University Press, 2000).
13. H. N. Parker, 'Plautus v. Terence: Audience and Popularity Re-examined', *AJP* 117 (1996), pp. 585–617.

FURTHER READING

Goldberg, S. M., *The Making of Menander's Comedy*. Berkeley: University of California Press, 1980.

Just, R., *Women in Athenian Law and Life*. London: Routledge, 1989.

Lape, S., *Reproducing Athens: Menander's Comedy, Democratic Culture, and the Hellenistic City*. Princeton: Princeton University Press, 2004.

McCarthy, K., *Slaves, Masters, and the Art of Authority in Plautine Comedy*. Princeton: Princeton University Press, 2000.

Omitomoju, R., *Rape and the Politics of Consent in Classical Athens*. Cambridge: Cambridge University Press, 2002.

Patterson, C. B., *The Family in Greek History*. Cambridge, Mass.: Harvard University Press, 1998.

Scafuro, A. C., *The Forensic Stage. Settling Disputes in Greco-Roman New Comedy*. Cambridge: Cambridge University Press, 1997.

8

HUGH DENARD

Lost theatre and performance traditions in Greece and Italy

Introduction

Browsing the Ancient Drama shelves of the average library, one could be forgiven for concluding that tragedy and comedy were by far the most frequent and important theatrical activities throughout antiquity, with just the occasional cameo appearance by the satyr play. But, from the protodramatic padded 'komasts' of sixth-century BC Greece to the exquisite musical dance theatre beloved of the Romans up to and beyond the sixth century AD, comedy and tragedy were surrounded on all sides by an extended family of other theatrical forms. If we ignore these lost traditions – festive mockeries, mythological burlesques, satires, farces, comical tragedies, history plays and dance dramas – we deny ourselves rich sources of knowledge and understanding about the array of theatrical activities in these ancient societies, as well as the nature and significance of their more famous cousins.

Alongside these more or less 'theatrical' traditions were a host of other performance activities by musicians, maskers, magicians, dancers, jugglers, poetry performers, exhibition speakers, tightrope walkers (in all shapes and sizes), sword-swallowers, storytellers, engineers, acrobats, escapologists, performing animals and others. Paratheatrical performances like these were to be found in the most unexpected places: at funerals, processions, dinner parties, in schools, on the streets, in front of temples, in the marketplace, in the countryside, at horse-races, at athletic and gladiatorial contests as well as on the stage itself; performance was a particularly flexible form of currency in the unceasing transactions of cultural change.

Precisely how various theatre and performance practices may have influenced each other is too large and, with often inadequate evidence, too complex a question to approach here, although I will suggest some possible connections. The present aim is to introduce the history of 'lost' extra-canonical theatre and performance traditions in classical antiquity, beginning within the Greek-speaking world and gradually moving towards Rome.

Theatrical traditions

Our evidence indicates the presence of broadly two theatrical traditions: mockery genres and serious genres, with some hybrid and extra-theatrical offshoots (adapted genres). From what we can tell, every single one of the lost theatrical genres shared some of the elements of form and content to be found in the surviving theatrical genres. The mockery genres were by far the most numerous and varied, although the serious genres tended to achieve higher status and greater longevity. The high degree of generic overlap in the Greek-speaking world suggests that each region contributed to a reservoir of theatrical forms, ideas and skills upon which other regions drew and which they gradually modified for local conditions – like dialects of a shared language.

In time, Rome absorbed and adapted some of these genres as pre-existing traditions, adapting them to serve its own aesthetic desires and cultural needs. The common wisdom is that Roman theatre is essentially a sub-species of Greek theatre and, at a certain level, this is undoubtedly true: the comic *fabulae (comoediae) palliatae* of Plautus and Terence were manifestly Latin adaptations of Greek plays. But it is also clear that there was a vibrant theatre tradition in and around the southern Italian peninsula from at least the fifth century BC, which not only was a direct co-tributary into Plautine comedy, but which, as I will discuss later, may have contributed to the formation of Greek drama itself at an early stage; Roman drama, even that of Terence and the tragedians, may be more 'Italian' than we are accustomed to think (see also Goldberg in ch. 7 of this volume).

Mockery genres

Each mockery genre appears to have ridiculed one or more of four basic targets: specific individuals, religion, social life and cultural forms. To have done so in everyday life would have been considered scandalous, indictable or even blasphemous; but the festive right to insult, abuse, parody and poke fun allowed communities temporary, symbolic dominion over the persons, powers, social conventions and cultural creations to which they were normally subject. Consequently, as today, a great deal can be learnt about a society through observing the nature and degree of festive licence that it extends to its members through the forms and conventions of its mockery genres.

Komasts, satyrs and animal choruses

There are traces of various types of light-hearted performance in the sixth century BC, particularly from the Peloponnese. Votive clay masks depicting wrinkled old women and men survive from the sanctuary of Artemis Orthia at Sparta in the late seventh century BC, perhaps remnants of the otherwise lost *Bryllicha*, a masked and cross-dressed fertility dance in which men and probably phallus-wearing women participated. We also hear of the so-called Dorian mime (not implying dumbshow) in Sparta, with portrayals of food thieves and itinerant physicians speaking in dialect. Other performance traditions, called *phallophoroi* (phallus carriers) and *autokabdaloi* (improvisers), remain relatively obscure. The title of one tradition, *sophistai* (wise guys), may hint at performances by a professional, or semi-professional, troupe.

However, hundreds of vase paintings have been discovered, mostly on scented oil bottles from Corinth around the 630s BC and then spreading further afield, which show that there may have been some sort of mocking, musical dance drama in the century or two before the dramatic festivals at Athens come into sharper historical focus. The earliest depictions show first individuals, then choruses of men in tunics and padded out with bulging bellies and buttocks and, in some examples, as in Old Comedy, a phallus. They are often to be found dancing around a wine-mixing bowl accompanied by a piper, and from around the 580s BC are joined by what appear to be women – all elements suitable for festivals and drinking parties. Sometimes mythological themes are also visually evoked, which may relate to the subject of the songs accompanying the dance. In a society that laid great premium upon the physical prowess and beauty of the younger male body, the padded komasts are in every way pointedly un-idealized: the incongruity of inviting aesthetic appreciation of a caricatured, mature body engaged in dance offers, through its affectionate parody of ageing revellers, a mocking retort to the powers of age and death.

In the 560s BC, the padded dancers gave way to drunken processions of relatively normal-looking men. During the first thirty years of the sixth century BC, Greek-style satyrs who were part-human and part-horse (with tail, horse-ears and sometimes hooves, in contrast to the Roman variety, which, like the god Pan, were goat-like), also began to appear on vases, becoming very popular from about the middle of the century. From an early time, satyrs were associated with transgressive behaviour. They became the *thiasos* of Dionysus (his band of revellers) escorting the god back into the city on a ship after his winter absence, hurling uncouth insults at the city-dwellers so that in time the Greek word 'to process' (*pomperein*) came to acquire the connotation of 'to insult'. If Aristotle is right, tragedy itself may have emerged from a non-serious form of drama with 'small plots' and 'ridiculous diction' (*Poetics* 1449a 19–21), which he tentatively associates with these riotous, dipsomaniacal, ithyphallic followers of Dionysus. After all, even mature tragedy sometimes represented heroes, gods, social conventions and cultural forms in a less than flattering light and, as vignettes such as the Nurse in Aeschylus' *Libation Bearers* shows, indulged in the occasional moment of social comedy. Perhaps in the more scurrilous genres, the anonymity of the mask served to shield mockers from the otherwise serious consequences of their festive taunts and abuses. By the turn of the century, both satyrs and human dancers were appearing together on vases with female companions in Dionysian contexts and, with the invention of the satyr play, the vases began explicitly to depict humans costumed as satyrs, rather than the mythical beasts themselves.

A different performance tradition may be indicated by the twenty Attic vases we have over the eighty years following *c.*560 BC, which show choruses of men costumed as and/or riding on horses, birds (**Figs. 4 and 5**), ostriches and (in at least six of the later vases) dolphins – all often accompanied by a piper. Interestingly, the horses and dolphins are often mounted by armed warriors. There is also a chorus of stilt-walkers. This immediately reminds us of comedy which at least from the 450s BC and well into the period of the so-called 'New Comedy' featured animal and other spectacularly costumed choruses, e.g. Aristophanes' *Birds*, *Wasps*, *Frogs*, *Clouds* and *Knights*, but also of the plays of at least another seventeen comic poets, some of which displayed presumably similarly costumed mythical entities such as centaurs, sirens and mounted Amazons. On some vases, the costumes are partially hidden beneath large cloaks, which would enable their spectacular novelty to be revealed as a *coup de théâtre*, reminiscent of the Aristophanic chorus 'stripping to dance'.[1]

However – and this is a major reservation – the vase figures do not have the grotesquely padded costume or oversized, red-tipped, flaccid leather phallus of fifth-century Attic comedy. The pictorial theme of animal choruses also trails off at about the same time as comedy was formally instituted at the Athenian City Dionysia (486 BC), which is interesting, to say the least. Perhaps the vases show a generic precursor to comedy; or perhaps it was a different comic tradition that declined once the organizers of the City Dionysia had selected its closely related but more ribald rival. Alternatively, the vases may show a serious genre of choral performance, which Old Comedy, characteristically, took upon itself to parody through caricature and grotesquery.

Personal mockery: Fescennine Verses

In parts of the Italian peninsula from at least the fifth century BC, fertility celebrations at harvests and weddings, perhaps not dissimilar to Greek *phallika* mentioned by Aristotle, included a form of improvised comic disparagement called Fescennine Verses, with laughter perhaps serving to avert evil spirits who might otherwise blight crops, or male sexual performance. The Augustan poet, Horace tells how 'earthy abuse poured forth from one side, then the other', and that 'such freedom, innocent and jolly, was welcomed each recurrent year'. However, as Aristophanes was later to experience, festive licence has its limits, and those in authority appear to have become sufficiently discomfited to have legislated against 'abusive slander in poems' some time around 450 BC. Horace, writing here as an apologist for censorship, notes:

> the jokes became cruel, and soon overtly savage, and stalked through innocent homes, fearless and unchecked. The slanderous tooth drew blood and even those who were spared felt concern for the welfare of all.[2]

We lack sufficient information to determine the full nature of these early performances or the sequence of places and times at which they arose, much less what gave rise to them or precisely how they relate to the textual survivors. The picture is further complicated by three interesting, and often interrelated, variables: adaptation, professionalization and scripting.

An entertaining form of performance will often be taken up and adapted for use outside its original context. So for instance, although the padded *komasts* and satyr dances depicted on vases may have originated in religious festivals, smaller versions may have been devised to provide attractive additions for banquets and drinking parties. In addition, popular traditions are often taken up by skilled individuals who refine their own performance beyond what the ordinary man or woman could easily achieve, with a view to making a living out of it. The 'professional' performer's versions of popular forms, ideal for private entertainments, may or may not in time even displace the public, 'folk' version altogether.

At some point, an attempt is often made to write down such entertainments, perhaps to record the live performance tradition, perhaps to improve upon it, or maybe simply to supplement it with a parallel literary version. Whether or not a scripted version will secure a foothold within a culture is subject to too many variables to be predictable, but scripted and unscripted forms frequently coexist for long periods of time.

The Sicilian school

Cumulatively, such performances provided a repertoire of elements upon which the first writers could draw. Aristotle claims that 'the making of plots originated in Sicily' (*Poetics* 1449b). If true, then the prime contender for the honour is Epicharmus, the earliest Sicilian comic writer of whom we have any mention or trace. Indeed, Plato, although a contemporary of Aristophanes, has Socrates deem Epicharmus the 'best of comic poets' (*Theaetetus* 152e). Epicharmus was one of a number of innovative and, as it turns out, important writers at the court of Hiero in Syracuse in the early fifth century BC. A later commentator credited one Phormus, alongside Epicharmus, with the invention of comedy, also claiming that Phormus robed his actors down to the feet and adorned the performance area with sumptuous, purple hangings: no mean display.

Epicharmus and Phormus each wrote a number of plays mocking myth – the stuff from which religious understanding and belief were woven. Epicharmus' burlesques often starred Heracles or Odysseus: *Heracles and the Girdle*, *Odysseus the Deserter*, *Odysseus Shipwrecked*. But his mythical range was much wider, with titles such as *Earth and Sea*, *Hebe's Wedding*, *Bousiris* (a mythical king of Egypt), *Amycus* (on Castor, Pollux and the eponymous pugilist king of the Bebrycians), *Sirens* and *Sphinx*. Scripting may have enabled the Sicilians to endow theatre with more ambitious dramatic structures and greater conceptual and verbal complexity than previously possible.

But what is most remarkable about the plays of Epicharmus is that, although probably quite short in themselves, they spanned three of the four main species of mockery that went on to dominate established comic genres for the next thousand years and more, from Old Comedy to the Roman Mime. Making fun of religion, social life and serious cultural forms, his oeuvre cuts through the traditional genre divisions of the comic canon.

The Male and the Female Argument, for instance, may have parodied philosophers, and his *Pilgrims*, religion. His *Chorus Members* and *Hephaestus* or *Revellers* may have been parodies of other styles of performance, perhaps imitated by or imitating the younger Deinolochus, whose title, *Comicotragedy*, was itself copied by later writers; around 300 BC, a Southern Italian playwright, Rhinthon, would become famous for his *Hilaritytragedies* – also in Doric dialect. Some of Epicharmus' titles, like *Hope* or *Wealth*, *The Megarian Woman* and *The Rustic*, reappeared in plays from the early fourth century through to the late Roman empire. In fact the only major mockery type obviously absent is satire of named individuals, which was to become such a major element in the comedies of Aristophanes and his contemporaries in Athens.

Epicharmus' plays required at least three speaking actors, and many of the dramatic conventions found in Attic drama are also detectable, including multiple scenes, narrative speeches, monologues, comic violence, debates, music and dance – both individual and choral, although it is not definitively known whether a chorus was a prominent element. Social (as opposed to mythological) character types also figure, as they do in later Athenian and Roman comedy, including cunning philosophers, outwitted idiots, tourists, trainers, athletes and drunkards.

The nature and extent of the influence of Epicharmus and his contemporaries upon Athenian comedy or vice versa is debated, but poets could hardly remain unaffected by accounts, whether oral or (increasingly in the fourth century) written, of how such writers had adapted unscripted performance traditions. With the early mockery genres borrowing from common sources and presumably from each other, it is not surprising that, even allowing for regional differences, they came closely to resemble one another.

Translation and adaptation

Attic comedy in southern Italy

Until the last years of the fifth century BC, comedy at the Athenian City Dionysia shared the broad range of Epicharmian drama, emphasizing mockery of religious, social and other domains, while extending to include mockery of specific individuals. The Dionysia commanded vast financial and human resources, and the theatrical pre-eminence of Athens was confirmed by the confluence of the careers of the canonical playwrights *par excellence*: Aeschylus, Sophocles, Euripides and Aristophanes. If Sicily took the early initiative, theatrically speaking, Athens established a hegemony that in the fifth century reflected, and in the centuries to come both replaced and eclipsed, its political influence, with the result that it attracted to itself many of the foremost playwrights and actors in the Greek-speaking world. Consequently, the earlier multilateral circulation of influence increasingly became a flow from the new 'centre' outwards.

So, in a couple of hundred theatrically inspired vase paintings from the Southern Italian peninsula dating from *c.*400 to 320 BC, we find what looks very much like Athenian drama (see Green, ch. 9 in this volume). The early fourth-century comic tradition in Southern Italy evidently either incorporated Attic Old Comedy, was closely modelled upon it, or effected some combination of the two. What is slightly perplexing, though, is that this style of comic performance was no longer being played at Athens itself.

From around the last decade of the fifth century BC, perhaps partly in response to their increasingly international appeal, Attic comedies shifted away from their former local specificity and generic diversity to develop one of the four comic strands – mockery of social life – to the exclusion of all others. The padded costume, dangling phallus and caricatured masks gave way to less exaggerated character masks and costumes representing a stock repertoire of types of slaves, sons, lovers, fathers, mothers, parasites, boastful soldiers and others. However, in around a hundred vases, mostly Apulian, from c.400 to c.365 BC – formerly known as '*phlyax*' (buffoon play) vases – the old comic tights, masks and phalluses are in full view; the comic subject-matter is entirely characteristic of Athenian Old Comedies, and some of the depictions even require a knowledge of specific plays by Aristophanes. However, during the 360s BC, even the Italian vases began to register a shift towards the kind of social comedy that by then dominated the Athenian stage.

Oscan and Latin drama

During the fourth century BC, the status of actors came to rest increasingly upon virtuoso performances of classical pieces, reflected in the admission of 'Old Tragedy' to the Dionysia on a regular basis from 386 BC and a prize for comic actors some time between 328 and 312 BC. Partly in order to service this new market, Athenian playwriting became increasingly formulaic, thereby losing much of the restlessly iconoclastic energies that had forged their revered antecedents.

Consequently, the next major innovations in playwriting came about as a result of Attic drama being translated into different cultural contexts. Oscan poets in Campania were adapting Greek comedies into their own language by 300 BC, and in about 240 BC (eighty years after the South Italian vases had moved on to other topics) a poet from Tarentum, Livius Andronicus, was the first to translate Greek comedies and tragedies into Latin, creating the *fabula palliata* (Greek-style plays) of which Plautus and Terence became the most famous examples. Within a few years of Andronicus' innovation, the Romans had gone on to create their own Latin versions, not only of plays, but of the theatrical genres themselves, producing the *fabula togata* (Roman-style plays) and *fabula praetexta* (*praetextata*), history plays, relatively little of which survives.

According to Livy, Roman theatre began with the adoption of an Etruscan dance (which, it has been argued, may have involved satyrs) some time around 363 BC, and out of these grew scenic entertainments with crude, versified jokes and correspondingly obscene gestures. Local actors subsequently developed *saturae*, the nature of which is not clear, although they did include songs with accompanying gestures that could be 'written down for the flute player' (*Ab urbe condita* 7.2.5–13).

Atellan farces

By the fourth century BC, the town of Atella near Naples had its own improvisation-based mockery genre, staged in the Oscan dialect. Like the seventeenth-century AD Italian *commedia dell'arte*, the original Atellan performers devised a great variety of comic scenarios using just a few grotesque characters: Bucco the braggart, Dossenus the trickster hunchback, Maccus the clown, Old Man Pappus, large-jawed Manducus and Lamia, an infant-eating ogress. These comic caricatures of social types and bogey monsters surely epitomize the thematic range of the *Atellanae*: pride, greed, envy, anger, lust and gluttony – later to reappear in the medieval Morality Play, with 'sloth', as 'the Seven Deadly Sins'.

The *Atellanae* became hugely popular, being performed by professional troupes throughout the region. Plautus' name (T. Maccius Plautus) suggests that he may himself have performed in them; he certainly drew heavily upon his knowledge of them in creating his Greek-style Latin comedies. Unscripted Latin versions of the *Atellanae* began to appear, we don't know when, followed eventually, in the first century BC, by scripted versions.

The Latin *Atellanae* – probably both scripted and unscripted – survived at Rome at least up to the reign of Domitian, by which time they were sometimes used to lighten the mood after tragic performances (Juvenal *Satires* 3.174ff; 6.71). But the hundred or so surviving titles of *Atellanae* by two Latin poets, Novius and Pomponius, show how radically the genre had changed since its earliest days in Atella. There are 'pure' Atellan farces, such as *Pappus the Rustic*, *The Marriage of Pappus*, *The Maccus Twins* and *Maccus the Soldier*. But, presumably under the influence of competing genres, the *Atellanae* also grew to encompass burlesques of myth and tragedy (e.g. *Andromache*, *Ariadne*, *Hercules the Bill-Collector*) and a further category of titles appears to be indebted to the Greek comic tradition also drawn upon by the comic *fabula palliata*: *Brothers*, *The Courtesan*, *The Twins* and *The Pimp*. Finally, there are earthy dramas of everyday social life: *The Rustic*, *The Prophet*, *The Fishermen* and *The Physician*. Fragments indicate that many of the comic tricks and tropes to be found in mockery genres from Epicharmus to Plautus, like comic transvestite disguise and adultery plots, were alive and well in the scripted Latin *Atellanae*.[3]

The *Atellanae* may have fulfilled a culturally specific need for a non-professional, public theatre tradition (alongside the professional) in which the well-born could perform without payment and without removing their masks, thereby avoiding the social stigma of *infamia* that tainted the Roman actor. Livy writes:

> the young Romans kept it for themselves and did not allow it to be debased by the professional actors. That is why the tradition remains that performers of Atellan plays are not removed from their tribes and serve in the army on the grounds that they have no connection with professional entertainment.
>
> (*Ab urbe condita* 7.2.12–13)

From the early Empire, as political freedoms became increasingly limited, so too did theatrical freedoms, and the licence to mock powerful individuals (at least indirectly) that the *Atellanae* had traditionally enjoyed was periodically withdrawn. This might be by regulation (Tiberius), or by exemplary punishments, such as that meted out by Caligula to one writer of *Atellanae* burned in the arena for, as Suetonius would have it (*Caligula*, 27), a single ambiguous line.

Greek and Roman *mimiamboi* and mime

At some point in the fifth century BC in Syracuse, and probably drawing on the same unscripted mockery performances as Epicharmus, a writer named Sophron wrote short prose playlets, *mimiamboi*, divided into *andreidi* and *gunaideiei* (about men/women). From Alexandria, in the middle of the following century, some seven other *mimiamboi* and parts of an eighth, all by the hand of Herondas (or Herodas), with titles such as: *Brothel-keeper*, *Women Making a Dedication and Sacrifice to Asclepius*, *The Jealous Woman*, *The Shoemaker* and *The Dream*.

Like Hellenistic comedy, the tone of Herondas' *mimiamboi* was domestic. In *Woman Visiting for a Chat*, the protagonist discreetly asks her friend where she had such a good dildo made. There is also the occasional slapstick element, such as in the *Schoolteacher*, in which Metrotime complains at length about her good-for-nothing son Cottalus who, she claims, has reduced the family to penury through gambling; she begs Lampriscus the schoolmaster to beat sense into the boy. An extended whipping ensues with animated vocal protests from Cottalus, until the schoolmaster is ready to hang up his maiming oxtail scourge. The mother, however, wants more: 'Don't stop now, Lampriscus, flog on till sunset!'

Depending on who one reads, these *mimiamboi* were either hugely popular with the masses, or so sophisticated that only educated Alexandrian courtiers could have appreciated them; either performed on the stage by several actors, or a purely literary genre designed to be read by a single actor. What is almost certain is that *mimiamboi* were an offshoot of the unscripted theatrical genre, the mime, into which they give us a tantalizing insight.

Protogenes, a mime (as the actors were also called) performing around 210–160 BC, is the earliest actor recorded on a Roman inscription. Traditionally, mimes acted barefoot, while the favoured (but by no means only) costumes were a colourful patchwork tunic (*centunculus*) and a square-hooded cloak (*ricinium*). A small curtain, the *siparium*, was used to stage entrances and exits which, when set alongside the grand theatre curtain, the *aulaeum*, suggests how the mime sought to retain an improvised, makeshift quality even when performed by internationally renowned actors on the grandest stages in Rome.

Pliny the Younger in the first century AD writes that the clownish buf-foonery of the theatrical mime was also a popular dinnertime entertainment in the houses of the wealthy (*Epistles* 1.36; 9.17; 9.36), and Augustus him-self was fond of them in this context. When, as periodically happened, the mimes were banned from performing in the theatres, they took refuge as crowd-pleasers at horse races.

The adultery mime

The mime, like the *mimiamboi*, appears to have been at liberty to deal head-long with a theme that, while perhaps broached by the *Atellanae* and other regional Italian comic traditions, occurs in Greek comedy or the comic *fab-ula palliata* only incidentally, namely the adulterous wife. In Herondas' *The Procuress*, for example, Gyllis visits Metriche, a young wife whose hus-band is away on business, with news that a rich and handsome citizen has proposed a financially advantageous affair. Metriche appears scandalized at first: 'Never come again to my house with any such words!' But the feigned pose quickly collapses: 'But, say they, that is not the talk that Gyllis wants to hear: so, Threissa, wipe the cup clean and pour out three mea-sures of neat wine; dribble some water over it and give her a good dose.'[4] The adultery plot capitalized on the fact that large swathes of the social lives of women and men in antiquity were segregated, protecting against illegitimate sexual liaisons that would disrupt inheritance lines and social networks. In tragedy the pretext for 'women behaving badly' tended to be the long-absent husband or guardian, but mimes also showed how sup-posedly preventative women-only zones could become a blind spot defeat-ing male vigilance. In a typical adultery mime a scheming wife and her lover or lovers use the secrecy, and if necessary furnishings, of the women's quarter to dupe a buffoonish husband. It may be one of these scenes that Cicero has in mind when he refers to the typically abrupt ending of a mime as an escapee flees (*pro Caelio* 65) – the implication of the adultery plot seems pretty consistent: only a fool allows a woman to control her own sexuality.

Translation and adaptation: the Roman mime

Like the *Atellanae*, however, the Roman mime's aim was not to preserve its own integrity as a genre, but to please. As the unmasked counterpart to the masked Roman *Atellanae*, the Roman mime annexed all the popular theatrical and paratheatrical influences it could, from slapstick buffoonery and miscellaneous assortments of acrobatics, song-and-dance routines, jokes, magic tricks and erotic shows, to some surprisingly beautiful and serious-seeming forms, including poetry performances and pithily expressed philosophical sentiments. So broad was its reach that, in the Empire, the term mime came to mean everything on the Roman stage other than tragedy and pantomime (discussed below).

The first institution of the mime at games in Rome was at the spring *Floralia* festival in 173 BC, from which date the prostitutes of Rome performed a theatrical piece, perhaps a mythical burlesque, at the end of which they stripped naked. In 55 BC, Cato the Younger, somewhat neglecting his reputation for dignified austerity (he can hardly have been unaware of the usual bill of fare at the Floralia!) tried to catch some of the action. The performers and spectators proved 'inhibited' by his august presence and Cato was obliged to leave, thereby apparently demonstrating 'tolerance'.

We have forty-two surviving titles of mimes by the wealthy Equestrian, Decimus Laberius, from the late Republic, including: *The Etruscan Girl*, *The Hamper*, *The Wedding*, *Poverty*, *The Twins*, *The Fisherman*, *The Fireman*, *The Prophet* and *The Saturnalia*, indicating just how far the mime overlapped with the territory of scripted comedy and the *Atellanae*. Indeed, some of Laberius' mimes, like the *Pot of Gold* and *The Flatterer*, took their titles directly from plays by Menander, Naevius and Plautus. His style, too, while uniquely obscene and inventively witty, shares many qualities of his comic sources, being also lifelike, elegant and polished.

Also like the *Atellanae*, the Roman mime played an important role in giving the Roman public a means, albeit indirectly, of mocking individuals. Some of Laberius' mimes, such as *The Six-Fingered Man* and *The Gauls*, may have been satires of contemporary poets, Volcacius Sedigitus and C. Cornelius Gallus, and he pointed lines against Julius Caesar particularly when forced by him, although a Knight, to take to the stage himself (Suetonius *Caesar* 39; Macrobius *Saturnalia* 2.7.2; 2.7.6–7).

Clearly then, whether or not the earlier *mimiamboi* were performed, Roman writers did script mimes for performance, allowing the genre to harness the distinctive energies of both unscripted improvisation and scripted plot and dialogue. Cicero was dismissive of what he deemed the mime's coarse and unsophisticated verbal and physical humour. Some mimographers, however, such as the dictator Sulla and Laberius, were also from the highest social echelons, and there are indications that this could result in a more 'cultured' species of mime. For instance, one mime mentioned by Cicero in the last half-century of the Republic placed Euripides, Menander, Epicurus and Socrates at dinner together (we cannot tell if the anachronism was deliberate or accidental), thereby simultaneously sending up tragedy, philosophy, and the opulent dinner parties of the elite – all of which were probably regular targets of mimographers. The mimes of Publius Syrus, a rival of Laberius, contained epigrams which one ancient connoisseur at least considered to have exceeded even tragedy in wisdom and literary quality; indeed some – such as 'Do unto others as you would have them do unto you' – are in common usage to this day.

The erotic and the spectacular

The fifth-century BC Athenian writer Xenophon describes in his *Symposium* professional after-dinner entertainments provided by a Syracusan, who also toured a marionette-show for the benefit of 'simple-minded folk' (*Symposium* 4.55). Following juggling, acrobatics and dancing, came a performance of Dionysus' visit, heralded by Bacchic flute music, to Ariadne's chamber:

> Ariadne reacted so that everyone would realize she was filled with joy at the sound . . . When Dionysus saw her, he danced up like one madly in love, and sat on her lap and embraced and kissed her. She affected modesty, but still embraced him most lovingly in return. (The guests when they saw this, applauded and shouted, 'Encore!') When Dionysus rose and drew Ariadne up to stand with him, there was a mimicry of lovers kissing and fondling each other. The audience gazed at a truly handsome Dionysus, a beautiful Ariadne, not pretending but really kissing with their lips; all were aroused as they watched. For they also heard Dionysus asking her if she loved him, and her swearing that she did, so that all those present would have sworn that the boy and girl really loved each other. For they seemed not like actors who had learned a role, but like those who were now allowed to do what they had long desired. Finally, the guests, seeing them embracing and apparently heading for bed, got up, the unmarried swearing that they would get married at once, while those already married mounted their horses and rode off to their wives, to enjoy them.[5]

Figure 2. 'A revolving stage for dance-drama?'

The genre achieves sexual titillation through sensual arousal, relying upon the youthful beauty of its unmasked performers and their skill; though not a 'high' genre, neither is it a mockery.

This rarely published fresco, now lost (**Fig. 2**), from the House of the Four Styles, Pompeii (I.8.17), dated to the third quarter of the first century AD, may depict a theatrical form of dance drama, and is unique in possibly depicting a revolving scenic device. To the left, a young man garlanded with vine leaves and grapes carries sympotic vessels. To the right, the light-coloured rear walls of the revolving platform, draped with curtains but otherwise now largely obscure, once depicted architectural features. Upon the mobile dais, a young man and woman stand, behind them a young man on horseback, carrying a spear, cloak flying in the wind. In the foreground, two near-nude female warriors dance, apparently in time – again suggesting a theatrical, rather than purely mythological or symbolic, context.

Despite some scholarly speculation, the subject of the painting is not known, but it perhaps suggests a kind of performance not dissimilar to that described by Apuleius in the mid-second century AD, who set a fictional account of theatrical entertainments in the Roman colony at Corinth. As in Xenophon, an erotically charged dance drama also figures prominently.

The show begins with patterned dance-cycles by 'boys and girls in the bloom of verdant youth, outstanding in beauty, resplendent in costume and graceful in movement', after which 'the curtain was raised, the screens folded back' heralding the Judgement of Paris. The scene is Mount Ida, a lofty wooden set 'planted with bushes and live trees' and a fountain pouring from its peak. Goats grazed in the low grasses:

> A young man, beautifully attired like the Phrygian shepherd Paris, with exotic robes flowing over his shoulders and a golden tiara covering his head, was feigning mastery of the flock. Then a radiantly beautiful boy appeared, naked except for an ephebic cape covering his left shoulder. He attracted all eyes with his blond curls, and from his hair projected little golden wings symmetrically attached; a caduceus and wand identifying him as Mercury.

Mercury is replaced by 'a girl of respectable appearance' playing Juno and one playing Minerva, but both are then overshadowed by a 'surpassingly beautiful' Venus:

> She displayed a perfect figure, her body naked and uncovered except for a piece of sheer silk with which she veiled her comely charms. An inquisitive little breeze would at one moment blow this veil aside in wanton playfulness so that it lifted to reveal the flower of her youth, and at another moment it would gust exuberantly against it so that it clung tightly and graphically delineated her body's voluptuousness.

Juno and Venus each have a pair of dancing attendants, but again Venus steals the show:

> Venus, amidst loud applause from the audience, delightfully took her position at the very centre of the stage, smiling sweetly and surrounded by a whole mob of happy little boys. You would have said that those soft, round, milky-skinned babies were real Cupids . . . Then in streamed handsome groups of

unwed girls, on one side the graceful Graces, on the other the lovely Hours, worshipping their goddess by throwing garlands and loose flowers; they formed a most elegant dance-pattern as they beguiled the Queen of pleasures with the tresses of Spring. Now flutes with many stops played Lydian melodies in sweet harmony; and while these tunes were delightfully charming the spectators' hearts, far more delightfully Venus started gently to move. With slow hesitant step and smoothly undulating body and gently moving head she began to walk forward, and to respond to the soft sound of the flutes with delicate movements. She gestured with her glances, now softly languid, now sharply threatening, and sometimes she would dance with her eyes alone.

Paris eagerly hands Venus the golden apple and Venus, victorious, dances with her chorus. As in Xenophon, great emphasis is placed on the physical beauty and artistic delicacy of the unmasked performers although, in this case, the young actors do not speak, perhaps lacking the vocal presence necessary to command such a huge and rowdy crowd. Apuleius' dance drama concludes with a piece of scenic wizardry:

> From a hidden pipe at the very peak of the mountain, saffron dissolved in wine came spurting up into the air and rained down in a fragrant shower, sprinkling the goats that were grazing all round, until, dyed to a greater beauty, they exchanged their natural whiteness for a yellow hue. Finally, when the theatre was filled with the delightful fragrance, a chasm in the earth opened and swallowed up the wooden mountain.[6]

This spectacular scenery is the kind of thing that had evidently been happening in the theatre for centuries. In the third century BC, Philon of Byzantium described how to build a fully operational miniature theatre. His automatic theatre, 'improved upon' in the first century AD by Heron of Alexandria, used a combination of intricate time-release mechanisms connected to all manner of rotating, sliding, raising, lowering and igniting objects, to perform a scenario called *Nauplius* including a coastal storm, complete with leaping dolphins (**Fig. 3**), lightning, live flame beacons on the shore and a pop-up Athena. It is clear from Heron's account that these automata were evoking the kind of scenic fare spectators could expect in an actual theatre.

Seneca the Younger, in the age of Nero, describes 'a structure that soars up by itself, or wooden panels that rise silently aloft, and many other unexpected devices such as objects fit together which come apart, or things separate which automatically join together, or objects which stand erect, then slowly collapse' (*Epist. Morales* 1.88.22), and in c.400 AD Claudian describes theatrical pyrotechnics: 'on the lofty stage let men circle like a chorus, scattering flames; let Vulcan mould balls of flame to roll harmlessly over the panels and

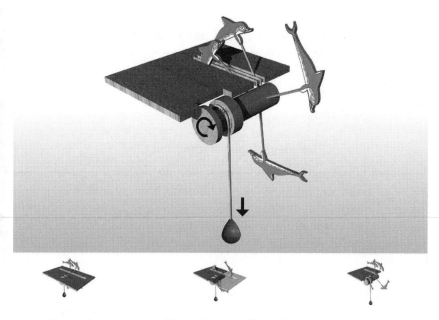

Figure 3. Reconstruction of the weighted spindle mechanism animating Heron's automated dolphins.

swift flames play about the painted beans, and a tame fire, not allowed to rest, roam amongst the untouched towers' (Claudius Claudianus *Panegyricus M. Theodoro* 323–30). Such mimes catered to a taste for the spectacular by showing in full what tragedy and comedy only reported.

The arena, too, constantly sought titillating novelties, and so looked to the theatre for ideas, 'theatricalizing' gladiatorial combats and exhibition executions by casting them as re-enactments of famous battles or events.[7] The theatre found it profitable to borrow back from the arena, bringing the gore of the arena onto the stage. Both theatrical domains – theatre and amphitheatre – became locked in an aesthetic embrace. At first, the mime only simulated arena-style entertainments, such as in the popular *Laureolus* of Catullus, 'at the close of which', Suetonius records, 'the leading character, a brigand, had to die while escaping, and vomit blood'. At one performance in *c*.40 AD, it was 'immediately followed by a humorous afterpiece – the comedians were so anxious to display their proficiency at dying that they flooded the stage with blood' (*Caligula* 57).

But with novel, spectacular titillation the goal, it was only a matter of time before stage blood was replaced by the real thing – what one might call the 'amphitheatrical turn' in Roman mime – and the mime was required to *become* what it previously only acted: the emperor Elagabalus (218–222 AD) stipulated that mimes should no longer only simulate, but actually have sex. Sex and death come together even in Apuleius' account: the beautiful mime in Book 10 of the *Metamorphoses*, described above, was to be followed by an 'animal act' in which a condemned woman was to be mounted by a donkey (the narrator) on a luxurious bed centre-stage, before being torn apart by wild animals.

Roman pantomime: tragic and comic

In around the second half of the first century BC, another theatrical genre began to take root in the theatrical culture of Rome, one that eventually exceeded even tragedy itself in popularity: tragic pantomime. Surprisingly, the appeal of tragic pantomime may largely be attributed to its *refusal*, in general, to surrender to the 'amphitheatrical turn' or the pursuit of novelty.

Roman tragic pantomime was visually and acoustically optimized for performance within the vast stone theatres that began to appear in the city of Rome from 55 BC, sharing with the dance dramas that doubtless influenced it an emphasis on graceful dance with musical accompaniment. However, in contrast to their overt eroticism and youthful unmasked performers, each dancing a single role, the Roman pantomime centred upon a virtuoso, masked performer who assumed several roles in the course of a performance, switching mask from role to role. He, or in time she, was accompanied by a second actor functioning almost as a human 'prop'.

Pantomime was also dissimilar to the mime in that it deliberately sustained aesthetic distance from reality by separating out the sign-systems of performance: the performer danced expressively, in particular with hand movements, but did not speak, and his or her beautiful masks, unlike tragedy or comedy, had closed mouths. In earlier versions of the pantomime, the words may have been sung by a single, non-dancing, performer but, perhaps as a result of innovations by two star dancers, Pylades and Bathyllus, the Italian-style pantomime used several musicians, rhythmically singing and playing instruments in chorus or individually.[8]

The tragic pantomime had a mocking counterpart: the comic pantomime. These mythological burlesques may have differed from the tragic pantomime more in mood than in form. The comic style was particularly associated with Bathyllus, but after a brief period of popularity during his lifetime, the genre fades from the historical record. There was nothing, it seems, that comic pantomime could do that was not already on offer in the all-encompassing mime or the *Atellanae* and, unlike them, the comic pantomime was, perhaps, insufficiently flexible to absorb or develop the theatrical spectacles and novelties, or above all the 'amphitheatricalism' that Roman audiences required of their mockery genres.

By contrast, the tragic pantomime (henceforth 'pantomime') became a beloved element in the collective memory culture of Rome, with individual plays repeated over centuries, sometimes scripted by prestigious poets. Ovid recounts how, during the festival of Anna Perenna when the city folk picnicked in the countryside, they 'sing whatever they have learnt in the theatre and move their hands easily to the words',[9] while in Nero's Rome, both men and women were evidently performing pantomime on private stages throughout the city (Seneca *Naturales Quaestiones* 7.32.3). The social and cultural elite could act as connoisseurs of poetic quality, while the mythological subjects, music and movement were intuitively and emotionally accessible to all. Theatre spectators were also highly partisan, supporting their favourites, shouting down rivals and creating rhythmic patterns of clapping and chanting which, from what we can tell, were so highly developed that mass cheerleading became something of an art-form in its own right.

The cult of the actor

In Rome, a popular professional actor enjoying the adulation of the crowd, whether mime or pantomime, could shape the political responses of the spectators, pointing lines for or against certain causes or individuals. Consequently, it was all too easy for the line separating symbolic from actual power – upon which theatrical licence depended – to grow faint. Rival pantomime factions came to blows in the reign of Augustus, and full-scale pantomime riots instigated by scheming politicians in later years killed thousands. By stimulating its spectators' imagination, rather than their taste for spectacle and titillation, the restrained aesthetic of the pantomime appears to have intensified rather than diminished the emotional immediacy of its performances to the extent that spectators, manipulated by scheming politicians, sometimes rioted, killing thousands. Already in the letters of the late Republic, we see politicians coordinating their movements to optimize theatrical approval or limit damage. In short, a political order that exercised power by manipulation of the religious and aesthetic domain could easily be threatened by its theatrical double.

Actors posed such a danger to elite interests that preventative measures were enacted. The more subtle approach was to appropriate the cultural currency of the theatre, which politicians and emperors did with gusto, styling and displaying themselves with the roles and attributes with which they wished to be associated, even at times adopting, like actors, the imagery and paraphernalia of gods. Some of the more theatrically inclined Roman rulers encouraged citizens of high rank to take to the stage themselves, both in private and in public; once, during games under Nero, a well-known Equestrian was to be seen riding an elephant as it walked down a sloping tightrope. Nero himself, of course, was a walking microcosm of the theatre: musician, tragedian, would-be pantomime: actor triumphant.

Alternatively, one could draw upon the popularity of the star actor; in the late Republic, for example, Sulla the dictator loved Metrobius the actor, while the famed actress, Cytheris, was beloved of both Mark Antony and Brutus. Cicero, acting as advocate for the great comic actor Roscius, captured the social ambivalence of such liaisons well when he described his client as 'an artist of such excellence that he alone seems fit to appear on the stage, and a man of such character that he alone seems fit not to go there' (Cicero *Pro Roscio Comoedo* 18). Even marriages were not out of the question: in the sixth century AD, the Emperor Justinian wedded the retired actress, Theodora. But appropriation and association were not always reliable means of neutralizing a performer's power – on the contrary: as courtiers and consorts to the powerful, actors could become highly influential (Juvenal 7.87 ff.).

When co-option proved too dangerous, difficult or distasteful, a less benign approach suggested itself; the ruling classes sought to defuse the power of actors by formally depriving them of the rights and privileges of citizenship (thereby branding them *infames*), from time to time subjecting them to additional, exemplary sanctions. The mimes were periodically driven out of Rome (Justinian himself shut down the theatres around 526 AD), and summarily executed for real or imagined transgressions. Pylades himself, the creator and darling of the Roman tragic pantomime, was temporarily exiled in 18 BC for merely gesturing at a hostile spectator. Actors, it seems, were useful for those seeking mass popularity, but could quickly be dropped if association with them became a liability with the powerful, conservative moral minority, or their manipulation of theatrical licence a direct threat.

The death of theatre

By the late Empire, both mime and pantomime were being periodically banned in response to the very real threat they represented to the ruling order, and subsequently rehabilitated in response to popular demand. To defeat the theatre altogether, an additional source of power was required – one capable of persuading and coercing the people themselves to desert the theatre: religion.

As Christianity became an increasingly powerful cultural presence, it predictably entered the mime's repertoire of religious burlesques, while through their myth-based performances, both mime and pantomime continued to promulgate and popularize Christ's religious rivals, the Roman gods. As its secular power grew, the Church exploited a long tradition of Roman anti-theatricalism and moral conservatism to encourage sanctions against the theatre, at the same time threatening his own followers with excommunication for theatrical attendance. By combining secular and sacred power, the Church finally succeeded in using the perceived 'immorality' of the Roman mime to discredit and destroy the great and ancient institution of the theatre, although it took some time: mimes were still being banned in 692 AD.

Officially frowned upon, legislated against and starved of funding, theatre disappeared from the official records. Late Roman mime and pantomime could not survive such economic privation; if theatrical activities persisted, it was in a much diminished form, probably by itinerant entertainers with no stage except what they could carry with them. Did the arts of writing and performing plays survive, or just a patchwork of tumbling, singing, dancing, jesting and juggling acts? We do not know. But weddings, harvests and other moments in the calendar will always be celebrated with song and dance, and what grew up once from those needs will grow up again if allowed, particularly if some traditions can be kept alive.

Only a couple of hundred years later, it was the Church itself that resuscitated theatre, realizing, as had earlier emperors, that it could with profit be appropriated as well as suppressed. The first 'liturgical dramas' in the tenth century AD harnessed again the power of personation for religious purposes, and as the veil lifts from the documentary record, extra-ecclesiastical performances begin to be mentioned that sound not unlike some of the forms that had been 'lost'.

It was the new religion's investment in the authority of the written word that caused the ancient scripted dramas to be preserved and venerated, enabling writers of the new age, like those of earlier centuries, very rapidly to adapt prior theatrical traditions for new purposes and conditions. Such were the dramas of Hroswitha of Gandersheim (935–1001 AD), whose neo-Terentian, devotional dramas are a quiet landmark in the rebirth of western drama. That the Church, erstwhile destroyer of the sacred art of the theatre, should be responsible for resurrecting it, and that it should do so by means of the written word – so often the latecomer at the theatrical feast in antiquity – are ironies that Epicharmus and his successors would have been the first to enjoy, and to mock.

NOTES

1. G. M. Sifakis, *Parabasis and Animal Choruses* (London: Athlone Press, 1971), pp. 76–7.
2. Horace *Epist.* 2.1.139ff., trans. R. Beacham in *The Roman Theatre and Its Audience* (Cambridge, Mass.: Harvard University Press, 1991), pp. 3–4.
3. C. T. Murphy, 'Popular Comedy in Aristophanes', *American Journal of Philology* 93.369 (1972), 182.
4. Herodas: *The Mimes and Fragments*, notes by W. Headlam, A. D. Knox (ed.) (Bristol: Bristol Classical Press, 2001), p. 9.
5. Xenophon *Symposium* (9, 1–7), Murphy, C. T. (trans.), in 'Popular Comedy in Aristophanes', *American Journal of Philology* 93.369 (1972), 175.
6. Apulcius *Metamorphoses* 10.29–34, J. A. Hanson (trans.) (Harvard: Loeb Classical Library, 1989).
7. See K. M. Coleman, 'Fatal Charades: Roman Executions Staged as Mythological Enactments', *Journal of Roman Studies* 80 (1990), 44–73.
8. E. J. Jory, 'Literary Evidence for the Beginnings of Imperial Pantomime', *Bulletin of the Institute of Classical Studies* 28 (1981), 147–61.
9. *Fasti* 3.535–6, E. Csapo and W. J. Slater (trans.), *The Context of Ancient Drama* (Ann Arbor: University of Michigan Press, 1995), p. 313.

FURTHER READING

Beacham, R. C., *The Roman Theatre and Its Audience*. London: Routledge, 1996.

Csapo, E. and Slater, W. J., *The Context of Ancient Drama*. Ann Arbor: University of Michigan Press, 1995.

Jory, E. J., 'The Drama of the Dance: Prolegomena to an Iconography of Imperial Pantomime', in W. J. Slater (ed.), *Roman Theater and Society*. Ann Arbor: University of Michigan Press, 1996, pp. 1–28.

Pickard-Cambridge, A. W., *Dithyramb, Tragedy and Comedy*, second ed. Oxford: Clarendon Press, 1996.

Sifakis, G. M., *Parabasis and Animal Choruses*. London: Athlone Press, 1971.

Taplin, O., *Comic Angels and Other Approaches to Greek Drama through Vase-Painting*. Oxford: Clarendon Press, 1993.

PART TWO

The nature of performance

9

RICHARD GREEN

Art and theatre in the ancient world

In assessing the relationship between art and the theatre in the ancient world, we must be clear about a number of issues, not least the importance of theatre itself in ancient society, since it was surely its perceived importance above all that prompted echoes of its activity in more permanent form.

From the perspective of the audience, Greek theatre possessed a number of significant attractions. They included the very spectacle of the presentation, with its processions, colourful costumes, music, and the element of competition between the writers, between the sponsors and between the actors. It was presented at key religious festivals which were themselves highlights in the communities' annual calendar. The audience therefore participated with a heightened sense of awareness and it must have recalled the festivals in much the same way. Important in the plays themselves was the enjoyment of the dramatic situation and of the competing agendas and motives of the participating characters; but one should not forget, either, the visualization of events, their instantiation before the eyes of the audience. We in our society have become so used to the process, so sated with images from cinema, television, newspapers, books, magazines, billboards in public spaces, that we tend to blot them out of our consciousness in self-defence at the overload of information. Classical Greeks had no such experience. Paintings were comparatively rare, and when they did exist – as in the Painted Stoa in Athens – they were found striking and became famous. The rarity of visual media also helps explain the importance of architectural sculpture in friezes and pediments, items that are by and large out of fashion in modern society where the need for images is catered for by other means. In a similar way, this search for a means of creating images of another world (that was at the same time their own) helps explain the way that pictures on pottery became such an important medium in the archaic and classical world. We cannot underestimate the importance and, in the early years the novelty, of having their own myth-history and more generally recognizable human situations played out before their eyes in a way that seemed reasonably convincing.

To see the lives of others played out for us is a human need which we all share, at least to some degree. The Greeks were the first to exploit this in a very creative way and, by contrast with other small-scale societies, in a way that went beyond the re-enactments associated with cultic festivals.

All this said, we need to bear in mind that Greek theatre was staged for the best part of a thousand years (roughly from 500 BC to 500 AD) and that, just as the performances themselves changed, at times almost beyond recognition, so too did their role in society and, conversely, society's reaction to them. Thus, the ways in which and the purposes for which they were recorded in visual media also changed enormously over the millennium.

Greek pottery is remarkable for the way it carried images and this is of course one of the reasons why it has attracted so much modern attention. As with other media, however, the approach of the vase-painter and the subject-matter he or she felt it appropriate to apply changed through time, and this in turn has its effect on what we should expect of the image in terms of its evidence for ancient theatre. It is arguable that vase-painting in general during the eighth, the seventh and a good part of the sixth centuries BC was not concerned with scenes of everyday life so much as with meaningful myth-history and, in the earlier years, fearsome and powerful creatures like lions and sphinxes that also had a symbolic value. This is not to say, of course, that the depictions were irrelevant to daily life; it is often demonstrable that they held a symbolic force relevant to the needs, problems and/or ideals of contemporary society. As a straightforward example, the heroic activity of Achilles as a warrior could be taken as something for a young Athenian to emulate. Thus, when we have depictions of proto-comic choruses in the second half of the sixth and the early fifth century, they represent a considerable break from tradition, but they were nonetheless acceptable because at one level they were representations of creations of strange, foreign and probably also mythical (at least in the sense of invented) people and animals. So, in turn, when in the fifth century we come to have depictions deriving from tragedy, they fit into the prevailing mindset because they show figures of Greek myth-history, even if the vase-painters were inspired to do so by the recreations of myth-history that they had seen in the theatre. It is only in the later part of the fifth century that we begin to find depictions of the actuality of theatre performance, and then it mainly concerns comedy.

At the same time, in assessing the importance of painted pottery as a source of visual imagery in the Athenian community, we need to remember that it was not inexpensive and that the bulk of it seems to have been exported. In Athens it is arguable that ownership tended to rest with the well-to-do. Theatre, on the other hand, seems to have had a broad popular appeal, and its audience included vase-painters, as the evidence clearly shows.

A further factor that we might bear in mind in reading the evidence is the way the vase-paintings, too, were constructed as recreating a situation for the viewer, one that involved movement and sound – as can be seen from the way that the participants are shown as making noise, singing, shouting, gesturing in ways that seem to us extravagant: occasionally they have words shown as coming from their mouths. These were not quasi-photographic pictures. We should also remember that they were created for a society that was still largely oral rather than one that was in the habit of reading texts: the scenes on the vases were not, as it were, passive depictions but ones that acted as a prompt for the viewer that he could explain, recalling the situations created on the vase and the stories that lay behind them.

This background helps explain the phenomenon of the so-called padded dancers of the second half of the seventh and the first half of the sixth centuries BC. The figures are taken to represent an early form of drama inasmuch as they appear to show men dressed up in costume performing dance and in rare cases enacting a story, such as the Return of Hephaestus – in essence a story to do with the power of wine – or being punished for misbehaviour with regard to wine.[1] We tend to associate them with the pottery of Corinth, but they are also found in that of Sparta, East Greece (e.g. Samos), a western colony (probably Reggio Calabria), Boeotia and Athens. There are occasionally names written alongside the performers, characterizing them as spirit figures rather than everyday humans. They are often shown with ritual drinking vessels and sometimes they are shown around a symposium, perhaps honouring assembled divinities. They seem therefore to be in some way associated with Dionysus as god of wine, and we for our part remember that Dionysus comes to be god of theatre. Nevertheless we should reckon that the figures may not necessarily have stood for precisely the same thing in all centres and the gods involved may not always have been the same in all regional cultures. The prominence of Corinth in the material evidence may not mean that Corinth was more advanced in primitive theatre than other cities: she after all had the most active pottery industry and therefore produced the most evidence, and probably inspired vase-painters in other centres to show their own versions of what was happening locally.

Padded dancers disappeared from the visual arts in the middle of the sixth century BC. One may ask whether two other phenomena which appeared at about that time took their place, at least in Athens: satyrs and early comic choruses. For now there can be no clear answer. Nor do we in fact know whether the players we call padded dancers themselves disappeared throughout the Greek world within this relatively short space of time. Their depictions may simply have gone out of fashion. The satyrs we see on vases give little hint of those later associated with the satyr play, but the early

Figure 4. Musician and mounted chorus, second half of the sixth century BC.

comic choruses are clear, specific and evident predecessors of the choruses of fifth-century Athenian comedy.[2]

The example on an amphora in Berlin belongs relatively early in the sequence, about 540–530 BC (**Fig. 4**).[3] It has three performers in front of the piper who provides the music. They act as knights, astride the shoulders of men dressed as horses. They wear corselets and helmets. Between them and the piper is written *eiocheochê*, which has reasonably been thought to mean 'giddy-up, giddy-up', presumably part of their song. Red was added for the tunics of the 'horses' (though apparently not for the tails attached at the back), for decorative dots on the tunics of the riders and for their helmets. The same colour is also used to decorate the cloak of the piper and for a festive fillet about his head. Although it is fairly simply done in this case, the applied colour gives us some idea of the importance of costume on these vases, and it seems from other cases too that it was an important factor in staging. The elaborate costume of the piper is also typical: for as long as we can trace them, they wore richly decorated clothing for this festive occasion (compare for example **Fig. 6**). Finally we may notice the crests of the helmets. They are all different. This variation of detail within the standard costume of a chorus is common to most of the series. But we may also notice that they are not standard Athenian helmet-types for the period: the first has long feathers, the second a crescent-shaped piece, and the third a cross-filled ring.

Figure 5. Two chorusmen in bird costume, early fifth century BC.

They are depicted as foreign cavalry. From our perspective we can see that they may have been thought of as coming from the hill country of southern Italy, but that may be reading too much into it. They may simply be strangers.

Our other sample is a jug in the British Museum (**Fig. 5**).[4] It dates from about 500–490 BC. The scene has two birdmen dancing before a piper against a background of ivy, which of course emphasizes the Dionysiac context. Their human faces have red beards and large pointed noses; on their heads are pronounced red crests or combs. They wear body-tights decorated for the most part with arcs or circles, probably to indicate feathers, although the one nearer the piper simply has short strokes on his body, right arm and right thigh. It is likely that they are intended to indicate the finer feathers of the under-body. Their wings seem to be relatively loose and pliable. The left figure has his chest towards us so that we see their underside; they fall over the arm and are gripped by a strap or cord near their ends (clearly visible at the dancer's right hand). The pose of the right dancer is more difficult to make out; he must have his back towards us and we see the back of his wings. The black of the wings here has turned slightly brown in the firing of the vase and it is just possible to make out two lines of a purer black which come down his left (rear) wing showing the outline of his arm. They must be where the added white has worn away. There are traces of actual white remaining at the edge of the other wing, and there are lines continuing from them which also seem to have shown the outline of the arm, but they are less clear. There are also traces of white touches by the upper and lower edges of the wing. That we can see the outline of the arm through the wing suggests that the wings were somewhat transparent and certainly lightweight, easily flapped with the arms but also tending to float.

A curious feature of their costume is the protrusion at each knee. Some are done in red, others in black. It seems that, as with the combs, the red here was added over black, and it is more than likely that they represent the birds' feet. They are above ground level as the dancers move: the 'bird' is therefore in its natural state of movement, flying. If they are to rest, it would not be difficult for the chorusmen to kneel, and a kneeling position would give a suitable imitation of birds at rest.

Here too we gain some sense of the perceived importance of the costume as it was presented in the theatre, not to mention the way that the vase-painters observed it and were able to reproduce it some time later in the workshop. In early comedy, the chorus stands for the comedy as a whole and identifies the performance. This is a convention that would last a long time in Athens, at least as late as the middle of the fourth century BC, and we can remember at the same time that the titles of the plays in the written tradition were those of the choruses (as *Knights*, *Wasps* or *Frogs*). The character of the chorus is again one of alien beings, this time non-human, and if we think of the transmitted titles of Old Comedy, this is what they are, even down to the time when the tradition is weakening, as with *Acharnians*, who are conceived as a special group, more belligerent than ordinary Athenians, or *Women in Assembly*, politicized women who are a figment of Aristophanes' imagination.

At around the time the Birds vase was made, in the first decade of the fifth century BC, we begin to find a wider range of scenes in vase-painting that seem to derive from theatre, from both tragedy and the satyr play. Those concerning tragedy are far more difficult to detect, for the reason that the audience (and therefore the vase-painter as a member of that audience) seems to have regarded its performances as recreations or re-enactments of myth-history. To put it another way, the dramatic illusion was near-complete; the performance, for all its conventions, was seen as a window on another world, not actors acting. So, when the vase-painter reproduced the situation on a pot, he showed the figures as 'real', as the performers had created them. For us it is therefore very difficult to know when a scene on a vase has been inspired by the theatre rather than a recital of a poem or some other event, even a request from a customer who had his own reason for wanting a pot decorated with a particular theme. We can sometimes guess that an image implies a dramatic context, for example when there suddenly appears a series of vase-paintings on a theme we know from historical evidence to have been the subject of a play or plays at that period, but it is difficult to know for sure unless they involve some strikingly individual innovation that we can pin down to a given writer. And then there are all the plays that must have existed but of which we have never heard. Our knowing or not knowing about them is hardly a valid criterion for estimating their popular impact at the time.

Satyr play is sometimes a little easier since, as a genre, it may be argued to have fallen between tragedy and comedy, and vase-painters sometimes showed it in the further reality typical of tragedy, and sometimes in the actuality of performance typical of the (more literal) representation of comic scenes. The late sixth and early fifth centuries seem to have been the heyday of the satyr play with authors such as Pratinas and then the early Aeschylus among its most noted practitioners. A good example is the scene on the shoulder of a hydria in Boston of about 480/470 BC (**Fig. 6**). This is the fullest literal depiction we have of a satyr play. On the right is the piper in his elaborate costume and behind him a man who may be the producer or the playwright. In front of him five satyrs of the chorus dance vigorously and begin to erect the various parts of a symposium couch and, at the far left, perhaps a table. The painter has made the artificiality of the masks evident as well as the typical drawers with a tail attached at the back and a *phallos* at the front. An excellent example of the further or interpreted reality is a depiction of Aeschylus' *Sphinx* of 467 BC.[5] A group of old satyrs, by their sceptres and cloaks a parody on the Elders of Thebes, sits before the figure of the Sphinx and doubtless will puzzle hopelessly and ridiculously over the riddle. Their elegant chairs are portable and could be carried in and out of the *orchêstra* without trouble in the course of the performance.

When we come to scenes deriving from tragedy, we may think, for example, of a series concerned with the deaths of Agamemnon and Aegisthus

Figure 6.   Satyrs and a musician, *c.*480–470 BC.

contemporary with and slightly earlier than Aeschylus' *Oresteia.*[6] What the sequence and chronology of the vases make clear is that the hero's entanglement in a net, often thought to be an Aeschylean invention, is seen earlier than the *Oresteia* and must have been due to an earlier playwright. There is no problem in this: it is simply another example of the shared, cumulative development of theatrical themes, between playwright-directors, as it were bouncing off each other, until a motif was felt to be exhausted. Athenian theatre in the fifth century was a communal effort and at the same time highly competitive, with new ideas and new staging constantly introduced to currently popular themes. Another such case is found with the Telephus story, first seen on a red-figure *pelikê* in the British Museum of the middle of the fifth century that seems to reflect Aeschylus' version.[7] Euripides wrote a somewhat later version which apparently increased the tension in the key scene, and that in turn was parodied by Aristophanes (presumably because he thought it could be regarded as rather over-the-top), first in *Acharnians* in 425 BC and a second time in *Women at the Thesmophoria* in 411 BC. A later performance of the latter in Taranto is to be seen on a vase now in Würzburg, datable to about 380–370 BC.[8] (See **Fig. 1**.) Despite its ongoing importance, we should remember that in many respects the theatre of Athens in the fifth century was a small world in which the key participants, both writers and actors, were well known to each other, whether as friends or rivals.

Another case of a recurring theme involves Andromeda. Although it was the subject of a play by Euripides, the earlier and highly creative version seems to have been one by Sophocles, written in the 440s. Only minor quotations from the text are preserved, but we have at least five contemporary vases by different painters that show slightly different moments of a critical scene of the play.

The storyline is a relatively simple one: Andromeda was the daughter of the king of the Ethiopians, Cepheus. Her mother, like so many in the ancient world, it would seem, was boastful, claiming that her daughter was finer than the Nereids of the sea. They were upset and called on their protector Poseidon to do something about it. He sent a monster up from the sea to ravage the land of the Ethiopians who, in despair at their deprivation and near-starvation, called on Cepheus to save them. An oracle advised him that he should sacrifice his daughter, the fair princess, to the monster. He was placed in a dilemma typical of Sophoclean theatre, whether to place family concerns ahead of those for the state. In the end he decided for the greater good and we see the result on the series of vases. On the one in Agrigento, a large white-ground calyx-krater (**Fig. 7**), Andromeda is in the centre tied to stakes.[9]

All the vases of the series show this in some fashion, whether she is in the process of being exposed and the stakes being fixed, or as here. They consistently show her in the trousers of an oriental, with a short tunic and an eastern cap, and this is surely how Sophocles depicted her on stage. (We may note in passing that the series is evidence of relatively naturalistic costume and bear in mind that it is roughly contemporary with the sculpture of the Parthenon.) Sophocles' talent as a stage-director as well as playwright is not always well recognized. In this case we have evidence that he must have made a stunning impact. Other vases show her being led onto the stage by a group of black (Ethiopian) slaves, the stakes set in place, and her being tied up, arms apart, exposed for the monster. While we are somewhat inured to such a pose, applied to a female in classical Greece, and exposing her as it did to the male gaze with its emphasis on her body, it was shocking. Furthermore the other vases show that the slaves also carried offerings, objects associated with weddings and/or funerals of women. Sophocles set before the audience the question of whether she was being sent to her death or set up for some travesty of a wedding for the pleasure of the monster. Cepheus, who was

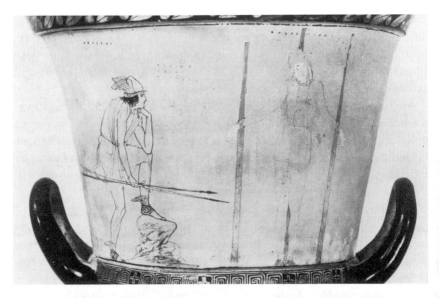

Figure 7. Sophocles' *Andromeda*, middle of the fifth century BC.

compelled to arrange this, is shown to the right of the scene, his head bowed. It so happened, however, that Perseus was flying across the Aegean after beheading the Gorgon Medusa. Looking down, he saw Andromeda tied up on the shore and flew in to investigate – we see him on the left. One senses something of the dialogue in progress. The next element was presumably not shown, his killing of the monster, nor do we know if Sophocles had them marry in the end or not. They do in later versions of the story, but it was not necessary here.

By the head of Perseus, the vase-painter wrote *Euaion kalos Aischylou* (Euaion the son of Aeschylus is fair). There are other indications that Euaion practised acting, it would seem (at this period at least) with a preference for the roles of youthful heroes and women. Theatre in the fifth century was the province of what we might call the gifted, distinguished amateur with an upper-class background. It also tended to be a family profession. The inclusion of his patronymic is by this period rather conservative, a last vestige, perhaps, of the old aristocratic way, suggesting the contemporary view of Aeschylus and his family.

The same painter decorated a vase now in Boston with a scene of two chorusmen preparing to enter the theatre (**Fig. 8**). Like all chorusmen, they are beardless young men. The one on the right already wears the tunic for the part (they will play women, perhaps maenads) and he is pulling on one

Figure 8.   Chorusmen with mask on the floor.

of his soft leather boots (*kothornoi*). His mask lies on the ground in front of him. It gives a very good idea of a mask of the classical period: it covers the head to the back of the neck, totally concealing the identity of the performer. The young man on the left already wears his mask and it is significant that he begins to perform: in wearing his mask he has taken on the identity of the part and so is shown as acting that part. One could point to other examples of the same phenomenon and it points to the thought-process that prompted vase-painters to show performers in tragedy as 'real'.

Here too the costume and the mask are relatively simple and naturalistic. The tragic mask with a tower of hair at the front (the *onkos*), heavy formal clothing and the platform boots would not start to emerge for over a century and in fact only became pronounced in the Late Hellenistic and Roman periods. One can read this style as reflecting the values of the high Classical Period when it was considered proper not to give much visible expression to the emotions. Compare, for example, the scenes of the battle between the Lapiths and the Centaurs on the metopes from the southern side of the Parthenon: the centaurs have faces distorted with the effort of the struggle whereas the Lapiths, as Greeks, have totally calm faces. So too Athena, even when shown fighting the Giants, is given a completely neutral expression. Tragic masks acquired wrinkles and frowns only from about 330 BC. Similarly, off the stage, upper-class Athenians were not supposed to dash about when in public, but to walk calmly and sedately, and to refrain from looking around wildly. Calm faces and straight noses were what was proper. Snub noses, as seen on satyrs, centaurs and Socrates, were considered a sign of subversiveness, on girls a sign of cheekiness.

In the later years of the fifth century, tragic costume became more elaborately decorated, in parallel with the so-called Rich Style seen in art of the period. At that point it began to move away from what might be worn offstage and to develop its own culture and conventions with their own levels of meaning. It slowly moved away from the naturalistic (insofar as theatre can ever be said to be naturalistic) as comedy moved towards it – exchanging territory, it could be said.

Athenian drama was already beginning to be performed outside the city in the later years of the fifth century. Pottery made in Taranto, Metaponto and soon afterwards Syracuse clearly reflects local performances of tragedy, satyr play and comedy. Identifiable examples include Euripides' *Antiope* and *Children of Heracles* and his satyr play *Cyclops*. (We shall look at examples of comedy below.) Like Athenians, the Greeks of Southern Italy followed the convention of depicting scenes as if they were drawn from myth. What is particularly interesting in this case is that tragedy was appealing to large audiences in these centres in a period before these plays could have been regarded as 'classics'. It must have been seen not only as attractive but as having universal values applicable to Greeks as a whole. Indeed it is arguable that drama was already coming to be regarded as standing for Greek culture by people in colonial contexts, something it demonstrably did later.

In the fourth century reflections of theatre became more common on the pottery of the Greek towns of Southern Italy, and especially Taranto, than on Athenian, and it has been suggested that this was due largely to a difference in cultural practice. The more elaborate Tarentine vases rapidly came to be specialist productions for the grave and that in turn seems to have encouraged the depiction of particular myths in a formal balance with funerary scenes. The choice of myth was therefore dictated by their relevance in the funerary context: Niobe, for example, mourning at the grave of her children; Alcestis as the perfect wife who would even give her life for her husband; young men taken away by the gods in the prime of their lives, doubtless for a better life in the company of the gods. It has been argued that these often elaborate scenes had a context in the funerary ritual when a speaker would retail the story and demonstrate its allegorical relevance to the deceased. Theatre and key scenes from the plays had come to be a common currency, certainly by the middle years of the fourth century, to be quoted at key moments of ritual, at times of stress for the surviving family.

The Tarentine vases have scenes from contemporary playwrights as much as from the tragedians we would regard as classical, and it helps demonstrate that in their day they were regarded as just as important. It is we, brought up in the inherited tradition of texts of the fifth-century playwrights, who have until recently thought of the fourth century as a period of decline – despite the fact that this was a major period of theatre construction throughout the Greek world.[10]

The red-figure technique of decorating pottery died away in the later years of the fourth century throughout the Greek world and with it the possibility of creating elaborate scenes. For tragedy there are hints of paintings of the Early Hellenistic period that were occasionally copied at sites such as Pompeii and they were unusual in that, as with comedy, they were shown in literal fashion, as actors acting. There are also terracottas and occasional small bronzes of actor-figures, but for the most part our evidence is restricted to depictions of masks, and they occur on a very wide range of media. Most notable are Roman sarcophagi of the second and third centuries AD which often have masks shown alone (whether for their Dionysiac implications or to hint at the cultured background of the deceased), or on Muse sarcophagi where Melpomene commonly holds a mask of the tragic Heracles. They sometimes have scenes of myths made popular in tragedy. Of some importance are the hexagonal mosaic panels from Porcarecchia on the Via Aurelia not far from Rome, datable to the third century AD. They were excavated before the end of the eighteenth century and one found its way to Berlin, twenty-two to the Vatican. They have suffered a lot from restoration but typically have pairs of tragic actors, presumably in situations that could once be related to specific plays. The figures have high masks, tall *kothornoi* and elaborate, heavy dress. There is still room for an exploration of the use of colour in tragic costume (see also Ley, ch. 14 in this volume). As a series they are interesting evidence for knowledge of traditional theatre at that period.

Depictions of comedy on pottery are more straightforward since they show the actuality of the performance, and even something of the stage business of which it is so difficult to gain a clear impression from the texts. Over two hundred scenes involving more than one figure are known. Most of them are from Southern Italy and Sicily but they demonstrably depict plays imported from Athens over a period from the late fifth century through to about 330 BC when their depictions seem to have gone out of fashion. Through them we can learn something of the evolution of the genre and its costume, as well as the changing practice of acting style. Alongside them we can place

Figure 9. Old man, slave and baggage.

hundreds of terracotta figurines of actors in characteristic roles made all over the Greek world, though largely based on archetypes created in Athens.

'I won't make those tired old jokes, master, at which the audience will always laugh,' writes Aristophanes at the beginning of *Frogs* in a splendidly comic dig at his fellow playwrights' slaves complaining at the weight of the baggage they have to carry. **Fig. 9,** a Tarentine vase of perhaps 380–370 BC, shows us how we should envisage such a scene from other playwrights.[11] The old man with receding white hair and beard comes to a halt as he listens to the remonstrations of his slave as he approaches from behind, carrying the heavy baggage. That the slave is speaking is made evident by the body-language given him by the vase-painter and by the two-finger gesture of his right hand, quite cleverly placed in the very middle of the composition. The man has been brought up short by what he has said and is shown as standing in amazement, as is implied by the way he rests his left hand on his hip. His posture as an old man is well captured by the painter who shows him as slightly round-shouldered, presumably something he copies from the way the actor created the character on stage. What the playwright as director had built into the performance is that, while the slave has the mask normal for such a character, with vigorous expression, snub nose and bristly hair, his owner wears the mask of a stupid man characterized by its large ears (a standard sign of stupidity in the ancient world) and a gross, bulbous, even pendulous nose. The slave is making smart remarks.

The costume is standard for Old and the earlier part of Middle Comedy, that is for Aristophanes and his immediate successors. All actors wear tights that contain padding on the belly and backside, carry a large *phallos* at the front, and cover the arms and legs to wrist and ankle. Over that they wear clothes appropriate to the part, whether male or female. In this case the figures both have short tunics. The older male wears a *himation* (cloak) over this and it conceals his left hand – this was regarded as fitting for a well-to-do citizen male and it indicated that he did not have to use his hands for work (much as our grandparents might have worn gloves). He also has a tall staff with curved top, again symbolic of his status by contrast with the shorter, more practical stick of the slave. They are on a journey. The slave has a yoke over his left shoulder, marked in white, to which is hooked a bed-roll at the back, and at the front a large (footed) basket of food for the trip.

An important piece of evidence from a slightly later date is the *krater* found a few years ago during the excavation of a cemetery in Messina (**Fig. 10**).[12] It was made in Sicily, probably in Syracuse, about 330 BC. We have a four-figure composition. From left to right are a young woman, a young man, a portly figure in long dress and white slippers, and then, watching from the right, a white-haired older man leaning on his stick. Between the two central figures is a *thumiatêrion* (incense-burner). In seeking to understand the plot, the key figure is the one with long dress in the centre. The attire is apparently that of a girl and it is, perhaps deliberately, comparable with that of the girl on the left. Yet when we look more closely, ignoring the dress and the finger-gestures, the mask is that of a slave and so is the fatness of the figure. It is a slave dressed up as a girl, and most likely as a bride (thus the incense-burner for a sanctuary in the context of a wedding). The body-language of the young man, and his gesture with the left hand, makes clear his surprise as he looks round to what was presumably his real bride as she comes in from the left of the stage. At this point the older man has no active part in the events and it is hard to know whose father he is, the real bride's or the young man's. What is likely is that he is the target of the hoax and the ruse has been blown apart by the girl's appearance.

We are here at the transition to New Comedy, in costume and in plot. Disguising oneself on stage has a long history – one thinks, for example, of the Heracles sequence in Aristophanes' *Frogs* – and for it to work, certain conventions have to be observed so that the audience can be participant in the

Figure 10.   Cross-dressing scene from a Greek comedy, *c.*330 BC.

fun. Ideally they should witness the dressing-up process, which can itself be comic, but most importantly the character needs to retain his normal mask. This not only has a practical function so that the audience can follow and identify him through the subsequent scenes, but a symbolic one, given the identity of mask and character in Greek comedy. The plot reminds one vividly of Plautus' *Casina*, which in turn was adapted from Diphilus' *Allotment*, a play of this very period and one to be considered as an inspiration for this painting.[13]

The painter has again attempted to capture the actors' movements and body-language. The slave-cum-bride hams up the part with dainty footsteps and fluttering fingers, head coyly to one side. The young man was presumably approaching the slave but starts back as he is actually touched by his real girl. This is a rare event. Girls did not normally do such things but, by convention, behaved very properly on stage. It is her reaction to a happening she must have found strange to say the least. Her cloak has slipped away from over her head, exposing her hair and even her arm (her face and hands were painted in white which has worn away). For the old man, the stance and the positioning of the arms in front of the body make him look uptight, as it were closed in on himself. As to costume, he is the only one of traditional appearance, with just a small *phallos* visible. It suits the conservative character of the part. The youth wears an up-to-date young man's mask, beardless and with wavy hair that indicates his lively nature. His costume now comes just below the knee, as one might see an active younger man about the streets of town, but one can see the bottom of his actor's leggings just above the sandals. His left arm, apart from the hand, was largely concealed, as was still considered proper at the time, and another sign of his social status is the staff shown in white and just visible between him and the girl. The males as a class carry more padding than the females. In the background are columns such as we see on many Sicilian vases connected with theatre. They must reflect semi-columns incorporated in the front of the stage-building itself. We know they were present on the stage-building in Athens too.[14] The supports are plain pillars but in this case we have two stairways of five or six steps leading up to it. On vases of the late fifth and the earlier part of the fourth century there were usually four, implying a stage-height of about a metre above the level of the *orchêstra*. After about 370–360 BC, six to eight steps are standard, implying a height of about 1.6 or 1.8 metres.[15]

It is at this critical point that the evidence of painted vases disappeared, with the narrative that they carried. We are left with figurines in clay and sometimes in bronze, but more often with models of masks. These last come in an elaborate series of about forty types of old men, young men, slaves and professionals, young women proper and otherwise, old women and so on that seem to have been instantly recognizable to the spectator in the audience or the viewer of the object. They were an aid in following the plot with all its twists and turns not least because they followed contemporary conventions and/or prejudices in physiognomy and general appearance, but also because the males, whose activities were still the most significant factors in the drama, were constructed according to type-systems that allowed one to recognize that a given father, son and slave belonged to a single family or household. As the comedies themselves revolved increasingly about the interplay of character-types as individuals, so their masks assisted in the process and were at the same time recognizable as standing for individuals with relatively predictable characters. All this forms some of the background to their reproduction in clay, metal, paint, glass, mosaic and marble models, whether in their own right or to decorate other objects in home or sanctuary. In the time of Diphilus and Menander, that is in the Early Hellenistic period of the late fourth and early third centuries BC, the most popular masks are those of old men and leading slaves, presumably because their interactions lay at the core of comedy, but on vessels designed for use in the symposium, masks of *hetairai* (girls from the escort agency) are far more popular, presumably because *hetairai* themselves were items of interest during or after the drinking – whatever the conversational interest of theatre plots involving young women of this kind. Art and life imitated each other.

Although we lack the evidence of narratives in vase-painting from the late fourth century onwards, the ancients found panel-paintings placed on walls, later copied in floor-mosaics, a significant alternative. It is evident that for comedy, as to a more limited extent for tragedy, there was a major series of paintings of key scenes. It is likely that it was created in Athens, and in some public place such as the Sanctuary of Dionysus. When one looks at the quality implicit in some of the reproductions, it is also likely that one or more major painters were involved. Their style would suggest that they were made in the first quarter of the third century BC, not long after the death of Menander (c.292 BC). The copies we can identify all seem to draw on plays by Menander (as those from tragedy seem to draw on Euripides), but that may be a result of later choice rather than the original presentation. On the other hand it is quite possible that they were created and exhibited to celebrate the poet's work soon after his death, just as a portrait-statue of him was set up near the theatre.

The best and best-known copies are the mosaic panels signed by Dioskourides of Samos in the later part of the second century BC and preserved in the floor of the so-called Villa of Cicero at Pompeii.[16] They illustrate Menander's *The Possessed Woman* (*Theophoroumenê*) (**Fig. 11**) and *Women at Breakfast* (*Sunaristôsai*) (**Fig. 28**). The scene from the former also survives in a wall-painting from Baiae, another, rather battered, mosaic identified recently in the storeroom at Pompeii, and a further mosaic from the set at Mytilene in Lesbos. The latter is also found at Mytilene as well as in a modified and essentially non-theatrical version in a mosaic found at Zeugma on the Euphrates.[17] Both had evidently become famous whether as paintings or as theatre-scenes, and in any given case it is not always easy to be sure which. The popularity of the scene from *The Possessed Woman* is also attested by clay figurines made at Myrina in Asia Minor at much the same period as the mosaics. It is fascinating that, although they were found as separate items, the types must originally have been created as three-dimensional reproductions of the paintings, recreating the scenes in the round and therefore even closer to their stage appearance.

If we look more closely at the mosaic version of *The Possessed Woman*, we can see something of the sophisticated nature of its composition. The title may be translated as 'The Girl Possessed by the Goddess', i.e. the Great Goddess, Cybele. Tambourines and castanets or cymbals were not normal instruments for Greeks to play, and especially not for men to play, but so far as we can tell from the preserved fragments of the text, they used them here to persuade the girl in question that the goddess was being

Figure 11. Mosaic from Pompeii of scene from Menander's *The Possessed Woman*.

celebrated by her eastern music and so entice her out of the house. Thus the painter included the house-door to the right as an essential part of the composition.

The mosaic gives an excellent idea of the appearance of Menander's comedy near the time of its original performance. The two young men are placed near the front of the stage. Their appearance is naturalistic and one has to look hard to see the conventional sleeves and leggings of their costume. The actor playing the role of the piper, who is placed closer to the rear wall, also has a mask and in this case white sleeves to simulate the colour of a woman's skin. (Compare those of the girl on the Sicilian vase, **Fig. 10**.) He is shown as slightly smaller, a convention for figures without speaking parts. The third speaker will be a slave who comes out of the house instead of the looked-for girl. The small attendant at the far left is maskless.

The period of the creation of the archetypes of these paintings and mosaics, the later years of the fourth and the earlier part of the third centuries, came to be regarded as a golden age. The work of Menander remained definitive as text for school and stage. This was the time of the classic description of the mask-types that is preserved in an abbreviated version by Pollux from the second century AD.[18] The stone masks used by Augustus to decorate the Theatre of Marcellus in Rome about 13 or 11 BC looked back to masks of the style of this period. The inscriptions created in Athens to record performances under the Flavians in the later first century AD consciously echoed those of this period (although it is worth noting that those carved under the later part of Hadrian's reign and the Antonines generally revert to the orthography and writing style of the fifth century).

In a similar way, other objects relating to performance, such as bronze figurines or miniature copies of masks that served as souvenirs and orna-ments, are regularly derived from archetypes of this same period, sometimes in the form of three-dimensional copies of key figures from the series of paint-ings. The costumes and masks of the actor-figures were sometimes updated to reflect later performance, but it must be emphasized that a lot of the material from Pompeii (mosaics and wall-paintings included), destroyed in AD 79, is not an up-to-date reflection of contemporary theatre but rather the sort of thing collected as souvenirs by collectors seeking to demonstrate their education and their knowledge of the Hellenistic world, a point that is not without its own importance for the perceived standing of what was regarded as classic Greek theatre.

NOTES

1. Discussions of padded dancers by a number of authors will be found in the forthcoming volume edited by E. Csapo and M. A. Miller, *Komasts and Ritual* (Cambridge: Cambridge University Press).
2. For a near-complete collection of this material, see J. R. Green, 'A Representation of the *Birds* of Aristophanes', in *The J. Paul Getty Museum. Greek Vases* 2 (Malibu: J. Paul Getty Trust, 1985), pp. 95–118.
3. See also G. M. Sifakis, *Parabasis and Animal Choruses* (London, Athlone Press, 1971), pl. 1. The reverse has satyrs and nymphs with a satyr-piper.
4. See also R. Green and E. Handley, *Images of the Greek Theatre* (London: British Museum, 1995), no. 3.
5. In D. Kurtz and B. A. Sparkes (eds.), *The Eye of Greece. Studies in the Art of Athens* (Cambridge: Cambridge University Press, 1982), pp. 141–2, pl. 37a–b.
6. See A. J. N. W. Prag, *The Oresteia: Iconographic and Narrative Tradition* (Warminster: Aris and Phillips, 1985). The fullest recent coverage of the *Oresteia* will be found in D. Knoepfler's catalogue of an exhibition of vases and

photographs on the theme organized for the Museum of Neuchâtel in 1991–2 (Kilchberg/Zurich, 1993).

7. See Green and Handley (1995), no. 15.

8. *Ibid.*, no. 27.

9. See J. R. Green, *Theatre in Ancient Greek Society* (London and New York: Routledge, 1994), pp. 20ff., fig. 2.4.

10. Recent work on the importance of new tragedy in the fourth century includes P. E. Easterling, 'The End of an Era? Tragedy in the Early Fourth Century', in A. H. Sommerstein, S. Halliwell, J. Henderson and B. Zimmerman (eds.), *Tragedy, Comedy and the Polis. Papers from the Greek Drama Conference, Nottingham, 18–20 July 1990* (Bari: Levante, 1993), pp. 559–69.

11. One should note that in Aristophanes' parody the slave is in fact riding on a donkey.

12. See J. R. Green, 'Towards a Reconstruction of Performance Style', in P. E. Easterling and E. Hall (eds.), *Greek and Roman Actors* (Cambridge: Cambridge University Press, 2002), p. 114, fig. 23.

13. See E. W. Handley in B. Le Guen (ed.), *De la scène aux gradins*, Pallas 47 (1997), 194–6.

14. R. F. Townsend, 'The Fourth-Century Skene of the Theater of Dionysos at Athens', *Hesperia* 55 (1986), 421–38.

15. Comments on developments in the Theatre of Dionysus at Athens which Townsend argues independently underwent a major make-over on similar lines about 370–360 BC, not later, under Lycurgus, as used to be supposed. See also Beacham, ch. 11 in this volume.

16. See J. R. Trendall and T. B. L. Webster, *Illustrations of Greek Drama* (London: Phaidon, 1971), colour-plate (facing p. 8) and frontispiece.

17. For the Mytilene mosaics, the primary publication is by S. Charitonides, L. Kahil and R. Ginouvès, *Les mosaïques de la Maison du Ménandre à Mytilène*, Antike Kunst 6 (Bern, 1970).

18. Pollux, *Onomasticon* IV, 133–54. There is a convenient translation in E. Csapo and W. J. Slater, *The Context of Ancient Drama* (Ann Arbor: University of Michigan Press, 1994), pp. 398–402.

FURTHER READING

Csapo, E. and Slater, W. J., *The Context of Ancient Drama*. Ann Arbor: University of Michigan Press, 1995.

Easterling, P. and Hall, E. (eds.), *Greek and Roman Actors. Aspects of an Ancient Profession*. Cambridge: Cambridge University Press, 2002.

Green J. R., *Theatre in Ancient Greek Society*. London: Routledge, 1994.

Green, R. and Handley, W., *Images of the Greek Theatre*. London: British Museum, 1995.

Taplin, O., *Comic Angels and Other Approaches to Greek Drama through Vase-Paintings*. Oxford: Clarendon Press, 1993.

Trendall, A. D. and Webster, T. B. L., *Illustrations of Greek Drama*. London: Phaidon, 1971.

IO

RUSH REHM

Festivals and audiences in Athens and Rome

In *The Messingkauf Dialogues*, Bertolt Brecht analyses the 'commerce' between stage and auditorium, the exchange that occurs between the actors and the spectators during a performance.[1] In the ancient theatre of Greece and Rome, festivals usually provided the context in which that exchange took place. But what was a festival, and what sorts of festivals included theatrical performances? How did these festivals change across time and place, and how were those changes reflected on stage? What was asked of the audiences in these varying circumstances, and what did they ask for in return?

What was a festival?

Festivals in the ancient world were religious occasions, in the root sense of *religio*, Latin for the 'tie' that binds people and places to the gods. The Greeks and Romans almost always characterized these deities as immortal anthropomorphic beings, more powerful and inscrutable than their human models. Given their power, the gods may have welcomed protestations of faith, but they required of their worshippers specific actions (rituals). These usually involved blood sacrifice or other offerings, performed in particular places and times as the means to please or placate them. Festivals provided important public occasions for such ritual worship.

Given the changing forces of nature (all ancient cultures lived close to the land) and the wide variety of human experience, polytheism represented the Mediterranean norm – many gods for many things, each god with several aspects.[2] In the great Athenian theatre festival, the City Dionysia, the city honoured the god Dionysus under his cult title *Eleutherios*, 'from Eleutherai', a border town between Attica and Thebes. The Athenians associated this traditional home of the god with *eleutheria* (freedom). The city set aside a sanctuary (*temenos*, land 'cut away') on the south slope of the Acropolis, erected an altar for sacrificial offerings and constructed a temple to house the god's image when it was brought from the Academy (on the route from Eleutherai) for the festival. They also built a theatre near the temple, where the community could watch performances dedicated to Dionysus, who encouraged the complementary moods of *ekstasis* (standing outside oneself) and *enthousiasmos* (the god within) associated with wine. As well as tragedies, satyr plays, and comedies, these performances included dithyrambs, narrative poems sung and danced by choruses of fifty men or fifty boys. Usually offered to Dionysus (the 'patron' god of theatre), dithyrambs in Athens also honoured Apollo and Athena at the Thargelia and the Panathenaea festivals respectively.

Unlike the Greeks, the Romans did not associate theatrical performance with any particular god, dedicating *ludi scaenici* (scenic games) to a variety of divinities, including deified emperors.[3] Surprisingly, it was not until 55 BC (almost two hundred years after the first performance of scripted plays in Rome) that the city allowed the construction of a permanent (stone) theatre (see Beacham, ch. 11 in this volume). Paid for by Pompey the Great, the theatre lay just outside the city walls in the Campus Martius, its central seats rising up like steps to the temple of Venus Victrix (Venus the Victorious). Making the theatre seating appear like an extension of the temple, Pompey avoided the strictures of the Senate, who feared that a permanent theatre might encourage political groups to gather there. No one doubted, however, that the goddess would enjoy the shows and spectacles that would take place in the new structure at the foot of her Roman 'home'.

Although the various theatrical festivals differed in detail, almost all included a procession leading to a sacrifice, pre-performance events, the performances themselves, and some sort of follow-up. The procession brought to the sanctuary the sacrificial offerings (both animate and inanimate), along with the cult image of the god. The movement of people, animals and divine image passed through places of importance to the city and its inhabitants, activating 'like an electric current the landscape's potential symbolism'.[4] Linked to territory (literally covering ground), these processions merged the political with the religious, like Catholic processionals on a Saint's day, intended (among other things) to mark out the parish boundary and offer apotropaic protection for the community.

As with other aspects of the festival, the procession united the worshippers in a grand display 'pleasing to the gods and spectators [*theatai*] alike', as Xenophon puts it (*Hipparchos* 3.2).[5] While drawing the community together, it also reinforced political and social differences among the participants, via their position, clothing, and other visible markers. At the City Dionysia in Athens, for instance, festival patrons and officials dressed lavishly, holding pride of place in the procession; citizens bore leather wineskins on their shoulders; resident aliens wore purple robes and carried trays of offerings; Athenian colonists brought *phalloi* as offerings to Dionysus; and so on. In Rome, festival processions followed a highly articulated dress code indicating political and economic class. During the empire, these codes of clothing and spatial location clearly distinguished the imperial entourage, the senators, knights (*equites*), plebeians, freedmen and finally slaves.

Roman festival processions shared the theatrical qualities of funerals, which in the case of the wealthy might include actors masked and dressed to imitate the deceased, musicians, mimes, professional mourners, along with the dead person's family and friends. Rome's delight in the paratheatrical extended to the grandest of its processions, the military triumphs, influenced by the highly theatricalized entries ('arrivals') of Hellenistic rulers, whose methods of political self-promotion Roman rulers imitated. Dressed and made-up (his face daubed with red paint) to resemble Jupiter Optimus Maximus ('Best and Greatest' of the gods), the triumphant Roman general rode in a chariot through the city. Behind him followed a vast array of musicians, mimes, banner carriers and victorious troops, who displayed the war booty, including abject human captives, often in their thousands. Shackled, caged and otherwise humiliated, most of them faced imminent death in the forum or amphitheatre, fodder for the blood sports that became the Romans' favourite form of theatricalized entertainment.

After the initial procession came the *sine qua non* of the festival, the sacrifice to the god(s), which constituted the ritual core of Greek and Roman religion. When the participants and animals arrived *en masse* at the sanctuary, the priests slew the beasts at the altar(s), wrapped the thigh bones with fat and burnt them, the savoury smoke rising as a gift to the god. Depending on the festival, the civic officials might distribute the butchered meat among the crowd, who could cook and eat it at the sanctuary or take it home for later consumption. Despite highly wrought theories linking blood sacrifice to guilt or institutionalized violence, the bloodletting itself seems to have evoked a mood of celebration rather than anxiety in the crowd, who anticipated the feast (meat was a luxury in the ancient world) and the theatrical events to come.

Before the performances began, however, smaller processions and proclamations took place in the theatre orchestra. At the City Dionysia, for example, the allies paraded their annual tribute (in the years of the Athenian empire); war-orphans who had reached their majority marched into the theatre wearing hoplite armour, the gift of the city that had raised them, then sat in reserved seats to watch the performances; officials announced the names of recently manumitted slaves, making the audience witnesses to their new status; the ten annually elected generals poured libations (the military campaign season began shortly after the festival); and heralds proclaimed special civic honours. Similar pre-performance activities occurred at Roman theatre festivals, including various displays of wealth and power. Following the performances and entertainments, the closing ceremonies might involve the awarding of prizes (if the performances were competitive) and the subsequent evaluation of the festival itself. To give these generalities greater specificity, let us briefly consider the major Athenian theatre festivals.

Theatrical festivals in democratic Athens

At the City Dionysia, the day after the sacrifice and communal feasting saw the dithyrambic competitions between ten men's and ten boys' choruses, each representing and sponsored by one of the ten *phylai* (tribes) of the city. The new divisions resulted from Cleisthenes' democratic reforms in 508/7 BC, shifting Athenian loyalties from noble families to the broader community. Although the sequence may have changed due to war or other factors, the following three days usually featured the contest in tragedy, each day given over to one of three playwrights, who presented three tragedies and a satyr play apiece. The final day of performances was dedicated to comedy, with five playwrights presenting a single play each. The magistrate in charge of the festival (the archon eponymous) had chosen the playwrights the previous year, although we don't know precisely how.

In all the events, the choruses consisted of Athenian citizens who had trained for many months. However, the professional actors and *aulêtai* (who accompanied the performances on the oboe-like *aulos*) frequently did not hail from Athens. Ten judges, one from each *phylê*, selected by lot to avoid bribery, voted on the best performance in each genre, with prizes awarded in the *orchêstra* to the producer and *phylê* for the best men's and boys' dithyrambs, to the producer and director (usually the playwright, who also composed the music) of the winning tragedies and comedy, and to the best actor in tragedy (an award introduced in 449 BC) and comedy (introduced between 328 and 312). The last day of the City Dionysia included a meeting of the Athenian assembly held in the theatre itself (normally the Assembly met on a nearby hillside, the Pnyx). Here citizens delivered a post-mortem on the running of the festival and began planning for next year's event.

The pre-performance festivities, the citizen choruses, the local (phyletic) nature of the dithyrambic competitions, the citywide support for tragic and comic contests and the follow-up assembly all underline the civic nature of the City Dionysia. We might contrast the Athenian audience's experience with our contemporary sense of theatre, a public event intended for the consumption of individuals, presented by artists unconnected with the audience's civic or political identity. The democratic support for theatrical festivals – part and parcel of what it meant to be an Athenian – stands in marked contrast to theatre as 'show-business', where 'show' represents one way (among many) of passing time, and 'business' indicates one way (among many) of making or losing money (see also Walton, ch. 15 in this volume).

A major Athenian showpiece, the City Dionysia took place in March after the end of winter storms. This allowed foreigners to sail to Athens and attend the festival, along with Athenian men (the majority of the audience), women, children and slaves. But Athens also held smaller theatre festivals in the winter, when agricultural work was at its least intensive (most Greeks and Romans made their living off the land) and local audiences could attend without neglecting their animals or crops. We find the most prestigious of these, the Lenaea (an old festival dedicated to Dionysus Lenaios, which added performances *c.* 440 BC), referred to by the Chorus of Aristophanes' *Acharnians* (performed in 425): 'We're by ourselves here; it's the Lenaea contest. / No foreigners are here yet, for the tribute / and allies from the cities have not come' (*Acharnians.* 504–6). As few non-Athenians would be present, the Lenaea offered an occasion for more unabashed criticism of Athenian politicians, a favourite target of Aristophanes. Celebrated in January, the festival featured competitions in comedy (three to five playwrights entered a comedy each, depending on external circumstances), with a prize for best production. In 432 tragic competitions were added (along with prizes for the best actor in comedy and in tragedy), with two to three playwrights presenting two tragedies each. Success at the Lenaea may have helped a playwright's selection at the City Dionysia in subsequent years.

At the 'rural' Dionysia held in December, local 'demes' (villages or inner suburbs) produced smaller theatrical festivals honouring Dionysus. Given the prohibitive cost of dithyrambs, these local gatherings concentrated on tragedies and/or comedies, with a flexible schedule that allowed Athenians to attend productions in several demes. In Plato's *Republic* (475d), Glaucon describes attending rural Dionysia one after another, and we have evidence for performances in at least fourteen of the 139 Attic demes.

In February, the city held its oldest celebration of Dionysus, the new wine festival called the Anthesteria.[6] The first day, the 'opening of the jars', included non-competitive choruses, and in the fourth century BC comedies were added on the third (final) day. Viewing the Anthesteria alongside the rural Dionysia, the Lenaea, and the City Dionysia, we recognize a Dionysiac mini-festival (December to March), within the larger, annual Athenian festival cycle.

The non-agonistic nature of the performances at the Anthesteria was anomalous for Athens and we should consider for a moment the Athenian love of competition, theatrical and otherwise. As indicated by the prizes at the City Dionysia and the Lenaea, productions and performers were scrutinized by the Athenian audience, which included the judges selected for that year's contests. Unlike the procession, sacrifice and pre-performance events, the festival's competitions introduced a critical element into the audiences' response, reinforcing their role as democratic citizens determining their city's future. As we shall see, no comparable agonistic/critical element operated in Roman *ludi scaenici*, which 'were only tangentially competitive, and [where] the instinct for impressive show . . . was greater'.[7]

The highest honours at the City Dionysia and the Lenaea went to those who produced the successful dramas or dithyrambs. Called *chorêgoi* (literally, 'chorus leaders'), these men paid for the choruses, as well as all production expenses (props, music, extras, scenic elements and so on) other than the principal actors and playwrights, who were paid by the festival directly. Twenty *chorêgoi* (two from each *phylê*) were enlisted to support the ten men's and ten boys' choruses (each with fifty members); three *chorêgoi* paid for the three tragic choruses (initially twelve, then later fifteen members each), and five *chorêgoi* funded the comedies (twenty-four members in each chorus). The *chorêgoi* provided food, rehearsal space, costumes and – if victorious in the dithyramb – a choregic monument erected near the theatre after the festival. Wealthy Athenian citizens (at the Lenaea they also could be prosperous resident aliens, called 'metics') served each year as *chorêgoi*, part of the Athenian system of *leitourgiai* ('liturgies', literally 'work for the people'). No one was forced to fulfil this function more than once every two years, and the city provided legal means to avoid a liturgy if it had overestimated a person's financial well-being. Generally, however, wealthy citizens interested in public careers wanted to serve as *chorêgoi*, viewing this form of *noblesse oblige* as a way of garnering glory and popular acclaim. After all, some 1,165 citizens served annually in choral contests at the City Dionysia, meaning that 'a substantial percentage of the citizen body was . . . effectively *under the pay of private individuals* . . . for several months every year'.[8]

A frequent 'liturgist' in fourth-century Athens, Demosthenes (20.108) contrasts an oligarchy, which strives for equality among those (few) who control the state, with 'the freedom of democracy [that] is guarded by the rivalry with which good citizens compete for the rewards offered by the people'. Liturgies exemplify the constructive rivalry between the elite and the masses in democratic Athens where, in exchange for support of the public good, the mass of citizens allowed wealthy aristocrats to maintain (and exercise) their economic and social status. We find this competitive ideology reflected in the performances themselves. Athena in Aeschylus' *Eumenides* claims that Athens' 'rivalry for good is the victor for all time' (974–5) and the Chorus of

Sophocles' *Oedipus Tyrannus* praise 'struggle which is advantageous for the city' (879–80). As these accounts suggest, Athenian democracy harnessed the competitive instincts of its citizens to the radical notion of popular rule. Festival performances showed this competitive ideology at work, putting the city 'on stage' so that Athenian and foreign audiences could view it critically and from a multitude of perspectives.

Festival developments in Hellenistic Athens

After decades of threats from the north, Athens surrendered unconditionally to the Macedonian regent Antipater in 322, marking the end of her democracy. During this period, important changes in the drama and the festivals that produced them had taken place. The Macedonian royalty already had established Dionysiac-style games to solemnize military conquests outside of Athens. Philip held games after destroying Olynthus in 348 BC, and Alexander staged a Dionysia at Dion to celebrate his sack of Thebes in 335, uprooting dramatic performance from its native soil of cyclic religious festivals.[9] In Athens, Lycurgus reformed the City Dionysia between 336/5 and 325/4 BC, establishing that the fifth-century tragedies and comedies remounted at the festival (popular reminders of Athens 'golden age') must be performed without interpolations or excisions. Some view this as Lycurgus' commitment to textual authenticity, but more likely his reforms aimed at keeping insertions critical of Philip of Macedon from finding a public voice before a sympathetic audience.

The interpolations in fourth-century productions also reflected the audiences' fascination with actors, often at the expense of the plays in which they performed. In the fifth century, each main actor ('protagonist', literally 'prime competitor') played in all four plays of a given tragedian at the City Dionysia and, from 449, each competed for the actor prize. About a century later that arrangement changed; each of the three protagonists performed in *one* of the tragedies presented by *each* playwright and *chorêgos* (what happened in the satyr plays is uncertain). This fundamental shift encouraged the actor to think less about the overall work of a given playwright and more about his own performance *per se*, a rift that led content-driven critics (Plato and Aristotle most famously) to condemn theatrical excess that aimed at pleasing the audience above all else.[10]

The growing popularity of tragedy and comedy outside Athens furthered the separation between playwright and performance. Touring companies, organized as the *technitai* (artists) of Dionysus, offered their services to theatrical festivals across Greece, in the Greek cities of Italy and Sicily (particularly Syracuse, which had a long tradition of tragic and comic performances), and in the Hellenistic cities of Asia Minor and Egypt. They frequently performed selections from classic tragedies and comedies, with greatly reduced choruses or without them altogether. The decline of the chorus represented a cost-cutting measure, but it also reflected the growing popularity of actors' monodies (solo arias), influenced by 'new music' that had become popular at the end of the fifth century. Whatever the cause, audiences increasingly witnessed the breakdown of the relationship between theatrical production and community, making obsolete the citizen choruses that had played a central role in most festival performances in democratic Athens.

Growing interest in actor virtuosity permeated the content and form of the drama being written at the time. The New Comedy of Menander, Diphilus, and Philemon, for example, eschewed the 'big questions' raised by fifth-century dramatists, focusing instead on domestic, nuptial and financial concerns. This shift required actors to convey different personalities rather than capture the primal power of mythic conflict. In place of Aristophanes' egalitarian and utopian vision, with comic heroes who get the best of political demagogues to make peace, or who imagine women's equality and the emancipation of slaves, Menander offers a scaled-down world of familial conflicts and less than heroic aspirations. In a typical New Comedy, a young man pursues an apparently unattainable young woman (already betrothed, or a slave) who inevitably turns out to be *both* well-born *and* available. Instead of the complex choruses of classical Athenian drama, composed and choreographed by the playwrights themselves, New Comedy inserted choral interludes, indicated simply by 'chorus' in the manuscripts. These boilerplate lyrical pieces operated like act-divisions, marking the passage of time in plays that depended on logic and realism for their effect, rather than on myth, passion and politics.

The abolition of *chorêgoi* in Athens near the end of the fourth century and their replacement by elected *agônothetai* (contest-arrangers) might seem like a democratizing move. However, elections in post-democratic Athens were limited to wealthy elites who ran the show. Indeed, the 'star-system' in the Hellenistic theatre reflected the dominance of elite individuals in political and military spheres, an early version of the 'cult of the personality' with which we are now so familiar. Uniting performance and power, the oligarchs (and increasingly the monarchs) who ruled Hellenistic cities set the stage for the consolidation of cultural and political leadership we find in late Republican and imperial Rome.

Spreading their influence from the third century on, the *technitai* of Dionysus dominated the Greek-speaking theatre for the next five hundred years. They received massive support from Hellenistic kings and rulers, who grafted their own names onto existing festivals or invented new ones, hiring *technitai* to celebrate their power. By amalgamating different artists and performers, these guilds provided a 'reverse' package tour for those who could afford it, leading to the inclusion of dramatic competitions at festivals not traditionally theatrical, like the Panathenaea in Athens and the Pythian games in Delphi. In 105 BC, to take one example, the *technitai* based in Athens supplied some 350 performers – *aulêtai*, singers, lyrists, poets (epic, tragic, and comic), actors, dancers and chorus directors – for a festival in Delos.

Boasting their own priests of Dionysus, the guilds played up their religiosity to secure freedom and safety of movement in a politically volatile world. The major guilds (Athenian, Isthmian-Nemean, Ionian-Hellespontine) constituted themselves as quasi-independent self-governing units, which sent members as official ambassadors (*theôroi*) to foreign cities and sanctuaries (like Delos or Delphi) to negotiate contracts, rights of travel and other details. On occasion a guild would offer free performances to drum up future business, offering their 'sacred art' in the service of Hellenistic ruler cults, especially in Asia Minor and Alexandria. The Hellenistic period witnessed a veritable 'agonistic explosion' both within and outside of Athens, but the festivals no longer represented the community to itself. Rather, cities and sanctuaries were now served by (nominally) independent guilds available for hire and eager to serve the interests of whoever paid them.

Theatrical festivals in Rome

The rise of theatrical performances and their inclusion in festivals at Rome involved the congruence of many diverse elements. Early Roman comedy (the plays of Plautus and Terence) and tragedy (the names of writers and titles survive, but no complete texts) did not emerge in a vacuum.[11] Revivals of Attic Tragedy, Old Comedy and the New Comedy of Menander constituted the formal theatrical fare in the Greek cities of southern Italy and Sicily. In addition, indigenous Italian farce from Umbria, the *Atellanae* (weak on plot, strong on music, dance and improvisation) and the even less formal 'mime' (anything from tumbling to striptease) remained extremely popular. Ancient Etruscan funeral games, which featured ritual killing, or the single combats popular in Campania, may have inspired the blood sports that eventually dominated Roman popular entertainment.

The performance of Greek plays became increasingly available to Romans who travelled to, traded with, and finally conquered the Greek towns of Sicily and southern Italy, Epirus, Delos, Delphi, Asia Minor, Alexandria; and eventually Athens (sacked by Sulla in 88 BC). From the time of the first Punic War (264–41), military conquest and territorial expansion played a crucial role in the political and cultural life of the Roman republic and the empire that followed. The first year of peace (240 BC) witnessed the inaugural performance in Rome of a Greek play in Latin translation. Composed by Livius Andronicus, a Romanized Greek who probably came from Tarentum, the play was performed at the *Ludi Romani,* one of the oldest Roman festivals, which included *ludi scaenici* as early as 364. Our earliest surviving drama in Latin, the twenty plays and 21,000 lines that remain of Plautus' comedies, 'show us what delighted a nation on the verge of world domination, in the only age when its [fully scripted] theater lived and flourished'.[12]

Plautus delights in vocabulary specific to military campaigns, and his plays feature soldiers, tradesmen, craftsmen, businessmen and slaves, reflecting their new importance after Rome's triumph in the first two Punic Wars. We see the influence of militarism on public performances most clearly in the gladiator games (*munera*) and hunting spectacles (*venationes*) that became popular in Rome. Formally included in the festival calendar only during the empire, gladiatorial combat offered Roman audiences an ersatz experience of war. The expanding empire recruited more and more of the army from the Italian countryside and the distant provinces, allowing Romans to substitute the voyeurism of blood sports for their own participation in military campaigns.[13] The animal hunts (often part of festival *ludi*) offered every variation on exotic bloodletting, dramatizing the 'civilization' that Rome introduced to its wild frontiers. In their tens of thousands, Romans gathered in the forum, and later in the Colosseum and other theatrical arenas, to gaze at the world's savage wonders and revel in their slaughter.[14]

As far as we know, 'dramatic performances' (*ludi scaenici*) were given only at 'games' (*ludi*), that is, at the entertainments that constituted an important part of many annual religious festivals. These included the *Ludi Romani* (dating from the fourth century BC), the *Ludi Plebeii* (220) and a quadriga of festivals instituted after the outbreak of the second Punic War – the *Apollinares* (212, made annual in 208), the *Megalenses* (204, reorganized in 191), the *Ceriales* (201) and the *Florales* (founded earlier, but made annual in 173). We do not know how many plays were presented on a single day, nor whether they included mimes in addition to fully scripted plays. Dramas also were performed (along with other *ludi*) on irregularly scheduled occasions, such as votive games for Jupiter Optimus Maximus (*ludi magni,* which often followed a triumph), funerals (*ludi funebres*), gladiatorial games (*munera,* described above), temple dedications and so on. Festivals that included *ludi scaenici* frequently featured chariot races (*ludi circenses*) on the final day.

We catch a glimpse of the eclectic atmosphere of Roman theatre festivals in the prologue to Terence's *The Mother-in-Law,* which he remounted at the funeral games for L. Aemilius Paullus in 160. The actor protests at having to compete with boxers, tightrope walkers and gladiators for the audience's attention. His complaint helps to account for the extraordinary relationship that the characters in Roman comedy (especially Plautus) establish directly with the audience, a means of holding their interest against the 'performance-surfing' possibilities at Roman festivals.

The festival schedule that included *ludi scaenici* began with the *Ludi Megalenses* and *Ludi Ceriales* in April (the late republic devoted seventeen of the thirty days in April to games) and ended with the *Ludi Plebeii* in November. The city organized markets and fairs to follow many of these festivals, maximizing rural attendance by offering farmers the opportunity to buy from and sell to a gathered throng. Within the spring-to-autumn festival 'season', the number of days dedicated to scenic entertainments grew from eleven during Plautus' lifetime (224–180) to fifty-five at the death of Julius Caesar (44), and to a hundred and one by the mid-fourth century AD. These figures do not include performance days during funeral and votive games, nor those occasions when a festival performance had to be repeated. This last observance, called *instauratio*, reflected religious concerns over an improperly performed ritual, but often provided a simple means to court audience favour by 'encoring' a popular show or event.

Paradoxically, the heyday of Roman theatre came during the empire, when Roman authors had all but ceased to write formal plays for public performance. Although the emperor occasionally commissioned a new tragedy, the imperial theatre featured revivals of older dramas, blood sports (gladiator contests and other staged killing), mimes (in which women performed) and the increasingly popular pantomime, an interpretive dance performed by a mute male soloist. Playing all the parts, the pantomimist acted out a tale from Greek mythology, accompanied by a small orchestra (*auloi*, pipes, cymbals, lyres, castanets, and sometimes even an organ) and a singer or chorus who sang the basic plot. The closed-mouth mask of the dancer appears in a myriad of Roman contexts – mosaics, wall paintings, sarcophagi – and individual solo artists achieved near cult-status for their sensuous and often lascivious portrayals of mythical figures (Ares, Aphrodite, Hephaestus in one tale; Atreus, Thyestes, Aerope, Aegisthus in another). Dazzled by a pantomimist's uncanny ability to imitate a woman, Juvenal (3.96–7) wonders if 'he has, not acts, a female part'.

The umbrella term 'mime' (as opposed to 'pantomime') covered a range of acts resembling burlesque and vaudeville. Whether after-pieces to other shows or intermezzi between them, mimes were performed in theatres (using small wooden stages erected in the orchestra), amphitheatres (during gladiatorial combats) and in the hippodrome (between chariot races), although they became part of regularly scheduled festivals only in the late empire. Played without masks, mimes included skits, improvisation, acrobatics, animal acts, magic and prestidigitation, physical stunts, striptease. Suetonius (*Caligula* 57) describes a mime in which the main actor spewed fake blood, setting off a chain reaction among the others that left the stage awash with crimson vomit. Uniquely for Rome, the mime offered women the chance to perform in public and they starred in popular 'adultery' mimes, which exerted a surprising influence on the 'high' art of Augustan elegiac poetry. 'Cytheris', the stage name of Volumnia, the most prominent female mime in the first century, also played her role in the corridors of power as the mistress of Mark Antony. The sophisticated Roman audience delighted at seeing her epitomize adultery so fully, bringing to the stage a version of what she had experienced in private.[15]

We can extrapolate a central aspect of Roman festivals from the title and practice of one of them, the *Saturnalia*. Held just before the winter solstice in December (Christianized Rome later turned the holiday into Christmas), the *Saturnalia* offered Romans temporary licence to reverse social and economic status, to suspend the mores of public behaviour and to dispense with traditional gender roles. Although the *Saturnalia* itself did not include *ludi scaenici*, its 'rule-bending' aspects influenced Roman theatre festivals, where the stage played an important role in the social formation of the audience.[16]

Like the *Saturnalia*, theatre festivals encouraged Romans to play with their own self-image, letting off steam that might otherwise explode in less predictable and more dangerous ways. The satyr plays that followed the tragedies at the City Dionysia in Athens served a similar function. With physical features and character traits opposed to those of the tragic hero, the satyrs provided the anti-type to the Athenians' image of civilized society. Rather than satyrs, the Romans used the image of the *Greeks* when putting their 'reversed world' on stage. Translating and adapting Greek originals, Roman dramatists developed the *fabula* (*comoedia*) *palliata* ('story in Greek dress'), which allowed audiences to delight in outrageous behaviour they might not have accepted from Roman characters. Setting his plays where 'anything goes', Plautus (and, to a lesser extent, Terence) satirized Rome and the Romans from the doubly safe distance of Greece and the stage.

The treatment of slaves in comic *palliatae* provides valuable evidence for the 'carnivalesque' roots of *ludi scaenici*. The *Saturnalia* festival featured various status and role reversals involving slaves and their masters, and the Roman *palliata* developed this motif. Plautine comedy abounds in slaves who outwit their masters, manifesting their intelligence and inventiveness at the expense of aristocrats, soldiers, tradesmen and citizens of all sorts. We can contrast this treatment with what we find in *fabula togata* (drama in Roman dress), which avoided any comparable reversals of power and status between masters and slaves. Such behaviour among *Romans* (even on stage) might challenge the status quo and weaken the foundations of the state, given that Rome's success depended on conquest, subjection and slavery.[17]

Whether *palliata* or *togata*, scripted Roman drama was performed primarily *by* slaves, owned by the company manager who usually took the lead roles. When that part was, in fact, a clever slave, the Roman audience enjoyed the tangled inversions of a real slave (playing a master) beating his real master (playing a slave). When slaves played the slave roles and addressed jokes to the rear of the theatre, they were in effect addressing their counterparts in the audience, where custom (and later the law) had them sequestered. The Roman citizens seated 'in between' may have suspected theatrical collusion between their own servants and those 'serving' them onstage. Because 'no actor [stood] behind the mask of the slave', the lowest non-criminal class in Rome experienced unprecedented freedom for the duration of the performance.[18]

As we might imagine, funding for festival performances changed as Rome grew from a large Italian town into the capital of an empire. In the early Republic, festival organizers (magistrates, or *aediles*) were responsible for whatever *ludi* took place, supported by a grant from the state (although we don't know how much). Called *lucar* (from *lucus*, a grove belonging to a god's sanctuary), this financial arrangement suggests the religious basis of Roman festivals. However, magistrates (selected annually from wealthy families) frequently supplemented the state grant with their personal funds, viewing the augmentation as the means to a political career. We find a strong correlation between those who served as *aediles* and those who subsequently held the more powerful offices of praetor and consul. The financial responsibilities for *ludi* figured less as a 'tax on the rich' than as a mark of status and an investment in future power (see also Walton, ch. 15 in this volume).

As part of Rome's transformation from republic to empire, Augustus centralized control of the most popular spectacles – gladiatorial *munera* and the *ludi circenses*. He also relieved the *aediles* of their traditional responsibility for organizing all festival *ludi*, entrusting it to the senior group of magistrates, the *praetores*. We find less and less freedom in aristocratic contributions to the empire outside of the emperor himself, who maintained a monopoly on spectacles (with carefully chosen exceptions) and garnered most of the public credit for mounting them. As he emphasizes in his *Res Gestae*, Augustus considered plays, *munera* and other spectacles as a significant part of his civic beneficence. Immortalized by Juvenal's phrase 'bread and circuses', this mode of internal political control traces its roots to the earlier efforts of Hellenistic kings, who turned the religious/democratic festivals in Athens into secularized propaganda.

Roman audiences reflected every social class, from aristocrat to slave. Although highly sophisticated in some contexts, they tended towards the raucous and the prurient. Admission was free, on a first-come, first-served basis, but restrictions on seating for different classes made the theatre 'a vivid representation of Roman social hierarchy'.[19] As choruses played little or no role in Roman drama, seats were set up in the orchestra for senators (and possibly their families), behind which sat recent civic honourees. The next fourteen rows were reserved for the 'knights' (*equites*). Behind them sat married (male) citizens, then unmarried citizens, then women, and finally slaves, who often stood in the back.

These restrictions on seating – as well as the siting of the permanent theatres themselves – aimed at 'normalizing' and controlling those who attended festival *ludi*. Drawing on Cicero's equation of the audience with the *vox populi*, however, some scholars see the theatre in Rome as one of the rare places where citizens could express their political views with relative safety, a vestige of the democratic tendencies of the early Republic. This argument departs from the usual 'content-driven' defence of the theatre, not surprising given the conservative nature of the extant plays, and it seems like a promising change from over subtle political 'readings' of texts to a performance-based politics of audience reception. However, by their attendance at, and gluttony for, imperial spectacles, the Roman audience already had ratified the political system in which the various *ludi* were an essential part. What sort of democratic expression resided in cheering a show or booing a performer, or in gesturing 'thumbs-up' or 'thumbs-down' at a gladiatorial contest? Influencing the fate of a condemned convict hardly constituted meaningful participation in the political process. With thousands of enemies awaiting their spectacular death, the emperor could afford to be merciful on occasion. However the audience expressed themselves, they had precious little influence over imperial decisions affecting their own lives.

Riots sometimes did break out at performances of pantomimes and at the circus, but these resembled the partisan outbursts of contemporary football fans rather than the acts of a citizenry in revolt. The significant politics at work on these occasions involved the spectators' failure to see that 'their' artist or team did not represent their own interests, but rather those of the organizers (who ran performance guilds for profit) and the emperor (who hired them to divert the crowds from meaningful dissent). As much as one admires the scholarly ingenuity that can ferret out democratic latencies in the Roman audience, a balanced look suggests that the spectators at festival *ludi* displayed little interest in – or capacity for – challenging the political power of the emperor.

When we consider the performances associated with the emperor Nero, the propaganda function of Roman festival theatre seems undeniable. Enamoured of acting and singing before the public, Nero guaranteed his success by hiring a claque of supporters who applauded his efforts and 'set the mood' for the audience at large. To add to his artistic lustre, Nero introduced a new festival to the Roman calendar, the *Neronia*, featuring athletics, chariot racing and musical contests (which he entered and won). Having conquered Rome with his talent, Nero tested his gifts in the land of the Muses (Greece had become the Roman provinces of Macedonia and Achaea). He rewrote the Greek festival calendar so that all the pan-Hellenic games took place in the same year, even adding musical competitions where they had never been. The emperor emerged victorious in every contest he entered, to the surprise of no one except (perhaps) Nero himself, who played the part of nervous performer to perfection.

Conflating the public performance of emperor with that of an actor playing a role, Nero realized a metaphor used by Augustus on his deathbed. According to Suetonius (*Augustus* 99), the founder of Rome's *imperium* asked his friends 'whether he had played the mime of life [*mimum vitae*] fitly'. He then died quoting the last lines of a Greek comedy: 'If I have pleased you, kindly signify / Appreciation with a warm goodbye.' Whatever resistance sounded in the theatres and arenas of Rome – boos aimed at an emperor's onstage (or offstage) favourite, pity for a herd of elephants slaughtered at a theatrical hunt, disgust at a particularly cruel example of imperial excess – that same audience also roared its approbation of the high and mighty. The institution of 'emperor' absorbed and transformed the traditional values of the Roman republic, the *mos maiorum* ('customs of our forefathers') that once included pride in popular rule. While flaunting its religious origins, festival theatre in imperial Rome came to celebrate political power, pure and simple.

The conversion of festival performances from occasions of liminality and licence to institutions of propaganda and state control appears most clearly in the *ludi* that included public executions. Frequently staged as a virtual history or as a twisted drama, these fatal charades turned state punishment into a spectacle. Consider the theatrical event Augustus arranged to celebrate his naval victory at Actium. Creating an artificial lake in present day Trastevere, the emperor re-enacted the battle of Salamis, with three thousand combatants (almost all condemned prisoners) and over thirty ships. Following his uncle's precedent, the emperor Claudius had nineteen thousand convicts and captives killed at the most spectacular *naumachia* (theatrical sea battle) in his reign, staged on the Fucine Lake in 52 AD.

Other confusions of the staged and the real proved popular in Rome. Costumed as the demi-god Attis (deified for mutilating himself in the service of the Great Mother), a convict was castrated in full view of a delighted Roman audience 'sophisticated' enough to get the joke. Another *condemnatio* wore a flammable pitch-smeared tunic, which consumed him in flames on the model of Heracles in Sophocles' *Women of Trachis*. At the games given by the emperor Titus for the dedication of the Flavian amphitheatre in 80 AD, a condemned man appeared on high (via a stage machine) bearing the attributes of Orpheus, famous for calming wild animals with his lyre. However, *this* Orpheus failed to cast a magical spell, and he fell to the dust where an un-bemused (and very hungry) bear devoured him. Other deadly theatricals included punishments adapted from such mythological figures as Prometheus, Daedalus and Pasiphae. When the time came to clear the arena of the masses of bodies and make room for new victims, attendants dressed as Mercury and Pluto (gods associated with guiding dead souls to the underworld) supervised the removal of the corpses 'off to Hades'. As Libanius (fourth century AD) put it, 'whatever legend rehearses, the amphitheatre provides'.

The theatrical spaces of the empire harnessed the myths of Roman religion to the bloody reality of the here and now. The emperor offered these delights to an appreciative audience, who demanded only more and greater spectacles, and occasionally the emperor's attendance at them.[20] Accepting the illusion of mutual allegiance, the festival audiences of Rome helped to guarantee the corruption of absolute power.

NOTES

1. Bertolt Brecht, *The Messingkauf Dialogues*, trans. J. Willett (Methuen: London, 1965).
2. In Athens, for example, Zeus had over thirty different cults, many associated with specific sites – Zeus as god of thunder, of guests, of libations, of justice, of safety, etc.
3. Early Rome accepted the worship of Dionysus or Bacchus under the name *Liber* ('Freedom'); in 186 BC, however, authorities held the cult responsible for an outbreak of crime and immorality, leading to restrictions and a severe decline in the cult's popularity.
4. M. H. Jameson, 'Sacred Space and the City: Greece and Bhaktapur', *International Journal of Hindu Studies* 1 (1997), 485–99; 486–7.
5. We get a sense of their splendour from the Parthenon frieze, which illustrates the procession at the Panathenaea. Although not originally a theatre festival, the Panathenaea included dramatic contests in the late Hellenistic period.
6. The Romans also held a new wine festival, the *Vinalia* (in April), as well as the *Liberalia* (the Roman 'Dionysia', n. 3 above) in mid-March. However, neither featured scenic games.
7. C. Garton, *Personal Aspects of the Roman Theatre* (Toronto: Hakkert, 1972), pp. 28–9.

8. P. Wilson, *The Athenian Institution of the Khoregia: The Chorus, the City and the Stage* (Cambridge: Cambridge University Press, 2000), p. 128; P. Cartledge reckons that in the late fifth century the total spent for the City Dionysia annually could have supported 350 Athenian families at subsistence level for a year; *Aristophanes and his Theatre of the Absurd* (Bristol: Bristol Classical Press, 1990), p. 8.

9. Anticipating this practice by 130 years, the tyrant Hieron of Syracuse *c.*476 commissioned Aeschylus' *Women of Aitnae* to celebrate the 'founding' of Aitnae (actually the settling of Syracusans after Hieron conquered and removed the indigenous inhabitants, the same pattern of colonization used by Israel in the occupied territories of Palestine). Here, as later, theatrical performance honoured military triumph and political reorganization rather than a religious/civic festival *per se.*

10. 'The actors are more important now than the poets' (Aristotle *Rhetoric* 3.1403b31); festivals have become a 'degenerate theatocracy' (Plato *Laws* 3.700e6–701a3). As main actors became 'stars' in Athens, some accrued sufficient wealth to serve as *chorêgoi* themselves (Demosthenes 18.114).

11. As an example of our lack of knowledge, all that survives of a lost play of Naevius called *Apella* is two remarks about onions.

12. E. Segal, *Roman Laughter: The Comedy of Plautus* (Harvard University Press: Cambridge, Mass., 1968), p. 14. The consequences of Rome's addressing social problems via military expansion included the institution of a large standing army (some 350,000–400,000 during the imperial period); the consolidation of aristocratic power; the rapid rise in merchants, craftsmen and slaves (on large agricultural estates); and a flood of peasants into Rome, forming the urban proletariat that became the target audience for theatrical festivals – G. Alföldy, *The Social History of Rome* (London and Sydney: Croom Helm, 1985), pp. 26–9, 36–61.

13. In these *munera* (shortened plural of *munus gladiatorium*, a 'gift consisting of gladiators'), the vast majority of human victims were war captives (*captivi*) and condemned criminals (*noxii*). Augustus made *munera* part of the regular festival season, acknowledging the importance of the military and anticipating the dying emperor Septimius Severus' advice to his sons (211 AD): 'Stay on good terms [with your troops], enrich the soldiers and don't take much notice of anything else' (Dio 76.15.2). On Roman women who idolized gladiators, Juvenal (6.112) concludes that 'the sword is what they love'.

14. Augustus averaged 1,250 gladiators at each of the three *munera* he sponsored in the Forum and 135 wild beasts at each of the twenty-six *venationes* he staged in the amphitheatre. By 107 AD Trajan (to celebrate his Dacian triumphs) gave gladiatorial contests and hunts over 123 days, involving ten thousand combatants in various deadly encounters and some eleven thousand animals for slaughter. Roman lust for killing exotic beasts devastated Central Asia and North Africa of many species, including lions.

15. Due to minimal cost, mimes survived into the Byzantine era in private venues, whereas shows like pantomime that demanded space, scenery and music died off. Even so, in the mid-fourth century AD, Rome still offered 175 days of *ludi* per year – ten of *munera*, sixty-four of circuses and a hundred and one of *ludi scaenici*. Discouraged by Christian emperors, however, theatrical festivals eventually died out.

16. In *Totem and Taboo*, Freud describes 'the festive feeling' as 'the liberty to do what as a rule is prohibited', in J. Strachey (ed. and trans.) *The Complete Psychological Works of Sigmund Freud* vol. 13 (London: Hogarth Press and the Institute of Psycho-Analysis, 1995), p. 140. Across cultures, theatre generally has exploited such licence.

17. Romans had good reason to fear their slaves: of the roughly seven million inhabitants of Italy under Augustus, three million were slaves. Fear of slave revolts haunted the upper classes (Seneca *de Clementia* 1.24), but Rome's 'divide and conquer' strategy ensured that the urban proletariat and resisters in the provinces rarely identified with rebellious slaves (Alföldy, 1985, pp. 56–73 and 81–2).

18. A. S. Gratwick, 'Drama', in E. J. Kenney (ed.), *Cambridge History of Classical Literature*: Vol II: *Latin Literature* (Cambridge: Cambridge University Press, 1982), p. 107. The Roman proverb *'non semper Saturnalia erunt'* ('the Saturnalia will not last for ever') reflected the true nature of the slaves' licence.

19. J. C. Edmondson, 'Dynamic Arenas', in W. J. Slater (ed.) *Roman Theater and Society* (University of Michigan Press: Ann Arbor, 1996), pp. 69–112; p. 80. The best theatre seats were reserved for a tiny fraction of Romans, who wielded, sustained and profited from imperial rule. Augustus never successfully extended these restrictions (the *lex Iulia theatralis*) to the amphitheatre (*munera*) nor to the hippodrome (chariot races), where classes and genders mixed.

20. Seneca (*Epistles* 7.3, 7.4) expresses disgust at the crowds, whose seductive bloodlust worried Augustine over three centuries later (*Confessions* 6.13).

FURTHER READING

Alföldy, G., *The Social History of Rome*, third ed., trans. D. Braund and F. Pollock. London and Sydney: Croom Helm, 1985.

Beare, W., *The Roman Stage: A Short History of Latin Drama in the Time of the Republic*, third ed. London: Methuen, 1964.

Csapo, E. and Slater, W. J., *The Context of Ancient Drama*. Ann Arbor: University of Michigan Press, 1995.

Pickard-Cambridge, A., *The Dramatic Festivals of Athens*, second ed., rev. J. Gould and D. Lewis. Oxford: Clarendon Press, 1998.

Scullard, H. H., *Festivals and Ceremonies of the Roman Republic*. Ithaca: Cornell University Press, 1981.

Wilson, P., *The Athenian Institution of the Khoregia: The Chorus, the City and the Stage*. Cambridge: Cambridge University Press, 2000.

11

RICHARD BEACHAM

Playing places: the temporary and the permanent

Early in the second century AD, during the reign of Hadrian, the proposed structural and functional conversion of the Theatre of Dionysus to stage gladiatorial combats within it led to rioting. The orator Musonius had earlier urged the Athenians to use peaceful persuasion to have the gladiatorial games banned from the sacred precinct of Dionysus. Subsequently the cynic philosopher Demonax went further, opposing gladiatorial games altogether and asserting that if the Athenians introduced them they should tear down the Altar of Mercy. The theatre had then been in use for some seven centuries.[1] Clearly the citizens of Athens conceived both the site itself and its associated functions as in some very fundamental and vital sense 'permanent'. During its long existence it had undergone numerous modifications, few of which, despite the determined and persistent efforts of generations of archaeologists and scholars, can now be identified or traced with much accuracy or confidence. At some point in late antiquity the theatre ceased to be used even for secular entertainments, and the site itself fell into ruin, was overgrown and all but forgotten. In fact, until the nineteenth century, its location was erroneously thought to be the more extensively preserved adjacent site of the late second-century AD Odeon of Herodes Atticus; an irony of history since the impulse to construct this second theatre arose in part from the wish to replace the desecrated venue. Although the location and general lineaments of the Theatre of Dionysus, the most significant of all ancient theatres, are identified and demarcated today, the whole site seems on the verge either of being submerged into the encroaching urban landscape, or alternatively, absorbed back into the living rock of the slopes of the Acropolis, out of which it had originally been fashioned.

Meanwhile in Rome, the great Theatre of Pompey, that city's first permanent theatre, erected in 55 BC, and a prototype for the thousands of theatres subsequently constructed throughout the Roman Empire, suffered an analogous fate. As late as the sixth century AD, it was still in use, and its enormous structure so imposing that the Chancellor of the reigning Ostrogoths,

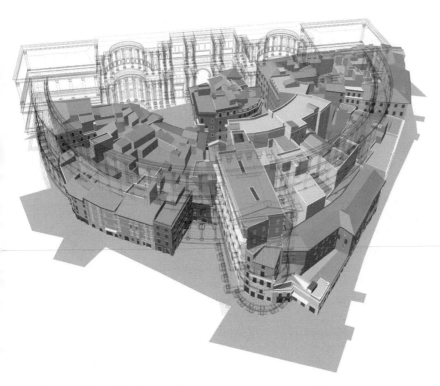

Figure 12. Outline of the Theatre of Pompey at Rome superimposed on a computer model of the existing state of the site.

Cassiodorus, described it as 'caves vaulted with hanging stones, so cleverly joined into beautiful shapes that they resemble more the grottoes of a huge mountain than anything wrought by human hand . . . one would have thought it more likely for mountains to subside, than this strong building be shaken'.[2] Yet by the sixteenth century, there was little to see of it above ground. Today its extensive physical remains may be discerned in the vast 'footprint' of the site imprinted upon the modern urban landscape, and viewed at first hand by examining the fabric of the array of buildings currently occupying the site, into which it was absorbed. To this day, the medieval and renaissance edifice that incorporates much of its enormous auditorium towers above the adjacent buildings of the Campo de Fiori area of Rome. The ancient structure, however, were it entirely extant, would stand a further fifteen metres or more, higher than the Palazzo Pio into which it was incorporated.

These two iconic examples urge us to bear in mind that the notion of 'temporary' as opposed to 'permanent' is not always a particularly useful or definitive term in trying to understand either the variety or, more crucially, the function and meaning of ancient theatres. We need to separate the issue of actual physical structures (that with the corrosive workings of time inevitably devolve into artefacts) from the question of how the site in which theatrical activities occurred was understood by its ancient users. In short, it is the *idea* of a theatre that is temporary or permanent, not the materials comprising it or the particular quality of the structural embodiment of the idea.

The most obvious distinction normally used in attempting to create such categories is, crudely, whether the theatre building was made of wood (temporary) or of stone (permanent). The logical basis for such an approach collapses when we consider that, for example (as we shall discuss later), some 'temporary' theatres at Rome were in part constructed of marble, while most Elizabethan theatres, including the great Globe itself, were wooden. The latter were hardly temporary, however, except in the sense that eventually, when Puritan ascendancy dictated a radically changed view of the role and meaning of theatre, they ceased to be used and in some cases were physically dismantled. Ultimately, as the most 'permanent' Elizabethan playwright noted of most things human, theatres, like other institutions and the edifices incorporating them, 'are subjects all to envious and calumniating time' (*Troilus and Cressida* 3.3).

At both Athens and Rome, long before the physical expression of theatrical activity was shaped into stone buildings, the no less permanent idea of theatre had already caused a variety of wooden and 'mixed media' structures to be erected. Through examining how these structures appeared and changed over time we can develop some insights about the shifting nature, function and ultimately the meaning of theatre in antiquity. Such an approach is likely to be more instructive than simply pursuing the rather sterile and uninformative distinction between temporary and permanent structures. But it demands that the scant information that literary and archaeological evidence tentatively provides be supplemented (like all historical investigations or assertions) by imagination and interpretation.

Whatever the precise physical nature and architectural configuration of the space, the essential thing to bear in mind is that for Greek and Roman actors and audiences the space itself was sacred – set aside and consecrated to honour and worship whatever gods were deemed to be associated with the place and the activities taking place.[3] The sites, once sanctified, remained holy, unless some event of desecration occurred – such as the gladiatorial combats the Romans proposed for the Theatre of Dionysus, which in Greek eyes was a sacrilege – requiring that they either be abandoned, or else purified and restored to the sacred condition essential for them to function as places of performance. At some point, many hundreds of years before – probably in the fifth century BC – the space on the south-west slopes of the Acropolis had been designated a theatre. Earlier dramatic performances had taken place within the Athenian agora, but the new location was determined by the twin advantages of being immediately adjacent to the Temple of Dionysus and of providing a convenient raised *theatron* (seeing place) for an audience seated upon the incline above an open area that could be configured to provide a sufficiently large and level space for presenting performances. Scholarly arguments have long raged – and continue unabated – over the shape and exact location of this first Theatre of Dionysus.[4]

Certainty is not possible; what on balance seems *probable* is that the performance space itself consisted at first of a large circular dancing area, the *orchêstra*, about twenty-five metres in diameter. Although elsewhere in Greece there were earlier non-circular theatre sites, their shapes (sometimes rectilinear or trapezoidal) were apparently determined primarily by a variety of specific and local conditions. But as theatres began to be built widely throughout Greece from the late fifth century and on into the fourth, they were almost always provided with circular orchestras, with the theatre at Athens itself serving as the most likely model. At the annual celebrations of the Athenian City Dionysia, it was here, in the circle, that the choral dithyrambs and earliest tragedies would have been performed, with no structural separation between actors and chorus. The audience was seated, probably initially upon the bare incline of the hill itself and then, somewhat later, upon wooden benches, which may have formed an angled area for seating, or, alternatively, were configured to provide a series of roughly curved tiers rising up the slope of the Acropolis. Analysis of the earliest surviving plays by Aeschylus strongly suggests that direct communication and contact was possible between chorus and actors, and that the plays unfolded within a circular space which was the most convenient and appropriate for the dithyrambic dances honouring the god, and out of which, according to Aristotle, tragic dramatic performance emerged.

At some point in the first half of the fifth century a wooden scene building, the *skênê*, was introduced, and it probably intersected and cut through the *orchêstra* (thus determining that the actors would continue to perform within the circular space), directly opposite the spectators, rather than as a tangent across the furthest edge of the *orchêstra*'s circumference. The *skênê* is likely to have had only a single large central door allowing access by the actors from within (or behind) it directly into the *orchêstra*.

It is not possible to determine whether a low raised stage was placed in front of it. In the course of the century (and possibly as part of the extensive building projects undertaken by Pericles) the *skênê*, previously of wood and canvas, may have been enlarged, made more elaborate in decor and provided with a serviceable roof for the appearance of gods. It is possible too that a limited amount of stone seating (*prodedria*) at the lowest level closest to the *orchêstra* and reserved for priests and dignitaries, may have been constructed during this period. The central structure of the Periclean stage building was erected to the north (and lined up along the back) of the new long hall or *stoa* that was probably constructed in the last phase of Pericles' building programme. It thus formed part of a Dionysian precinct of a temple, theatre *stoa* and, as described below, an Odeon.

From at least the middle of the fifth century, the façade of the *skênê* was decorated with painting (*skênographia*) which may have enhanced its flat surface with perspectively rendered depictions of architectural embellishments. Alternatively, there may have been painted emblems (a tree to suggest a grove, a statue or column to indicate a temple) of the sort Attic vases of the same period used conventionally to signal elements of the mythological scenes and the locale of narratives depicted upon them.

The structural organization of this, the earliest Greek theatre for which the texts of plays performed within it survive, suggests that the primary function of its space was to assist in creating within the imagination of the audience, not an illusionistic or imitative representation of places or actions, but rather a mental *scenescape*. Physical space and movement in this venue were employed to provide imaginative access to emotional, ethical and political issues. These issues populated a compelling, but insubstantial, imaginary realm generated out of highly stylized and image-laden poetry, within the 'mind's eye' of spectators. Such language was employed partly to enact and partly to recount narratives, and was in turn conjoined with the evocative powers of music and what was almost certainly highly figurative mimetic dance. It was the essence of such 'total' works of art, fashioned from these expressive elements, that they could not be adequately conveyed by purely realistic means; neither language, movement, gesture, nor scenic depiction attempted to imitate the appearance of ordinary behaviour or physical reality. The very occasion and act of theatre established that quite different conventions of communication and understanding governed and determined the transactions taking place.[5]

The manner in which the audience gained access to this imaginative realm was conditioned and coloured not only by the elements of the actual performance space itself and its use, but also by the larger urban environment in the vicinity of the theatre. Many of the spectators would have had in constant view before them the old temple of Dionysus beyond the far side of the *orchêstra* and *skênê*, while the Acropolis and its temples rose behind and above them. Here were located by the last decades of the fifth century the Parthenon and other great temples and monuments

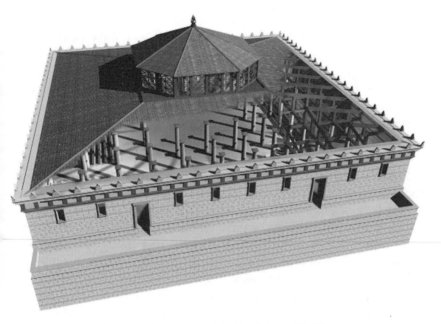

Figure 13. Computer model of the Odeon of Pericles.

built under the leadership of Pericles (495–429), following the destruction of much of the city by the Persians in 480. From 460 until his death, Pericles dominated Athenian politics and under his leadership the city became the cultural leader of the Mediterranean world. Thus, while watching and responding to the dramas presented before them in the theatre, the Athenian spectators (and foreign visitors) were constantly aware of the visible monuments which in part embodied and reflected the culture whose values or meaning were themselves continually the concern of the dramatic presentations.

One of the greatest achievements of Pericles' building programme was the construction of the Odeon which bore his name; probably the first roofed theatre-like structure of antiquity. It was immediately adjacent to and due east of the *orchêstra* and seating area of the Theatre of Dionysus. At this period the theatre had little or no architectural structure of stone: its *skênê* built of wood; most if not all of its seating insubstantial and resting upon an earthen embankment; its *orchêstra* a flat, unornamented and empty space. By contrast, for the audience who viewed the plays within their insubstantial theatre (which to accommodate the encroaching Odeon was probably shifted somewhat to the north and west) the great mass of Pericles' structure rose monumentally to the left in their field of vision; most of it visible to everyone as a colossal dominating presence.

Pericles had explicitly underscored the importance of works of monumental architecture for the celebration of Athenian cultural values and their enduring capacity to impress upon future generations the glory and achievements of her people. Although relatively few details are reliably known about the Odeon, what is clear is that it functioned in part to remind Athenians both of Pericles himself and of the defeat of the Persians, an event that was decisive for the very survival of the city and its fledgling form of government, democracy. Its shape, and in particular its great slanting roof converging to a single point at its apex, was said to have been modelled to recall the war tent of the defeated Persian King, Xerxes, while the array of pillars and beams within it allegedly incorporated the masts of the ships of the vast Persian fleet defeated by the Greeks under the leadership of Athens at the battle of Salamis.[6] So, the display and recycling of such trophies would indeed have been both 'sweet and useful' as, some centuries later, the Roman critic Horace would demand of great works of art. The Odeon was probably built between 446 and 442. Research, recently augmented by the creation and analysis of 3D computer models, suggests that it measured about sixty metres square, and at its highest point stood over twenty metres tall. The colonnaded front terrace was around eight and a half metres high, and would have been ideal for viewing the *proagôn*, a great festive procession that preceded the Dionysia, as it travelled along the Dionysian precinct and entered the theatre. One side of the Odeon actually intruded into the seating area, the *theatron*, of the Theatre of Dionysus and into the slope of the Acropolis. The site was cut into the hillside on the north, west and east, and was supported by retaining walls, parts of which have been recovered in recent excavations. Built mainly from timber (but by no means temporary!), the Odeon is believed to have stood for almost four centuries, before being destroyed by fire and later rebuilt using stone. It was regarded as one of the greatest architectural achievements of ancient Athens.

About a century after Pericles' construction of the Odeon, its neighbour, the Theatre of Dionysus, was given monumental form at the instigation of the Athenian statesman and orator Lycurgus (390–324 BC). He controlled the city's finances in the period 338–326, following the defeat of Athens by Macedonia. Believing it essential to restore Athenian morale (and morality), he undertook a number of important civic reforms while also encouraging extensive building and other projects. As part of this process of renewal he evidently wished to monumentalize and memorialize Athenian achievement, including its great theatrical tradition. He ordered that official copies of the plays of the three great tragic poets, Aeschylus, Euripides and Sophocles, be established and 'fixed' – in effect making them permanent. In an analogous fashion, the architectural features of the theatre itself were no longer

Figure 14. Computer model of the Theatre of Dionysus in the Lycurgan phase.

left contingent upon possibly periodic architectural adjustments, but (more) permanently embodied in stone and masonry. He succeeded on both counts; the texts that survive today are probably based on the versions he preserved, while the stone auditorium he ordered to be built, to replace the earlier wooden seats resting upon the natural slope of the hillside, substantially comprises the archaeological remains we see today.

This enables scholars to make reasonably informed guesses about the architectural format of the Lycurgan theatre, and in turn gain a better sense of other Greek theatres constructed or renovated during the same period. The foundations of the *skênê* are substantially preserved, but their precise characteristics somewhat obscured by later modifications. It was composed of a solid masonry wall about twenty metres in length, probably broken by three doorways. The surface of its roof might have been flat to allow performers to act on top of the *skênê* as well as in front of it. Normally, however, it seems likely that the actors continued to perform in front of the scene building, either on the surface of the *orchêstra*, or possibly upon a wooden raised stage.

The most striking element of the stone *skênê* (and a feature that gave its name to this type of theatre) were the two large – probably columned – square

Figure 15. Computer model of the Theatre of Dionysus in the Hellenistic phase.

structures (*paraskênia*) which extended out approximately five metres from either end of the central wall into the orchestral area (itself a circle twenty metres in diameter), thereby forming projecting wings. From an architectural perspective, through the provision of these prominent new elements the stage building acquired not only solid stone structures but also columns and pediments (instead of mere painted indications of these) which were the 'hallmarks' of imposing public edifices, and thereby perhaps emphasized the institutional and cultural importance of the theatre, helping to fulfil what we infer was one of Lycurgus' objectives.

The new type of stage appears to have been emulated widely throughout the Hellenistic world. The great theatre at Epidaurus in southern Greece, for example, in its earliest fourth-century form, had a *skênê* employing substantial *paraskênia*. In terms of the dynamics of performance and the mental scenescape of the audience, these structural developments were significant. The performance of the actors was more tightly framed and focused – and in effect contained – in a manner that possibly reflected the prominence now given to the skills and virtuosity of individual performers in an era when acting had become the province of professional performers. The works of New Comedy were domestic and concerned with everyday events and plausible situations; not with the imaginative exuberance, linguistic acrobatics and impossible fantasies of the 'cosmic' comedies dreamed forth by Aristophanes and his contemporaries. Such domesticated plays, no longer surfing the waves with the spectators' unfettered imaginations, required solid and well-defined architecture to moor them.

The Lycurgan *theatron* was divided with twelve narrow stairways (each of which was sixty centimetres wide) into thirteen wedge-shaped blocks or *kerkides*; two other staircases (making fourteen in all) ran just inside the two supporting walls at either side of the structure.

In the late third or early second century further structural changes were made to the theatre, primarily in regard to its *skênê*. A permanent, high stone stage (*proskênion*), probably only three metres deep, was erected upon columns in front of the *skênê* itself. At the same time the *paraskênia* were also rebuilt to reduce their previously prominent projection out from the *skênê* to perhaps just over two metres. It is likely that these changes signal the definitive transition of performance out of the *orchêstra* and up onto the raised structure of the *skênê*'s stage. One consequence of this was that actors and audience members no longer entered the theatre, as previously, by the same route: the two *parodoi* giving access from outside the theatre into either side of the *orchêstra*, which had been used both by actors and chorus to enter the playing area of the *orchêstra*, and by spectators to gain access into the seating areas. Now the raised stage required that actors approach it either by stairs affording entrance from the rear or the sides of the *skênê*, or perhaps along a sloping ramp. It seems plausible that a consequence of these new modes of access was to further distance the audience psychologically and imaginatively from the sense of direct participation in the theatrical experience. Although, in the absence of extant tragic texts for the period, it is difficult to be certain, it seems probable too that, except when revivals of earlier tragedies were staged, plays no longer employed choruses – at least not as an element central to the plot and action of the play. Therefore the theatre's *orchêstra* was now used primarily for choral or danced presentations, including dithyrambs, but no longer as a regular playing space for the enactment of contemporaneous dramatic works.

In attempting to understand these changes of physical focus we should bear in mind a shift of emphasis arising from the changed political circumstances of the Athenian audience. The works presented now were either revivals or selections from the 'classics' of the fifth century, or works intended as demonstrations of the professional skills of the individual actors, rather than, as in the earlier period, meant to employ the theatre as a forum for discussing and debating the great political questions of the day. Although, as the plays of Menander and what we can discern of the works of the other dramatists

Figure 16. Computer model of a Greek Hellenistic theatre, based upon the Theatre at Epidaurus.

1. *Skênê*   2. *Thyrômata*   3. *Proskênion*   4. *Pinakes*   5. *Parodos*   6. *Orchêstra*
7. *Proedria*   8. *Diazômata*   9. *Klimakes*   10. *Kerkides*

of the Hellenistic period establish, the theatre continued to explore social and moral issues, particularly those relating to the life of the individual citizen, performances were no longer the participatory community events that defined earlier Athenian theatre, but rather showcase performances, in which increasingly the audiences' experience and evaluation of performance was conditioned by a sense of artistic connoisseurship.

According to Aristotle, writing in the late fourth century, 'theatre actors are more important now than playwrights' (*Rhetoric* 1403b33), and it seems likely that this condition continued and indeed became more pronounced in the later Hellenistic period. Another element which received greater emphasis and presumably increased attention from the spectators was the provision of scenery to adorn the increasingly elaborate stone-built scene buildings, such as that at Epidaurus. These now frequently had spaces (called *thyrômata*) into which painted wooden panels (*pinakes*) could be inserted. These openings between pillars or pilasters were located at the level of the *orchêstra* along the front facade of the stage (*proskênion*) itself, while above, wider apertures were provided along the front wall of the scene building which

Figure 17. *Phlyax* vase, from the J. Paul Getty Museum.

opened onto the stage. Painted depictions intended to evoke different settings could be presented and changed by removing and replacing these panels. Once again, we are probably justified in perceiving in this practice a further transition away from the transformative and multivalent concept of theatrical space that characterized the presentation of drama in the fifth century towards a more literal notion of stage space and the fictive environments in which the dramas were conceived to take place.

In addition to the evidence for Hellenistic performance provided by the architectural remains of the stone theatres, we have valuable information from a large number of vases, found in southern Italy and Sicily and dating from around 400–325 BC. These so-called *phlyax* vases were earlier erroneously believed by scholars to depict a type of farce drama indigenous to southern Italy. But recent research has established that many of the vases in fact are directly influenced by Athenian Old Comedy – in several cases specific works can be reliably identified – and its staging.[7] The characters depicted on the vases are usually grotesque, wearing padded costumes and tights, masks, cloaks, tunics and armour, and the males are invariably outfitted with a prominent phallus. They show a raised platform stage, varying in height, resting on wooden posts, with a decorated rear wall made from panels of wood or canvas. This wall often has a double doorway usually opening

Figure 18. Computer model of a *phlyax* stage.

inwards, through which the actors would have entered onto the stage, and occasionally it has window openings that may have been employed for comic purposes. The space behind the rear stage wall was probably used as a tiring area and to store stage properties. A short flight of steps, varying in number from six to eight, is sometimes shown standing at the front of the platform, suggesting a stage height of something between a metre and a metre and a half. Draperies are often hung in swags from the edge of the stage to the ground, either to mask the wooden posts supporting the stage platform, or perhaps as an embellishment of the structure. The vases indicate that both the stage and the ground around it were used for performance, as some depict actors climbing the stairs leading up to the platform or standing away from the stage looking on (see also **Fig. 27**).

The stages as represented on the vases sometimes had a small roof protruding from the rear wall over the stage, held aloft by wooden supports attached to the posts of the main structure. These supports were usually decorated, often to resemble one of the classical orders. Other stage properties depicted on the vases include small porches and altars, baskets, chests, tables, weapons and chairs. It is impossible to determine whether the stages were in a fixed location (but possibly only erected for particular occasions), or portable and the property of travelling troupes. As depicted, they appear simple in structure, implying that they were capable of being dismantled and transported. However, the conventions of vase-painting may have determined that such depictions imply a less substantial, and significantly smaller, structure than may actually have been the case. The later vases, from the second half of the fourth century, tend to depict more elaborate structures. Some scholars have argued that the stages were depicted in a simplified manner because of the limited space available to the vase-painters, and that in fact they reflect, if only incompletely, large wooden stages (at least some 8 to 10 m. in width) constructed in the permanent theatres of *Magna Graecia*, the area colonized and settled by the Greeks in southern Italy.

In any case, throughout southern Italy and Sicily, both during the fourth century when the vases were produced and later, numerous theatres with what were eventually masonry *skênai* were constructed, and the evidence suggests that, broadly, these followed a pattern of development parallel to that which we believe to have been the case at Athens: the stage buildings tended to acquire *paraskênia* which later, in the first and second centuries BC, were diminished in size; but, unlike in the Hellenistic East, the structures do not appear to have been transformed into the *thyrômata* format. For centuries, the Romans were in close and ever-increasing contact with the Greek cities to the south of them in Italy; many spheres of Roman culture were profoundly influenced by Hellenistic traditions, and both Roman drama and stage practice reflect this. The stages shown on the southern Italian vases strongly resemble what other evidence, both written and visual, suggests the earliest Roman stages may have been like. These wooden structures were put up for particular, usually established, annual holidays (*ludi*) at Rome and then dismantled. Thus, from at least the late fourth or early third century the theatre as an established cultural, political and religious institution became ever more firmly fixed and prominent in Roman society – *permanent* – but the structures on which plays were presented continued for centuries to be *provisional*. Historical accounts describe in some detail the nature of these sometimes highly elaborate structures. In addition, the extant plays of Plautus and Terence give us some idea of what they may have been like, by enabling us to analyse the information they contain about the use of doorways, stage action and the exits and entrances of actors. However, by far the best visual evidence comes from surviving Roman wall-painting, which may actually preserve depictions of such stages. The Roman architect Vitruvius, writing at the time of Augustus, states that painters 'depicted the facades of stages of the tragic, comic or satyric type' on the walls of Roman houses (*De Architectura* 7.5.1–2). By closely examining such paintings (principally those surviving at Pompeii and Herculaneum), most recently with the aid of 3D computer modelling technologies, it is possible to discern in some

Figure 19. A reconstruction of a Roman temporary stage, based upon a Roman wall painting, created by the author at the J. Paul Getty Museum in Malibu.

detail the probable nature of the temporary wooden stages used at Rome for several centuries before the construction of the first permanent theatre in 55 BC.

The basic format of these stages closely resembles the relatively simple trestle stage depicted with variations in detail and decor on the *phlyax* vases and it is certainly possible that Roman practice drew directly upon the examples of stage architecture at hand in the neighbouring Greek communities. However it is equally plausible to assume that such stages were developed independently at Rome: their basic elements – raised stage, background of wood or canvas, broken by one or more openings – are so simple and utilitarian that such *Ur*-stages have appeared and reappeared with only minor variations throughout the history of the theatre.

What is particularly notable about the Roman temporary structures is that, despite their provisional nature, such stages tended over the several centuries in which their use is documented (which continued even after the city had acquired several enormous stone-built theatres) to become increasingly, and sometimes extraordinarily, elaborate, both in size and the sumptuousness of their decor. The evidence of the wall paintings collaborates and helps to illustrate the ancient written descriptions of some of these extravagant *scaenae*. The annual series of games at Rome in which these stages figured were organized and sponsored by Roman state officials – primarily the *aediles*, although other officials were also responsible for giving public entertainments from time to time. Because the office of aedile was a relatively junior one, and the future electoral success of its holder in obtaining higher office depended in part upon the impression his one-year tenure of the post made upon the electorate, there developed a profoundly competitive dynamic which dictated and could greatly reward one-upmanship. Indeed, it is likely that the determined and successful resistance which Roman officials displayed over several centuries to the construction of a permanent stone theatre structure was based quite as much upon their desire to reserve for themselves the option for such beneficial 'showcasing' of their largesse as it was upon moral reservations. In the wider sense too, the Roman elite wished as far as possible to exercise broad control over taste and culture; in particular it tended (at least officially) to regard many of the defining elements of Hellenistic civilization, including of course the theatre, with a degree of suspicion and unease, and wished to monitor and modulate their dissemination to the inhabitants of Rome.

Ancient literary evidence provides us with some tantalizing descriptions of some of these temporary, but nevertheless sumptuous, theatres, erected by aspiring politicians over several centuries. At the beginning of the first century BC, Claudius Pulcher provided what was described as the first *scaena* to be painted in a variety of colours, and to use illusionistic techniques of *skênographia* to depict 'fake' architecture. This was so convincing that according to one account, 'crows were deceived into flying to the painted image of roof tiles' (Pliny the Elder, *Nat. Hist.* 35.23). The stages themselves became, in effect, performative, and part of the delight which audiences evidently took in them was their visual and playful extravagance. In order to ensure that spectators could view both the stages and performances in comfort, patrons began to provide a great awning, the *vela*, which stretched out over much of the *cavea*, offering both shelter from the sun, as well as additional scenic splendour, through the colourful designs painted or embroidered upon it, which also created a pleasing 'special effect' as the sunlight played through its red, yellow and purple colours (Lucretius, *De Rerum Natura* 4.75–83). The *vela* was such a crowd-pleaser that, as surviving announcements for games written upon walls at Pompeii attest, when a performance was to take place employing one, the news featured prominently in the advance publicity. Other accounts trace an accelerating process of increasing showmanship, with stages decorated in silver, then gold, and finally even in ivory.

The most awe-inspiring example of the impulse towards ever-increasing and competitive extravagance was the theatre of M. Aemilius Scaurus, erected in 58 BC. The ancient account describes a three-storied structure, supported by some 360 columns, the lowest range of which was some twelve metres high. The first level of the facade was fashioned of marble, the second of wood inlaid with glass and the uppermost of gold-gilded boards. In addition, it displayed several thousand bronze statues, and a vast array of other scenic and architectural decor (Pliny the Elder, *Naturalis Historia* 36.114–15). The visual evidence of the wall paintings serves to corroborate the incredible imaginative exuberance of Roman architectural design, suggested by accounts of the temporary stages.

Even after Rome acquired its first permanent theatre, which as we shall see might well have been thought of as 'the last word' in architectural splendour, we hear of temporary structures continuing to be erected. In 52 BC, C. Scribonius Curio constructed one which, though it impoverished him at the time, evidently boosted his political career (he was tribune two years later in 50) and certainly ensured lasting fame in the annals of theatrical history. In fact, Curio's structure, or 'major folly' as Pliny deemed it (*Nat. Hist.* 36.116–120), was two large wooden theatres cunningly constructed to adjoin one another, back to back, but balanced upon a revolving pivot. In the mornings they were used for the simultaneous presentation of various theatrical entertainments, and then, in the afternoon, with spectators clinging precariously upon them, they could be revolved and conjoined to create a single double theatre (an amphitheatre, in fact) for the presentation of gladiatorial displays.

The yearly cycle of theatre-building was deliberately and conspicuously extravagant and wasteful. Rome was in many ways a highly 'theatricalized' society, in which the devising and provision of visual displays of status, dignity and power was an important form of communication and cultural signification. Consequently, the means through which such display could take place was subject to continuing negotiation and regulation. This included in particular the right to provide enduring and monumental public buildings to glorify one's name and achievements. During the last years of the dying Roman Republic the traditional political system and institutions began to disintegrate, essentially because a constitution that had originally evolved for the governance of a city-state could no longer adequately meet the needs of a great imperial power. These changed circumstances led to many years of instability, including chronic civil discord and war, while one aspiring leader after another sought to secure and retain power, including the most important power of all, that of ensuring one's memory; a hope that could be significantly enhanced by providing an enduring public memorial.

In 55 BC the triumphal general Pompey the Great – a vastly successful 'warlord' who had emerged from his military campaigns with sufficient

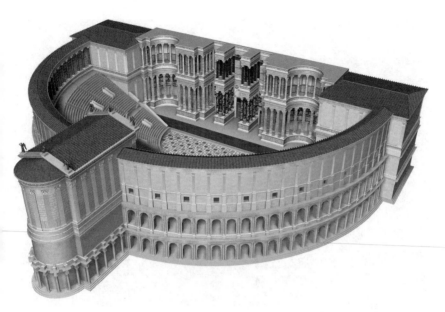

Figure 20. Computer model of the Theatre of Pompey, showing the Temple of Venus.

power both to dazzle, and if necessary intimidate, the Roman people – 'persuaded' the authorities to allow him to construct Rome's first permanent theatre. It was the largest the Romans ever built, anywhere. And Pompey named it after himself; a name it retained during the six centuries in which it remained in active use as one of the principal monuments of ancient Rome. Pompey's sumptuous and grandiose edifice comprised in addition to the theatre itself (crowned by a temple dedicated to his patron goddess, Venus *Victrix*) an extensive 'leisure-complex' of gardens enclosed within a colonnade. It was located just outside the formal boundaries (*pomerium*) of the City; a boundary that by law men with pro-consular status (such as at times Pompey himself) could not cross without forfeiting the very special power (*imperium*) that status allowed them to exercise. By including in the complex a senatorial assembly room or *curia* available for meetings of the Senate, he enabled such individuals to participate in senatorial politics with impunity.

It was the first major example of 'imperial' architecture at Rome, decisively influencing the style of much subsequent building as well as Rome's urban development, and throughout its history was one of the great showplaces of the City as well as the venue for many of its most momentous events. Its importance extended far beyond permanently commemorating Pompey's own political and military power. It was an audacious example of 'performing architecture', providing a venue so vast, grand and above all 'permanent',

Figure 21. Computer model of the stage facade (*scaenae frons*) of the Theatre of Pompey.

that (like the Colosseum built a century and a half later) it appears to have embodied and signified for its popular audience some fundamental sense of what it meant to be Roman. Eventually laws determined where all classes and categories of spectators were seated, and what they wore; the theatre audience thus assembled served as a potent visual expression of the Roman Empire in microcosm. And nothing epitomized this more than the high wall that curved through the upper region of the auditorium (*cavea*), graphically and physically segregating citizen spectators from non-citizens. As befitted such a major public institution, a special government official, the '*Procurator operis theatri Pompeiani*', oversaw the theatre's maintenance.

The Theatre of Pompey has more claim than most ancient performance venues to the status of 'permanent'. Its legacy of entropy and reuse has determined to this day much of how we perceive the area of Rome in which it is located. In the Middle Ages, the local inhabitants built houses and palaces into the theatre, buildings which even today preserve its very extensive remains in their cellars and walls. The *curia* was dominated by a statue of Pompey himself, provided by the Roman people to demonstrate its gratitude (Plutarch, *Brutus* 14); and it was here, as Shakespeare would dramatize many centuries later, 'even at the base of Pompey's statue which all the while ran blood, great Caesar fell' (*Julius Caesar* 3.2.189–90), assassinated in 44 BC, after his own forces had been responsible for the murder of

Figure 22. Computer model of a Roman theatre.

1. *Postscaenium*   2. *Scaenae frons*   3. *Versura*   4. *Portae hospitales*   5. *Porta regia*
6. *Pulpitum*   7. *Frons Pulpitum*   8. *Orchestra*   9. *Scalaria*   10. Parapet   11. *Proedria*
12. *Aditus Maximus*   13. *Praecinctio*   14. *Cuneus*   15. Tribunal   16. *Vomitoria*
17. *Porticus in summa cavea*   18. Supports of the *Vela*

his rival Pompey. Both this assembly hall and a nearby house which Pompey provided for himself were located within a spacious park extending some two hundred metres behind the theatre. In addition to its use in connection with performances in the theatre (Vitruvius 5.9.5), this amenity soon became one of the most popular places in Rome to escape from the summer heat, or arrange amorous assignations. Within it were rows of trees, and shaded streams and fountains. Along its north side the *Hecatostylon*, 'portico of the hundred pillars', was festooned with golden curtains from Pergamum, and displayed a large and impressive collection of valuable statues and paintings.

According to Pliny (*Nat. Hist.* 36.115) Pompey's theatre could seat forty thousand spectators, a figure which has long been doubted, but which a recent detailed scientific survey 'The Pompey Project', led by the University of Warwick, indicates may not have been too vastly exaggerated. The diameter of the auditorium was 150 metres, the actual length of the stage itself, astonishingly, almost a hundred metres! Behind it the great facade of the *scaena*, which may initially have been of wood, probably rose to the full height of the upper tiers of the auditorium opposite: three storeys. The fact that the theatre (and specifically its *scaena* in AD 80) is reported several times to have been damaged by fire lends weight to the theory that during its early history the stage facade was at least partly constructed of wood, later replaced by stone.

Apart from its immensity, the most striking architectural element of the theatre itself was the temple to Venus *Victrix*. It was the largest of several shrines along the colonnade at the upper rim of the *cavea*; for the Romans, as for the Greeks, performances in the theatre were acts of worship, and the games, however entertaining, were also highly important religious occasions. Possibly this temple was constructed in such a way that a monumental ramp of steps leading up to it formed the central bank of seats in the auditorium. It was said that when Pompey's political rivals objected to a permanent theatre, he claimed that in fact he was building a temple (a traditional privilege of victorious generals), beneath which steps would be provided for watching games honouring the goddess (Tertullian *De Spectaculis* 10.5; Tacitus *Annales* 14.20).

At regular intervals around the external perimeter of the upper colonnade were attached the vertical masts from which projecting horizontal booms suspended a huge brightly coloured linen awning, the *vela*, that shaded the audience. The building also was provided with a form of air-conditioning. Writing three quarters of a century later, Valerius Maximus recorded that 'Pompey was the first to have water flowing down the aisles [of the Theatre] to cool the summer heat' (2.4.6). Other ancient sources refer in addition to the provision of an invention for spraying a fine-scented saffron mist.

Pompey's complex was an amenity with a message; one of the major precursors of the type of 'performing architecture' which would figure so prominently under the patronage of the emperors. To walk through the central court of the park was to be impressed with both the munificence and military accomplishments of its patron. Moreover, the site and its architecture communicated an ideological concept. Because the complex was located in the Campus Martius, which – in addition to its venerable military connection as a parade ground and training area – had long been a place where voters were impressed by monumental architecture (and from time to time bribed with gifts or hand-outs), in effect it extended and refined associations which this area already had. The layout of the buildings and in particular the placing of the theatre and the *curia* at opposite ends of the central axis, tended to raise the status of the former (crowned by its temple) to that of a formal political space when faced from the front porch of the *curia* which was also itself a sacred precinct. The entrance to the latter was dominated by a huge painting of a warrior by the fifth-century painter Polygnotus, which may have served to remind visitors of the military prowess of its builder. The political/religious nature of the building dominating each pole of the axis was therefore visually emphasized by being mirrored in its opposite.

Rome eventually acquired two more stone theatres, which, though extremely impressive, were on a smaller scale than Pompey's edifice. Not only the provision of such theatres, but indeed a great many of their specific details of design, building technique and decoration were soon widely imitated throughout the Roman world. Together with the arena, these monuments were viewed by both patrons and citizens throughout the far-flung Empire as an important and binding example of *Romanitas* – the sense of being part of Roman culture – and this intangible but crucial and highly 'permanent' aspect of Roman imperial identity and ideology led to the widespread construction of theatres broadly based upon the same prototype. Enabling and contributing lustre and grandeur to the participation of their vast audiences, these venues were places in which, in effect, the Romans performed themselves.

In addition to the awe-inspiring richness of their décor and architectural splendour, the most striking aspect, and an important difference between such theatres and their Greek and Hellenistic equivalents, was that the Roman structures were usually built on flat land (levelled and configured as necessary by the architects and builders), free-standing and integrated as a single architectural entity comprising scene-building, stage, *orchêstra* and auditorium. Like the Theatre of Pompey, Roman theatres often included a temple and colonnade (*porticus post scaenam*) as part of a complete architectural ensemble. By contrast, the earlier theatres tended to be not purpose-built, but appropriated spaces, fashioned out of naturally sloping hillsides, and their structural elements usually were not conjoined into a single autonomous edifice.

The Romans also developed a further form of theatre, or more accurately refined the design of earlier Hellenistic assembly halls, called *bouleuteria*. The new Roman structure, an Odeum, modified their architectural format by creating a smaller orchestral area, limiting the lateral extensions of the curved tiers of seating in the *cavea*, and dispensing with the columns which traditionally had been used to provide support for the roof spanning over the auditorium and stage. In creating this new building the Romans achieved a structure which, of all ancient theatrical venues, was closest in its design and organization of space between performers and spectators to theatres with which modern audiences are familiar. One of the most impressive examples was built in Athens.

Marcus Agrippa, who had decisively contributed to defeating the forces of Mark Antony and Cleopatra in the renowned naval victory at Actium in 31 BC, was a close adviser and son-in-law of the Emperor Augustus. To

Figure 23. Computer model of the Odeum or Odeon of Agrippa.

perpetuate his name and dignity, and to offer public patronage on a suitably lavish scale, he built an elegant Odeon at Athens in the period 16 to 14 BC, which bore his name. It was one of the best-designed and most architecturally detailed of ancient indoor theatres, and indeed amongst the most elegantly proportioned and sumptuously decorated buildings of antiquity. It stood several storeys high, completely dominating the neighbouring buildings. Its original function was to serve as a concert hall, although it is likely that dramatic performances took place within it as well. Its interior, which was essentially square, seated some twelve hundred spectators and was remarkable for the huge span of its roof, which was twenty-eight metres; one of the largest in antiquity – with no internal supporting columns. Thus the Odeon avoided the problem of poor sightlines which characterized the much earlier Odeon of Pericles. Its walls were decorated with elegant marble inlay, and the upper portions strengthened with pilasters between which there may have been windows for ventilation and illumination.

Because of its orientation, and the open colonnades to the rear of the structure, the sunlight fell directly from the front upon the stage; probably the first time that such a design feature was used in an indoor theatre. At the rear of the auditorium there was a double-columned wall composed of two parallel rows of six enormous Corinthian columns, which allowed cross-ventilation and also served as a foyer for members of the audience to assemble, after they had entered the building from the rear through a large loggia.[8]

All of the materials used to decorate the Odeon were costly, with the stage (*pulpitum*) and *cavea* made of the same white pentelic marble used to construct the temples on the Acropolis. The floor of the semicircular *orchêstra* was paved with a variety of multicoloured marbles – blue, green, purple and pink – as well as red and yellow limestone and black slate. The auditorium (*cavea*) was formed of a series of rising curved rows, which were truncated at the sides to fit into the rectangular form of the building.

The stage facade was broken by three doorways which led into the scene building (*scaena*), behind the stage. Unlike most Roman outdoor theatres, including that of Pompey, this facade did not have the elaborate decoration of columns, sculpture and other architectural embellishment of the sort which characterized such structures. Instead it was decorated with alternating slabs of coloured marble and shafts (herms) topped by heads of white marble. Both the acoustics and the sightlines of this auditorium are believed to have been excellent, and its general layout is remarkably similar to that of Richard Wagner's Bayreuth Festspielhaus, built almost two thousand years later.

The Odeon was constructed in the agora, probably upon or adjacent to the very site where the earliest performances in honour of Dionysus had taken place (and wooded bleachers, *ikria*, erected), before these were relocated to the Theatre of Dionysus on the slopes of the Acropolis. Thus, in one sense the 'permanence' of the agora as a site for performance was reasserted after a lapse of some five centuries. In the second century AD, the roof of the Odeon collapsed, the structure was drastically altered, and – ironically perhaps for students and scholars of theatre history – it was converted to a lecture hall. It is likely too that at the time of this renovation and re-purposing, a new and much admired cedar roof was provided. The benefactor was that same Herodes Atticus, with whose provision of a building to bear his name, and to compensate for the loss of the desecrated Theatre of Dionysus, we began our account. It was a building that not only replaced that theatre, but, as noted earlier, in time also displaced it from memory, not to be recalled again until scholars identified the authentic site of Dionysus' theatre and began their study of both its story and that of the later theatres, temporary and permanent, it had helped to inspire.

NOTES

1. Dio Chrysostom, *Orationes* 31.122; Lucian, *Demonax*, 57.
2. *Variae*, 4.51; 3.39.

3. Vitruvius, the most important ancient literary source for our knowledge of Greek and Roman architecture, describes where within a city the sites sacred to various gods should be located. He states that the temples of Apollo and of Dionysus (the two gods most closely associated with theatre) should be close to the site of the theatre (*De Architectura*, 1.7.1). Elsewhere he notes the importance of a theatre's proximity to the gods' temples so they can observe the plays and associated rites dedicated to their worship.

4. For a comprehensive treatment and analysis of the evidence see D. Wiles, *Tragedy in Athens: Performance Space and Theatrical Meaning* (Cambridge: Cambridge University Press, 1999).

5. These in turn drew upon codes of visual culture that embraced architecture, painting and sculpture (see Green, ch. 9 in this volume).

6. However, according to the theatre historian and architect George C. Izenour, this account by the ancient historian Pausanias, can only be a 'good story': '. . . naval vessels of the time were not large enough to support masts and spars of sufficient cross-section to serve either as columns or roof beams in a structure as large as this one. Purlins between beams perhaps, but not the columns and main beams.' *Roofed Theatres of Classical Antiquity* (New Haven and London: Yale University Press, 1992).

7. The evidence is usefully summarized and evaluated by Alan Hughes, 'Comic Stages in Magna Graecia: the Evidence of the Vases', *Theatre Research International* 21.2 (1996), 95–107.

8. For a description and structural analysis see Izenour, 1992. He follows the reconstruction by Homer Thompson and John Travlos in the first publication of the building in *Hesperia* 19 (1950), 31–141.

FURTHER READING

Beacham, R., *Spectacle Entertainments of Early Imperial Rome*. New Haven and London: Yale University Press, 1999.

— *The Roman Theatre and its Audience*. London: Routledge, 1991.

Bieber, M. *The History of the Greek and Roman Theater*. Princeton: Princeton University Press, 1961.

Izenour, G., *Roofed Theatres of Classical Antiquity*. New Haven and London: Yale University Press, 1992.

Rossetto, P., and Sartorio, G., *Teatri Grecie e Romani*. Rome: Edizioni, SEAT, 1996.

Vitruvius, *Ten Books of Architecture*, trans. I. Rowland and T. Howe. Cambridge: Cambridge University Press, 1999.

Walton, J. M., *Greek Theatre Practice*. Westport: Greenwood, 1980; second ed., London: Methuen, 1991.

Wiles, D., *Tragedy in Athens: Performance Space and Theatrical Meaning*. Cambridge: Cambridge University Press, 1999.

12

YANA ZARIFI

Chorus and dance in the ancient world

The cosmic dance

The performance of ancient dance is largely irrecoverable. Any attempt to recover it involves many technical problems and this essay does not make the attempt. Nor will I provide an encyclopaedic summary of information and views about ancient dance in its immense variety in time and place. My main focus will be on the ways in which the functions and the associations of dance in ancient society differ from those of dance in modern society. A crucial place in this argument will be occupied by *theatrical* dance.

In Hindu religion Shiva dances the Anandatandava (the dance of bliss), symbolizing the cosmic cycles of creation and destruction, the rhythms of birth and death and the perennial movements of the cosmos. In the hymns of the Veda, the dawn, Ushas, is described as a dancer who appears on a stage. This has no parallel in the Judaeo-Christian tradition. But in Sophocles' *Antigone* the chorus invoke Dionysus as a *choragos* (dance-leader) of the fire-breathing stars (1146–7). Plato (*Timaeus* 40c) describes the heavenly bodies with their 'juxtapositions and their approximations . . . circling as in dance',[1] and in another work ascribed to Plato the stars are said to move 'through the figures of the fairest and most glorious of dances' (*Epinomis* 982e). Five centuries later Lucian writes that:

> Dance came into being contemporaneously with the primal origin of the universe, making her appearance together with Love – the love that is age-old. In fact, the concord of the heavenly spheres, the interlacing of the errant planets with the fixed stars, their rhythmic agreement and timed harmony, are proofs that Dance was primordial.[2] 　　　　　　　　　　　　(*On the Dance* 7)

For the Greeks heavenly bodies dance, and so do the gods. In the *Homeric Hymn to Pythian Apollo* of the sixth century BC, Aphrodite dances with the *Charites* (the Graces), the *Horai* (the Seasons), and with Harmonia and Hebe 'holding each other's hand at the wrist' (*epi karpô cheiras* – a familiar configuration of dance), while Ares and Hermes dance playfully in their midst. Apollo himself 'plays the lyre, stepping high and beautifully, and around him shines a radiance and gleamings of his feet and his well-sewn tunic'. Leto and Zeus look on with pleasure (194–206).

The procession of gods in a mystic vision described by Plato (*Phaedrus* 247a) is a divine *choros*, i.e. a group that dances and sings. In a fragment of the lost epic cycle, from the *Titanomachy* (fr. 5), even Zeus, the dignified father of the gods, dances at the centre of a group.

Lesser divinities such as Muses, Nereids (sea-nymphs) and Graces are persistently linked to dance in art, myth and literature. Hesiod's *Theogony* begins with the Muses, who 'dance on tender feet around the deep-blue spring and altar of the almighty son of Cronos'. Nereids are depicted dancing in Greek iconography and in choral passages of tragedy, as in Euripides' *Ion*:

> Zeus' starry sky began the dance, and the moon dances, and Nereus' fifty daughters who in the sea and whirlings of ever-flowing rivers dance for the gold-crowned maiden [Persephone] and her holy mother [Demeter].
>
> (1078–86)

Finally, it is not just the cosmos and the deities that dance. Fawns are imagined as dancing (e.g. Euripides *Alcestis* 582–5), and so are dolphins (in vase-painting and at Euripides *Electra* 860). Dionysus makes herds of animals 'dance' (Pindar fragment 70b); and the whole mountain and its wild animals join in the bacchic movement of the maenads (Euripides *Bacchae* 726–7).

Pre-modern peoples often imagine the cosmos, deity and nature in terms of socially central institutions and practices. When the Greeks project dance onto cosmos, deity and nature, this is a symptom of the social centrality of their dancing. It is significant that what makes Lucian see dance in the heavenly bodies is the *coordination* of their movement. In our postmodern world, the arts are distinct from other areas of significant activity, economic, social, political and religious. Dancing occurs at times and in spaces designated for entertainment. The ancient Greeks also danced simply for enjoyment (for instance the suitors feasting in the house of Odysseus in the *Odyssey*), but frequently not only for enjoyment: they had what may be called a *dance culture*, in which much of their dancing contributed to processes needed for the coordination, survival, reproduction and prosperity of the community. These processes or contexts included agriculture, warfare, rites of passage, festivals, celebrations of athletic victory, deliverance and theatre. In the next section I will confine myself to a few examples of this functionality of the ancient Greek dance.

Contexts of dance

In agriculture, as in warfare, the coordination of movement is crucial, and this is sometimes achieved by music. Celebrating or rehearsing such coordinated activities may take the form of dance. The joy and the grief attached to the fruitfulness of death in the agricultural cycle found expression in the Linos dance-song described in the *Iliad*:

> Young girls and young men, in all their light-hearted innocence,
> carried the kind, sweet fruit away in their woven baskets,
> and in their midst, a youth with a singing lyre played charmingly
> upon it for them, and sang the beautiful song for Linos
> in a light voice, and they followed him, and with singing and whistling
> and light dance-steps of their feet kept time to the music. (18.567–72)[3]

Ailinos came to mean lament and was derived from the cry *ai Linon* ('alas for Linos'), a lament for a legendary musician said to have died young. *Linon* also means 'flax' and so, in the performance of the dance song, the plant and the musician merge. In the inscribed 'Hymn of the Kouretes' to the 'Greatest Kouros (Young Man)' the young men urge him to leap into the jars, the flocks, the fields – an idea surely deriving from the impetus to promote fertility through vigorous leaping.

The *pyrrichê* was, according to Lysias (*c*.459 BC–*c*.380 BC), danced at the Athenian Panathenaea festival by naked youths brandishing shields (21.1–4). Plato (*Laws* 815a) describes it as imitating avoidance of blows and missiles by dodging, pulling back, leaping on high and into a crouch, as well as aggressive postures, the shooting of arrows and javelins and all kinds of blows. It is referred to also by Aristophanes (*Clouds* 988–9). Euripides in his *Andromache* describes Neoptolemus' avoidance of a shower of missiles with the memorable metaphor of dancing the *pyrrichê* (1135). Armed dancing was of course not confined to Athens. Plato (*Laws* 796b) speaks of armed dances at Athens for Athena, at Sparta for the Dioscuri and on Crete for Zeus, and his contemporary Xenophon (*Anabasis* 6.1.11) mentions Arcadians putting on a show by marching in armour to pipes and singing a paean and dancing 'just as they do in their processions to the gods'.

Armed dancing by youths was likely to mark their entry into the status of warrior, and so to belong, loosely or specifically, to a rite of passage to adulthood. Groups of girls too would sing and dance to mark their passage to womanhood. In seventh-century BC Sparta Alcman composed *partheneia*, songs performed by dancing girls on the threshold of womanhood, apparently at festivals of the whole community. Herodotus in the sixth century BC reports that 'the Samians instituted a festival (which is in fact still celebrated in the same way nowadays), which involved unmarried girls and boys dancing every night . . .'.[4] A passage of the *Homeric Hymn to Delian Apollo* (146–64) describing the performance of the Delian maidens (*kourai*) as the highlight of the Ionian festival of Artemis and Apollo on Delos is quoted by Thucydides (3.104), who adds that the Athenians and island cities revived the practice of sending (probably adolescent) *choroi*. Girls danced for Artemis in Karyai and boys danced at the Spartan Gymnopaidia for Apollo (Pausanias 3.10.7; 4.16.9).

A formal ceremonial was the wedding. Homer (*Iliad* 18.491–5) describes a representation, on the shield of Achilles, of brides being led through the streets, with wedding-song, while youths dance to the sound of pipes and lyres. In what survives of Euripides' play *Phaethon* the chorus of girls sings a wedding-song, to which presumably – as is normally the case with choral songs in tragedy – they dance. Then the girls are taken inside the house and told to dance in a circle as they sing wedding-songs (227–44). In Euripides' *Iphigenia at Aulis* we hear of fifty girls whirling in a circle as they 'dance the marriage of Nereus' (1055–7) and in *Trojan Women* (308–40) Cassandra calls on the chorus and on her mother to 'dance for her wedding' as she herself performs her mad dance song invoking Hymenaios, the young marriage-god. We may well imagine that some of the surviving wedding-songs, for instance the one at the end of Aristophanes' *Peace*, were accompanied by dance.

Another rite of passage involving choral dance was mystic initiation. In the second century AD Lucian maintained that 'not a single ancient mystic initiation (*teletê*) can be found that is without dancing' (*On the Dance* 15). According to Plutarch people believe that by being purified in mystic rituals they can 'continue singing and dancing in Hades' (*Moralia* 1105a). Mystic initiation was a preparation and a rehearsal for death, and the next world was imagined by initiates as experienced in their initiation. And so, because this initiation included group dancing (e.g. Oppian 4.246 'mystic dance'; Plutarch fragment 178), Hades is often imagined (for instance in epitaphs) as containing dancing. Particularly striking, and within the sphere of Greek aesthetic influence, are the Etruscan depictions of music and dancing, probably imagined as in the afterlife, painted on the walls of tombs in Tarquinia in the sixth and fifth centuries BC (**Fig. 24**).

Death ritual is a formal rite of passage. Greek lamentations were generally performed by women. We know that their performance was often accompanied by coordinated and rhythmical bodily movement, for instance the beating of the breast. One Euripidean lament evokes a '*choros* which Hades honours' (*Suppliants* 73–5), another a '*choros* of Hades' (*Heracles* 1025–7), and tragic choruses sometimes lament while dancing. But none of this means

Figure 24. Etruscan wall painting, 'Tomb of the Triclinium', c.500 BC.

that the lament was generally accompanied by dance in the narrow sense of patterned movement of the whole body, including the feet.

An occasion for group dancing was provided by athletic victory. Pausanias (6. 22. 1–4) mentions the dancing of the orgiastic *kordax* around the sanctuary of Artemis in celebration of Pelops' victory at Pisa. But we also have the magnificent epinicians (victory odes) of Pindar (518–438 BC), which were clearly written to be simultaneously sung and danced.

For the obtaining or celebration of deliverance it might be appropriate to sing a choral paean (e.g. in warfare: Aeschylus' *Seven Against Thebes* 267–70; deliverance from plague: *Iliad* 1.472–3). Occasionally the paean is said to have been danced: in Euripides a chorus mentions the girls of Delos whirling in dance around the temple of Apollo as they sing a paean (*Heracles* 687–90), and Iphigenia, before her sacrifice which she believes will bring victory for the Greeks, tells the chorus of girls to sing a paean to Artemis and to whirl around her altar and temple (*Iphigenia at Aulis* 1467–81). Sophocles makes a chorus of girls sing and dance a paean on the return of Heracles to Deianeira (*Women of Trachis* 210–24).

Pollux in his *Onomasticon* (4.104) reports that 'the dithyrambic dance' was called *tyrbasia*, a word that implies riotousness. The dithyramb was a hymn in honour of Dionysus, which – it seems – was originally sung in a procession, probably to escort Dionysus to his festival, but was transformed into a song sung in a fixed position by a 'circular chorus'. The dithyramb continued to be associated with a Dionysiac context, being performed most notably at the City Dionysia in fifth-century Athens, but might be performed with little or no Dionysiac content: a surviving dithyramb by Bacchylides, for instance, narrates a story about Theseus. The transformation of the dithyramb was from a processional danced song, that probably had the function of bringing in Dionysus for his festival, to a danced song that was fixed to a single place. Having lost its processional function, the dithyramb may have acquired new roles – perhaps the evocation of Dionysus and certainly mere narration of myth (Dionysiac or non-Dionysiac). Already in Homer storytelling (by the bard) may be accompanied by a group of dancers (*Odyssey* 8.262–7, in Phaeacia). Functional songs, for instance the wedding-song or the epinician (victory song), might include the mythical stories, but this is distinct from danced song whose function is to narrate myth. It seems that such wholly narrative songs were being composed by the sixth century, most notably by Stesichorus, whose name refers to the establishment of a chorus on a single spot and whose elaborate songs were almost certainly danced, although we do not know in what context.

It is from such functional contexts that the genres of archaic song arise (wedding-song, paean, epinician, dithyramb and so on), many of which were danced by a group. Most of the surviving examples of these songs were composed by individual poets such as Alcman and Pindar. But the genres – despite stories of poets inventing them – pre-exist individual authors, and are slow to change: they continue to retain the specific characteristics derived from their function (for instance to praise a victor or a bride). The lament has retained many of its ancient elements even up to modern times.

The festival, and especially the Dionysiac festivals (Lenaea, City and Rural Dionysia), seems to have been the context for the development of a new kind of dancing chorus, such as the dithyrambic, detached from any immediate ritual function. Tragedy, which developed out of the dithyramb and was influenced by Stesichorus, contained in its *stasima* (songs sung and danced by the chorus) a mixture of mythical narratives and of elements of genres that were now – as part of fictional drama – divorced from their traditional functional contexts.

The meaning of dance

It has long been realized that most Greek poetry (at least of the archaic and classical periods) was performed. But even those who remind us of this fact do not necessarily draw out its implications for the meaning of the performance. The survival of the words, together with the loss of the music and dance, determines their basic orientation. And so, for example, in 1960, A. M. Dale,[5] though emphasizing the importance of dance in Greek drama, declared nevertheless that the dance was 'a *pictorial clarification* for the spectators' (my italics). The implication here is that it is the words which embody the fundamental meaning of choral poetry: the dance merely clarifies or embellishes the meaning.

We are used to the division of creativity in the making of opera, musicals and dance. One person composes music for which another devises dance, or one person writes words for which another composes music, or vice versa: there is a prior or fundamental medium, whether words, music or dance. But it seems that, at least in the early history of Greek choral poetry, including Greek drama, the words, music and dance were composed by the same person, who might also even be a performer. Because only the words of the songs have survived, it is difficult for us to avoid privileging them, to imagine the possibility of meaning being created not by the words independently of music and dance but by – at every moment – the synthesis of all three.

In restoring, to the limited extent possible, the element of dance we are assisted by three kinds of evidence. One is the survival into our world of something like this synthesis. In the dances of Bali and in modern Japanese Butoh, for instance, there is a more co-operative relationship between dancer and musician in the devising of performance than anything we are familiar with in the West. It is probably not coincidental that the culture of Bali was in the relatively recent past a dance culture, not only in that dance had a socially central position, as it still does, but also in that the socially fundamental occasions were marked by dances specific to them.

The second kind is the evidence for dance preserved in ancient writings and visual representations. This may be of great interest, but of very limited value for restoring the dance to any particular song.

The third kind of evidence is the metre in which the words of the choral songs were written. This provides an abstract model of the rhythm of the music and dance, and so constitutes a trace of the original unity of all three elements of the synthesis. But the trace is very faint. In the classical period metre was distinguished from rhythm, and there are numerous aspects of bodily movement to which the metre gives little or no access: hand gestures, vigour, mood, pace, intensity, variations arising from the specific musical mode and from the volume and pace of the music, the flow, and so on.

Finally, we noted at the end of the last section that the choral songs of tragedy contain elements of genres that were now divorced from their traditional functional contexts. This enables tragic choral song to evoke a variety of genres. We may now add that the synthesis of words, music and dance in tragic choral songs should, as a vehicle of meaning, be taken together with its evocation of various genres and their traditional contexts. For example, when a chorus sings a song containing elements of a wedding-song it is obvious that the mood of the wedding is evoked, but not so obvious that for an audience thoroughly familiar with wedding performances it was evoked not only by the words but also, in all probability, by the music and the bodily movement. The same person, whom we call the 'poet', was able to create a synthesis of words, music and movement because he inherited just such a synthesis in the traditional genres of what we call 'poetry'.

Theatre: a *mélange* of genres

If irreligious acts are honoured, say the chorus of Sophocles' *Oedipus Tyrannus*, 'why should I dance (*choreuein*)?' (896). Civic choral dance is sustained by religion. In contrast to the individuals of the self-destructive ruling families of tragedy, the chorus always survives, and its danced song may prefigure the danced song that will be celebrated for ever in the civic cult that is so often founded at the end of tragedy.

The metrical schemes inherent in the words of tragic songs are based on combinations of long and short syllables. The schemes are elaborate and varied, and yet are generally repeated identically between one stanza (the *strophê*) and the next (the *antistrophê*).

This combination of complexity and discipline reflects the dance, in which the elaborate dance movements of the 'turning' (*strophê*) of the chorus are followed by the same movements in its 'turning back' (*antistrophê*).

This double movement was often followed by an epode, giving a triadic structure that is also found in the danced choral song of 'lyric poets' such as Stesichorus or Pindar. The metrical units (of a few syllables each) are also on the whole shared with non-theatrical choral song.

Also derived from pre-theatrical choral danced song is composition in genres, but this works very differently in tragedy. Because the dramatized myth of tragedy is divorced from any particular context, tragic choruses can move from one genre (or its mere evocation) to another, sometimes within the same song. The genre (and its associated context, such as the wedding) is represented, or evoked, by means of typical, traditional themes and verbal forms.

Here is an example, from Euripides' *Hippolytus*. A danced choral song (525–64) is divided into two parts, each containing a *strophê* and *antistrophê*. The first pair is a propitiatory hymn to *Erôs* (sexual passion) pervaded with a sense of his potential for destruction exemplified by his power to shoot missiles. Of the second pair the *strophê* evokes the myth of Heracles' violent capture of Iole and his consequent violent death. These events are called a 'murderous wedding', Heracles is 'wretched in his wedding-songs', and there is an image from the wedding-song (Iole as a yoked filly). The *antistrophê* evokes the myth of Semele destroyed by a thunderbolt as she gave birth to Dionysus, the typical myth of the dithyramb, and ends with the image of Aphrodite floating around like a bee. We have then in sequence evocations of hymn, wedding-song and dithyramb, but the Dionysiac subversion of the reproductive process (Semele) is prefigured even in the wedding-song by calling Iole *bacchê* (maenad), a word whose position in the *strophê* corresponds with *Bacchou* (Dionysus) in the *antistrophê*. It is extremely likely that generic performance, such as danced wedding-song, contained much that was traditional and typical beyond the words: dance steps, but also other aspects of bodily movement such as speed, vehemence and hand gestures, as well as musical mode, pace, volume and intensity, and rhythm, which was distinguished from metre. These elements too, we may well imagine, belonged to the tragic invocation of context through genre. But we cannot know that, for they are all lost. Therefore, and because ancient writers agree that choral dance was *imitative*, it is worth imagining the performance of tragic song in which the vacuum is filled by elements from a surviving traditional signifying system of bodily movements. This assumption was embodied in the performance of songs from the *Hippolytus* in Javanese idiom by Thiasos Theatre Company (Cambridge, 1998). Images in the text were expressed by traditional dance movements, repeated exactly in the *antistrophê*, such as respect for the god, the shooting of an arrow, the riding of horses and the floating of a bee (from an erotic dance). Just as Euripides' *Hippolytus* concerns the failed transition of Hippolytus to reproductive adulthood, so his *Bacchae* concerns the failed initiation of Pentheus into the Dionysiac mysteries. Though a relatively late tragedy, the *Bacchae* sheds light on the origins of tragedy (set before the royal house) in the processional dithyramb. At the end of the prologue Dionysus tells the band (*thiasos*) of his female followers (maenads), who form the chorus, to sound their Phrygian drums around the royal house 'so that the city of Cadmus (Thebes) may see'. They then sing what is formally known as the *parodos* (entry-song). This danced song has many of the features of a dithyramb, including the traditional theme of the double birth of Dionysus. It contains much self-presentation, with descriptions of their rituals (dancing, mystic initiation, escorting Dionysus, rushing to the mountainside) as well as of the sacred accoutrements of the *thiasos*, namely *thyrsos*, ivy crowns, fawn-skins, drums and pipes, all of which are no doubt on show: besides the drum-playing ordered by Dionysus, the song is presumably also accompanied by the pipe that was a regular feature of tragic choruses. The metre consists largely of the unit of two shorts followed by two longs: this form is known as 'Ionics', conveys a sense of excitement, is associated especially with the voluptuous and the Oriental, and occurs also in two other hymns to Dionysus (Philodamos' paean and Aristophanes' hymn to Iacchus at *Frogs* 324–52). It may thus be especially associated – together with concomitant bodily movements – with the cult of Dionysus.

It is inconceivable that a song so pervaded with the visual specificity of the Dionysiac *thiasos* (and its music: Aristotle associates the dithyramb with the Phrygian mode, *Politics* 1342b) was not also integrated with the bodily

Figure 25. Maenads around Dionysus' cult statue, fifth century BC.

movements typical of the female Dionysiac *thiasos*. These movements are still visible in numerous Athenian vase-paintings contemporary with Euripides, of which I give an example in **Fig. 25**. One of our contexts for dance song was mystic initiation. Later in the play Dionysus, who is disguised as his priest, is imprisoned by Pentheus. Then Dionysus appears in an epiphany to his *thiasos*, amid thunder and lightning and an earthquake that demolishes the house of Pentheus. This scene is pervaded with details that correspond to initiation into the Dionysiac mysteries. As for the metre, we will have to confine our focus to the climax of the terror, just before Dionysus himself appears to bring reassurance and joy to the *thiasos*. The metre of this passage – for which the technical terms are dochmiac, dactyl and trochee – is characterized by much resolution (the substitution of two short syllables for a long syllable), which results in long runs of short syllables, especially in the description of the appearance of cracks in the house and in the maenads' call to each other to hurl their trembling bodies to the ground, which is followed by a rocking motion in the words (*ho gar anax anô katô titheis*) that describe the god turning the house upside down. Just as land can 'dance' at an earthquake (Callimachus *Hymns* 4.139), so an earthquake can be danced. Each chorus-member suffers 'isolated desolation' (609), which belonged, as did falling to the ground, to the experience of mystic initiation. Another theatrical earthquake occurs (probably also with mystic associations) at the end of the tragedy *Prometheus Bound* (1080–93) where the chorus, the daughters of the Ocean, could well have danced the earthquake as they disappeared.

The excited runs of short syllables express the fragmentation of the normally unified *thiasos* and of the house, which would render the staging of an actual collapse of the house unnecessary. Mystery-cult was secret, and so Euripides cannot reveal it all, but for the initiated the scene may have connoted also bodily fragmentation (suffered by the failed initiate Pentheus later in the play) and perhaps even the psychic fragmentation of the initiate, as well as the bodily movements of mystic initiation. The earthquake scene of the *Bacchae* (576–610) was danced in strict accordance with the rhythm of the original Greek lyrics in a performance of the play by Thiasos Theatre Company (London, 2003; Cyprus, 2004). This demonstrated that the unity of verbal rhythm, music, bodily movement, imagined collapse of palace, and ritual context can be made apparent only in performance.

Dance and social order: Plato

Having indicated the role of dance in (1) imagining the cosmos, (2) central social processes, (3) its combination with words, music and contextual associations in the creation of meaning, and (4) tragedy, we turn now to the general features of dance that qualify it for its central role in Greek society.

Dances in socially central contexts were generally performed, not by an individual but by a group, the *choros*. In this respect too – as well as through its ubiquity and social centrality – Greek dancing expressed and confirmed the identity and the cohesion of the community. The unanimous movement of numerous individuals coordinated by music and song in the dance is an aesthetically and emotionally powerful image of communal cohesion. The *thiasos* of the *Bacchae* claims in its danced song that the Dionysiac initiate 'joins his soul to the *thiasos*' (75). The central benefit of ritual – to create a guiding image of perfect control in an unpredictable world – is especially attainable by means of dance, not just because of its apparently effortless unanimity, but also because in the dance – more so even than in (most) ritual – the material that forms the powerful image consists only of ourselves, without anything that may be beyond human control. This symbolic significance of the collective dance is likely to be especially important in societies that – like the ancient Greek city – depend on the human body (rather than on advanced technology) for their productive and military capacities.

For the Greeks dance might seem to be an embodiment of order, and used to make peace. Xenophon says that 'there is nothing so useful or beautiful as order', and gives as an example of this principle the *choros* (*Oeconomicus*

8.3). Pausanias (5.16.5–6) recounts how the sixteen most esteemed women of Elis were appointed to establish two *choroi* in order to 'make peace between the cities of Pisa and Elis'. But the richest text on the importance of dancing for the social order is by Plato, who wrote not long after the end of the most creative period of Athenian tragedy.

In the *Laws* Plato describes the 'right' kind of education. The young of all species are always moving and crying out. But whereas the animals have no perception of order and disorder in their movements, humans have been appointed by deities to be their companions in the dance, and these deities have given humans a sense of pleasure in rhythm and harmony, with the result that they lead us in the dance, joining us to one another in dances and songs (653e–654a, 664e). And so religion is central to dance, and dance is central to education: 'one who is not trained in the chorus (*achoreutos*) is uneducated (*apaideutos*)' (654b). But choral performance is not to be confined to the young. In the ideal city, choral performance is to be divided into three age groups, with the Muses and Apollo leading the boys' and young men's choruses, and Dionysus the chorus of men between fifty and sixty – with their vigour restored by wine.

So, dance through rhythm and harmony expresses the god-given coordination of the group and is central to the life of the ideal *polis* and to the education of its citizens. And yet it is important for Plato that there are good dances and bad dances. The person who is well educated will be able, not just to sing well and dance well, but to sing what is good and dance what is good (654bc). Choral dancing imitates character and ways of doing (655d), and is good or bad according to whether it expresses, and so tends to inculcate, virtue or vice (655b). In the *Republic* it is asked which rhythms are 'those of an orderly and courageous life' and 'which movements suit meanness and insolence and madness and other badness, and which rhythms are to be left for the opposite qualities' (399e–400b).

Another quality desired by Plato in choral performance is internal consistency, but of a very special kind. The Muses, unlike certain human poets, would not set masculine language to a female scale and melody, nor would they put together the song and (bodily) figures of free men and then attach rhythms of slaves and base men, and so on (669c). For Plato the main kind of inconsistency in choral performance is the mixing of a superior social group with an inferior one. He goes on to deplore the contemporary disintegration of the unity of words, music and dance: poets separate the rhythm and (bodily) figures from the melody, setting bare words to the metre, and also separating the melody and rhythm from the words (669e). Here again, Plato's objection is moral and social as well as aesthetic: in the absence of words, it is difficult to know what the rhythm and harmony mean and whether anything worthy is being imitated, and this sort of thing produces coarseness (agroikia, literally 'rusticity').

Later, in the Laws, Plato produces his classification of dances (814e–817a). They are to be divided into the serious, which imitates the more beautiful bodies with a solemn (semnon) effect, and that which imitates uglier bodies with a vulgar (phaulon) effect. The serious category is itself divided into war dancing (the pyrrichê), in which Plato recommends the upright and braced posture that imitates good bodies and souls, and dances of peace, in which the dancer should maintain the naturalness and gracefulness appropriate to law-abiding men. The dances of peace are subdivided into thanksgiving dances for the restoration of prosperity following turmoil and dances that give thanks for the continuation or augmentation of prosperity. Plato goes out of his way to praise the naming of peaceful dancing as emmeleia, which means 'in tune' as well as more generally 'appropriate'. As for vulgar dancing, the imitation of ugly bodies and thoughts, which includes comedy, this must not be performed by free citizens, but must be left to slaves and hired aliens.

Plato's classification of dance is quite different from the classification by social context that we adopted earlier. Although he proposes some descriptive classification (within his category of the serious), the main thrust of his categorisation is evaluative. Whereas the multifarious contexts listed above preceded the polis (and were more or less absorbed into it), the perspective of Plato derives exclusively from concern for the unity and incorruptibility of the polis and for the single value (virtue) on which a unified and incorruptible polis depends. In his conceptualization of the dance a variety of contexts is largely replaced by a single value – largely, but not entirely, for his chorus of young men are to sing a paean, and he pays attention to the pyrrichê, which as military training is essential for the well-being of the polis as a whole. But most instructive is his reference to the performance of 'purifications and initiations' by people dancing under the influence of wine in imitation of Nymphs and Pans and Satyrs (815c). This belongs to our category of dances in mystic initiation, specifically Dionysiac mystic initiation. Plato is puzzled about how to classify it, finally deciding to 'leave it aside' because it 'does not belong to the polis' (ou politikon). Finally, it must be emphasized that despite the enormous difference between the classification of dance above and that of our fourth-century philosopher, they are both based on the social dimension of dance.

Further evidence

Information about Greek dancing is contained, often incidentally, in numerous ancient authors from Homer onwards, as well as in visual representations. My purpose in this section is to give a small sample from this vast range of information, so as to indicate how the picture given in the previous sections might be complemented and extended.

In his *Deipnosophistai* (*Philosophers at Dinner*), a compilation of learning presented as dinner conversation, Athenaeus (second century AD) preserves ideas of dance from the fifth century BC:

> The followers of Damon the Athenian are right to say that songs and dances are the result of the soul's being in a kind of motion; those songs which are noble and beautiful produce noble and beautiful souls, whereas the contrary kind produce the contrary . . . For whether in dancing or in walking, decency and dignity of bearing are beautiful, whereas immodesty and vulgarity are ugly. For this reason from the beginning the poets arranged dances for free men, and they used the dance-figures (*schêmata*) only to illustrate the theme of the songs, always preserving nobility and manliness in them . . . But if anyone arranged his figures with undue exaggeration, or when he came to his songs said anything that did not correspond to the dance, he was discredited.[6]
>
> (628c)

Athenaeus at this point (628d) cites the example of Hippocleides (reported in Herodotus, vi. 128–133) who 'danced away his marriage' by standing on his head and 'beating time with his legs in the air' to display his dancing skills to his prospective father-in-law. This had the opposite of the desired effect since, according to Athenaeus, the performance revealed not the skilfulness of his body but the vulgarity of his soul. Athenaeus then continues (628e) to praise the 'decent' and 'dignified' choral dancing of the fifth century BC which emulated the movements of men under arms, so that 'Socrates in his poems says that those who dance most beautifully are the best in warfare . . . For the art of dancing was virtually like armed manoeuvres, and a display not merely of discipline in general but also of care taken for the body.'

Damon was an older contemporary of Plato, and the passages above embody the Platonic concerns with the effect of dancing on the soul, with the social hierarchy of dancing ('free men'), with the danger of excess and the unity of words and movement, and with dancing as training for warfare. But another contemporary of Plato, Xenophon, provides a very different picture. His *Symposium* is about an evening party, in which dances are performed to entertain the guests. Unlike the dancing mentioned in previous sections, this is dancing in a private space and with no ritual function. There is a dance with whirling hoops (2.8) and dances in which the body bends to imitate hoops (2.22). There is a dangerous acrobatic dance involving a circle of upright knives (2.11–12) and mention of 'dancing, to the pipe, of figures in which Graces and Seasons and Nymphs are painted' (7.5). As a finale, Ariadne enters and sits on a throne, a Bacchic rhythm is played on the pipe, and Dionysus dances towards her. They embrace, and 'there were many figures (*schêmata*) to behold'. In the end the guests depart in a state of erotic excitement.

Plutarch (*c.*46–120 AD) advocates a close correspondence between dance gestures and words so that the lines of the poetry 'dictate representation in dancing, summoning our hands and feet' as if connected by strings which the words pull (748c1–4). This is followed by a condemnation of the pantomime popular in his day where the caprices of this theatrical dance are said to have debased poetry and music by bringing them 'under her sway' (748d).

In his *Table Conversations* (747b–748d) Plutarch sets out an analysis of the dance into three elements: *phora* (movement), *schêma* (pose) and *deixis* (pointing). *Schêmata* (plural of *schêma*) 'is the name of the representational positions in which the movements end, as when dancers compose their bodies in the attitude of Apollo or Pan or a Bacchant, and then retain that aspect like figures in a picture'. *Deixis* is not imitative but indication or pointing, as when poets use proper names.

The *Onomasticon*, a Greek lexicon compiled in the late second century AD by Pollux, contains, in the section on theatre terminology, a list of words about dance (4.95–110). Some of the words are grouped under various categories, such as adjectives for the dancer, qualities of dance, verbs and adverbs of the dance and words related to the chorus. There is also a somewhat haphazard list of names of 'dances' and occasionally of 'kind(s) of dance(s)', although there seems in effect to be no real distinction between these two categories.

One entry covers the three dramatic genres: 'Kinds of dances (are) tragic *emmeleia*, comic *kordaxes*, satyric *sikinnis*' (in this Pollux is preceded by the fourth-century BC expert Aristoxenos). The *emmeleia* is described by a later writer as 'solemn and grandiose, with many long pauses between movements'.[7] Athenaeus describes the *kordax* as a ludicrous and indecent dance-form characteristic of comedy (631d) and the *sikinnis* as a fast and unrelentingly vigorous dance involving shaking (618c and 630b–631a).

As for *schêmata* (figures), we find the messengers' *schêmata* imitated by the 'messenger dance', and the '*schêmata* of tragic dancing'. The latter include

- the *simê cheir* and *cheir katapranês* (hand upturned and hand down-turned).
- the *kalathiskos*, meaning 'little basket', which has been taken to indicate the gesture of holding hands above the head like a basket-bearer.
- the *thermaustris*, meaning 'tongs'. But this occurs elsewhere in the list as a dance involving leaping, and is said by another writer (Critias 88B 36

Diels-Kranz) to be an energetic dance step in which the dancers 'leapt high into the air and crossed their feet several times before hitting the ground again'.[8]

What we read in Pollux is an unsatisfactory summary of earlier scholarship, which brings together material from widely divergent times and places (e.g. classical tragedy and contemporary pantomime) and is sometimes at odds with what we discover elsewhere. It raises numerous complex problems (such as whether a given dance is individual or choral) and the access that it gives us to ancient dancing is rather limited. Nevertheless, we cannot fail to be struck by the fact that many of the *names* of the dances suggest imitation – of an action or an animal or a person – that is without social significance. For example the *maktrismos*, from *maktra* meaning 'kneading-trough', is a gyration of the hips ('ludicrous' according to Athenaeus 629f). The *skôps*, which means 'owl', is 'a kind of dancing having a twisting round of the neck in imitation of the bird, which is caught when stunned at the dancing' (although at Athenaeus 629f. it is an imitation of someone gazing into the distance and curving their hand high over their forehead). The *geranos*, 'crane', was danced in imitation of Theseus' exit from the labyrinth. It is difficult to judge in each case the extent to which the names entered into the creative consciousness of the dancers and choreographers (as opposed to observers and scholars). If they did generally and to a great extent, this would suggest a coded system of dancing, exemplified rather differently by the *mudras* of Indian classical dance.

Whatever the truth of this – whether the names come from the process of creation or of reception – Pollux's account, together with our passages of Xenophon and Plutarch, imply a conceptualization of the dance that is in a sense at the opposite pole to defining dance by context and function or by its moral and social character and effect. Military training, transition to adulthood, wedding, mystic initiation, athletic victory, communal crisis, even the harvest – these are all contexts important enough for the well-being of the community to require that the dancing embody (imitate) the human qualities needed for that well-being. For the community, ritual is always positive. But dancing outside ritual context or crisis, dance performed exclusively for entertainment, is likely to be more widely and variously imitative. The symposiatic dances described by Xenophon imitate hoops, the Graces, Seasons and Nymphs, and the sexual union of Dionysus and Ariadne. And from such merely entertaining imitation emerges the taste for pictures in the dance, which may tend to dissolve the unity of words, music and song: Xenophon, we remember, writes of a dance containing 'figures in which

Graces and Seasons and Nymphs are painted', and during the embraces of Dionysus and Ariadne 'there were many figures (*schêmata*) to behold'. It is uncertain whether the word '*schêmata*' here refers to specific movements, or whether it means what it will later be defined as in Plutarch, i.e. still positions representing e.g. 'Apollo or Pan or a Bacchant . . . like figures in a picture'. But in either case, the dance is conceptualized as consisting of discrete temporal components. There may have been a chronological development from (roughly speaking) functional to merely entertaining dance, but this is not necessarily what happened: it is better to think of the functional and the merely entertaining as two antithetical models (both imitative) of dance, provided that we allow them to contain elements of each other. Greek dance might be imagined as a series of joined-up 'pictures'.

But what of the actual ancient visual representations of dance? There are, in particular, numerous surviving vase-paintings of dance from the classical period, many of them clearly inspired by the three dramatic genres, not least by satyric drama. They are of great interest, and enhance our understanding of dramatic performance. But they can only rarely be successfully related to specific dramatic texts, or (as attempted by Lillian Lawler)[9] to the names listed by Pollux. They are therefore quite unlike the numerous Indian visual representations of the named positions of a codified system of dance. Greek visual representations of dance are not of static positions but of movement. A fine example from the middle of the sixth century is the circle of females (probably Nereids) located (like the tragic chorus, but before the birth of drama) in a mythical sphere, moving around Heracles and a Triton (**Fig. 26**). By portraying signs of movement such as the backward bending of the maenads, their flying hair, the swirling skirts (**Fig. 25**), Greek painters can sometimes indicate movement at least as effectively as the video-camera. Despite the occasional ambiguity between dance and other kinds of movement (such as running), the rarity of unmistakable signs of the theatre, and the potential for distortion by the conventions and limitations of vase-painting or by the imagination of the vase-painter, vase-painting gives us invaluable access to the Greek perception of dance, including choral dance in the theatre.

Pantomime

Our argument finds its natural conclusion in the pantomime, a theatrical form that flourished in the Roman empire, but had some antecedents such as the performances we noted in Xenophon's *Symposium*. Pantomime was the ancient successor to tragedy, in six respects. Firstly, though it could be

Figure 26. Dancing Nereids; Heracles and a Triton, mid-sixth century.

performed in private, it was generally a public show. Secondly, it was very popular, throughout much of the Roman empire. Thirdly, its themes were generally taken from myth, in particular the myths of tragedy (Lucian, *On the Dance* 60 and 61). Fourthly, the continuous plots of pantomime were more reminiscent of tragedy in the classical age which by Roman times was being performed only in excerpts. Fifthly, it sometimes claimed similarity to tragedy: its solo dancers were described in inscriptions as 'actors of tragic rhythmic dance'. And sixthly, it consisted of dance, music and words.

The relation between the dance, the music and the words was however quite different from that of tragedy. The dance was performed by a silent masked dancer (the *pantomimos*), the song by a chorus that did not dance. There might also be other individuals involved, such as an actor assisting the solo dancer. Lucian, in the work he wrote in defence of the pantomime, claims – perhaps as a mere inference – that originally the dancer also sang, but that the resulting panting distorted his singing, which was therefore transferred to others (*On the Dance* 30). Lucian goes on to say that tragedy and the dance (his name for pantomime) have the same themes, except that the themes of the dance are more varied and from a wider range and contain countless vicissitudes. We also know that the solo dancer could assume many mythical roles.

Tragedy and pantomime share subject-matter but differ profoundly in performance. Dance in pantomime is separated from the tragic unity of words, music, and song. That tragic unity was, as we have seen, inherited from traditional genres of danced song performed in socially significant ritual contexts associated with myths. After their absorption into tragedy the danced songs retained – at least in the fifth century BC – their association with the ritual contexts and with socially significant myths. At the opposite extreme, in the pantomime, the emotional and aesthetic power of dance belongs not to the group but to the imitative ability of an individual body (the *pantomimos*, 'imitator of everything'). Myth now embodies not social contradictions but emotional or pictorial moments. The auditorium is vast, but the separation of dance from ritual context and social significance is complete.

NOTES

1. All translations of Plato are taken from E. Hamilton and H. Cairns (eds.), *The Collected Dialogues of Plato* (Princeton: Princeton University Press, 1964). Unless otherwise identified, translations are my own.
2. All translations of Lucian are from E. H. Warmington (ed.) and A. M. Harmon (trans.), Loeb edition, *Lucian*, Vol. V (Cambridge, Mass.: Harvard University Press; and London: William Heinemann Ltd., 1936).
3. All translations of Homer are by Richmond Lattimore from *The Iliad of Homer* (Chicago and London: University of Chicago Press, 1951), and *The Odyssey of Homer* (New York: Harper Collins Publishers, 1975).
4. *Herodotus* 3.48, trans. Robert Waterfield (Oxford: Oxford University Press, 1998).
5. In her inaugural lecture at Birkbeck, 'Words, Music and Dance', in *Collected Papers of A. M. Dale* (Cambridge: Cambridge University Press, 1969).
6. All translations of Athenaeus are from E. H. Warmington (ed). and C. B. Gulick (trans.), Loeb edition, *Athenaeus*, Vol. VI (Cambridge, Mass.: Harvard University Press and London: William Heinemann Ltd., 1937).
7. M. Psellos (?), 'On Tragedy' 77 Browning, in E. Csapo, and W. J. Slater, *The Context of Ancient Drama* (Ann Arbor: University of Michigan Press, 1994), p. 364, 317B.
8. Critias 88B 36 in Hermann Diels (ed. and trans.) and Walther Kranz (ed.), *Die Fragmente der Vorsokratiker*, Vol. II (1903; rpt. Dublin/Zürich: Weidmann, 1970), p. 393.
9. Lillian B. Lawler, *The Dance in Ancient Greece* (London: A. & C. Black, 1964) and *The Dance of the Ancient Greek Theatre* (Iowa: University of Iowa Press, 1964).

FURTHER READING

Barker, A. (ed.), *Greek Musical Writings. Vol. I: The Musician and his Art; Vol. II: Harmonic and Acoustic Theory*. Cambridge: Cambridge University Press, 1984/1989.

Fitton, J. W., 'Greek Dance'. *Classical Quarterly* 23.2 (Nov. 1973): 254–74.

Lawler, L. B., *The Dance in Ancient Greece*. London: A. & C. Black Ltd, 1964.

— *The Dance of the Ancient Greek Theatre*. Iowa: University of Iowa Press, 1964.

Naerebout, F. G., *Attractive Performances – Ancient Greek Dance: Three Preliminary Studies*. Amsterdam: J. C. Gieben, 1997.

West, M. L., *Ancient Greek Music*. Oxford: Clarendon, 1992.

Wiles, D., *Greek Theatre Performance*. Cambridge: Cambridge University Press, 2000.

13

GREGORY McCART

Masks in Greek and Roman theatre

We know with certainty that the mask was an essential feature of theatrical performance in ancient Greece and Rome.

We are frustrated by the paucity of evidence relating to why it was adopted and how it functioned.

We are encouraged by the fact that, like the actors of old, we can don similar masks and learn from the experience of performing in them something about their use and significance in the ancient theatres.

Over a period of fifteen years, I conducted a series of productions and workshops of tragedy and comedy with a view to discovering what we might learn through performance. Specifically, each production was designed to test certain hypotheses about theatrical performance in ancient Greece. It was clearly understood that it was impossible to recreate the original productions or their context. But particular aspects of those performances could be tested in isolation.

The tragedies and comedies performed or workshopped in whole or in part were Sophocles' *Oedipus Tyrannus, Oedipus at Colonus, Antigone, Philoctetes* and *Ajax*; Euripides' *Medea* and *Bacchae*, Aristophanes' *Women at the Thesmophoria* and *Lysistrata* and the lyrical *Homeric Hymn to Demeter*. The methodology sought to test aspects of the ancient theatre through

- comparison of masked and unmasked, indoor and outdoor performances;
- confronting the challenges an actor faces in using masks;
- the application of clues to performance in the texts themselves;
- obedience to generally accepted conventions of ancient performance such as the distinctive performative modes of actor and chorus sequences, the significance of entrances and exits to the actor's left (downtown) and right (out-of-town), the use or non-use of a high or low stage or of a central altar, and so on.

At the very least these practical explorations generated a greater respect for what Aristotle called *opsis*, the visualization of performance; beyond that they opened up debated issues to alternative methods of scrutiny.

The dominant forms of dramatic fiction in our time are the cinema and television. These media introduced to enacted fiction something that is not achievable in the live theatre. That new component is the close-up. In fact, the close-up of an actor's face is arguably the defining characteristic of contemporary dramatic fiction. Because of this, actors adopt a minimalist approach to their craft with respect to facial expression, physical posture and emphatic gesture. In comparison even with barefaced acting on the stage, acting for film and television more often than not requires restriction. The slightest movement of the lips, the tilt of the head, the tear in the eye can in close-up convey so much.

This is entirely different from acting in mask. The mask demands that actors work at the limit of their vocal and physical energies. After an initial hesitancy, they learn to thrust out their chests, open their shoulders, raise their arms, clench their fists or extend their fingers, adopt an open stance and stride purposefully over the ground. The outcome is a demonstrative performance that serves as a clearly observable contrast to unmasked acting.

The experience of rehearsing Euripides' *Bacchae* for a masked performance attested to this observation. In the final scene, Cadmus tries to comfort the distraught Agave who has just come to realize that she is responsible for the dismemberment and death of her son, Pentheus. During rehearsals of this scene, the actors were initially unmasked. The relationship between the characters they played prompted them to adopt muted tones of voice and to use comforting gestures such as stroking or embracing. As soon as the actors donned masks and rehearsed the scene with them, however, physical contact disappeared almost entirely and a more declamatory delivery of the lines substituted for the earlier intimacy.

The ancient Greek actors did not of course encounter such difficulties. They were born into a culture that celebrated the use of mask. They witnessed performances in mask and as trained performers it was the only option available to them. Acting was masked acting. They did not need to unlearn naturalistic techniques. A consequence of acting in mask is the demonstration of emotion rather than the creation of an illusion of emotion.

Vocal impediment

One other consequence experienced by modern actors was certainly also experienced by actors in ancient Greece. Human sounds are projected by the use of various connections between parts of the vocal apparatus incorporating the tongue, the soft and hard palates, the teeth, the lips and a number of resonating chambers. These resonating chambers include the thorax, the throat, the mouth, the nasal cavities and parts of the skull. Wearing a mask impedes the projection of these sounds. The mask particularly affects facial resonance associated with upper registers and the clarity of plosive consonants. It would appear that the ancient Greeks tried to overcome this problem in various ways.

Tragic masks featured a wide-open mouth, allowing the actor's voice some unhindered passage. Contemporary experimentation confirms that although a wide-open mouth, as is found in some ancient portrayals of actors, helps projection of the voice, it is not nearly enough to compensate for the general impediment. Even when a mask is made from a mould of an actor's face so that the cavities of the eyes and mouth correspond perfectly with those of the mask and the contours of the individual face inform the interior of the mask, vocal projection remains restricted. Masks used in our experimental productions were made from papier-mâché, to create a thick, durable product, or fine cloth and glue, to create a light, flexible product, in an effort to match the stiffened linen that the ancient Greeks might have used.[1] Their use demonstrated that, unsurprisingly, the harder the material, the more the voice is impeded. It was also discovered that a mask that covers the entire head and face of an actor creates an additional resonance between the inside of the mask and the face and skull. This was very disconcerting initially for the actor but with diligent practice, it could be used in performance to create an enhanced resonating effect, which served dramatic delivery. Masks that cover the face only and were topped with a wig to represent the scalp of the character do not allow for this additional resonance, nor do they markedly improve projection because the crucial facial resonances are still veiled.

Our actors soon realized that working in mask required a much greater physical performance than unmasked acting. This was especially the case with the musculature of the vocal apparatus. Peter Arnott records that for the ancient Greeks a good voice and good acting were synonymous; he cites authorities of the time who speak of the euphony, power and strength of the actor's voice as well as the athletic training, voice exercises and diet that ensured the development and maintenance of such a voice.[2] Our experience confirmed that acting in mask in an expansive outdoor setting today requires similar rigour on the part of the performer.

Most importantly, however, the ancient Greeks addressed the problem of reduced vocal projection through theatrical design.

Acoustics

To understand more comprehensively the use and significance of the mask in classical performance, we need to study the space for which its use was designed.

The theatre at Epidaurus in the north-eastern Peloponnese is the best-preserved theatre from ancient Greece. It was built in the late fourth century, many decades after the last canonical tragedy, *Oedipus at Colonus*, had been performed in Athens. Contemporary performance validates its reputation as a site of exceptional acoustics. Today, a flat stone marks the centre of the performing circle, which is some twenty yards in diameter. The slightest sound made at this spot can be heard clearly throughout the towering arc of seating. There are supplementary spots a yard or so to the left and right of centre that also afford strong support for the human voice. Apart from these sites of remarkable acoustic, the circularity of the seating ensures that a strongly projected human voice is clearly audible throughout the theatre no matter where the actor delivers lines.

Actors and speakers today, however, are drawn to that central position in delivering lines because the magnification of the voice is greater than anywhere else in the space. The experience of delivery on that spot is exciting and dramatically powerful. It can have been no different when actors first performed in that venue.

The theatre at Epidaurus has exceptional acoustics, but experiments that I have conducted in sites of other surviving theatres, such as the Theatre of Dionysus in Athens and others in Delphi, Argos and Kourion in Cyprus, also attest to the pre-eminence of the centres of these performing areas as the sites for maximal acoustic support. The level of support varies from theatre to theatre in much the same way that acoustics in modern indoor theatres vary. In its present state, the acoustic support provided by the remains of the Theatre of Dionysus in Athens is nowhere near that provided by the space at Epidaurus. But it is clearly evident from experience that even now there is greater support in the centre of the existing space than nearer its perimeter. In classical times, the space would have provided far better acoustic support than today's ruins do.

The support provided by the acoustics in any of the ancient theatre spaces was crucial to the use of the mask. It is also observable from existing remains that the theatre spaces were engineered to lend this support. The theatres were not 'found spaces', handy hollows in the sides of a hill, although that might have been a good starting point. Examination of surviving sites in, for example, Athens and Delphi verifies that the ancient Greek architects went to a great deal of trouble in their design and construction to ensure that the curve of the seating and the placement of the performing area ensured the best acoustic support possible for the masked performer.

Efforts to overcome the vocal impediment created by wearing a mask had a profound effect therefore on the performance of tragedy and, as we shall see, on the significance of the mask in that performance.

Watching the performance

The place where the spectators at tragedy sat was called the *theatron*, a word derived from the ancient Greek word 'to see'. The Athenians and their guests went to *watch* the drama and the vast majority of the fifteen thousand or so who attended the Theatre of Dionysus had to ascend the side of the southern slope of the Acropolis to take their seats. In doing so, they physically enacted something that computer graphics these days have so accustomed us to enjoy: moving from a level view of a space to a view from above. The difference is startling. The spectators at the performances looked down on the action.

And what did they see? They saw up to three speaking masked actors impersonating a number of characters in each drama. Given the strong acoustic at the centre of the performance area, it is tempting to visualize the actors using this central position for much of the time, especially in the delivery of the lengthy and vocally demanding long speeches. They were accompanied during these scenic engagements by the chorus of singer/dancers who also represented a group of people with a vested interest in the outcome of the argument dramatized. From time to time there was interaction between the individual actors and between actors and members of the chorus. From their perspective above the action, the spectators watched the enacted relationships powerfully conveyed by the range of visual dynamics available to the performers.

The third scene of Sophocles' *Oedipus Tyrannus* (513–862) is a particularly dynamic one, involving as it does three speaking actors and a chorus of involved witnesses. It features an argument between Oedipus and Creon concerning the charge that Creon has attempted to displace Oedipus from the throne. Creon is furious because Oedipus has called him a traitor to the city. The chorus just concluded explored the dire consequences of the conflict between Tiresias and Oedipus. The chorus asserted its support for Oedipus, but now in this scene they are forced to reconsider their position.

In our production, the spatial interactions between Oedipus and Creon as they argued their case against each other, moving into and out from the visual and putative acoustic centre of the space, were matched by the movements of the divided chorus physically bracketing them. The entrance of Jocasta added another dimension to the choreography of the scene, which was made even more complex by the sung intervention of the chorus on Creon's behalf. On the basis of this experience, it is not difficult to allow the informed imagination to visualize the dynamics available to the original performers.

Masks in action

And what couldn't the spectators see? They couldn't see the faces of the actors or of the chorus. Even if they had not been masked, facial expression would have been lost on most of the spectators because of the distances involved. Yet the face is our most powerful visual tool of communication. How did the actors and the singer/dancers compensate for this deprivation?

Our experiments with tragic mask provided us with some clues. Initially when actors who are not accustomed to the mask put them on, they suffer disorientation and restriction. They forget lines they have learned. They do not know what to do with their hands. Their movement around the stage is impaired by the removal of peripheral vision. They have to turn their whole bodies rather than just their heads in order to see a fellow masked actor. Their voices echo alarmingly inside the full mask. To the observer it appears that their bodies are too small for the mask; they look, comically enough, like walking tadpoles.

It takes time and practice to overcome these disabilities. Ideas and concepts need to be 'embodied' and this involves the development of what we might call a vocabulary of gesture. The ancient Greeks had a word for this: *cheironomia*, meaning, literally, gesticulation. The word later came to mean 'shadow-boxing' and 'pantomimic movement'. We know that related disciplines also employed considerable use of gesture. Oratory and dancing are two of the most closely related.[3]

No less an authority than Aristotle attests to the substantial use of gesture in performance (*Poetics*, 1455, 1462a). He advises the composer of tragedy to enact appropriate gestures during the composition process itself in order to feel the relevant emotions, ensuring greater conviction in the subsequent performance, and he criticizes the acting styles of his own day, which he says, by comparison with the older tradition, encourage excessive gesture, amounting to overacting.

We do not know if the actors inherited a set of instantly recognizable gestures that had been developed over time or whether they were inventive in the use of gesture in different performances. Certainly by the time Pollux recorded his observations on theatrical practice in the second century AD (*Onomasticon*, IV, 103–5), the Roman actors had developed what appears to be an established vocabulary of sign. There is no evidence that the Greeks had one. What is certain is that gesture accompanied speech, especially in formal situations, and this gesture, Aristotle tells us (*Poetics* 1448b), was largely mimetic. Gestures were used to imitate or represent some thing, person or action. Vase illustrations of probable dramatic action in the theatre are another source of evidence that gesture was widely used in performance.

If we take these clues to masked performance of tragedy and apply them today, we find that it is not too difficult to find appropriate mimetic gestures to underscore ideas, phrases or words. The simplest of all are invocations of the gods. Hands raised to the sky in prayer are both 'natural' today and recorded in ancient writings as far back as Homer's *Iliad* (e.g. I: 447–74). If a chthonic deity is addressed, it is appropriate to gesture to the earth. Pointing gestures are used in naming another person or in accusing a character. Mimicry allows for a degree of inventiveness in finding other gestured patterns that support more complex dramatic utterance.

Apart from gesture, the use of the mask itself in different ways also conveys meaning beyond or in support of language. The tragic mask is not neutral; it is a powerful dramatic tool characterized by suffering or endurance. The actor can use the body in various ways to qualify this characteristic. If the mask is lowered, it might convey reflection; if it is raised through arching and thrusting out the chest, it might indicate superiority or challenge. These physical stances, called *schêmata* by the ancient Greeks, helped the actor promote the mask to imitate thought and feeling and support this with mimetic gestures and stances. Our experience resulted in a dance-like style of performance governed by mask and space. Understanding the nature of masked performance led us to conclude that the spectators in the Theatre of Dionysus looked down on a remarkably athletic interaction between the masked protagonists and chorus.

It also helped us understand features of tragedy that are not readily perceived in the texts themselves. Two features in particular stood out: the use of silent masks and the distribution of roles among two or three speaking actors.

Silent masks

Some tragedies feature masked actors who play silent characters. These instances are always significant but can only be fully appreciated when the theatrical power of the silent mask is understood.

Aeschylus made three uses of the silent mask in the *Oresteia*. In the first play of the trilogy, *Agamemnon*, the third actor performs Cassandra, who is brought on stage in a chariot. She is silent for the entire exchange between Agamemnon and his wife Clytemnestra that leads to the returned victor walking on enriched tapestries in a foolhardy gesture of *hubris*. She continues to be silent during Clytemnestra's attempts to draw her into the palace. By the time Cassandra performs her dramatic song and dance foreshadowing her death and that of her captor, her lengthy silence to that point serves to give greater significance to her predicament. Later in the same play,

Clytemnestra and Aegisthus stand over two dead bodies – extras or dummies wearing the masks of Agamemnon and Cassandra. This use of silent masks, representing death, recurs in a parallel revelation in the second play of the trilogy, *Libation-Bearers*, when the victors become victims and the masks of Clytemnestra and Aegisthus adorn inert bodies.

Although there is no evidence that children wore masks in theatrical performance, our experimentation with silent masks on child characters provided their most dramatic use. Two examples repay close attention: the son of Ajax in Sophocles' play of that name and the children of Jason and Medea in Euripides' *Medea*.

Sophocles' use of masks in *Ajax* is ingenious, considering that the hero commits a prominent act of suicide just over halfway through the performance. But it is the way in which the playwright uses the silent masks of Ajax himself, his wife Tecmessa and his son Eurysaces that contributes so much to the final fifteen minutes or so of performance.

After Ajax has committed suicide, his brother Teucer attempts to ensure that he has a hero's burial rather than have his body thrown to the dogs as Menelaus and Agamemnon demand. In order to win the argument, Teucer establishes a tableau engineered to elicit sympathy. He describes in detail how Eurysaces is to kneel like a suppliant beside the body of his father, represented by an extra or a dummy wearing the mask of Ajax, and place a hand on the corpse (lines 1171–81). His mother and the widow of Ajax, now played by an extra wearing the mask of Tecmessa, stands beside him. It is this tableau of the three masks, so expressive of loss, suffering and vulnerability, that is the riveting visual focus of the play while the tawdry arguments of Menelaus and Agamemnon in favour of dishonouring Ajax are played out.

Nowhere, however, in surviving tragedy are the silent masks of children put to such profound theatrical effect as they are in Euripides' *Medea*. The two sons of Medea and Jason appear alive in three scenes and dead in one. The masked faces of the children are visible for over a fifth of the performance. Scenes involving them incorporate intimate action designed to heighten their youthful innocence and vulnerability. They are first seen when the Tutor brings them home from playing (49–110). Medea makes much of them in her second scene with Jason, urging them to embrace their father who responds to her duplicitous instructions, and she gives them the gown and headband impregnated with poisons intended for Jason's new bride (898–975). Medea herself embraces them and agonizes over her determination to kill them before dismissing them with cold resolve (1002–77). For the entire final sequence of the play, while Medea and Jason argue and apportion blame, their masks and bloodied costumes are visible in their mother's chariot.

This use by Euripides of the significant theatrical power of the silent mask is mirrored to varying degrees in other surviving tragedies of his: the children of Heracles in Euripides' play of that name, the boy Astyanax in *Trojan Women* and the young son in *Andromache*. At times sung lines are assigned to children, but these are either offstage, as in *Medea*, or can be sung by someone other than the masked child actor, as in *Andromache*. The presence of the silent masked children playing the young Antigone and Ismene in the last scene of our production of *Oedipus the King* demonstrated the power of the silent mask to evoke sympathy through the depiction of powerlessness, as they stood bewildered beside their bloodied and distraught father/brother.

Allocating masks

Logical analysis of the entrances and exits of characters in tragedy allows us in some instances to work out how three masked speaking actors, and on occasion two, were able to present up to three times as many characters. The results appear to suggest that the playwrights might have used the multiple masked role-playing to comment on the very nature of the theatre and its imitation of life.

Sophocles' *Oedipus at Colonus*, first performed posthumously in 401 BC, is an example of flexibility in the allocation of mask to enact a tragedy that involves eight characters and scenes requiring multiple entrances and exits.

The play tells the story of how Oedipus was exiled from Thebes after it was discovered that his wife Jocasta was also his mother. The blind Oedipus is guided by one of his two daughters, Antigone, to the village of Colonus outside Athens. It is here that Oedipus makes peace with the gods, is pardoned by Theseus, the ruler of Athens, blesses his daughters who have cared for him and curses his sons who have not, and miraculously departs the earth.

If we apply rigorous logic to the allocation of masks under the convention that allowed for a maximum of three speaking actors, we arrive at the following possible scenario for the 'behind-the-scenes' action in the use and exchange of masks.

- Oedipus and Antigone enter; given their significance and presence on stage throughout the play, it is safe to assume they were performed by the first and second actor, respectively. A scout from Colonus, played by the third actor, enters and exits during the opening scene.
- After the first chorus, the third actor re-enters as Ismene, the other daughter of Oedipus, with news affecting her father. At the conclusion of this scene,

this third actor exits, following instructions from the chorus, to perform a rite of purification for Oedipus.

- The third actor next appears as Theseus who welcomes Oedipus. He exits at the end of the scene.
- This same actor re-enters in the following scene as Creon who has come to take Oedipus hostage. During the argumentative exchange that follows, Creon tells Oedipus that he has already taken Ismene hostage. This is quite believable because Ismene disappeared earlier, logically in the same direction from which Creon came, to perform the ritual of purification. As the scene develops, Creon orders his guards to abduct Antigone. They drag her off.
- While Oedipus and Creon argue, Theseus re-enters. In this instance, he can *only* be played by the second actor who was dragged offstage as Antigone. At the close of this scene, Theseus conducts Creon off to pursue the women.
- After the following chorus, Theseus reappears and presents both Antigone and Ismene, whom he has rescued, to Oedipus. So now Sophocles had four main characters in full view, but only three speaking actors. So what did he do? He simply assigned no lines to Ismene for the next four hundred and fifty-nine lines (about a quarter of the entire play) after which she exited. The character of Ismene was probably played by an extra during these scenes, while the first actor played Oedipus, the second actor again played Antigone and the third actor resumed the role of Theseus.
- When the reunion is complete, the third actor as Theseus departs in order to resume the sacrifice from which he has been distracted. This actor next appears as Polynices, a son of Oedipus. After a bitter exchange with Oedipus, he exits before returning after the next chorus as Theseus. At the end of this scene, the blind Oedipus miraculously leads Theseus, Antigone and Ismene out through the sacred grove.
- At the close of the subsequent chorus, a Messenger enters from the grove to inform the people of Colonus how Oedipus disappeared from the face of the earth. At the end of his address, Antigone and Ismene immediately appear for a scene in which they both sing. So in this instance, Ismene is played by the third actor again, not an extra. This means therefore that the first actor must play the role of the Messenger. And it is appropriate that the voice of the first actor, which the spectators recognize as the voice of the actor who played Oedipus, should inform them of the last actions and words of Oedipus.
- The Messenger departs and Antigone and Ismene lament Oedipus' departure until Theseus reappears to comfort them. The role of Theseus in this instance must be played by the first actor. So all three actors have played the character of Theseus at some stage in this performance.

In this scenario therefore, the first actor plays Oedipus, the Messenger and Theseus in the last scene. The second actor plays Antigone and Theseus in one scene. The third actor plays the Scout from Colonus, Ismene in her first and last (speaking) scenes, Theseus in three scenes, Creon and Polynices. A supernumerary plays Ismene as a silent mask for three scenes.

The use of mask and multiple role-playing in this drama is particularly complex, both ingenious and convoluted, but all tragedies incorporate multiple role-playing to some degree. In *Antigone*, for example, since the tragedy dramatizes the rise and fall of the house of Menoeceus, it is reasonable to expect that the first actor played the role of Creon while the second actor played the roles of Antigone, Haemon and the Messenger who reports so vividly on the horrific events that took place in the cave where Antigone was entombed. In *Women of Trachis*, it is tempting to believe that the first actor played Deianira as well as the husband whom she kills, Heracles. In *Libation-Bearers*, the second actor can play the roles of Electra and her murdered mother, Clytemnestra. In *Ajax*, presuming the suicide took place out of sight of the spectators, the actor who played Ajax was available to play his brother and saviour, Teucer, who first appears after the suicide of Ajax.

The three-actor convention might have been sustained because the ancient Greeks applauded economy and wanted to see and hear only the best perform. Also, the allocation of masks among speaking actors solved the practical problem of having more fictional characters than speaking actors. But multiple role-playing in mask also reflects a difference between the ancient Greek view of the world and that of modern times. The ancient Greeks did not see tragedy principally as an outcome of individual choice or action. They were more inclined to give pre-eminence to circumstance as the cause of a happy or a disastrous life. And the gods determined circumstance arbitrarily. If disaster struck, the Greeks did not go looking for psychological causes. They knew that it was in the hands of the gods whether an individual played victor or victim, Electra or her murdered mother, Deianira or her slaughtered husband, Pentheus or his mother/murderer Agave. The masked performer in tragedy embodied this existential dilemma.

Old and New Comedy

The first recorded victory in a comic competition was at the City Dionysia 486.[4] Despite considerable output from renowned comic writers such as Cratinus, Eupolis and others for over a hundred years, only eleven plays by Aristophanes have survived. The first of these surviving works was produced in 425 (*Acharnians*) and the last in 388 (*Wealth*).

A substantial record of what the comic masks might have looked like can be found in illustrations on vases in the late fifth and early fourth centuries. These have been discovered in Greece and in southern Italy and Sicily where Greek colonists preserved their theatrical traditions. Masks represented human faces distorted for comic effect, gods in anthropomorphic disguise and animals; these last appear notably in choruses of Aristophanes' *Wasps*, *Birds* and *Frogs*. The comic character represented humans as grotesque, parodic figures with masks, padded costumes and phalluses.

A vase painting from Tarentum in south-eastern Italy, dated to the first quarter of the fourth century, depicts what may be a scene from a comedy that deals with the punishment of a thief caught in the act.[5] The character in the centre of the scene stands naked on his toes with his hands raised above his head. He wears a comic mask featuring a ring of tousled white hair, eyes wide with fear, and an open, distorted mouth. He is clothed in an actor's body suit that covered him entirely except for head, hands and feet. The suit is embellished with a large pot-belly, a padded rump and a phallus, characteristics that appear regularly in the plentiful reproductions of comic scenes from the period. This particular figure also has false breasts attached to the body suit and is a clear pictorial representation of the gender-crossing that was the foundation of Old Comedy.

This image of the 'naked' male playing a female role is found elsewhere in Aristophanes. One example occurs in a scene from his play, *Women at the Thesmophoria*, first produced in 411. The play satirizes the women's festival in honour of Demeter and Persephone as well as parodying the playwright Euripides and some of his works. Early in the play (236–317), the character Euripides coerces his servant, Mnesilochus, to dress as a woman in order to infiltrate the festival and save him from an expected condemnation. With the help of the transvestite playwright, Agathon, Mnesilochus is stripped, leaving his phallus and padding exposed; his body hair is singed and his beard is shaved from his mask. This male body is then dressed in women's clothes to complete the burlesque gender transition.

A red-figure bell-krater also from south-eastern Italy and dated to around 380–370 BC depicts a scene probably from the lost play, *Cheiron*[6] (**Fig. 27**). Two male characters assist a third, who struggles with the additional help of a crooked staff to mount a flight of three steps to a low stage. Each of the masks incorporates exaggerated facial features with grey or receding hair while the costumes feature the familiar phalluses dangling at different angles below the short tunics. The assisting characters pull and push the old man in an ungainly fashion indicative of knockabout, slapstick performance. The mouthpieces of the masks are open, like the tragic mask, only this time in a

Figure 27. Cheiron goes on stage.

parodic fashion, and the representation suggests a great deal of energy, even athleticism, in the enactment.

Experimentation with facsimile comic masks today helps us appreciate the nature of masked comedy and in particular its rambunctious, parodic style. We can apply this appreciation to any surviving comedy. Aristophanes' *Lysistrata*, also composed around 411, is a case in point. It is an anti-war play in which the older women of Athens seize the treasury on the Acropolis so that the men cannot get access to funds to promote the war with Sparta, while the young women refuse to have sex with their military husbands until they lay down their arms. The entire conceit of the play therefore lies in gender differentiation and conflict. It is the most commonly revived play by Aristophanes in modern times and that is precisely because the gender lines are so clearly drawn and stereotypical differences are comically exploited. It also resounds with modern sensibilities relating to gender equity and indeed to the superiority of conciliatory women over bellicose men in the matters of war and peace.

Two thirds of the way through *Lysistrata*, a young Athenian, Cinesias, arrives at the Acropolis with baby in arms begging his wife Myrrhine to come and care for the child (862). When she does come, Cinesias abandons the baby and reveals his swollen phallus. The sexual tease scene that follows as Myrrhine constantly runs back inside the Acropolis to fetch successively stretcher, mattress, blanket, pillow and aromatic oil plays well even today with unmasked actors.

But even with a scene like this that translates from ancient Greek cultural humour to our own, the reception of the scene would change markedly when played by masked male actors. The scene takes on a burlesque character grounded in the cross-dressed nature of the performance. It is one thing for a male actor masked or otherwise to offer his phallus to a female actor masked or otherwise; it is another thing entirely in a robust comic context for both actors to be male.

Later in the play when Lysistrata has finally brought the warring parties to the negotiation table, the text requires a silent character called Reconciliation to be brought onstage (1160), and her body is used as a referent for the peacemaking allocation of land between the Athenians and the Spartans. Modern translations invariably describe this character as a nude or unclothed girl. However, it is well to bear in mind the naked thief caught in the act discussed above. When a male actor wearing a silent mask and a costume that parodies rather than accurately portrays a female body plays the character of Reconciliation, the nature of the comedy is again distinctly distorted.

As a style of comic performance, Old Comedy lasted barely a century. New Comedy, which prevailed from the late fourth to the second centuries, superseded it and also provided a model for comedy in the Roman Empire. The Greek playwright, Menander (*c*.342–*c*.291) is credited with its introduction. It was thought that none of his works survived until a fortuitous discovery in 1905 by Gustave Lefebvre revealed the remains of five plays in what came to be called the Cairo Codex. Since then two more or less complete plays, *The Bad-Tempered Man* and *The Woman from Samos*, and substantial parts of several others, have been translated and performed[7] (see also Goldberg, ch. 7 in this volume).

Menander invented the comedy of manners with its emphasis on stereotypical characters that have served comedy, in various adaptations, from that time on. The most popular of his stock were contrasting types such as the strict father and the lovelorn son, innocent maidens and streetwise courtesans, slaves that overstepped their status and cooks that acted more like clowns. His plots moved away from the political and social satire of Old Comedy and dealt with quotidian matters like romance and domestic intrigue. In fact, Euripides was more likely a stronger influence on Menander with his creation of non-heroic characters than was Aristophanes.

Figure 28. Mosaic from Pompeii of Menander's *Women at Breakfast*,
*c.*100 BC.

There is not a great deal of evidence available that might help us appreciate
the theatrical style of this comic genre. A floor mosaic from Samos dated
to the late second century BC represents a scene from a play, most likely
New Comedy. Its precise referent is unsure though it has been ascribed to
the opening scene from Menander's *Synaristosai* (translated variously as *The
Hen's Party* or *Women at Breakfast*). It might be a reproduction of an original
from *c.*300 BC[8] (**Fig. 28**).

The mosaic depicts three masked women seated on cushioned chairs
around a table, attended by an unmasked young girl. The masks are far more
realistic than those from Old Comedy. The main characters are swathed in
cloaks and tunics, suggesting a static style of performance, in contrast to
that of Old Comedy where the costumes allowed for considerable freedom
of movement. One of the characters represents an old crone with a cup of
wine in hand who gestures emphatically to the other masked figures. Each

of these adopts a posture that indicates attention from one and indifference from the other. The scene appears to represent the domestication of comedy with its emphasis on familiar surroundings, fashionable clothing and recognizable characters that featured in New Comedy.

The masks of Rome

The theatre of the Roman Empire was eclectic and multi-faceted, incorporating mime, spectacle, recitations, literary drama and comedy. The mask seems to have figured in most of these entertainments, but there were two developments that warrant inspection: the use of the open-mouthed mask in imitations of Greek comedy and tragedy and the use of the closed-mouthed mask in the spectacular pantomime deriving from folk culture.

The two heralded comic playwrights of the period were Plautus (died *c.*184 BC) and Terence (*c.*184–159 BC) who reflect both similarities and differences in their efforts to create Roman versions of Greek comedy. For both of them, the works of Menander were an inspiration.

Plautus wrote knockabout comedies such as *The Swaggering Soldier* (*Miles Gloriosus*) and *The Liar* (*Pseudolus*), on which Stephen Sondheim's 1960s Broadway musical hit *A Funny Thing Happened on the Way to the Forum* was based. One of his works that incorporates a number of characteristics of his style is *The Rope* (*Rudens*). The plot has an Athenian context and its romantic theme concerns the discovery of abducted sisters. There is a reference in the text to one of Menander's contemporaries, Diphilus, as its author. This indicates that it was probably a translation or version of an earlier Greek work. Its characters include an old man who doesn't know what is going on, a slave who is aggressive and comically offensive, a scabrous procurer and two sweet, innocent young maidens whose lives and virtue are saved despite prolonged risks that drive the comedy. It is not great literature but serves as an excellent springboard for the antics of gifted comic actors, one of whom, the masked actor, Roscius (*c.*120–62 BC), was celebrated for his interpretations of both Plautus and Terence a century after their deaths.

Terence strove to match the literary standards of Menander. He completed six plays in six years then died during a sea journey in an apparent search for additional surviving plays by his idol to use as models. A fascinating aspect to these remaining plays by Terence is the disputatious prologue that introduces each of them. In the guise of the Prologue, Terence takes issue with older, established Roman comic playwrights who have subjected his own work to severe critique. What is surprising to modern eyes, with our disapproval of plagiarism, is to read his passionate justification for 'borrowing' scenes

Figure 29. Manuscript miniature of scene from Terence's *Phormio*.

and even entire plays from Menander and other earlier Greek writers.[9] He argues that such 'borrowing' rescues scenes and plays from oblivion and does everyone a favour. He recognizes, however, that a scene or play should only be 'borrowed' once; in fact, he apologizes for mistakenly copying a scene that an older playwright had previously used.

There is no mention of the use of masks in Plautus and Terence's surviving plays, but by the same token there is no mention of the improvised spaces they had to use, given the absence of a theatre building in Rome at the time. However, such is their evident devotion to Menander and admiration for the style and standards of the ancient Greeks that it would be entirely out of character for them to ignore what was such a vital theatrical component in the production of their mentor's plays. It is highly likely that they adopted the comic mask of New Comedy along with the other facets of Menander's exemplifiers as they appear in medieval manuscripts of Terence (**Fig. 29**).[10]

But whereas the comic mask appears to become more realistic in New Comedy and its Roman imitations, the open-mouthed tragic mask became more stylized in a way that served both Roman tragedy and theatre architecture. The style of dramatic writing seems to have suited developments in theatre architecture and the tragic mask. After the classical period, the *orchêstra* no longer served as the performing space for the actors. They performed on a stage of varying heights at different times, initially tangential to the top of the circle. The changes resulted in the typical Roman theatre with a wooden stage, ten to twelve feet high, a semi-circular *orchêstra* used for seating some members of the audience, and a lofty *scaena* or scene-building at the back of the stage. This provided the principal sounding-board for the masked actors now that the centre of the *orchêstra* no longer served that purpose. The mask itself changed; it did not affect to represent the natural human face but was embellished with an *onkos* or elaborate crown. The actor on the high stage took to wearing *cothurni* or boots with raised soles. The nature of performance no longer relied on athletic and choreographed movement but on a towering presence and vocal delivery.

Seneca (*c.*4 BC–65 AD), tutor to the Emperor Nero, was the leading tragedian who also based his work on Greek models. His versions however revelled in gore and brutality in a manner that suited his own time. His play *Thyestes* recounts the ancient Greek legend about the character who seduced his brother Atreus' wife. In an extreme act of revenge, Atreus killed Thyestes' children and served them up to him in a stew. Seneca's drama dwells in detail on the hideous dismemberment of the children and the unabashed glorification of the act of vengeance. Like Seneca's other works, the play does not rely on stage management but on its literary qualities and the demonstrable power of recitation. It is highly doubtful that Seneca's plays were ever performed in public, masked or unmasked.

The open-mouthed mask was confined, it seems, to imitations of Greek theatrical practice and did not enjoy universal approbation. Lucian (*c.*120–90 AD), in his Socratic dialogue *The Dance* (see Zarifi, ch. 12 in this volume), wrote, 'What a repulsive and frightful spectacle is a man tricked out to disproportionate stature, mounted upon high clogs, wearing a mask that reaches out above his head, with a mouth that is set in a vast yawn, as if he meant to swallow spectators.'[11] Inside it, Lucian continues, 'you have the man himself, bawling out, bending backwards and forwards, sometimes singing his lines and (what is surely the height of unseemliness) melodizing his calamities'. In contrast, Lucian finds the closed mouth of the pantomime mask a thing of beauty, with the performer adorned in silks and accompanied by the flute and sweet voices of singers.

The pantomime was a spectacular indigenous invention of Rome deriving from folk traditions in Italy. This style of entertainment originated in the third century and was firmly established by the 80s BC; it constituted the most significant development in the theatre at that time.[12] The *pantomimus* was a masked dancer whose choreography was informed by Greek myth and legend. The functions of the miming storyteller and the singing chorus were separated. My own experiments with actors singing and dancing in mask confirm the difficulty of doing both at the same time with sustained vigour. We found that there was simply not sufficient breath support, given the impediment of the mask, to produce a performance of any appreciable length. When the task is shared with other choral members, the weight of numbers helps surmount the problem, but the solo performer faces a prodigious task.

Libanius, writing in the fourth century AD in defence of the pantomime, records the rigour of the training that was a prerequisite for such an energetic and spectacular performance:

> the gymnastic trainer will twist him round into more numerous and more remarkable bends than a wrestler, bringing up both his feet over the back onto his head and in addition even forcing them back to project further past the face so that his heels approach his elbows. And when he has made the body into a circle, like some willow cane, he sets it in motion for running like a hoop, and it runs . . . Such will the trainer render the body for the dancing teacher, and he, when he has taken it over, will render the framework of the limbs obedient with a view to the imitation of each figure.[13]

The dancer is required, he records, to imitate a range of tools associated with women's work – the distaff, the spindle, the wool, the warp and the woof – to Diomedes with his trumpet and Achilles shaking his ashen spear, dragging Hector's corpse and 'leaping further than the pentathletes'.[14] Lucian records an instance in which the emperor Nero refuted criticism of the pantomime performer by Diogenes the Cynic through commissioning a performance. After it, Diogenes was compelled to shout out: 'I hear the story that you are acting, man, I do not just see it; you seem to me to be talking with your very hands.'[15]

These testimonies give us some indication of the athleticism, ingenuity and spectacle of the Roman pantomime dancer telling stories from ancient Greece through imitative mime and manipulation of the closed-mouthed mask. There is evidence that not all *pantomimi* were male; women certainly performed at private functions and on occasion in public by the fourth century AD.[16]

Mask-making was quite an industry in ancient Rome. Pollux, writing in the second century AD, records that in his time there were forty-four different types of theatrical masks (*Onomasticon*, IV, 133–40). Representations of the open-mouthed masks employed in theatrical developments of Greek originals have been found in a variety of reproductions in the period on caskets, jewellery, household items, murals, frescoes, terracotta statuettes and sarcophagi. The closed-mouthed masks of pantomime were also reproduced in abundance on numerous monuments by the second century AD.

This reproduction of representations of mask associated with histrionic performance subsequently bequeathed to posterity the enduring symbols of theatre itself: the grieving mask of tragedy and the grinning mask of comedy.

NOTES

1. For stills and videotape excerpts from these productions, see the website: playingwithtragedy.usq.edu.au
2. P. D. Arnott, *Public and Performance in the Greek Theatre* (London and New York: Routledge 1989), pp. 74–104.
3. *Ibid.*, pp. 56–73.
4. A. Pickard-Cambridge, *The Dramatic Festivals of Athens*, second ed. rev. by J. Gould and D. M. Lewis (Oxford: Clarendon Press, 1968), p. 82.
5. A. D. Trendall, *Red Figure Vases of South Italy and Sicily* (London: Thames and Hudson, 1989), pp. 74f., 104 (plate 105); see also A. D. Trendall and T. B. L. Webster, *Illustrations of Greek Drama* (London: Phaidon, 1991), p. 130 (plate IV.13).
6. J. R. Green and E. Handley, *Images of the Greek Theatre* (London: British Museum Press, 1995), pp. 53f.
7. J. M. Walton and P. D. Arnott, *Menander and the Making of Comedy* (Westport, Conn.: Greenwood, 1996), pp. 39–40.
8. Green and Handley, 1995, pp. 77f., 116. The mosaic is illustrated on p. 78. See also Trendall and Webster, 1991, opp. p. 8, p. 145; on the Mytilene mosaics, Walton and Arnott, 1996, pp. 62–5 and Ill. 9–12.
9. P. Bovie, C. Carrier, and D. Parker (eds.), *The Complete Comedies of Terence* (New Brunswick, New Jersey: Rutgers University Press, 1974), p. 308 (Prologue to *The Brothers*), p. 155 (Prologue to *The Eunuch*).
10. E. Fantham, 'Orator and/et actor' in P. E. Easterling and E. Hall (eds.), *Greek and Roman Actors: Aspects of an Ancient Profession* (Cambridge: Cambridge University Press, 2002), p. 365.
11. 'The Dance' in *Lucian*, trans. A. M. Harmon, Loeb edition, Vol. V (Cambridge, Mass.: Harvard University Press, and London: William Heinemann, 1936).
12. E. Hall, 'The Singing Actors of Antiquity', *Greek and Roman Actors*, p. 28.
13. 'The Dancers', 104–5 in Margaret E. Molloy, *Libanius and the Dancers* (Hildesheim, Zürich and New York: Olms-Weidmann, 1996), pp. 171f.
14. *Ibid.*, 68, pp. 160f.
15. *Lucian*, 'The Dance', 63.
16. R. Webb, 'Female Entertainers in Late Antiquity', *Greek and Roman Actors*, pp. 282–303.

FURTHER READING

Arnott, P. D., *Public and Performance in the Greek Theatre*. London and New York: Routledge, 1989.

Easterling, P. E., *The Cambridge Companion to Greek Tragedy*. Cambridge: Cambridge University Press, 1997.

— and E. Hall (eds.), *Greek and Roman Actors: Aspects of an Ancient Profession*. Cambridge: Cambridge University Press, 2002.

Rehm, R., *Greek Tragic Theatre*. London and New York: Routledge, 1992.

Walton, J. M., *The Greek Sense of Theatre: Tragedy Reviewed*. 1984; rev. Amsterdam: Harwood, 1996.

— and Arnott, P. D., *Menander and the Making of Comedy*. Westport, Conn.: Greenwood, 1996.

Wiles, D., *Greek Theatre Performance: An Introduction*. Cambridge: Cambridge University Press, 2000.

14

GRAHAM LEY

A material world: costumes, properties and scenic effects

In a reading of scripts, costume and properties may be barely noticed, emerging sharply into view only when critical attention attributes to them a particular significance. In this chapter, I want to emphasize the material nature of classical theatre and to indicate the diversity of their use as essential components of all ancient performances.

One approach to the ancient dramatic texts that survive is to consider them as language intended to be delivered by performers. Another is to treat classical stage practice through the surviving remains of its theatre structures. But in both cases, the transient and the perishable are missing. The transient is everything that belongs to a culture of live performance, from established conventions of artistic expression through to idiosyncratic nuances and specific blunders in the work of performers; the perishable is, in many respects, the subject of this chapter.

Decay affects far more than the pigment applied to stone temples, or the pillage of precious objects. Even metals only survive either in bits (e.g. the clamps that hold stone blocks together) or by chance, when bronze statues that were part of a ship's cargo are discovered more or less intact in the sea. Armour may be found, as may some personal and more domestic items, often in burials. Glass and ceramics are fragile but durable, and complete items do survive. But timber and wood, bone, fabrics of all kinds, ropes and binding materials, basketwork, leather for work (buckets, harnesses) or dress (belts, jerkins, boots and sandals) will be found rarely, almost always in fragments.[1] Substances were also vital: resins of various kinds, pastes or plasters, pigments, grease must have been liberally deployed to create the material and functional world. An awareness of this material world should lead to an enlargement of our sense of the personnel of theatre production, and raise interesting questions. Some machinery with a specific function will have been made exclusively for the theatre, but techniques may have been drawn from other spheres of activity. The theatrical *mêchanê* or crane of the fifth-century Greek theatre would have had a specific function, but the principles of its construction would surely have been based on hoists used for everyday purposes. Similarly, the rolling platform known as the *ekkuklêma* from the same period would undoubtedly have drawn on principles of controlled traction applied elsewhere.

For properties, we need to consider either special manufacture or the use of adopted objects. Carriages are used in a number of surviving Greek tragedies, from which performers must descend with ease. It seems likely that adaptations would need to be made to any existing model. When armour or weapons are introduced, will these be real or simulations, made of lighter materials? So, amongst the personnel of production we need to acknowledge those who have made the buckets or baskets, the jerkins or tunics, the domestic implements, or the doors in the *skênê* building. Included in these we would find the other classes of Athenians, the women, the migrants and the slaves. Many migrants were artisans, and women were traditionally the domestic creators of garments, while slaves were employed not just on hard labour (agricultural, in the metal-ore mines, in the stone quarries, in the mills) but also in skilled tasks of all kinds.

There is little reference to these makers of theatre, but we do have titles for some leading professionals. For the fifth-century Greek theatre we hear of the *skeuopoios* (Aristophanes *Knights* 232), and for the republican Roman comic theatre of the *choragus* (Plautus *Curculio* 785; *The Persian Girl*, 157). The context in *Knights* refers to the creation of masks, but elsewhere *skeuê* means properties, and so the *skeuopoios* remains our leading term for 'props-maker'.[2] In Plautus, the *choragus* comes on and speaks in *The Persian Girl*, and is plainly associated in both passages cited with the provision of costumes and personal ornamentation. Elsewhere in Aristophanes (*Peace*, 174) we hear of the *mêchanopoios*, literally the 'crane-maker' and clearly in that context the crane-operator. But we must allow for numerous 'makers' and operators who were, directly or indirectly, involved in theatrical production.

The comedies of Aristophanes delight in the presentation or distortion of the material world, and add to that the realization of fantastic images. In Aristophanic comedy, the chorus numbered twenty-four, and this allowed for spectacular display. Athenian comedy had from its origins drawn much of its inspiration from animal choruses, which Aristophanes at least aligned with metaphorical suggestion.[3] In *Wasps*, the chorus represents the vindictive sting of Athenian jurors and the swarm will have been unified in a distinctive costume bearing a rear end and sting. These are mentioned before they appear and, as the Wasps attempt to rescue their fellow juror, they brandish them (*Wasps*, 457). Later Aristophanes uses the costume to suggest the sting of past military success against the Persians and elaborates on the visual metaphor in relation to the Athenian democratic jury system (*Wasps*,

1060–1121, in what is known as the *parabasis*). These characters are also old men, caricatured by Aristophanes as typical of the composition of juries in the democracy, and the upper part of their costume and their mask may well have fitted this aspect of their dual insect-man personality. When they first appear they are escorted by their paradoxically young sons, and much play is made of their slow progress in the dark, suggested by the oil lamps and wicks held by the children. These boys are later sent away before the knockabout action begins, with their cloaks thrown over their shoulders, in a gesture which recurs throughout ancient comedy for characters running (*Wasps*, 408).

Aristophanic choruses may be unified, and may be animal or human, but there are other variations on these patterns. It is difficult to be sure how the chorus of *Clouds* was portrayed, and the aristocratic cavalry of *Knights* might have been disappointing if they appeared without 'horses', but texts in these cases tell us little about visual representation (see **Fig. 4**). In the case of *Birds*, the script emphasizes the variety of birds that make up the chorus as they appear. It seems from the action and the list of birds that there were even more than twenty-four outfits, because four other named birds appear separately. We can then add to that the character of the Hoopoe and the door-keeper to the Hoopoe, and the elaboration and expense of comic production begins to be clear. This is colourful and visually extravagant performance, exciting in dance and agitated movement, a brilliant extrapolation from the lifeless property birds, crow and jackdaw, which the human protagonists use as their guides at the opening of the comedy.

It would be impossible to summarize the variety of costume in ancient Greek comedy satisfactorily, since undoubtedly invention must have been at a premium in the competition, and we have only eleven surviving plays of Aristophanes, a number of fragments, and a collection of titles. Laura Stone has written an excellent survey for Aristophanes, and it is proba- ble that alongside invention we should also expect to find some relatively standard items.[4] It seems that comic performers wore a body stocking, and human characters may not have been clothed in anything other than every- day garments, such as what we might call a tunic or undergarment (*chitôn* or *peplos*) and a cloak or overgarment of some sort (*himation*, *chlaina*), which was wrapped around the upper body. The material in both cases was wool. Shoes and slippers of various kinds and occasionally boots may be mentioned, notably when identifying a character. So for instance, in *Wasps*, Procleon, the old juror whom the chorus comes to collect from his house, is transformed by his son Anticleon by means of a change of costume. His old cloak, of the kind known as *tribôn*, is replaced with an expensive Persian cloak, and his old slippers with more luxurious 'Spartans', as they were called. This replacement gear prompts him to accuse his son of revealing pro-Persian or pro-Spartan sympathies.

Mask and costume may well be exploited in the portrayal of non-Athenians, since ancient comedy delights in indulging the prejudices of its audiences. In the opening of Aristophanes' *Acharnians*, the official known as the (Persian) King's Eye is accompanied by at least two non-speaking performers costumed and identified as eunuchs. The mask of the King's Eye (perhaps with a single eye) is a ridiculous feature, but incidental mention of Sardian dyes and Persian gold are probably suggestive of ornamentation in the costume. If characters are non-Athenian Greeks, there may be nothing specific about their costume that we can detect from the script, but properties or accompanying extras will add to the ethnic characterization. The Boeotian in *Acharnians* arrives (*Acharnians*, 860) with Theban pipers and another Boeotian carrying produce from that region, and the delicacy of an eel is singled out for admiration from the chorus. Earlier a similar scene introduces a Megarian, who has brought his starving daughters for sale as piglets, since he has nothing else. Despite our temptation to see this as a moment for comic animal costuming, the Megarian has great difficulty in maintaining that they really are piglets, and costume may be subordinate to the opportunity for sexual innuendo and animal babble.

The performance fact that exclusively male performers will be transvestite when playing women characters is regularly exploited. As the non-Athenian women join the Athenians in the opening of *Lysistrata*, we have no particular impression of distinctive clothing. But the Spartan protests that she is being felt over like a sacrificial victim after her breasts have been praised, and sexual and physical approval greets the accompanying Boeotian and Corinthian. Padding was a universal resource of comic performance in this period, accommodated easily within a body-stocking, and it is most likely that supposedly seductive or naked female figures were portrayed in this way. Male characters who dress up as women, either for preference or artistic inspiration (the tragic playwright Agathon in *Women at the Thesmophoria*) or for subterfuge, will prompt sexual innuendo. Agathon's womanly costume and accoutrements are mixed with some properties with male associations to point up the humour, and his confusing image is supported by crucial omissions: his mask has no beard and he lacks the exaggerated comic *phallos* or penis, but conversely he has no padding for breasts.[5] In *Acharnians*, Euripides provides an impoverished costume and properties to suit a pitiful appearance for the protagonist Dicaeopolis, who has to plead his case for peace to a hostile chorus (*Acharnians* 393–479). In *Women at the Thesmophoria*, Agathon provides the relative of Euripides with what he needs to dress up as a woman: he is shaved with a razor and a mirror, singed by torches brought out from the house, given a yellow *himation* and a breast-band or bra, a hairnet and headband, and a shawl and shoes (101–268). Of course, the relative's body-stocking has no padding and he still has his comic *phallos*, both of which are a source of humour later, when he is discovered by the group of women at the festival that he has infiltrated (635–48). When women characters dress up as men, as they do in *Women in Assembly* (1–284), they are seen to purloin their husbands' shoes, sticks and cloaks to create the effect, but they also need property beards and wreaths of good omen.

Properties, or items of clothing as properties, abound in Aristophanic comedy. Some may be pre-set, waiting to be picked up, some may be brought on by characters and then discarded, some may be brought out to characters and removed.[6] Properties provide sequences in the script, either by composing a relatively stable focus for a scene, or by contributing to comic repetition through variation. In *Women in Assembly*, the women practise speaking in the public assembly by assuming the speaker's wreath, while in *Lysistrata* they take an oath. They start by using the shield carried by the Scythian archeress and look for the butchered parts of the sacrificial victim. When this strikes them as too warlike, they take their oaths from a cup and a jar of wine, in a realization of the male prejudice about the fondness of women for drinking. Later in *Lysistrata*, Aristophanes has Myrrhine frustrate her aroused and phallic husband by repeatedly leaving him to fetch properties from the scene-building. Initially Aristophanes constructs the sequence around a child to whose cries Myrrhine comes, but the child is conducted away by an attendant and the husband demands the rites of Aphrodite. Myrrhine fetches in turn a small bed, a rush mat for the bed, a pillow, a blanket and Rhodian perfume, since the perfume she had just brought out was not good enough, and then leaves him with an instruction to vote for peace (829–958). In *Acharnians* the peaceful indulgence of Dicaeopolis is contrasted with the warlike duties of Lamachus in a sequence in which properties relating to festival dining and military subsistence and equipment are apparently brought to each respectively and in sequence.

Material objects and substances, either shown or alluded to in the script, suggest a state of being. Food is associated with peace and festivals and a life at home, as a guest or on one's own property, and the equipment for preparing or carrying or cooking it is immediately suggestive of its enjoyment.[7] Domestic equipment may also be used preposterously, as it is in *Wasps*, when items from the kitchen and the house are deployed to conduct a trial of a house-dog (798–1008), whose 'puppies' are finally brought on to create sympathy. The paraphernalia of a public courtroom are created from utensils and furniture, and the witnesses are a cup, a pestle, a brazier, a cooking-pot and a cheese-grater, which is briefly interrogated either as a property or a personification, to no purpose. Properties are also personal attributes, as may be some costumes. Dionysus at the opening of *Frogs* is dressed as Heracles, with lionskin and club, but also as 'himself', in a yellow *chitôn* and the soft boots worn by performers in tragedy: the combination leaves the 'true' Heracles in consternation. More simply, the sickle-maker and the jar-maker bring their wares with them to thank the protagonist Trygaeus in *Peace*, and the military tradesmen are identified by crests, helmets, breastplates, trumpets and spears (1197–1264).

Scenic effects in Aristophanic comedy are as dependent on costume, properties and a sense of setting conveyed by words and action as they are on any machinery. So Aristophanes at the opening of *Acharnians* can evoke the atmosphere of the Athenian assembly by redefining the theatre audience as the assembly of citizens, and later in the comedy can bring on his protagonist with his family in a celebration of a rural festival of Dionysus. Similarly, the opening of *Frogs* sees Dionysus and his slave embark on an eventful journey: firstly with a donkey and baggage to the house of Heracles, then past a cortege of the dead and across the river Styx by means of Charon's boat, surrounded by a chorus of frogs, past fearful sights and then through a secondary chorus of initiates, and finally back to the scene-building and the door of Pluto's palace. But Aristophanes is not averse to technology, placing the protagonist of *Peace* astride a gigantic dung-beetle suspended on the crane (*mêchanê*). The ride on the dung-beetle calls to mind the tragic hero Bellerophon riding Pegasus, while Socrates suspended in a basket contemplating higher things in *Clouds* slyly suggests the godlike pretensions of philosophy. Euripides flies past in the tragic role of Perseus in an attempt to rescue his relative in *Women at the Thesmophoria* (1008–15), who sings the part of Andromeda appropriately; in *Birds* the chorus of birds and the human protagonist contest the air-space with Iris, messenger and representative of the rights of the gods, swinging in on the *mêchanê* (1188–1266). It is interesting that Aristophanes' relatively sparing use of the *ekkuklêma*, a machine that could bring performers and properties into view through the main doors of the *skênê*, is also confined in the surviving comedies to parody of tragedy, with the tragic playwrights Euripides and Agathon 'wheeled out' to be interrogated, exploited and abused by comic protagonists in *Acharnians* and *Women at the Thesmophoria* respectively.

The *skênê* is the construction that houses this machinery, and it is subject to all kinds of (re)definition in Aristophanic comedy. Its door is essential to the action, whether used to indicate subsequent locales as it is in the long, opening sequence of *Frogs* mentioned above, or made the location of a complex interaction between those inside or on the *skênê* and those outside, as it is when Procleon is struggling to evade house-arrest in *Wasps*. There are some gestures towards this realization of the *skênê* in tragedy: Antigone and her mentor appear on its roof in Euripides' *Phoenician Women* (88), as do Orestes and Pylades, brandishing torches and threatening to murder Hermione and set fire to the building in Euripides' *Orestes* (1567). Euripides combines this disturbing picture with the introduction of the god Apollo on the *mêchanê*, and he repeatedly makes use of the crane to achieve these effects of divine resolution to the crisis or the aftermath of a tragic action.[8] In Aeschylus' *Libation-Bearers*, there is furious use of the door in the murderous climax to the tragedy, as a slave, Clytemnestra, and then Orestes and Pylades emerge in succession from the *skênê* (870–930). In tragedy, the *ekkuklêma* displays disturbing scenes of slaughter, the implication being that the audience is allowed by this means to see the result of actions that have taken place inside the *skênê*. Some striking effects cannot be reconstructed with any certainty: in Euripides' *Bacchae*, the text suggests that part of the palace may be seen to collapse as a result of a Dionysiac earthquake (576–607); Prometheus is shackled to a rock by Hephaestus in the opening of *Prometheus Bound*; and Evadne speaks and then leaps from a high rock which is not the temple (*skênê*) in Euripides' *Suppliants* (980–1071).

But, in general, it would be a mistake to believe that the action of tragedy in the fifth century was ever heavily dependent on the machinery attached to the scene-building. The *skênê* was a relatively late introduction to the tragic theatre, first clearly in evidence in the *Oresteia* of Aeschylus, when it probably already contained the *ekkuklêma*, if Orestes' display of the dead bodies of Clytemnestra and Aegisthus in *Libation-Bearers* was made on it (973). Aeschylus died only two years after the production of the *Oresteia*, and the bulk of his tragedies must have been produced without the *skênê*. The three that survive from before the *Oresteia* (*Persians*, *Seven Against Thebes*, *Suppliants*) rely for their power and conviction substantially on the impetus of the chorus in conjunction with individual performers, who sing with, or speak to, the chorus. The playing space of the *orchêstra* may contain images of the gods, as would seem to be the case in both *Seven Against Thebes* and *Suppliants*, while in *Persians* the appearance of the ghost of the king Darius on top of his burial mound must have been intended as an impressive *coup de théâtre*, however the mound was represented. The *orchêstra* also accommodates the carriage of the Persian queen earlier in the tragedy and the tented carriage that returns with Xerxes later in *Persians*, and Aeschylus uses this effect again with the arrival of Agamemnon and Cassandra in *Agamemnon*. From this carriage Agamemnon descends to walk

Figure 30. Aeschylus' *Libation-Bearers*: Electra at the tomb with hair and libations, *c.*350 BC.

across dyed tapestries into the *skênê*, leaving Cassandra to jump down from it later, in a visionary madness (1072).

Tragic costume makes a distinctive contribution. In *Persians*, it seems likely that ornamental, orientalizing garments or patterns would have been worn, and it is evident from the script that the conclusion of the tragedy has the Persian king Xerxes returning in tatters with an empty quiver which he pathetically displays[9] (**Fig. 31**). Selected properties and elements of costume carry immense significance.[10] The audience's eyes will fix themselves on Agamemnon's boots as he has them finally removed, before he steps on the tapestries (*Agamemnon*, 944–5); a lock of hair, so similar to that on her own mask, will divert Electra away from the libations to reunion with Orestes in *Libation-Bearers* (164–204), **Fig. 30**; the branches decorated with woollen filaments define and ultimately protect the young women in *Suppliants*. But in comparison with Aristophanic comedy, the material world is sparsely represented in all fifth-century tragedy, as if there was a conscious process of abstraction; or, alternatively, as if comedy sensed the need

275

Figure 31. Costumes and furniture in a fourth-century *Persians*, *c*.340 BC.

or the opportunity to take the restricted material qualities of costumed and propertied tragic performance and exaggerate them exuberantly. Comedy rarely exploits a property for long, discarding objects quickly and absolutely. Tragedy, in contrast, may cling to a property throughout its action. This is the case with the bow of Philoctetes in Sophocles' tragedy, about which we hear before we see it, and which never leaves our minds until the close, by which time it has defined the ethical and heroic status of all the leading characters, and mediated crucially in both deceit and trust.[11] This sense of mediation is exploited again by Sophocles in his *Electra*, when the delivery of the urn supposedly containing Orestes' ashes prompts a pitiful lament from his sister. In *Philoctetes*, the bow is everything: it has secured

Figure 32. Sophocles' *Electra:* Orestes with the urn of 'ashes' and Electra, 360–350 BC.

Philoctetes his food on the island, and is the key to the capture of Troy. In *Electra* the urn is nothing, an empty vessel, merely a property in the deceit conducted by Orestes and the Tutor (**Fig. 32**).

In Sophocles' *Ajax* we see the sword that Ajax received as a gift from his proper enemy Hector (660–5), but which he is forced by his own disgrace to turn against himself (815–20). It was perhaps with this sword that Ajax went in distraction to murder the Greeks (284–7), and slaughtered animals instead. But the heroic Ajax of Homer's *Iliad* was pre-eminently a spearman: it was with his spear that he destroyed Tecmessa's land (514–19) and with his famous hide-shield that he protected his half-brother Teucer in battle, who arrives in Sophocles' tragedy to defend his corpse. Ajax bequeaths his shield to his son Eurysaces, and expresses the wish that his other armour and weapons should be buried in his grave (572–7), a wish that Teucer recalls at the close (1408). From this one, visible property ranges a series of unseen properties, with the armour of Achilles as the ultimate source of the quarrel, and cause of the tragedy. We have a similar sense of unseen objects radiating in to a visible property in Sophocles' *Women of Trachis*, where the casket not only hides the robe itself (a *peplos*), but is the reference point for the woollen tuft with which Deianira applied the ointment to the robe, and which she reports has dissolved in the sun's heat, and beyond that for the arrows that struck the centaur Nessus (672–722). The casket is sealed by an imprint from Deianira's ring, and our growing sense of the robe's vicious potency allows the performer playing Heracles to make a horror out of his costume when he appears in agony.

The casket, box or basket may contain something deadly, as it does also in Euripides' *Medea* in which we do not see the death agonies inflicted by the robe (again a *peplos*) and gold tiara it contains, or it may precipitate the tragic action in other ways. Euripides' *Ion* is a tragedy that resolves happily, and this is due to the recognition achieved between mother and son by a basketwork cradle, a baby's woven swaddling clothes, a gold necklace and a wreath of olive leaves. The cradle passes from the Priestess of Apollo to his temple attendant Ion, and is then snatched by Ion's threatened mother, Creusa, who enumerates the cradle's contents successfully, in loving detail (1320–1438). The cradle itself is carefully described to us – it has wheels and a lid – by the god Hermes at the opening of the play. Other recognitions may be achieved through properties playing a more cursory role, with Agamemnon's signet ring sufficient to identify Orestes to his sister in Sophocles' *Electra* (1222–4).

A property may also speak more directly through the words written on it, or subtle variations of that idea. In Euripides' *Iphigenia among the Taurians* the recognition between Orestes and Iphigenia is begun by means of a letter to her brother that Iphigenia has had written down to her dictation, but whose contents she repeats from memory as she entrusts it to Orestes and Pylades (578–826). But the visible property cannot here confirm the identity of Orestes and, under interrogation, he reveals knowledge of the designs of two separate weavings made by Iphigenia in Argos, and the spear of Pelops that she used to keep in her room there (811–26).[12] By contrast, writing speaks fatally in Euripides' *Hippolytus*: Phaedra's corpse displayed on the *ekkuklêma* holds a writing tablet, which falsely denounces Hippolytus to his father Theseus. Even the slightest of properties may work subtly in the action. In this same tragedy, Hippolytus has offered a wreath to an icon of the goddess Artemis at the opening of the play. On his return his father Theseus wears a wreath in celebration of his homecoming which he throws away in anguish when he hears of his wife's death, and orders the doors to be opened to reveal her body (806–10). Similarly, in the opening scene of Sophocles' *Oedipus Tyrannus*, Creon is seen returning from Delphi wearing a wreath of laurel, which the Priest of Zeus interprets as a sign of the good news that proves to be pitifully absent in the ensuing action.

Costume in tragedy was probably an elaborate, decorated version of everyday clothing, but it is rarely used to provide a specific focus for the action.[13] Wedding garments will carry clear connotations, and Hermione appears in hers (a gold diadem, and an embroidered *peplos*), racked with jealousy, to emphasize her status in Euripides' *Andromache* (147–54); later, when distraught, she pulls them apart in an attempted suicide (825–65). Clothes appropriate to mourning also convey a message; in Euripides' *Helen* Helen decides to appear in mourning to deceive her Egyptian captor, Theoclymenus, changing white for black garments (1186–92). Euripides was mocked by Aristophanes for presenting heroic characters in rags, and we gain some sense of this from the appearance of the shipwrecked Menelaus in this play, and from the rustic clothing that we undoubtedly see on the Farmer and Electra in Euripides' *Electra*, which she herself contrasts to the clothing suitable for a festival (175–89). By far the most remarkable sequence comes in Euripides' *Bacchae*, with the appearance of Talthybius and Cadmus in Dionysiac costume, carrying the staff (*thyrsos*) and wearing a fawnskin and ivy wreath, anticipating the final, transvestite appearance of the tyrant Pentheus, dressed as a woman worshipper of Dionysus (912–70).

The tragic playwrights also wrote the satyr plays, and while there is little doubt about the satyric costumes, the survival of only one complete script (Euripides' *Cyclops*) makes exploration of the theatricality of these plays difficult in this context.[14] Granted the nature of the satyrs, wineskins, cups and jars will have been regular properties, and food of various kinds, but the central attraction of *Cyclops* is the giant himself, whose one-eyed mask will have been set off by costume and club. Other fragments, notably those from Aeschylus, are tantalizingly suggestive of a major role for properties, and the fascination of the satyrs for any unusual sound or object would seem to be as characteristic of them as their love for food and drink, and their cowardice.

Menander's comedies were played in front of a domestic facade of two front doors, with occasional use of a third opening, which might represent a shrine. Characters frequently emerge from these doors and re-enter them, engaging in dialogue and heart-searching monologue that involve us intricately with an immediate, and often erotic, crisis implicating the neighbouring households.[15] Though the costumes and masks together presented social status unequivocally, the masks concentrated on grotesque caricature for slaves and the elderly in particular, while the costume remained closely related to everyday garments.[16] Menander, from the limited evidence of the surviving plays and fragments, had a flexible and dynamic attitude to the use of properties, which in its economy and some characteristics owed much to tragedy. The birth tokens that were critical in Euripides' *Ion* of a century earlier became a staple means for achieving the formulaic recognitions, which transform the lives of Menander's characters by restoring (free or citizen) status and reestablishing family relations. They are clearly central to *Arbitration*, which takes its title from a scene in which these tokens are

Figure 33. 'Robbing the Miser'. Costumes, furniture and masks in a Middle Comedy, c.350 BC.

kept with the foundling child, and used to clarify paternity. A single signet ring, engraved with the maker's name, and belonging to the father of the child, does most of the work of the plot. A similar climactic role is played by tokens in *The Shorn Girl* (*Perikeiromenê*), and although these scripts are incomplete, Menander seems to have given the tokens prominence here by keeping the action otherwise free of properties.

Another fragmentary play, *The Shield*, takes its title from a battered shield brought back from the battlefield by a slave, who takes it to be evidence of his master's death. The pathos of this opening not only recalls the use of property armour in heroic tragedy (e.g. the shield of Hector on which his child's broken body is brought in towards the close of Euripides' *Trojan Women*, 1123–1250), but also connects with common experience, in the gruesome account in the comedy of the unidentifiable dead bodies. But the scene expands from the shield carried by the speaker, since he is accompanied by plunder, in the form of captives, and by mules carrying booty, which includes silver cups and gold coins.[17] This human and material hoard captures the attention of a caricatured miser, and so binds the evolution of the scene firmly back in to the comic action, helped by the explanation provided by the presiding deity, Chance. (See **Fig. 33** for a Middle Comedy scene about a miser.)

There are other glimpses of the diversion of tragic moments. In all that remains of *The Girl from Perinthos*, a slave who has taken refuge at an altar is threatened with the sight of logs and torches, which will be used to smoke him away from his asylum, an action threatened by Lycus against the wife of Heracles in Euripides' *Heracles* (240–52). In *The Bad-Tempered Man*, it is possible that the injured misanthrope of the title is wheeled out on an *ekkuklêma*, in a parody of the traumatic scenes of tragedy (758), and mosaics make it clear that an *ekkuklêma* was used for the display of a scene of women taking breakfast from a lost play with that title. In the rustic setting of *The Bad-Tempered Man*, a girl is helped to fill a water-jug, which looks back to Electra's refusal of help in Euripides' *Electra* (54–81). But the material world may be purely comic: the apparatus of cooking and feasting provides the occasion for much of the knockabout action of *The Bad-Tempered Man* and a mattock is the instrument of the painful transformation of a city boy, temporarily, into a labourer. There seems to be a relatively sparing use of costume for effect. At the climax of *The Woman from Samos* a son threatens to leave by having a travelling cloak and a sword brought out to him, while in *The Shield* an Athenian is provided with a hairpiece, a cloak and a stick to act the part of a comic doctor (376–9).

The comedy of the Roman Republic emerges as a highly professional entertainment, derivative of the theatre of Menander and his approximate contemporaries. These broad adaptations by Plautus and Terence similarly rely on a facade of two neighbouring front doors, and differentiate between the social status of characters readily by costume and (almost certainly) mask.[18] The *choragus* was responsible for this provision, and there is one intriguing description of a character's appearance, which might give an impression of mask and padding: 'Red hair, fat belly, thick legs, dark skin, big head, sharp eyes, red face and very large feet' (Plautus *Pseudolus* 1218–20).[19]

The use of properties is often recognizably similar to that in Menander, but has its subtleties and variations. Food and drink for a feast are brought on at the opening of Terence's *The Girl from Andros*, but it is only later that we discover from the script that it may have been noticeably less lavish than usual (353–61). In Plautus' *The Swaggering Soldier* a ring is passed between characters and ultimately used to deceive the sex-mad and vain soldier of the title (771–812, and 947–87). In Plautus' *Curculio* a signet ring is stolen from a similar comic type, but used to seal a forged letter (605–785). In Terence's *The Mother-in-Law* the climactic recognition is achieved by means of a ring that is worn by a character, but we only hear about this by report, and no attention is drawn to the ring beforehand. At the opening of *Pseudolus* a letter that is read out reveals the erotic crisis that will provoke the comic action, while in *Curculio* and in Plautus' *The Persian Girl* (449–548) letters are used in faked transactions.

In this last instance, the deception is guaranteed by the assumption of Persian costume by the girl who is to be bought, and by travelling clothes for the man who is pretending to have brought her from abroad (154–65, and 459–69). A sailor's outfit – a broad-brimmed hat and a short cloak, both rust-coloured, and a woollen eye-patch – is assumed for a deception in *The Swaggering Soldier* (1175–82) and that of a soldier's slave in *Pseudolus* (722–66). Rustic clothing has a thematic relevance in the contrast between city and country lifestyles in Terence's *The Self-Tormentor*, where a mattock adds to the effect, and possibly in *Brothers*, recalling Menander's *The Bad-Tempered Man*. In Menander's *The Woman from Samos* an unseen baby is the cause of the central confusions and in his *Arbitration* a babe-in-arms witnesses the contention; in Terence's *The Girl from Andros* the baby is brought on as an object to provoke confusion (721).

More radical effects are achieved with cross-dressing. In the prologue to *Casina* Plautus acknowledges that some may be shocked by the spectacle of slaves taking wives, and later he parades one in white wedding gear, accompanied by a cook and his attendants. At the climax of the comedy, the bridegroom is brought out of the house, garlanded and with a wedding torch, accompanied by a piper for the wedding-song, and the bride is escorted to him, to be embraced and fondled. The harsh and violent discovery that the bride is a cross-dressed male slave is obscenely reported, and eventually the 'bride' bursts out of the house to shame the old man who had hoped to bed 'her' in his slave's place (1137–end). In these final moments the old man's loss of his cloak and stick, left behind in the bedroom, is decisive in the proof not just of his lust but also of the loss of his self-esteem and status. In Terence's *The Eunuch*, a young man assumes the costume of a eunuch in order to gain access to the room of a girl, whom he proceeds to rape: we gather that his costume convinces those who do not know him of his status (575–7), that it is multicoloured (682–4), and that physically the eunuch does not look remotely like the young man when dressed in his clothes (665–85). At the opening of the action in Plautus' *The Brothers Menaechmus* one of the brothers appears from his house wearing a gown he has purloined from his wife's wardrobe to give to his mistress. His cross-dressing is not instrumental to the plot, but the gown is, and once he has handed it over it proves a linking thread in the confusions of identity that spread through the action.

The material world is present in abundance in Plautus' comedies, in allusions to the marketplace, the possessions of the household, the interior of the house and its walls, and the enticements of food and dining. What we actually see is only a selection, and at times even a central 'property', such as the pot of gold in the play of that title, may remain hidden from us. But just as slaves are an object of fascination for Plautus and his audience, in the fantastic licence allowed to them, so the material objects that symbolized their oppression are constantly cited. Slaves may indulge in a drinking bout (*The Swaggering Soldier*, 813–66), but we hear repeatedly of fears of the treadmill, of stone quarries, of fetters and chains, of birch-rods and whipping, and of crucifixion; we see a slave taken off to be bound hand to foot (*The Girl from Andros*, 861–5) and watch as a pimp abuses his slaves with a whip in his hand (*Pseudolus*, 133–69). It is not only the actual properties, but this lived reality of subjection that determines the sober action and atmosphere of Plautus' *The Captives*.[20]

It remains uncertain whether the tragedies of Seneca were composed for public recitation, private reading and circulation, performance in excerpts or in private houses, or for the Roman public theatres. In such circumstances, the discussion of material elements of performance is difficult.[21] There are some specific problems for a practical vision of the texts that remain extremely awkward. The introduction of Cerberus, the three-headed hound of hell, in *The Mad Hercules* (592–617) seems a bizarre choice for a stage tragedian, and the evisceration of a bull and heifer in sacrifice in *Oedipus* (291–402) is harder to explain than the presence of live draught or pack animals, lambs or even sheep in earlier tragedy and comedy. The most plausible conclusion must be that we are surprisingly unsure of the kind(s) of performance for which the texts were intended, and so will find it more difficult to distinguish satisfactorily between the seen and the unseen than we do with the other scripts we possess.

As I have suggested, ancient performance is imbued with the presence of the material world, and we should in principle resist the tendency to read scripts exclusively as a set of verbal texts for actors. Costume and properties are constant components of classical theatre and our vision of ancient scripts must just as constantly account for them. Both the selective austerity of Greek tragedy and the abundance so evident in Aristophanic comedy are aesthetic exploitations of the sensual and sensory awareness of their audience, who like their Roman counterparts lived in a material world, as well as in a world of words.

NOTES

1. On ancient manufacture, see R. J. Forbes, *Studies in Ancient Technology*, Vol. IV for fabrics and Vol. V for leather (Leiden: Brill, 1964/1966).
2. Aristotle, *Poetics* at the end of ch.6 mentions the *skeuopoios* disparagingly in relation to visual effects.
3. G. M. Sifakis, *Parabasis and Animal Choruses* (London: Athlone Press, 1971).

4. L. M. Stone, *Costume in Aristophanic Poetry* (New York: Ayer, 1981).

5. F. Muecke, 'A Portrait of the Artist as a Young Woman', *Classical Quarterly* 32 (1982), 41–55.

6. J. P. Poe provides a detailed catalogue of objects/properties in Aristophanic comedy. Attendants may have been more regularly involved in these activities than the incidental references in scripts reveal; 'Multiplicity, Discontinuity and Visual Meaning in Aristophanic Comedy', *Rheinischer Museum*, 14.3 (2000), pp. 256–95.

7. J. Wilkins delightfully reviews the 'comic discourse of food', and incidentally the properties themselves, in both Aristophanes and Menander; *The Boastful Chef: The Discourse of Food in Ancient Greek Comedy* (Oxford: Oxford University Press, 2000).

8. D. J. Mastronarde studies the deployment of the *skênê* roof and the *mêchanê* in tragedy, 'Actors on High: the *Skênê* Roof, the Crane, and the Gods in Attic Drama', *Classical Antiquity* 9.2 (1990), 247–94.

9. The choruses in Aeschylus' *Suppliants* and Euripides' *Phoenician Women* and *Bacchae* may be comparable. Andromeda, on a vase-painting probably reflecting tragedy, may give an impression of this kind of costume for an individual actor from *c.*400 BC (Graham Ley, *A Short Introduction to Greek Theater* [Chicago: University of Chicago Press, 1991], Plate 5, p. 93).

10. Oliver Taplin has interesting discussions of tragic properties, *Greek Tragedy in Action* (London: Methuen, 1978), pp. 77–100.

11. This property inevitably attracts an unusual range of critical attention: e.g. P. W. Harsh, 'The Role of the Bow in the "Philoctetes" of Sophocles', *American Journal of Philology* 81(1960), 408–14; C. P. Segal, 'Visual Symbolism and Visual Effects in Sophocles', *Classical World* 74 (1980), 125–42; C. Gill, 'Bow, Oracle and Epiphany in Sophocles' "Philoctetes"', *Greece and Rome* 27 (1980), 137–46. See also the notes to *Philoctetes* by Ley who also did the translation in M. Ewans (ed.), *Sophocles: Three Dramas of Old Age* (London: Dent, 1996).

12. Aristotle in *Poetics*, ch.13 has a low opinion of recognition by tokens and of their physical absence in this particular scene.

13. A. Pickard-Cambridge gives a useful summary of evidence from vase-paintings, *Dramatic Festivals of Athens*, rev. J. Gould and D. Lewis, second ed. (Oxford: Clarendon Press, 1988), pp. 180–3 and 198–203.

14. On the evidence from vase-paintings, see Pickard-Cambridge, 1988, pp. 184–7.

15. N. Lowe helpfully examines the implications of interior/exterior space and locality in relation to Menander's *The Bad-Tempered Man*, 'Tragic Space and Comic Timing in Menander's "Dyskolos"' in E. Segal (ed.), *Oxford Readings in Menander, Plautus and Terence* (Oxford: Oxford University Press, 2001).

16. There is some possibility that comic costume from this period was colour-coded to a degree: see the summary in Pickard-Cambridge, 1988, pp. 230–1.

17. Compare the return of Lichas with the captives secured by Heracles in Sophocles' *Women of Trachis*.

18. Only one house is required for Plautus' *The Captives* and *Amphitryon*. Standard items of clothing were *tunica* (for the Greek *chitôn* or *peplos*), *pallia* (for *himation*), and *chlamys*: see G. E. Duckworth, *The Nature of Roman Comedy: A Study in Popular Entertainment* (Princeton: Princeton University Press, 1952),

pp. 73–101, and W. Beare, *The Roman Stage*, third ed. (London: Methuen, 1964), pp. 184–95.

19. There is no good reason to doubt the use of masks: the issues are summarized by Duckworth, 1952, p. 92.
20. For the social context, see K. Bradley, *Slavery and Society at Rome* (Cambridge: Cambridge University Press, 1994), pp. 57–80.
21. For the debate on the performance of Seneca's tragedies, see H. A. Kelly, 'Tragedy and the Performance of Tragedy in Late Roman Antiquity', *Tradition* 35 (1979), 21–44 and the essays by E. Fantham and J. G. Fitch, in W. M. Harrison (ed.), *Seneca in Performance* (London: Duckworth, 2000).

FURTHER READING

English, M. C., 'The Diminishing Role of Stage Properties in Aristophanic Comedy', *Helios*, 27.2 (2000), 149–62.

Harrison, W. M., *Seneca in Performance*. London: Duckworth, 2000.

Ketterer, R. C., 'Stage Properties in Plautine Comedy I', *Semiotica* 58.3/4 (1986), 193–216; 'Stage Properties in Plautine Comedy II', *Semiotica* 59.1/2 (1986), 93–135; 'Stage Properties in Plautine Comedy III', *Semiotica* 60.1/2 (1986), 29–72.

Mastronarde, D. J., 'Actors on High: The *Skênê* Roof, the Crane, and the Gods in Attic Drama', *Classical Antiquity* 9.2 (1990), 247–94.

Poe, J. P., 'Multiplicity, Discontinuity, and Visual Meaning in Aristophanic Comedy', *Rheinische Museum* 14.3 (2000), 256–95.

Segal, E. (ed.), *Oxford Readings in Menander, Plautus, and Terence*. Oxford: Oxford University Press, 2001.

Stone, L. M., *Costume in Aristophanic Poetry*. New York: Ayer, 1981.

15

J. MICHAEL WALTON

Commodity: asking the wrong questions

In an interview published in *New Theatre Quarterly* in 1994, Ian Watson asked the American theatre historian Bruce A. McConachie whether he believed that theatre history was 'no longer an hermetic history of playscripts, performances, and/or personalities but, rather, their history in the light of their social and cultural milieu'.[1] McConachie's response raised a number of issues relating to the nature of 'historical facts' as they may be reflected in the study of acts of theatre, leading to the assertion that '. . . for the theatre, one needs to go beyond empiricism and formalism to get at larger issues of how theatre works in history, how it works in society and culture'.

Until relatively recently, with a few notable exceptions, the study of Greek and Roman theatre was tied to the study of its texts. Not surprisingly this left a residue of feeling that classical theatre suffered from a kind of inverted Darwinism. Its zenith, history seemed to be telling us, was with Aeschylus, descending, gradually at first, and then by leaps and bounds, to end up with the grotesqueries of the Roman arena and the eventual excommunication of the mimes. That may be a fair comment on the drama as art, theatre as an aesthetic experience. From a historical perspective it is nothing like the whole story, though what that story is has to be gleaned not from a treasury of the world's greatest plays, but from threads and patches, anecdotes and incidentals. Most of the classical historians wrote of the major events: Herodotus, the conflict between Greece and Asia; Thucydides, Athens' great war against Sparta; Livy, the early years of Rome; Tacitus, the reigns of the first emperors; Plutarch, across the board. The theatre and, in McConachie's words, 'how it works in society and culture', until well into the time of the Roman empire, has to be distilled from less targeted sources but is maybe none the worse for that. With a throwaway art the unguarded comment can often be more revealing than the systematic narrative.

Much of the physical detail of costume and mask, settings, stage architecture and machinery, choreography and acting, originates in the Graeco-Roman world of the late Republic and the Roman Empire. If the lack of historical reliability offers more controversies and paradoxes than solutions, there is at least raw material from which the diligence and ingenuity of contemporary scholarship is gradually unearthing a broad perspective on performance cultures.

There are some questions about the classical theatre which are of little interest to most readers of texts. How long did a performance last? What happened when it rained? Were there understudies? How much did a player or a musician make? Where did rehearsals take place and for how many weeks/months? If the theatre was competitive, did that involve betting? Or even bribery? How much did audiences pay, and to whom? Were there 'season tickets'? Who controlled the auditorium and what happened to latecomers? Were there intervals between plays? If so, for how long? Where did the Athenian audience go for refreshment, or for relief, after sitting on a stone seat to watch a group of four, sometimes five, plays, in a single day at the City Dionysia in spring; never mind the Lenaea in midwinter?

Some of these questions do have immediate answers and have already been addressed earlier in this book. Others come down less to drama as an art than to the theatre as an organization: and that in its turn comes down to practicalities, to questions of commodity.

The idea of theatre as commodity involves two separate strands. The first is the extent to which the theatre may have featured within the eco-nomic framework of various communities in various periods. This instantly launches entertainment onto a particularly contentious battleground. Lined up on one side are modernists for whom the application of modern values in matters of social structures, no less than in aesthetics, is the only appro-priate means of creating links between the twenty-first century AD and the worlds of ancient Athens and Rome. Ranged against the modernists are the primitivists. For the primitivists employment of contemporary notions of economics, or, indeed, a whole lot of universalizing judgements from the moral to the cultural, is as misguided as treating the oracle at Delphi as though it were some sort of a cross between a newspaper 'agony aunt' and a fairground Gypsy Petulengro.

Issues that are raised may often best be addressed by the manner in which the questions are formulated. If, for example, in tragedy in Athens only three actors seem to have been employed, rather than raking through the existing playtexts in order to find ways to distort theatre practice, like fitting ugly sisters into Cinderella's shoes, the *reason* might be sought. Was it something to do with the number of trained actors available, or something to do with festival tradition? Or was it all about money? There are other questions relating to contracts of one kind or another, rational answers to which may reveal the theatre in Athens not just as a religious festival but as a commercial enterprise. And even if such a view is anachronistic or misplaced for the theatre of Aeschylus or Aristophanes, there must be a time when commerce comes into it somewhere, if for no other reason than that by the time of Plautus and Terence in the second century BC, drama was part of the market fabric. It continued to be so and arguably had been ever since the actor became a professional, when prizes were first awarded and Aeschylus was still alive.

The second aspect of commodity intertwines with the first. However much, or little, dramatic festivals from the earliest times were commercialized, there were a number of people who depended on theatre for their living, or part of it. There are Greek words for 'theatre attendant' (*rhabdouchos* – a man with a rod to regulate the audience), crane-operator (*mêchanopoios*), mask-maker (*skeuopoios*), costumier (*himatiomisthês*), lessee of the theatre (*architektôn*, *theatrônês* or *theatropôlês*). In Rome there were ushers (*pedisequi* or *dissignatores*), a superintendent (*curator*), a manager (*imperator histricus*), a herald (*praeco*). What did they do, these people? They clearly formed part of the management. Theatres need people to run them, from accountants to carpenters. Stars rely on satellites. The management may have consisted of independent operatives, slaves, or hired hands. Somebody, perhaps many people, stood to profit from a successful festival: and if something went wrong, there had to be a chain of responsibility right up to the *archôn* in Athens, or the *aedile* in Rome, who would have to answer to the Assembly or the Senate, both for the spending of the public purse and for the maintaining of public order.

First, something about money. Equivalents in the currency of any other country or era are always misleading. Inflation remained low in Greece, but became uncomfortably high in Rome during the time of the Empire (late first century BC onwards). The changes that occur over hundreds of years inevitably fluctuate according to political circumstance as well as supply and demand. What follows is the roughest of guides to monetary values.

Greece (fifth century BC and beyond)

6 *oboloi* = 1 *drachma*
100 *drachmai* = 1 *mna* (or *mina*)
60 *mnai* = 1 talent (*talanton*)

The cost of a slave could be as low as 1 *mna* (100 *drachmai*) but might be six times as much. The Greek general Nicias is reputed to have paid a whole talent (6,000 *drachmai*) for an overseer for his silver mines.

Dillon and Garland[2] have a section on slave prices and compute the average cost of a slave at an auction of property confiscated from an Athenian, after the mutilation of the Herms in 414 BC, as 157 *drachmai*.

The wage paid to a juryman was two *oboloi* per day, a bare minimum living wage.

Two *oboloi* was probably the cost of a seat in the theatre for one day's performances: that was the amount awarded to applicants from the theoric fund.

Ninety per cent of the free population of Attica probably lived on an annual income of between 180 and 400 *drachmai*.

The daily wage of a craftsman or a soldier was one *drachma*.

A tunic would cost about five *drachmai*.

Csapo and Slater[3] suggest from a variety of sources the following as likely costs of liturgies required by the city of Athens from the wealthiest citizens on an annual basis:

Upkeep of a warship for one year 5,143 *drachmai*.

Costs which Lysias claimed that he had incurred (in his defence against a charge of bribery)

for a group of tragedies	3000 *drachmai*.
for a comedy	1600 *drachmai*.
for the men's dithyramb	5000 *drachmai*.

A simple estimate of the possible box-office take at a City Dionysia, lasting for five days with a paying audience of 15,000, is 25,000 *drachmai* (a little over four talents).

Csapo and Slater include sections on performance costs and commitments in the Hellenistic world of the third and second centuries BC, and through to Roman times, based on inscriptions. These can be bafflingly confusing over detail but seem to include items such as 600 Demetrian *drachmai* for a piper, 300 to a costumier: and prizes established by Flavius Lysimachus (late second century BC) as 2,500 *denarii* (see below) for a tragic actor, 800 for the man who came second; 1,500 for the comic winner, 500 for coming second and also for a trumpeter and for a tragic chorus.

Prize-money at Tanagra in the first century BC was banded, with musicians, reciters and actors in revivals earning 169 *drachmai*, playwrights of new plays 135, down to minor awards of between forty and fifty.

Rome (from late third century BC)

4 *asses* = 1 *sestertius* (sesterce)
4 *sestertii* = 1 *denarius*
25 *denarii* = 1 *aureus*

Suetonius' *Life of Terence* states that the playwright was paid the high sum of 1,500 *denarii* for *The Eunuch*.

A week's supply of bread might cost around 6 *asses*.

An unskilled worker might earn 1 *denarius* a day, a soldier 120 *denarii* a year (all found), increased by Julius Caesar to 225 *denarii*.

A top gladiator in the time of the Empire was reputed to be able to make as much in a single day as a soldier in a year.

A senator at this time (first century BC) had to have property worth 200,000 *denarii*, later raised to 250,000.

The price of a slave could be between 500 and 2,000 *denarii*.

Jo-Ann Shelton[4] estimates that a carpenter could expect to earn 250 *denarii* per year.

Prices in Plautus and Terence, as might be expected in a world that is poised in some stage world halfway between Greece and Rome, are very variable. Usually the currency is Greek, though the Roman *nummus* is the equivalent of two *drachmai*. Buying out a girl from slavery or prostitution (the most common purpose for which money is sought) can be as high as 100 *minae*, though as low as twelve (600 *nummi*) for the girl whose freedom Toxilius is trying to buy in Plautus' *The Persian Girl*.

The Roman Empire

Inflation increased rapidly under the Empire.

By the time of the poet Martial (first century AD) a carpenter might be paid 50 *denarii* per day.

The poet Varius Rufus wrote a *Thyestes* for Games paid for by Augustus to celebrate victory at the battle of Actium, for which he was paid a million *sestertii*. The play has not survived.

Cost of olive oil and honey, twenty-four to forty *denarii* per pint.

Wine, between eight and thirty *denarii* per pint.

Maths teacher's pay, twenty-five *denarii* per boy, per month.

The cost of the *Ludi Romani* (Roman Games) under Claudius (one of the less extravagant emperors despite a fondness for the Games that attracted criticism), 200,000 *denarii*.

Most of the essays in this book review their subjects more or less chronologically from classical Athens through to the Roman empire. With 'commodity' it is different. Detail about organization and procedures is better documented for the Roman world than it is for the Greek. At the risk of confusing the issues I am choosing here to look first at imperial Rome; then to work backwards to the theatre of Plautus and Terence under the Roman Republic of the second century BC; from there through the Hellenistic period in Greece of the third and fourth centuries BC when the Guilds of actors first turned the acting profession into part of what Richard Findlater called 'the unholy trade'; and finally back to the fifth and fourth centuries BC when tragedy and comedy were first developing and when the spectre of professionalism first began to influence how the festivals in the Theatre of Dionysus in Athens were conducted.

Imperial Rome (27 BC–sixth century AD)

Gaius Octavius who, as Octavius Caesar, appears as a character in Shakespeare's *Julius Caesar*, became the first emperor of Rome in 27 BC, when the Senate conferred on him the title of Augustus. A reluctant autocrat, he presided over a court that was famous for its patronage of poets and artists. Virgil, author of the *Aeneid*, the only epic poem in Latin to rival the Greek epics of Homer, was a prominent member of the literary circles at court. So were Propertius and Horace, the latter the author of a letter of advice on playwriting (the *Ars Poetica*)[5] which is sometimes published in tandem with Aristotle's *Poetics*. The poet Ovid was one of their number until some scandal resulted in his exile to the far end of the Black Sea from where he wrote gloomy letters home, asking vainly for a pardon. Ovid was a playwright too: his *Medea* was held in high esteem though it has not survived. A less prominent writer of plays was Maecenas whose real claim to fame was as a patron. Vastly rich, it was Maecenas who supported and encouraged the artistic coterie at the first Roman court.[6]

Some plays by such writers, often based on the stories of Greek mythology, did receive public performance at the Games during Augustus' reign; others may have been recited or were played on private occasions. Tragedy was not what filled the theatres for most of the time and, as the first century of the Christian era proceeded, fell further out of the public taste. Seneca, whose tragedies are the only Latin tragedy to survive, may have received some kind of closet enactment, but they do not read as though the author had much notion or expectation of staging or performance.

For the populace it was the pantomime that reigned supreme from almost the same time as did Augustus. This involved a single masked performer dancing or miming to the accompaniment of a musical chorus. So fashionable did a certain Pylades become that the emperor felt bound to intervene. The writer Dio Cassius tells the story of Augustus summoning Pylades and reproaching him for the uproar caused in the city by his 'quarrels and rivalries'. Far from being abashed, Pylades told Augustus that it was in the emperor's own interest that the public of Rome should concentrate on a stage performer rather than on the emperor. Bread and circuses were well on their way to becoming the means of controlling a Roman public, eventually almost two thirds of which were wholly dependent on the state. But perhaps, culture has always functioned in such a fashion, as advertising or distraction.

The popularity of the theatre made it prone to domestic disaster, sometimes on a scale that beggars belief. The historian Tacitus wrote a vivid account of the collapse of an amphitheatre in 27 AD at Fidenae, just to the north of Rome, because of shoddy construction. The wooden building caved inwards, trapping most of the audience. The number of those killed or severely injured in this single accident is given as fifty thousand. The reaction of the senate was to prohibit anyone from putting on a gladiatorial show who did not have a substantial income. The jerry-builder, a former slave called Atilius, was subsequently exiled.

As Augustus' rule gave way in the beginning of the Christian era to a series of less stable emperors, so the wildest excesses of the arena were given every opportunity to flourish. The building of new amphitheatres to house the various forms of gladiatorial contest pandered to palates that became more and more jaded with ever more novel forms of ingenious bloodletting. There was clearly big money in this for those who were in a position to meet the demand. North Africa was scoured and eventually deprived entirely of its large beasts. Human life was, if anything, cheaper, various forms of criminal or captive being herded into the Colosseum to meet their deaths in a variety of nasty and ingenious ways. What was not cheap was the gladiator. Only the most promising were chosen for training but, if they were good enough, they could earn vast sums and, in rare cases, retire unmaimed. On average about one in ten was killed in any set of Games. Contemporary parallels are mostly simplistic and best left to the individual imagination, but there is no doubt that the entertainment industry in imperial Rome was one of its biggest businesses: it was also, as Pylades seems to have warned Augustus, one of its most necessary.

When women first became involved is difficult to establish. The historian Pliny the Younger talks in a letter to a friend, some time around the beginning of the second century AD, of the death of a woman who owned a pantomime company and enjoyed their performances rather more than was appropriate for someone of her station. But her players were male. Under the emperors women did appear as performers, at least in the mimes, the non-legitimate theatre of short unmasked farces which became ever lewder as time went on. They also appeared as combatants in the arena in the time of Domitian. Eventually, after Constantine had the seat of power moved from Rome to Byzantium in 330 AD, Christianity flourished and some of the excesses of the old empire diminished. Entertainments associated with pagan religions do seem to have continued but evidence is marginal. The Christian church did have all mime actors excommunicated in the fifth century AD, but that failed to stand in the way of Theodora, who had enjoyed a career as a mime actress before marrying the emperor Justinian, thus establishing a precedent for all manner of intriguing unions of opposites in centuries to come. Justinian was eventually to close the theatres, at least for a time, in 526 AD and the Trullan Council of 692 AD banned all forms of entertainment (see Griffith, ch. 1 in this volume).

By this far end of the empire actors, entertainers, mimes or *histriones* presumably lived by their wits, staying alive by whatever means they could, preserving the skills of musical and mimetic playing that ensured the survival of their art through the dark ages. Pure speculation suggests that part of the ability to survive related to the close-knit company structure first created by the Guilds of Hellenistic Greece, and working effectively in the Italy of Plautus and Terence, to whom we can now turn.

Republican Rome (third century BC–27 BC)

The Romans of the republican period had had an ambivalent relationship with theatre and spectacle. From as early as the third century BC, public entertainment over all of the more populated areas of Italy had included dramatic performances, including music and dance. The Guilds of Greek actors (of whom more later) had ensured that touring companies could be hired for local festivals in any part of the Greek world. By the third century BC, the century in which Menander died, there were Greek communities spread as wide as Italy, Sicily, the Middle East and the Black Sea, even North Africa and Spain. The touring circuit ensured that Greek tragedies and comedies survived in performance in Greek alongside newer material, history plays and local farces, frequently in Latin. Theatre, in the broadest sense of the word, remained linked both to the individual community and to the wider fraternity derived from a common language and a perceived heritage. Much of the most successful of the dramatic fare was by its very nature transient, unrecorded and unrecordable except in the passing reference. There were no scripts for improvised comedy, for the puppet show or for the purely local dramatic sketch (see Denard, ch. 8 in this volume).

A revival of interest in Greek culture in the second half of the third century BC, when Roman soldiers were based in Sicily, led to the performance in Rome of a Greek play in a Latin translation at the *Ludi Romani*, the Roman Games of 240 BC. The translator, Livius Andronicus, a slave who had been captured at the siege of Tarentum, went on to write a number of tragedies and comedies of his own but, for whatever reason, none of his plays or those of his contemporaries survive. In fact no Roman tragedy survives at all until Seneca writing during the reign of Nero, three hundred years after Andronicus. What we do have are a series of comedies. The plays of Plautus and Terence, all adapted from Greek originals and presented first between 200 and 160 BC, are both the first Latin literature to come down to us and a mine of information on the whole theatrical enterprise in early Rome. No permanent theatre was permitted in the city during the second century BC – these were stern and upright Romans, a far cry from the mobs who would later throng the amphitheatres and howl for the blood of victims thrown to wild beasts, or the gladiators grimly described by one commentator as 'having a job for life'. Instead, the charming but harmless plays of Plautus and Terence were performed in purpose-built temporary theatres (see Beacham, ch. 11 in this volume).

Though such theatres were easy enough to erect, they appear to have lacked that element of audience control which divides organized theatre from that of the streets. The prologues of the two comic writers offer unique insights into the circumstances of performance. Terence opens *The Mother-in-Law* by reminding the audience that the first performance had had to be cancelled because of the intervention of '*vitium* and *calamitas*'. This 'failure and disaster' is explained as a rope-dancer who so distracted the audience that the play could not continue. The second performance (165 BC) was also doomed to failure. The manuscript also has the prologue to a third (160 BC), complaining that, second time round, after the first act had gone well, a rumour spread that gladiators were on next. In the resulting influx of noisy audience the comedy again had to be abandoned.

Lucius Ambivius Turpio, who delivers this third prologue, is best described as an actor-manager, in the style of the nineteenth century in England. Later in the same prologue he tells the audience, 'If I've never been so greedy as to have a fixed price for my art – I have always thought of serving your interests (*commodis*) as my greatest profit – then give a proper hearing to this playwright [Terence] who has entrusted his efforts to my care.'[7] The title of *dominus*, 'lord', for the leader of such a company probably gives a fair indication of his influence and how he could exert it over the rest of the actors, the *grex*, Latin for 'a flock of sheep'. The status of the actors, however, is more complicated than that. Shadowy details of the life of Plautus suggest that he had started out as an actor in Atellan farce and had made enough money to lose it all on a dodgy business venture. Reduced to manual labour in a mill, he began to write and subsequently became a *professional* playwright.

Many actors were slaves, but the opportunities for a slave to become a freedman were numerous in Rome, if erratic. Freedom could be bought, if you managed to save up enough, or you could be declared 'free' by your master. Gaining their freedom for services rendered is the prime motivation of most of the slaves in Roman comedy. The playwright Terence, Publius Terentius Afer, had been brought to Rome as a slave from Carthage in North Africa, gaining his freedom, one rather dubious story has it, thanks to the enlightenment of his master Terentius Lucanus who educated him and gave him his independence.

Such relationships were more complex than simply slave and master. Though in later times the simple declaration '*civis Romanus sum*' was enough to ensure safety in out-of-the-way parts of the Empire, there were plenty of citizens in Rome itself whose financial situation was at best precarious. Part of the perceived duty of the patrician family was to ensure the welfare of all its members, however distant the relationship. In addition, the propertied classes attracted clients who would offer their services, not as slave labour, but as moral and visible support; at times of canvassing for office, for example, or on civic occasions where status was significant. In Rome, the notion of 'commodity of prestige' was well established – the stage character of the parasite depends upon it – and was one of the relationships of society that lasted through and across the transition from republic to empire. The patron/client system was embedded in the structure of Italian society: perhaps it still is.

The standing of the professional actor in society may even have been slightly higher then than it has been in any society up to the conferring of a knighthood on Henry Irving in 1895. Players as well as playwrights could belong to the prestigious *Collegium Poetarum*, the College of Artists in second-century BC Rome, and actors may have been exempt from military service: whether this was a reward or an indication of scorn is a moot point.

During the second century BC when new/adapted plays, the *comoediae palliatae*, formed the mainstay of the repertoire, the arrangements the manager had with individual playwrights were wholly commercial. The *dominus* purchased the play from the playwright for an agreed sum: on occasion the aedile in charge of the Games may have bought the play himself. Either way the playwright lost any rights in his work.

These plays were presented at Games connected with specific religious festivals in honour of Jupiter, Apollo or the Great Mother. Theatrical performances of all kinds were still created long after the death of Terence, with fashion and public taste dictating what was presented. But the where, the when and the how of it all came down, not to art, but to what the public wanted – when doesn't it? However pleasing it may be to welcome Plautus as the first Latin literature it is probably appropriate to think of him and his *dominus* in professional terms as the Mack Sennetts of their day, providing comedy to order that was unsophisticated, easily presented and cheap. William Beare summed up the position of the playwright succinctly when he wrote in *The Roman Stage*, 'But if anything is clear about Roman drama as a whole, it is that no one wrote for the stage except to make money.'[8]

Throughout all of this period, from Livius Andronicus and the first plays in Rome; through the growth of the Games in their various guises; the plays of Plautus and Terence; the first permanent theatres in Rome; the huge amphitheatres and the colossal spectacles of the second half of the first century AD, and beyond when over half the year might be given over to public entertainment: that is what it all was, public entertainment. It was a complex national industry. Expenses were met by the state through senatorial funds; through the goodwill and the purses of various officials, aediles and praetors, who oversaw and organized the Games; through the private incomes of those seeking office, or public favour, or just publicity; to celebrate funerals, weddings, military victories; or via the privy purse of the emperors, for whom the mob became a huge and demanding hydra. All these individuals paid, with or without taxpayers' money. But admission was free, for everything.

There is a paradox in charging for entertainment. The exchange of money implies a contract for 'x' amount of diversion, even if the precise value of 'x' is never quite defined. The price of a ticket makes the effort of attending a conscious one, involving a sacrifice, however small. Free admission, on the other hand, leads to a mindset of assuming that somebody else *should* supply all sorts of things. Bread and circuses may be all very well, but it takes little time for the right to have bread to escalate to a demand for butter on it; for circuses to involve greater novelty with more beasts, more wonders and more danger.

The result was that the less theatre became a commodity, in the sense of giving value for money to the audience, as opposed to value for money to the sponsors, the less possible was it for any serious artistic endeavour to survive. Novelty was defined by sensation and the search for novelty became ever more difficult for producers to satisfy. Audiences preferred battles to the death between the handicapped and the mutilated to Euripides or even Plautus, so that is what they had to be given – a warning, perhaps, to all those for whom the ratings are the ultimate arbiter of public taste. It also serves as a platform for returning to the Greek world of the classical and Hellenistic periods to see how far, if at all, commodity did influence the theatre of the fifth and fourth centuries BC.

Hellenistic Greece (late fourth–third centuries BC)

With the rise of Macedon in the fourth century BC under first Philip, then his son Alexander, Athens had ceased to be at the centre of world affairs. As sometimes happens with loss of empire, the cultural residue hangs on long after the disappearance of political influence. Athens, where tragedy and comedy were born and found their shape, continued to act as a magnet for theatrical performance but the popularity of the theatre spread quickly. Most of the surviving Greek theatres date from the fourth or third centuries BC. The acting profession first became fully commercialized when it became effectively full-time. To protect themselves from the unscrupulous, both players and local civic authorities, the *technitai*, the artists of Dionysus, banded together and created a number of agencies known as Guilds.[9] First evidence of them comes in inscriptions and public records from 288 BC in Euboea, off the eastern seaboard of mainland Greece. A few years later there is a reference in Delphi to the Athenian Guild, probably the first to have been established. More were to follow, an Isthmian-Nemean Guild in the Peloponnese, others in Egypt, Cyprus and eventually Naples.

Though they seem to have managed musical as well as dance and dramatic performances, their initial commitment was to companies of performers, four in a troupe: three actors and a musician. The records may be incomplete but what have survived are numbers of painted vases from the late fourth and third centuries BC which appear to record scenes from popular plays; it is now established beyond reasonable doubt that the works of Aristophanes were performed outside Athens long after their apparent Athenian bias might have seemed to render them museum pieces.[10]

The travelling companies would contract to turn up for a specific fee at a local festival with a play or set of plays. The commissioning community would rehearse the chorus separately and slot them into the production, presumably, in a couple of days of rehearsal. Many a local arts festival today will present opera productions under some similar arrangement. The amount of money to be earned must have varied considerably as must the regularity of the work. Fines could be instituted for failure to arrive on time or fulfil a contract, whatever the reason. Considering the vagaries of travel in the ancient world the performing professions could have been at best precarious, but at least the Guilds offered some sense of order. And when has the freelance player ever been given to expect security? Sadly, the records that do survive are partial and give little indication of how their behaviour as agents might be compared with any modern equivalent. Nor is there any way of knowing the fate of the performer who defaulted or who crossed the Guilds, beyond surmising from the effects of blacklisting by the syndicates in America at the end of the nineteenth century.

The artists may have been organized in a highly professional manner, but the financing of entertainment was inevitably a local affair. The great festivals of Greece which served as a focal point in the calendar had either ceased to exist or lost much of their importance. The Olympian or Olympic Games, so consequential that in the Greek world they were used as a means of dating subsequent events, suffered a decline in significance that matched the realigning of the ancient world, away from Greece and in the direction of Italy where, as we have seen, a new Italian tradition would emerge, though one that was steeped in recollections of the Hellenistic world.

The acting and kindred professional worlds were fully professionalized by the third century BC, but where and when did it all begin? It should now be possible to return to the Athenian beginnings and see if there is a case for suggesting that the festivals in Athens, the theatre of Aeschylus, Sophocles, Euripides and Aristophanes, did all rely on some commercial imperative that could have influenced their organization and development.

Classical Athens (sixth–fourth centuries BC)

The drama in Greece may have been sheltered beneath the umbrella of sacred festival and civic occasion, but even from the time of Aeschylus it was always competitive with honour, prestige and possibly prize-money at stake. Any snapshot of the organization of one of the dramatic festivals at which plays were performed (see Rehm, ch. 10 in this volume) can at best be a composite of a variety of circumstances created by a variety of factors. One of these seems to have been fiscal.

Consider the following four independent but linked practices:

1. A playwright who wished to be considered for inclusion in the City Dionysia submitted a group of plays to an *archôn* who 'awarded a chorus' to three applicants who would compete for prizes.

2. In any one year a large number of Athenian citizens identified as the wealthiest were required to undertake a liturgy (*leitourgia*), that is, they had to pay for some necessary civic expense amongst which financing theatrical performance (acting as *chorêgos*) was prominent and prestigious.

3. Plutarch (writing in the second century AD) says that Pericles, who initiated the building of the Parthenon and the Precinct of Dionysus which housed the Theatre and the Odeon, was the first to offer a grant (the theoric fund) for attendance at festival performances.

4. Theophrastus, who wrote a series of character-studies in the late fourth century in Athens, includes 'the stingy man', so mean he only takes his children to the theatre when the manager has declared free entrance.

The award of a chorus was the mechanism that linked playwright to production. It ensured that whatever was put on had the backing of the state, financially and in other ways too. Of the two major public festivals at which plays were presented, one at least, the City Dionysia, was an occasion when the city was on display, a significant proportion of the audience being foreign guests. In Athens this was less part of a coercive process to ensure that some party line was pursued, as Boal suggests in *The Theatre of the Oppressed*, than a proud demonstration of a civic system in action which encouraged personal expression in a spirit of freedom, even at the risk of criticism: or, more cynically, a demonstration of state *hubris*. The theatre's place in society in Athens was as a medium for debate and for display. It was, therefore, as worthy of financial backing as was any other institution that contributed to the maintenance of the democratic process.

Liturgies were a vital supplement to state finances. The number delegated to undertake a liturgy may have been as many as a hundred in any one year, perhaps more, from an eligible population, variously estimated as from no more than forty thousand to as many as a hundred and twenty thousand Athenian citizens, which by the end of the Peloponnesian War had fallen considerably. At various times, including the final years of the war against Sparta at the end of the fifth century, the burden of the *chorêgia* became simply too great for a single individual and was shared, till it eventually ceased to function. Assignments could set an individual back up to five thousand *drachmai*. Those who volunteered for, or were allocated, the office of *chorêgos* paid for the choruses in a group of four plays by a single playwright, their costumes, masks and incidental expenses including their keep during the rehearsal period. The *chorêgos* also paid for a professional choreographer and a musician, perhaps for a director. He had to meet all the production expenses, including additional actors, should any be required. The state paid for three actors and anything to do with the theatre and its maintenance. It was also the state that paid the playwrights, though how much they paid goes unrecorded. That there was no formal association between dramatist and *chorêgos* says something, but by no means everything, about the intriguingly elusive relationship between dramatist and paymaster. Peter Wilson has delved into all the evidence for direct involvement of the *chorêgos*, some of whom may even have wanted to appear in person.[11] 'The *khoregos*', he concludes, 'provided a spectacle, and the *khoregia* was a spectacle of self-presentation.' In this curious relationship of all the interested parties lies the true commodity of the Athenian stage, the commodity of prestige, the *philo-timia* (love of honour) which could work either altruistically for the good of the state, or selfishly, as it did in later times, for personal glory or simply self-preservation.

Plutarch's attribution of what was known as the theoric fund to Pericles is no longer accepted by many scholars who suggest that the fund is from the following century. The idea of subsidizing the audience to the tune of two *oboloi* was certainly introduced at some time in Athens, and that is what is important in the present context. It was felt that poor citizens were being excluded from attending the theatre, either through poverty or because the rich were buying up all the tickets (though how the latter was helped by the theoric fund is far from clear). At any rate, anyone, poor or rich, whose name appeared on the citizen list, the *lêxiarchikon grammateion*, became entitled to apply for the two-obol subsidy. Most probably this was for a single ticket for one day: there is a suggestion that half of it was for food which was probably available between individual plays, depending on how the day was organized (see Rehm, ch. 10 in this volume).

The question that does arise is why, if the state was so keen on as many citizens as possible attending, there was any charge at all. What would be the point of the state paying someone two obols in order that they could go to the theatre and pay it back again to the state? It seems like bureaucracy gone mad. If the theatre could hold only about fifteen thousand, and recent estimates seem to be heading down rather than up, it is possible that competition for seats may have been fierce and that this was the best means of regulating entry.

There is another possibility, hinted at by the reference above to Theophrastus and the stingy man who waits for free entrance before taking his children to the theatre. Theophrastus is writing at a time when Sophocles and Euripides have been dead for seventy years. The world has changed. The theatre building is now stone. Management and finance are no longer in the hands of the earmarked wealthy. This story makes sense only if free entrance was unusual but offered under special circumstances. But by whom? This is where the rather shadowy figure of the *theatrônês* or *theatropôlês* crops up. Though first mentioned only in the fourth century, there was surely a job for the theatre-manager, or lessee, from as early as the first move from the Agora in Athens to the Precinct of Dionysus.

Someone who takes gate money but has the discretion to waive it; who may also be providing the catering; who has the responsibility of seeing that the house is 'managed', anything from getting the play started and seeing that the audience behave with due decorum to clearing up afterwards, is more than a minor state official. The possibility is that a private individual leased the theatre from the state, perhaps on an annual basis. The lessee's responsibility could then be for all the incidentals of upkeep and probably the provision of stage, as well as front-of-house, staff.

It may not be possible to give answers to all the questions raised at the outset about how, at any period, the theatre functioned as a theatre, in Greece or in Rome. Two things emerge from all this, however. The first is that the theatre in Athens may have been part of a religious and ceremonial occasion but that occasion, however festive or solemn, was inevitably underpinned by the organization that supervised it: and that organization may have been more the result of private than of public involvement. The second is that, despite the rapid slide downmarket of Roman taste, entertainment in Rome before and after the constitutional change from republic to imperial government was a hundred per cent subsidized. If this is all an unconscious form of economy, lacking both theory and analysis, it remains enough to claim the theatre from its earliest organization as both a profession and an industry and, at times, an exercise of artistic endeavour.

NOTES

1. *New Theatre Quarterly* 10.39 (Aug 1994), 217–22.
2. M. Dillon and L. Garland (eds.), *Ancient Greece: Social and Historical Documents from Archaic Times to the Death of Socrates* (Routledge: London and New York, 1994; revised ed., 2000).
3. E. Csapo and W. J. Slater, *The Context of Ancient Drama* (Ann Arbor: University of Michigan Press, 1994).
4. J.-A. Shelton, *As the Romans Did* (Oxford: Oxford University Press, 1988).
5. Horace, *Letter to the Pisos*, also known as the *Ars Poetica* (c.12–8 BC).
6. See Richard Beacham, 'The Emperor as Impresario: Producing the Pageantry of Power', in Karl Galinsky (ed.), *The Cambridge Companion to the Age of Augustus* (Cambridge, Cambridge University Press, 2004), pp. 151–74.
7. Terence, *The Mother-in-Law* (*Hecyra*), 49–52.
8. W. Beare, *The Roman Stage* (London: Methuen, 1950; revised ed., 1964), p. 235.
9. See G. M. Sifakis, *Studies in the History of Hellenistic Drama* (London: Athlone Press, 1967).
10. See Oliver Taplin, *Comic Angels and Other Approaches to Greek Drama through Vase-Painting* (Oxford: Clarendon Press, 1993).
11. Peter Wilson offers an exhaustive investigation of every aspect of this Athenian institution in *The Athenian Institution of the Khoregia: The Chorus, the City and the Stage* (Cambridge: Cambridge University Press, 2000).

FURTHER READING

Beare, W., *The Roman Stage*. London: Methuen, 1950.
Carcopino, J., *Daily Life in Ancient Rome*, trans. E. O. Lorimer. Harmondsworth: Penguin, 1956.

Csapo, E. and Slater, W. J., *The Context of Ancient Drama*. Ann Arbor: University of Michigan, 1994.

Gold, B. K., *Literary Patronage in Greece and Rome*. Chapel Hill and London: University of North Carolina Press, 1987.

Sifakis, G. M., *Studies in the History of Hellenistic Drama*. London: Athlone Press, 1967.

Wilson, P. *The Athenian Institution of the Khoregia: The Chorus, the City and The Stage*. Cambridge: Cambridge University Press, 2000.

16

MARIANNE McDONALD

The dramatic legacy of myth: Oedipus in opera, radio, television and film

This chapter will investigate what happens to ancient drama in performance as opera, radio, television and film. Understanding the media is like learning a new dramatic language. Drama is as old as man if we believe Aristotle and associate it with the mimetic instinct. One might say the first act of communication for all of us – the infant's first cry as it greets the world – is a form of drama.

Drama was used to propitiate the gods and amuse viewers. Flourishing in both Greek and Roman theatres, and later on elaborate stages, opera married music to text as it revived mythical themes. Modern media transformed drama further. George Eastman first manufactured transparent celluloid film in 1889, and Auguste and Louis Lumière showed the first motion picture using film projection in 1895. Guglielmo Marconi first sent radio waves across the Atlantic in 1901. Television can be traced to John Logie Baird in 1926. Whereas the modern media are just about a hundred years old, drama has been staged in front of live audiences for thousands of years.

To illustrate the transformation that takes place when classical drama is reproduced in modern media, I will take as an example Oedipus plays and the varieties of treatments they have received from those media. For ease of comparison, I shall discuss only those plays, but the discussion applies to almost all Greek and Roman drama because of the media used for performance.

Oedipus is a singularly fitting choice since, throughout the centuries, his myth has served as a Rorschach for philosophical and psychological theories from Freud to Nietzsche to Lévi-Strauss. This parable of a man who unwittingly commits the vilest crimes – murdering his father, marrying his mother, and engendering children with her – also describes a man who will not give up, and is certainly a memorial to man's capacity for survival.

The original Greek drama was presented in fifth-century BC Athens in a roughly circular outdoor theatre as is described by Richard Beacham (ch. 11) in this volume. Masks were worn, and Gregory McCart (ch. 13) tells us how the voice was projected and heard in these spaces. Over the centuries, the theatres of the Greeks evolved into other forms, such as the Roman, medieval and renaissance stages, the proscenium arch, and now modern theatres that range from stark black boxes to stadiums with stages of all sizes and shapes.

Opera

Opera, as we know it, is a latecomer to drama. The Florentine Camerata thought they were reviving ancient Greek tragedy when they 'invented' opera in the early seventeenth century, and with some justification because music and dance are integral elements of Greek tragedy.[1] Opera's many antecedents include, among the earliest, Hildegard von Bingen's *Ordo Virtutum* in the twelfth century. Some of the earliest operas – for example, Francesco Cavalli's account of Medea and Jason's story in *Giasone* (1648) – incorporated themes from Greek tragedy as they freely reworked classical myths.

If we accept Aristotle's account of the elements of tragedy – we would also assume they applied to comedy – most are retained in opera: plot, character, thought, language, spectacle and music. In opera, spectacle and music (particularly the music) prevailed to the point of overwhelming the other elements. The baroque stage with its lavish effects and scenery was overwhelming by comparison with the classical restraint of ancient stages. Until modern times, only rarely did opera incorporate spoken sections (like Mozart's *Magic Flute*, deriving from the German Singspiel tradition). In Greek tragedy, the *aulos* (a double pipe with finger-holes and a reed mouthpiece) and drum accompanied sung and danced sections.[2] As the chorus became less important in Greek tragedy and comedy from the fourth century BC on, musical interludes took their place. Both Roman and Greek comedy included musical sections accompanied by dance and mime. In ancient drama, music was handmaiden to the words; however, the debate as to whether the words or the music were more important lasted for centuries.

Operas were often longer than ancient dramas, yet the addition of music usually resulted in the ancient text being shortened, usually by cutting poetical passages and dialogue that in the original play advanced the action. These abridgements were simplifications of the originals, whereas music added new complexity; music was like the ancient chorus in that it provided additional commentary.

Theories about the possible emotional effects of different types of music date back millennia. Plato spoke of the emotional content of the various modes used in the music of his time, and even noted the political significance of music in his *Republic* (4.424c). He considered certain modes, like the Dorian, ethically inspiring, whereas others, like the Lydian, could lead people astray. Although some of today's music analysts may consider major and minor keys simply as sequences of notes arranged in particular intervals with no obvious emotional significance, many listeners still associate major keys with happier, more positive emotions, and the minor keys with sadder ones. Composers drawing on these emotional connotations frequently choose these keys to illustrate the ideas being expressed, or in certain cases to add new subliminal information.

However it comes about, humans have for centuries appeared to believe that music can communicate the meaning of words and emotional states. Historically, for example, the descending tetrachord (four descending notes) was popular in the seventeenth century for conveying sadness; one need only think of Purcell's final lament for Dido in his opera *Dido and Aeneas* (1689). Earlier, Monteverdi's *Il ritorno di Ulisse in patria* (1640) used music programmatically: for instance, rhythmically stressed repeated chords suggest battles (*stile concitato*). In the nineteenth century, this approach culminated in Wagner's development of an entire system of musical themes (later called *leitmotifs*) that identified and were associated with characters, objects, and concepts in his operas.

Some might object to the idea of music telling people what they ought to be thinking and feeling, but in the early years of film musical accompaniment did exactly that, and even the first 'talkies' used music to inform and comment on the action of the film. Over the decades, scores have come to be seen as supporting the visual images in ways ranging from subtle to blatant. The overuse of 'suspense' music can be especially irritating. Horror movies abound in attempts to create spinetingling scenarios that too often feature vulnerable, attractive young women wandering, in defiance of all common sense, through menacingly dark houses in the middle of the night to the accompaniment of an equally menacing soundtrack. Sentimental music used to underline reunions and happy endings in film can also be tedious, but in opera it can be sheer genius in the hands of a gifted composer. For example, in Strauss's *Elektra*, the music for the moment in which Elektra and Orestes recognize each other after years of separation turns it into an ecstatic love scene that earns the applause of most music lovers. Music is the most important way in which ancient texts are translated for opera.

The structure of musical units can interfere with or even contradict the dramatic flow. In earlier operas, for example, arias often involved repeated passages. Thus, in Monteverdi's *Il ritorno di Ulisse in patria*, Athena tells Ulysses that, among his other difficulties, Penelope is being besieged by suitors, but the score makes him a victim of the reprise by calling for him to continue rather mindlessly, 'O fortunato Ulisse' (O fortunate Ulysses). Singers themselves also rarely undergo the training in acting that professional actors in theatre, radio, television and film do, so the musical director and the dramatic director have to reach compromises.

Modern opera combines many more elements than did ancient drama, which nonetheless was also costly and depended on both state and private patronage (see Walton, ch. 15 in this volume). The expenses associated with opera – orchestra, opera singers, sets and costumes – made it, even more than ancient drama, a pursuit of the elite. Opera began as a pastime for royals, but became accessible to the public as early as the seventeenth century in Venice.

The production by the American designer and director Julie Taymor of Stravinsky's *Oedipus Rex*, mounted in 1992 in Japan, provides an example.[3] Although music usually expands the original text, Stravinsky drastically reduced the text in his libretto so that the focus would be on the music, and the performance ended up being less than an hour.

Opera based on Greek tragedy usually lacks the dramatic impact of the original play. Though many operas use choruses, composers who restage the classics often reduce them to allow for repetitions. Consider the chorus in Sophocles' *Oedipus Tyrannus* that follows Oedipus' discovery of who he is:

> Oh, generations of men,
> Your lives add up to nothing.
> What happiness
> Man thinks he has
> Is only an illusion.
> It glitters for a moment
> And then fades away.
> (OT 1186–1192)[4]

Stravinsky's *Oedipus Rex* eliminated this chorus, besides the final scene of Oedipus with his daughters. He appeared as a silent blinded outcast at the end, with the chorus bidding him farewell. The music and the spectacle of opera expanded the ancient palette to show another way that ancient tragedy is as vital as ever (see **Fig. 34**).

For his libretto, Stravinsky used a Latin translation by Abbé Jean Daniélou which abbreviated Sophocles's *Oedipus Tyrannus*. His Latin hardly equaled the rich Greek of Sophocles, or even the richly poetic Latin of Virgil, but was an etiolated Church Latin, and even contained errors. In short it was almost a parody of the original Greek text.

This was symptomatic of what often happens in adaptation. Stravinsky said he was interested in 'composing an opera in Latin based on a universally

Figure 34. Jessye Norman as Jocasta in Julie Taymor's production of Stravinsky's opera *Oedipus Rex*, 1992.

known tragedy of the ancient world'.[5] He was inspired, he said, by St Francis of Assisi using French to express what he wanted to express because his native Italian 'had become for him vulgarized and debased by daily use'.[6] Stravinsky thus sought a libretto written in a language that he considered elevated and perhaps exotic because it was inaccessible to most people, so that it would not interfere with what he wanted to highlight, namely, his music. The language became another instrument to be used for its percussive and sometimes lyrical texture.

In addition to the sung text, Stravinsky had Jean Cocteau write a commentary which e.e. cummings translated into English (and in other languages to suit the audience before whom this opera is performed). Cocteau interpolated monologues that advanced the plot in ways that Daniélou's libretto did not. However, Stravinsky rejected Cocteau's interludes initially because they were too florid.

Stravinsky wanted a language that was 'imperfectly remembered' but had an 'incantatory' element.[7] His aim was for his opera to be 'monumental' and the language, in addition to the choice of play, added to this quality. He also proposed what he called a 'wooden Indian staging' because he considered 'the music more important than the action' (not to mention the words).[8]

Taymor's production departed from Stravinsky's static concept. She had her singers moving about the stage and added spectacle with puppets, moving machinery and dance. Stravinsky's original intent seemed to be to approach the symphonic, with singers added, so that his music would be the star. In fact, an early version was presented in simple oratorio form with the singers seated, and this was probably Stravinsky's preferred mode of presentation: less distracting drama.

Taymor's production had a suggestive Japanese set consisting of wooden slats over water with a stone textured background. Elaborate mobiles re-enacted the drama of Oedipus's contest with the Sphinx and other incidents from his life. Her costume design for the chorus, rags and monochromatic ash, made them resemble victims of Hiroshima, and also apparently drew from the make-up used in Butoh, a post-Hiroshima dance form. Thebes' plague was equated with Hiroshima.

She retained monumental elements in her elaborate costumes for the principal singers. For example, Cycladic heads from the Neolithic period (c.3000 BC) surmounted the elaborately made-up faces of the main performers, and this made them look eight feet tall. This Cycladic art resembled the early Japanese Haniwa sculpture from the Kofun period (300–710 AD). The singers also had oversized hands to heighten the expressivity of their gestures. Tiresias, in addition, had eyes painted on the palms of his hands.

Taymor's narrator, Shiraishi Kayoko, moved with the grace of a Kabuki actor. Taymor complicated the action by having Oedipus represented by both a dancer (Min Tanaka) and a singer (Philip Langridge). After Jocasta hanged herself – the mask was torn off the top of her head – Langridge and Tanaka became one as Tanaka stabbed the eyes in Langridge's mask. When Langridge turned around red ribbons streamed from his eyes to indicate the blood:

> The red line was the recurring image throughout our [Taymor's] production: the umbilical cord from which the infant Oedipus was suspended, roads of taboo, the noose by which Jocasta hung herself, and finally the bloody tears that streamed from the pierced eyes of Oedipus.[9]

When Tanaka first appeared, he wore a type of stone armour and, because he was suspended by a red cord, he resembled a puppet. By the end of the opera, he had shed the armour and appeared in a thong: Oedipus's vulnerable nakedness was revealed as he discovered who he was and what he had done.

Another type of doubling was used in Lee Breuer's *Gospel at Colonus* (1982), an opera based on Sophocles' second play about Oedipus that shared elements with a black gospel service. Breuer chose to have portions spoken in addition to being sung; he had the actors who played the spoken roles double the singers who performed the main characters.

Both Breuer and Stravinsky incorporated Christian ritual into conventional opera, and coupled it with Greek tragedy. Particularly in its early stages, western opera showed the influence of Christianity in its music and in its librettos, so this was another layer imposed on the classical text in performance. Although Oedipus might seem an odd choice for a Christ figure, both Stravinsky's and Breuer's works showed him as someone who sacrificed himself for his people, and in both versions the portions of the ancient play corresponded to the traditional sections of the Christian mass.

Music provided commentary for the text. In Stravinsky's opera, Jocasta's music was more florid than Oedipus's – she may have died at the end but she triumphed in her divahood. Her operatic role gave her immortality. Also, she was introduced by a 'Gloria' section that left no doubt as to who ruled. Oedipus's music was more timid and his arias wove in and out of his wife-mother's powerful *cabaletta*.

This reflected the increased power afforded women in opera. One can attribute this, in part, to the influence of Christianity and the Virgin Mary cult in early opera. Part of it has to do with the medium of opera *per se*. Opera today would be almost inconceivable without women, but Greek tragedy featured men playing women. Castrati (castrated men who sang in the upper ranges) dominated opera in the seventeenth and eighteenth century, but once the power of the soprano voice was discovered, and with it the passing of the castrati, the diva came into her own. Penelope in *Il ritorno di Ulisse in patria* and Jocasta in *Oedipus Rex* are more powerful and have bigger roles than their classical prototypes.

In the Breuer production, the chorus was representative of a religious congregation, and sang in something resembling plainchant. In the Stravinsky opera both Jocasta and Oedipus were more chromatic, and their keys wandered. They were out of Italian opera, blithely ignoring the clues that point to Oedipus' identity. Tiresias sang in a straightforward major key as representative of God, fate and the truth. The shepherd delivered a *berceuse* (lullaby) as he described the abandoned baby he found; but the audience never learned the complete story of the infant's abandonment (another operatic omission). Oedipus finally sang the words 'Lux facta est' in D major (Tiresias' key), after all had been illuminated for him. These were his last words. He said nothing when he returned blinded and left the stage – and why did he leave the stage with the chorus bidding him farewell? This implied he was leaving the city at that point, but in the original play he stayed until word came from Delphi about what should be done with him. In the Taymor production, purifying rain began to fall and wash the ash and clay caked on the bodies of the chorus as Oedipus left, and this seemed to represent the washing away of the pollution caused by Oedipus' sin because he was leaving the city.

Truncated texts, elevated and expanded roles for women, and a world after Christ have all influenced operatic renditions of Greek tragedy. Much is lost as the finality of death for the Greeks is replaced by an implied resurrection. But what one gains is the genius of the composer and music as the ultimate commentator as it attempts to approach the ineffable behind the ancient myths. Stravinsky's *Oedipus Rex* shares much in common with other operas that incorporate myths. The texts are generally shorter than their ancient predecessors' because the addition of music means that it takes longer to render the same amount of text.

An opera is a musical translation of ancient drama that often uses only the skeleton of the ancient text as a type of scaffolding. The product is something new.

Radio

Radio was the first technological tool capable of reaching a mass audience. It reaches an audience more than any live play or opera can and is only limited by transmission range and listener interest. Recordings and re-broadcasts make the listening audience potentially limitless.

In March 1997, Peter Hall directed his 1996 Oedipus plays for BBC Radio; his producer was Peter Kavanagh. Ranjit Bolt's translation was in the verse form favoured by Hall, namely rhymed pentameters (his *Oresteia* was in a part-rhymed version by Tony Harrison). In Hall's stage production of the plays, masks muffled the delivery of the words, so the radio production was an improvement for the listening audience. Nevertheless, Hall seemed to have added an extra mask by having the performers adopt an exaggerated style of delivery. Like Stravinsky, he seemed to go for the monumental and the obscure.

Bolt said of his verse, with 'rhyming couplets for the scenes and varying rhythmical schemes for the choruses', that 'the first choice was made in the hope of giving the piece a kind of heightened quality.' In actuality, it could not compare to the stark poetry to be found in the original Sophoclean work, which featured metre but not rhyme. Bolt's first four lines illustrate this well:

> My children, latest harvest of the seed
> That old king Cadmus sewed [*sic*], what pressing need
> Has brought you to me? Something grave it's clear:
> Why else would you be sitting, silent here –[10]

Bolt reduced the chorus that followed Oedipus' discovery of his true identity from Sophocles' forty-four lines to thirty-six, and the first seven lines become five:

> The generations come and go.
> Shadows are what we are – not men.
> No man is truly happy – none.
> We only dream we're happy – then,
> Almost at once the dream is gone.
>
> (p. 52)

He also truncated the choral presentations and Oedipus' lamentations at the end of the play. For instance, Oedipus asked Creon twice to banish him (*OT* 1432–45 and 1517–23), but this production retained only one request. Perhaps this cut was required to fit a radio time-slot, or perhaps due to considerations that, in the absence of the visual element, the listening audience's tolerance called for a shorter performance time.

A more successful BBC radio performance was the June 1983 broadcast of Ted Hughes's adaptation of Seneca's *Oedipus*.[11] Directed by Martin Jenkins, it starred Martin Jarvis as Oedipus, Sian Phillips as Jocasta, John Rowe as Creon and Hugh Dixon as Tiresias, with music by Ilona Sekacz. Hughes brought his poetic genius to bear on the text. The performance lasted a little over an hour. The production avoided exaggerated delivery and showed how effectively spareness could create intimacy between the audience and the actors. This quality is almost unique to radio, of all the current mass media, because of its ability to harness the listener's imagination as an integral part of the production.

In 1927, T. S. Eliot wrote, 'It is pretty generally agreed that the plays of Seneca were composed, not for stage performance, but for private declamation' (*Selected Essays*, p. 54).[12] He continued by suggesting that many of the horrors 'could hardly have been represented on a stage, even with the most ingenious machinery, without being merely ridiculous', and went on, 'Seneca's plays might, in fact, be practical models for the modern "broadcasted (*sic*) drama"' (Eliot, p. 55). For these reasons, radio is the ideal medium for Seneca, just as it certainly was for early horror programmes like *Inner Sanctum*, which were more terrifying than explicit 'slasher' films because they harnessed the human imagination.

This version of Seneca's *Oedipus* retained much from the original. Nevertheless, Hughes could not resist adding lines for Jocasta that showed her obsession with the baby she thought had died, and her meditating on her final role after learning she was both wife and mother to her lost son. Hughes both reduced and added to Sophocles at various times while retaining the main sequence of events in Seneca's version. For example, Jocasta committed suicide in front of Oedipus, who had earlier blinded himself by ripping out his eyeballs with his own hands (no brooches for him).

Seneca himself freely altered the Sophoclean original by adding dark rhetorical descriptions of rituals and deformed sacrificial beasts, invoking the ghost of Laius, and including a sight of the monsters in Hades. However, what his version gained in gore, it lost in dramatic tension. Seneca liked maxims and the macabre; his awe was for fate and stoic acceptance thereof.

The performances were muted and a strange music suggesting ghosts and the supernatural, punctuated by muffled screams, played in the background. The ritual chorus to Bacchus beginning 'ooo-ai-ee' suggested an African chant. By contrast to Seneca's version, choruses began and ended the production. Hughes also added some lines at the beginning to interpolate the riddle of the Sphinx (here spelled Sphynx), which was also the riddle of man: 'What has four legs at dawn / two legs at noon three legs at dusk?'[13] The chorus became a musical chant at the end.

Radio both captured and heightened the eerie atmosphere, particularly with this aural background, and the listener's imagination could run freely on hearing the descriptions of gore like this – 'the liver is rotten breaks in my hand oozing black bitter gall' (Eliot, p. 28) – or:

His fingers had stabbed deep into his eyesockets   he hooked them gripping the eyeballs   and he tugged twisting and dragging with all his
strength   till they gave way   and he flung them from him . . . there
were rags of flesh strings and nerve ends still trailing over his cheeks   he
fumbled for them snapping them off every last shred.   (p. 51)

This gory, ghost-ridden, superstitious play oozed blood over the airwaves
better than it could have over a stage.

Both plays retained the humour of the original. For instance, when Jocasta
began to speak to the blind Oedipus he claimed, 'You are spoiling my comfortable darkness' (p. 53), or, after she had killed herself and her body was
lying in front of him, he muttered sensibly, 'Do not stumble on the body of
your mother' (p. 55). Seneca might not have shared our modern delight with
these lines, but the radio kept the jokes going.

Radio broadcasts of Greek or Latin plays will be faithful to the text if the
translator is faithful. However, rhymes cannot be faithful to the Latin originals in any literal sense because rhyming was not consistently used before
the medieval period.

What radio performances lack are the visual elements and immediacy of
live performance, even if they are heard simultaneously as in a live broadcast.
Live radio offers something of the same excitement and 'danger', because of
the possibilities for error and surprise, as live theatre, but the audience is not
in the same room with the actors and actresses. There is always some danger
in a live performance. Either actor or audience has the potential for violence
or surprise. No radio audience can be threatened by a radio broadcast in
any immediate sense, unless they are sitting in the broadcasting studio. Of
course, one cannot underestimate the human imagination as we recall the
major panic that followed Orson Welles' broadcast of *War of the Worlds*.[14]

Radio performances also suffer from or are enhanced by the added factors of reception and transmission. The quality of reception depends on the
receiver, and the quality of transmission is limited by the transmitter. There is
also a focus on the aural. The blind who listen to a radio performance are on
an equal footing with any other member of the listening audience, whereas
radio excludes the deaf who can only enjoy the visual aspects of a live performance since they cannot hear words.

There is so much that is conveyed by the actions, gestures and facial expressions of an actor or actress that is lost in a radio transmission. Radio performances also eliminate any possibility of mime as well as any element of
dance or movement, and it is highly likely that ancient choruses mimed some
part of what they conveyed, as they danced their parts. Sets and costumes

are non-existent. But the Greek dramatists wrote for visual performance. Oedipus and Tiresias must wander about the stage blind, and are generally led. Jocasta communicates with her physical reactions as well as words when she finally understands the truth. Silent figures, such as Oedipus' children at the end of the *Oedipus Tyrannus*, also appear, hardly something to be replicated by radio unless some announcer draws attention to them.

A radio transmission allows fewer actors to play all the roles, just as the mask allowed the performance of an entire play that had many parts with only two or three actors. A voice might be recognized, but a clever actor could change pitch and expression when he assumed a new role. The voice became the costume.

Any audience attending a live performance has the added advantage – or in some cases, disadvantage – of having access to three of their five senses (sight, hearing, smell), whereas the radio limits them to one. A live audience can be titillated by odours. Incense can be burned on stage. As actors become excited, those in the closer rows can smell the sweat. Flowers can add to the staging, even if real ones are now rarely used in performance, because seeing them can evoke the memory of their perfume. A cigarette is shared with the audience. Sometimes the fourth sense, touch, comes into play when a director has the actors enter the audience, brush against audience members, or even invade the audience and involve them directly in the action of the piece. One concert I remember featured a blender mixing drinks, which were shared with some lucky audience members, so in this case even taste was included!

Live theatre differs from all the other media and heightens the aspect of danger. There is nothing to equal the stilled hush as a play begins and, at the end, the applause. The fourteenth-century Japanese Noh actor, playwright and critic, Zeami, called this audience–actor interaction the *hana*, or 'the flower': a mutual creation necessary for the success of the performance.

Radio seems the ideal medium for the spare simplicity of Samuel Beckett and Harold Pinter.[15] Many consider the medium freeing because it simplifies. It is certainly less expensive than opera, live stage productions, television, or film. In radio, the storyteller is king, and language is supreme.

At the same time, because an actor can refer to a script, the delivery for radio is usually more accurate than on the stage. Although most radio directors ask that the actors memorize their parts, the lines are always available.

Radio, even more than theatre, engages the imaginative faculty. Because the imagination can roam limitlessly through space and time, the setting described by the words can generate as many different mental images as there are listeners. Operas and plays limit an audience 'visiting' places to the suggestions offered by the sets. Of course, the text can also evoke different settings in the imagination. The same is true for television and film, which can present pictures of the actual locales described and can take place anywhere in the world (or, given digital technology, out of the world). Nevertheless, sometimes what one gains by explicitness, one loses in imagination.

The multitude of technical and technological 'tricks' available to stage, television and film are useless in radio, unless those 'tricks' relate to sound. The voice is an important instrument, sound the only medium.

Radio was the most popular and available form of mass entertainment until television, which can offer all that radio offers with the addition of a visual image. Radio is still popular among commuters who drive to and from work daily. It is the perfect medium for people in transit. Although small automobile-mounted television sets are now available for passengers to enjoy, drivers still rely on their radio for news, commentary, interviews, music – or the occasional dramatic show.

Television

Television has the same access as radio to a home audience. Television gets us back to the visual. Television and film share an advantage that any live stage production, play or opera lacks – the close-up that can catch even the slightest nuance in an actor's expression. Acting techniques for television and for film necessarily differ from those for the stage. Some actors do well in all three, but many times a stage actor is hopeless on television or in film because their style is too 'big', while film or TV actors may be too 'small' for the stage because they don't know how to fill the space or command an audience. Part of the problem, of course, may simply be bad direction.

Many television stations pay for programmes by soliciting advertising; in addition, prime-time has to satisfy the requirements of family viewing which one might typify as a 'sunshine mentality'. Cable and HBO (Home Box Office, which allows viewers to order and pay for specific programmes) have been more venturesome because they have a paid sponsorship. The BBC also has channels BBC3 and BBC4 for 'minority' programmes that provide a haven for taste. One could, however, make the case that radio and television are more subject to censorship than live theatre and films.[16] Sarah Kane, who modernized the Hippolytus legend in her play *Phaedra's Love*, said:

> I would never work in television, and they wouldn't let me. There is too much censorship. As you cannot say what you want to say, I will not do it . . . Film is another matter. I've written one eleven-minute film, which was made for television but they would not show it till after midnight. That says it all.[17]

Television productions tend to blunt the sharp edges and danger of stage productions. The advantage of the television broadcast is its availability for a large audience, but that very advantage can be a liability when choices have to be made to suit that large audience, and potential audience numbers based on the economic premise of delivering audiences to sponsors are used to make programming decisions. Both radio and television have regulations that theatrical performances and films can avoid.[18] Films are given ratings to allow for personal choice, but something unsuitable for family viewing on television is either shunted to late hours or not shown.

A limited time-slot is mandated for most performances on television or radio; this is avoided by the film that can have repeated showings, and a play can be seen on continuous nights during a run. The limited availability of videos and DVDs has also extended runs, as have the reruns available on cable and its equivalents.

The colour quality and visual detail of television is also poorer than a film can deliver. The audio systems for television home viewing are also not of the calibre that good theatres can provide, both for live performances and for film. Cinema sound surpasses what can be found in most homes, but this may be changing.

The television production that I shall be discussing here is the two-hour 1986 BBC production of *Oedipus the King* from Sophocles' *The Theban Plays*, starring John Gielgud as Tiresias, Claire Bloom as Jocasta, John Shrapnel as Creon and Michael Pennington as Oedipus. The translator and director Don Taylor's additions to the Sophoclean text and his variations of it resulted in a 'translation' which might more aptly be called a version.

Taylor renders the seven-lined chorus following Oedipus' discovery of his identity as:

> Like a shadow thrown in the dust
> Is the short life of man:
> The sunlit generations
> Pass into the night,
> And happiness, like a bird in flight,
> Flutters and is gone.[19]

He omitted Sophocles' suggestion that happiness is an illusion that diminishes, but introduced the idea of 'sunlit generations' passing 'into night' (man dies?) and associates happiness with a bird ('bluebird of happiness'?), two notions not mentioned by Sophocles in these lines (1186–92). His expansions of the original increased Sophocles' text by close to a third; for example, Sophocles' closing seven lines were doubled to fourteen.

Taylor's attempts at vernacular diminished the poetry: 'He's shouting / Repeatedly that he must be kicked out of the city'; 'She was scared stiff'; or: 'Let sleeping dogs lie'. He introduces modernisms, such as calling Tiresias a 'shaman' and Creon 'maestro' and later a 'guru'. Did he choose mass language to suit a mass (television) audience?

This version also contained errors about Greek mythology in addition to the Greek language. The Sphinx was called a monster 'with the face of a woman and the body of a dog'. Sophocles called her a singing dog (*rhapsodos kuon*, OT 392) metaphorically, but as Greek art testifies, she had the head of a woman, the wings of an eagle (or large bird of prey) and the body of a lion, not a dog.[20]

In the modern text, the Messenger said that Oedipus' ankles would bear witness to what he has just announced, namely that Oedipus had his ankles pierced: 'Look to your ankles! They're still / Swollen up, more than normal'. Such a wound would certainly leave scars, but hardly cause swelling after all these years. Also, given the fact that, in this production, Oedipus wore shoes rather than sandals, the messenger could not have seen his ankles. A canny director might have taken the costumes into account and cut this line.

When the chorus spoke their lines together they sometimes shouted unintelligibly. They often lined up like church choirs. The costumes, music and set reflected such 'church' references with solemn organ music accompanying Oedipus' exit at the end. The chorus were dressed like deacons, and Ismene and Antigone wore white as if they were communicants. A type of cross hung with a white sheet was also part of the set, and a black sheet was added at the end presumably to indicate Jocasta's death or Oedipus' fall or both.

The extras at the beginning and end resembled something out of Dickens. The modern dress detracted more than it added. What is the point being made? Using rose-pink and powder-blue as the main colours of the sky as the final tragedy unfolded added to the incongruity.

Derek Bourgeois's musical score told the audience what to think. Eerie, muffled, rolling chords accompanied Tiresias as he appeared, presumably suggesting he was a seer. As Jocasta made offerings to Apollo, flutes and dance-like music underscored the optimistic turn the drama supposedly took at this point. Finally, the organ music that accompanied Oedipus' departure seemed to be signalling the end of a ritual.

The set, a palace of polished stone on the right and a rough-hewn stone entrance for the people on the left, does not change, and an unchanging set is faithful to most ancient dramas as well as convenient for television. On the other hand, the single set gave the production a 'studio-bound' look.

This production reduced *Oedipus Tyrannus* to fit the TV screen while at the same time expanding its text to fit a two-hour slot. Besides the censorship for mass media, television imposes both length and production considerations. Nevertheless, like radio, it can potentially make great productions available to every person who has a set. In the many disasters plaguing the world now, along with the refrigerator and stove, the television set is among the first items to be repaired or replaced.

Film

Literally hundreds of technical books describe the technical aspects of film, film-making techniques and the philosophy that underlies film-makers' cinematic choices. Film has greater potential for technological tricks than either stage or radio. Its use of colours and light and dark (*chiaroscuro*), including digital manipulation, surpasses the capabilities of stage lighting. Seeing a film, the audience can literally travel in space and time, and the close-up provides added commentary.

Just as opera translates much of the ancient text into music, so film translates it into visuals (sometimes coupled with music). Suddenly the set can expand to the world (or not the world, but some virtual construct).

Tyrone Guthrie's ninety-minute film *Oedipus Rex* (1957) exemplifies how film can make better use of time and space than television can. Douglas Campbell is Oedipus, Eleanor Stuart is Jocasta and Douglas Rain Creon. The composer Louis Applebaum provides spare music, which is appropriate and never dominant. He offers a wonderful balance of music and silence, which enables all the words to be clearly heard.

This film featured the text of William B. Yeats, modified by E. F. Watling. Sometimes these modifications are infelicitous, as in the addition of lines like a 'cataract of scarlet' to the simpler 'dark shower as it were hail' in Yeats, to describe the blood from Oedipus's pierced eyes.

Yeats' own text was sparse and he himself cut the choruses and dialogue to make it more workable for the stage. He also changed the meaning in many places, expanding when he liked and reducing when he thought that reduction would make the drama more effective. He drastically reduced Oedipus' final lamentation. Yeats' *Oedipus the King* (and it is rightly called a version) was taught for many years in schools as if it were a faithful translation. What it may have lacked in fidelity is compensated for in poetic genius. For example, he reduced the seven-lined chorus describing the unreliability of human happiness to three magnificent lines:

> What can the shadow-like generations of man attain
> But build up a dazzling mockery of delight that
> Under their touch dissolves again?[21]

Guthrie himself directed the film, which was closely based on his own 1955 stage production in Stratford, Ontario. His use of large stylized masks lent a majesty to the texts and returned to an ancient use that forces the

Figure 35. Douglas Campbell as Oedipus in Tyrone Guthrie's film of *Oedipus Rex*, 1957.

body to provide the expressions that a face usually does. His masks were also symbolic: a large gold mask for Oedipus (later with crown removed and veiled in black to indicate his blindness and renunciation of the king-ship), a silver mask for Jocasta, and a frightening, ghostly birdlike mask for Tiresias, who also had claws for hands. In all cases, the mouth openings were large enough not to muffle speech. Guthrie's masks made the actors into ageless monuments of an immortal text and also infused the produc-tion with a primitive element that brought one into the realm of gods and archetypes – something the Japanese understood with their Noh masks, as did the American Indians and native Africans with their ritual masks. The stylization of the entire production, with the chorus hovering and winding about the single characters, and Tiresias clawing at Oedipus' robe to try to make him face the truth, was very effective and more convincing than more literal productions either on stage or in film.

Figure 36. Pasolini's *Edipo Re*, 1967.

The film did not use the usual common film techniques such as elaborate pans, creative montage, or even close-ups to show a facial expression (for obvious reasons, since the main actors were masked). I have included this example simply to show that some mask-work can be effective in a film when a director knows what he or she is doing. Guthrie started with a gripping masterpiece and translated it amazingly well into film. His chorus was always intelligible and the movement was well directed. When stage productions are made into a film, bad directing can multiply pre-existing flaws exponentially.

Perhaps Greek tragedy is served best in other media by wholesale reinvention, as illustrated by Pier Paolo Pasolini's 1967 film, *Edipo Re*. It was filmed in Northern Italy, Morocco and Bologna and ran for 104 minutes in the British version and 110 minutes in the Italian original. The camera techniques are superb and show film's capabilities (**Fig. 36**).

Pasolini both wrote the minimal script and directed the film which starred Franco Citti as Oedipus, Silvana Mangano as Jocasta and Julian Beck from the Living Theatre as Tiresias. Pasolini himself played the high priest who says that Laius' murder must be avenged.

Of all the reinventions of Greek tragedy discussed in this article, Pasolini's was the furthest from Sophocles, both in time, being set mainly in the modern era, and in approach, which was visual/mythical.

The director took the myth of Oedipus and filtered it through Freud to provide commentary on his own life and experiences growing up with a rather remote father in the military and a mother he adored.[22] This film, with its depiction of an innocent man as the victim of his inner drives, was a strange portent of Pasolini's own death, murdered at the hands of a man whom fate seemingly led him to approach.

Pasolini tried to capture Oedipus' essential innocence. He showed, as much as Sophocles did, how free will and fate seem to operate at the same time. In both works, audiences saw Oedipus commit crimes, but at the same time how he struggled to avoid those very crimes he had been told would be his fate.

Pasolini said of *Edipo Re* that he had 'two objectives: first, to make a kind of completely metaphoric – and therefore mythologized – autobiography; and second to confront both the problem of psycho-analysis and the problem of the myth'.[23] The visual approach seems to be particularly suited for depicting psychological drives and myths, and Pasolini's approach here often seems to replicate the dream state. Although events unfolded before the viewers' eyes, they seemed to replicate the inner life more than actual things that took place in time. He aptly described his approach as 'the contemplative and lazy taste for beauty' (Pasolini, *Oedipus Rex*, p. 8).[24] One only misses, at times, the sonorous lilt and flow of Sophocles' language.

The sequences set in 'ancient' time blended dress appropriate for Morocco in addition to Pasolini's imagination – for instance, as the high priest he wears an elaborate headdress of straw and seashells – whereas the 'present' time was set in modern Italy. Primitive contrasted with civilized, and the primitive was often identified with the subconscious. Pasolini made powerful use of suggestive settings and creative montage to create effective visual sequences.

In terms of the story, Pasolini followed the outlines of the Sophoclean original, but with variations. He forced the viewer to guess at the motives for Oedipus' father killing him. Jealousy was one factor, as shown in the modern father's complaint to his wife at the beginning of the film: 'Here he is, the child who is gradually going to take your place in the world . . . He will kill you . . . The first thing he will rob you of is your wife' (Pasolini, p. 20).[25]

Also, the Sphinx, a woman wearing an elaborate African mask, said she saw that Oedipus had a riddle. He threw her into an abyss, but she told him that that was futile because the abyss was inside himself. The scene as filmed differed from the published script that said they spoke together silently, and then Oedipus was seen dragging her corpse by the tail as 'his trophy' (Pasolini, p. 58). However, both scenes differ radically from Sophocles' play, which did not enact the Sphinx episode but only referred to it in general terms.

Amidst much rejoicing, Oedipus was made king of Corinth and married Laius' widow, Jocasta, his queen. The consummation of their love ended

Part One. When Oedipus suspected who he was, and even after Tiresias had delivered his dire prediction, Oedipus called Jocasta 'mother' but made love to her yet again. Jocasta finally hanged herself and Oedipus blinded himself, but then, in an abbreviated version of Sophocles' sequel, *Oedipus at Colonus*, the film shifted to modern time again and a modern location (Bologna, 1967). Oedipus' guide now is not Antigone (as in Sophocles), but a young boy named Angelo, the earlier messenger (*aggelos* = messenger = angel) who met him when he first arrived in Thebes and told him about the Sphinx.

Pasolini exploited the full range of cinematic resources, including montage, to create visual dramatic impact. For instance, after Oedipus condemned Creon to death, there was a cut to Jocasta braiding her hair after she and her husband-son had made love. She said nothing, but there was a cut back to Oedipus saying he would pardon Creon for her sake. There are other visual illustrations of the verbal, such as the scene in which Oedipus killed his father and his armed retinue, but one servant escaped.

This director who was notorious for his explicit visuals stopped at showing nothing: lovemaking between mother and son, the graphic killing of the father, Oedipus finding his mother hanging (he revealed her naked body as he tore off her dress to get the brooches with which he would put out his eyes, also shown explicitly in all its gory details). No long messenger speeches were used because everything was shown.

Pasolini also used visual imagery to create resonances and to presage future action. For instance, the young Oedipus was shown going to a balcony to look for his mother, only to be frightened by both the sound and the sight of fireworks. He tried to shield his eyes and block up his ears, a premonition of his later self-blinding, and his statement claiming he would make himself deaf if he could, in reaction to the violent acts that he committed. Also, the fireworks may have symbolized his inner 'explosions' as well as those inflicted on him by fate. Shots that panned away from Oedipus and show him the size of an ant in a vast landscape also provide visual commentary: he was a small creature lost in his myth and fate.

Pasolini used montage for special effects. In the Delphi scenes he intercut shots of Oedipus alone with shots of him in a crowd. In the last part of the film, set in Bologna, he 'used distorting wide-angled lenses because coming back suddenly to the modern world could not be done naturalistically . . . the physical distortion made the transition from meta-history to contemporary history less brusque, and helped to maintain the dream atmosphere'.[25]

The aural technology was as sophisticated as the visual, and the music was chosen for its mythical value: 'As I wanted to make Oedipus a myth, I wanted music which was a-historical, a-temporal' (*Pasolini on Pasolini*, p. 126). (Pasolini later corrected 'a-historical' to 'meta-historical'. He wanted to claim it included all of history, no particular period.) For the most part this specific intent was never made obvious, but the film did achieve that monumental dimension which Stravinsky tried to achieve in his opera. The myth of Oedipus more than other myths may have inspired Pasolini to render it iconically, drawing more attention to the universals than the particulars. Pasolini reduced the Sophoclean chorus that described the illusion of human happiness to the picture of a blind man playing a flute. Film can abbreviate a text by its visual representation, just as opera's music offers its own elucidation as it abbreviates and replaces the text.

Pasolini used Romanian songs and Japanese music, besides his own original music, to add commentary. He accompanied a nursing scene with Mozart's Quartet in C major ('Dissonance', K465). The last frame of the film showed a meadow, and the same quartet that began the film ends it as Oedipus says, 'Life ends where it began.' The personal life parallels the musical development and recapitulation. Mozart is decidedly appropriate, along with the Romanian and Japanese music, as part of the stylized palette used by Pasolini.

At the end of his film Pasolini showed Oedipus re-entering modern society in Bologna in an act of Freudian sublimation, as Pasolini saw it. Like Socrates at the end of his life, he 'played music' or, as Pasolini said, he defined himself metaphorically as a poet. He played both Japanese music and a Russian folk tune associated with the Italian resistance as a revolutionary song. One can see Pasolini as Oedipus using 'decadent' aesthetically elite art (*Salò, o le 120 giornate di Sodoma*, 1975) besides more publicly minded forms of art (*Il Vangelo Secondo Matteo*, 1964). Oedipus is a symbol for all men, yet for Pasolini he was specifically a musician and a poet, and a man with whom he could identify: *un monstre sacré*.

The final scene of the film was of Oedipus playing next to the river Livensa where his mother, Susanna, had taken Pier Paolo as a child. Oedipus claims that this sunlight warms him for the last time, and the reference to the sun parallels a comparable reference in *Oedipus at Colonus*. Colonus, where Oedipus died, was also Sophocles' birthplace.

Compared to the Guthrie and other versions investigated here, Pasolini's mythical depiction was only remotely related to Sophocles. I chose it to illustrate how a creator like Pasolini could exploit the vast resources of the film medium, such as varied locations, camera devices, and techniques. Some might argue that Pasolini erased Sophocles from the picture, but that master playwright's trace still remains in what was emotionally and visually translated.

These versions in the various media show the resilience of Greek or Roman drama to survive in the human imagination. Their songs will be forever sung and reproduced. There will always be a place both for attempts at original staging and for translations that try to remain faithful to the originals. Productions at Herodes Atticus, Epidaurus, and in Syracuse take their place among the world's greatest performances.

The technologies used to present ancient plays in modern forms all have their own requirements. Each needs artists to master them to attain a valid avatar that matches the originals in their beauty and dramatic effectiveness.

NOTES

1. See 'The Birth of Opera and the Use of Classics', in my *Sing Sorrow: Classics, History and Heroines in Opera* (Westport/Connecticut/London: Greenwood Press, 2001), pp. 9–16. For a discussion of the operas and other modern versions, see also my *The Living Art of Greek Tragedy* (Bloomington, Indianapolis, Indiana University Press) and my *Ancient Sun, Modern Light: Greek Drama on the Modern Stage* (New York/Oxford: Columbia University Press, 1992) for other discussions of adaptations and the techniques used.
2. See M. L. West, *Ancient Greek Music* (Oxford: Clarendon Press, 1992), p. 81.
3. For details of this production, mounted at the Saito Kinen Festival, Matsumoto, Japan in 1992, see both the award-winning Cami video (which featured Seiji Ozawa conducting, Philip Langridge singing Oedipus, with Min Tanaka dancing the part, Jessye Norman singing the part of Jocasta, and Bryn Terfel, Creon; George Tsypin designed the set), and Eileen Blumenthal and Julie Taymor's *Julie Taymor Playing with Fire: Theatre Opera Film* (New York: Harry N. Abrams, 1995).
4. I am using my translation.
5. Letter cited by Stephen Walsh in *Stravinsky: Oedipus Rex* (Cambridge Music Handbooks) (Cambridge: Cambridge University Press, 1993), p. 6.
6. Eric Walter White, *Stravinsky: The Composer and His Work*, second ed. (Berkeley: University of California Press, 1984), p. 327.
7. Mikhail Druskin, *Igor Stravinsky: His Personality, Works and Views*, trans. Martin Cooper (1979; rpt. Cambridge: Cambridge University Press, 1983), p. 153.
8. Robert Craft, *Stravinsky: Chronicle of a Friendship* (1963; rev. and expanded, Nashville, Tenn.: Vanderbilt University Press, 1994), p. 452. Such a production is in fact available on video directed by Hans Hulscher with the Concertgebouw Orchestra and NOS TV's Men's Choir conducted by Bernard Haitink (NOS Holland production in association with RM Arts, Munich and London Weekend Television, 1984). Neil Rosenshein plays Oedipus and Alan Howard is the narrator who also plays the Sophocles Oedipuses for the Hall/Bolt radio productions of the Oedipus plays.
9. *Playing with Fire*, p. 160.
10. Quotation from *The Oedipus Plays: Oedipus the King/Oedipus at Colonus by Sophocles*, trans. Ranjit Bolt (Bath, England: Absolute Classics, 1996), p. 9. He gives the cast list for this production: Alan Howard as Oedipus, Suzanne Bertish as Jocasta, Pip Donaghy as Creon and Greg Hicks as Tiresias.

11. Hughes's translation had been used by Peter Brook for his production at the National Theatre in 1968, which featured John Gielgud and Irene Worth as Oedipus and Jocasta. The radio production was in June 1983: *Seneca's Oedipus*, adapted by Ted Hughes (London: Faber and Faber, 1969).

12. 'Seneca in Elizabethan Translation', in T. S. Eliot, *Selected Essays* (1932; rpt. and new ed. San Diego/New York/London: Harcourt Brace Jovanovich, 1964), p. 54.

13. *Seneca's Oedipus*, adapted by Ted Hughes, p. 11.

14. See 'Radio's War of the Worlds' (Orson Welles) in Dermot Rattigan, *Theatre of Sound: Radio and the Dramatic Imagination* (Dublin: Carysfort Press, 2002), pp. 39–65. See also 'The War of the Worlds Effect: *Spoonface Steinberg?*' in Tim Crook, *Radio Drama: Theory and Practice* (London/New York: Routledge, 1999), pp. 136–43.

15. Dermot Rattigan sees Beckett's *Krapp's Last Tape* as 'curiously significant to the exploration of sound perception and, by extension, radio drama' (2002, p. 97).

16. See Nicholas Fraser, 'To BBC or Not to BBC: Independent Journalism Suffers an Identity Crisis', *Harpers* 308 (May 2004), p. 58. One could argue classics are exempt from this type of censorship, but classics often mask political criticism (*Antigone*), and moral content is a factor, e.g., England's banning of *Oedipus Tyrannus* from the stage until 1910; see Marianne McDonald and J. Michael Walton, *Amid Our Troubles*, *passim*, and Fiona Macintosh, *Dying Acts: Death in Ancient Greek and Modern Irish Tragic Drama* (New York: St Martin's Press, 1995), p. 13. In the United States in the 1950s 'television was clean and most shows carried the seal of the Code of Good Practices . . . illicit sex relations are not treated as commendable', and such censorship now risks reinstatement; Jeff Jarvis, 'Can the FCC Shut Howard Up?', *The Nation* 278.19 (17 May 2004), 14.

17. Graham Saunders, *'Love me or kill me': Sarah Kane and the Theatre of Extremes* (Manchester/New York: Manchester University Press, 2002), p. 14.

18. See 'TV and Business' in *The Television Annual, 1978–79*, ed. Steven H. Scheuer (New York/London: Collier Macmillan, 1979), pp. 195–211. See also 'Studies in Television' in Tania Modleski (ed.), *Studies in Entertainment: Critical Approaches to Mass Culture* (Bloomington and Indianapolis: Indiana University Press, 1986), pp. 39–95.

19. Don Taylor, trans. and intr., *Sophocles, The Theban Plays: Oedipus the King, Oedipus at Colonus and Antigone* (1986; rpt. London: Methuen, 1998), p. 49.

20. See marble sphinx (550 BC) in John Boardman, *Greek Art* (1964; rev. and rpt. London: Thames and Hudson, 1985), p. 76.

21. *Sophocles' King Oedipus* in *The Collected Plays of W. B. Yeats* (London: Macmillan, 1934), p. 510.

22. See my chapter on Pasolini in *Euripides in Cinema: The Heart Made Visible* (Philadelphia: Centrum, 1983), pp. 3–50.

23. *Pasolini on Pasolini: Interviews with Oswald Stack* (Bloomington and London: Indiana University Press, 1969), p. 120.

24. Preface to *Oedipus Rex, A Film by Pier Paolo Pasolini*, trans. John Mathews (New York: Simon and Schuster, 1971), p. 8. Pasolini discusses his relationship with Sophocles and the reasons for certain choices in *Pasolini on Pasolini*, pp. 119–31.

25. *Pasolini on Pasolini*, p. 127.

FURTHER READING

Bignell, J., *An Introduction to Television Studies*. London/New York: Routledge, 2004.

McDonald, M., *The Living Art of Greek Tragedy*. Bloomington, Indianapolis: Indiana University Press, 2003.

— *Sing Sorrow: Classics, History and Heroines in Opera*. Westport/Connecticut/London: Greenwood Press, 2001.

— *Ancient Sun Modern Light: Greek Drama on the Modern Stage*. New York/Oxford: Columbia University Press, 1992.

— *Euripides in Cinema: The Heart Made Visible*. Philadelphia: Centrum, 1983.

Monaco, J., *How to Read a Film: Movies, Media, Multimedia*, third ed. New York/Oxford: Oxford University Press, 2000.

Rattigan, D., *Theatre of Sound: Radio and the Dramatic Imagination*. Dublin: Carysfort Press, 2002.

Wrigley, A., 'Stages of Imagination: Broadcasting Greek Plays 1920s–1970s'. E-seminar paper/discussion. Milton Keynes: The Open University, May 2006.

PLAYWRIGHTS AND PLAYS

The dates of no more than a small number of plays are known with any certainty, either from the fragmentary surviving records or from other sources. They are included, where known, in the following lists of extant Greek and Roman drama in possible chronological order by playwright. The titles are given in an English version (often one of several) with the original transliterated from Greek or Latin in brackets.

AESCHYLUS	c.526–456 BC; wrote about eighty plays, of which seven survive.
Persians	(*Persai*), 472
Prometheus Bound	(*Promêtheus Desmôtês*), believed by some critics not to be by Aeschylus
Seven Against Thebes	(*Hepta epi Thêbas*), 468 or 467
Suppliants	(*Hiketides*), possibly 463
The Oresteia	(458)
Agamemnon	(*Agamemnôn*)
Libation-Bearers	(*Choêphoroi*)
Eumenides	(*Eumenides*)
SOPHOCLES	496/5–406/5 BC; wrote more than 120 plays, of which seven survive in their entirety.
Ajax	(*Aias*), before *Antigone*
Antigone	(*Antigonê*), 443–441
Women of Trachis	(*Trachiniai*), possibly 430s
Oedipus Tyrannus	(*Oidipous Turannos*), c.429, possibly 427–425
Electra	(*Êlektra*), 425–413
Philoctetes	(*Philoktêtês*), 409

Oedipus at Colonus	(*Oidipous epi Kolônôi*), produced posthumously in 401

EURIPIDES	485/4 or 480–406 BC; wrote about ninety plays, of which nineteen survive, one of them our only complete satyr play.
Alcestis	(*Alkêstis*), 438
Medea	(*Mêdeia*), 431
Children of Heracles	(*Herakleidai*), c.430
Hippolytus	(*Hippolutos*), 428
Andromache	(*Andromachê*), c.425
Electra	(*Êlektra*), 425–413
Hecuba	(*Hekabê*), c.424
Cyclops	(*Kuklôps*)
Suppliants	(*Hiketides*), 424–420
Trojan Women	(*Trôiades*), 415
Heracles	(*Hêraklês*), c.415
Iphigenia among the Taurians	(*Iphigeneia hê en Taurois*), c.414
Ion	(*Iôn*), c.413
Helen	(*Helenê*), 412
Phoenician Women	(*Phoinissai*), c.409
Orestes	(*Orestês*), 408
Iphigenia at Aulis	(*Iphigeneia hê en Aulidi*), performed posthumously in 405
Bacchae	(*Bakchai*), performed posthumously in 405
Rhesus	(*Rhêsos*), believed by some critics not to be by Euripides

ARISTOPHANES	c.445–c.385 BC; wrote about fifty plays, of which eleven survive.
Acharnians	(*Acharnês*), 425
Knights	(*Hippês*), 424
Clouds	(*Nephelai*), first version 423 – this is revised
Wasps	(*Sphêkes*), 422
Peace	(*Eirênê*), 421
Birds	(*Ornithes*), 414
Women at the Thesmophoria	(*Thesmophoriazousai*), 411 or 410
Lysistrata	(*Lusistratê*), 411
Frogs	(*Batrachoi*), 405

| Women in Assembly | (*Ekklêsiazousai*), *c*.392 |
| Wealth | (*Ploutos*), *c*.388 |

MENANDER — *c*.342–*c*.292; wrote over a hundred plays, of which only two survive in a performable state, with substantial fragments of five others.

| The Bad-Tempered Man | (*Duskolos*) |
| The Woman from Samos | (*Samia*) |

HERODAS — *c*.300–250 BC; wrote at least nine mimes, *mimiamboi*, possibly many more, of which seven are complete.

The Bawd or Go-Between	(*Prokuklis ê Mastropos*)
The Pimp	(*Pornoboskos*)
The Schoolmaster	(*Didaskalos*)
Women Worshippers of Asclepius	(*Asklêpidi Anatitheisai kai Thusiazousai*)
The Jealous Woman	(*Zêlotupos*)
A Friendly or Private Chat	(*Philiazousai ê Idiazousai*)
The Shoemaker	(*Skêteus*)

TITUS MACCIUS PLAUTUS — *c*.254–184 BC; had 130 plays attributed to him, but probably incorrectly, all based on Greek originals. The Roman scholar, Varro, identified twenty-one as authentic, twenty of which survive complete.

The Comedy of Asses	(*Asinaria*), 212–207
The Carthaginian	(*Poenulus*)
The Merchant	(*Mercator*)
The Swaggering Soldier	(*Miles Gloriosus*), 206–204
The Casket	(*Cistellaria*), before 201
Stichus	(*Stichus*), 200
Amphitryon	(*Amphitruo*)
The Pot of Gold	(*Aulularia*)
The Rope	(*Rudens*)
The Captives	(*Captivi*)
Epidicus	(*Epidicus*)
The Haunted House	(*Mostellaria*), 200–194
The Persian Girl	(*Persa*), 200–194
Curculio	(*Curculio*), *c*.200 or 193

The Brothers Menaechmus   (*Menaechmi*)
The Threepenny Day   (*Trinummus*), after 194
Pseudolus   (*Pseudolus*), 191
Truculentus   (*Truculentus*), 191–186
Two Sisters Named Bacchis   (*Bacchides*), 189–184
Casina   (*Casina*), 185–184

PUBLIUS TERENTIUS AFER   *c.*195–159 BC; wrote six plays based on
  (TERENCE)   Greek originals, all of which have survived.
The Girl from Andros   (*Andria*), 166
The Mother-in-Law   (*Hecyra*), 165
The Self-Tormentor   (*Heautontimorumenos*), 163
The Eunuch   (*Eunuchus*), 161
Phormio   (*Phormio*), 161
Brothers   (*Adelphoe*), 160

LUCIUS ANNAEUS SENECA   *c.*4 BC–65 AD; wrote nine tragedies, with
   a contemporary history play also
   attributed to him. These are listed
   alphabetically. None of the plays is dated
   and it is widely believed that no Senecan
   tragedy received a full stage production
   under the Roman Empire.
Agamemnon   (*Agamemnon*)
The Mad Hercules   (*Hercules Furens*)
Hercules on Oeta   (*Hercules Oetaeus*)
Medea   (*Medea*)
Octavia   (*Octavia*), a play about recent history and
   the only surviving *fabula praetexta*. It
   seems unlikely that it was written by
   Seneca.
Oedipus   (*Oedipus*)
Phaedra   (*Phaedra*, also known as *Hippolytus*)
Phoenician Women   (*Phoenissae*, also known as *Thebais*)
Thyestes   (*Thyestes*)
Trojan Women   (*Troades*)

GLOSSARY OF GREEK AND LATIN WORDS AND TERMS

Greek

Acropolis	The citadel of Athens where the Parthenon was built. Below and to the south-east is the site of the Theatre of Dionysus; to the south-west the Odeon of Herodes Atticus.
Agôn	A competition, contest or trial.
Agônes	Competitions.
Agônothetês	A Festival and Games organizer or judge.
Agora	The marketplace area of Athens, to the north-east of the Acropolis, where the first performances of tragedy were staged.
Anagnôrisis	'Recognition', as an aspect of play construction (Aristotle).
Anapiesma	A stage trap.
Antistrophê	The circular, turning dance-movement in a choral sequence, balancing and complementing a *strophê*.
Architektôn	The lessee of the theatre. See also *Theatrônês*.
Archôn	One of a number of officials with responsibility for organizing Festivals.
Aulêtês	An *aulos*-player.
Aulos	The double-pipe used to accompany dramatic and dance performance.
Autokabdaloi	Improvisers
Barbaros	A non-Greek, barbarian.
Boulê	The Athenian Council.
Bouleutêria	Meeting chambers (and performance spaces) found in some Hellenistic theatres.
Bronteion	A thunder-machine (Pollux).

Charônioi klimakes	'Charon's Steps', an underground passage leading from backstage to the centre of the *orchêstra* in some later theatres.
Cheironomia	Language of gesture.
Chitôn	An undershirt.
Chlaina	A woollen cloak worn over the *chitôn*.
Chlamys	A short military cloak.
Chorêgia	The office of being a *chorêgos*.
Chorêgos	Private financier of part of an Athenian festival, or other state *leitourgia*. The word is also used for the leader of the Chorus: sometimes found in a choral ode as *choragos* (Doric dialect).
Chorodidaskalos	Choreographer.
Choros	Dance, hence the word became used for the Chorus in dramatic performance.
Deixis	A demonstrative dance.
Dêmos	The Athenian people.
Deuteragonistês	Second actor in a company of three.
Diazôma	The horizontal aisle in a Greek theatre.
Didaskaliai	Catalogues and victory-lists compiled by Aristotle, among others, and official records that have survived (imperfectly).
Distêgia	The upper level of the stage acting-area (Pollux).
Dithyrambos	Dithyramb. A competitive dance for fifty performers from which, Aristotle believed, tragedy was derived.
Drachma	Greek currency, in use in Athens until finally supplanted by the Euro.
Ekklêsia	The Athenian Assembly which all male citizens were entitled to attend, with voting rights.
Ekkuklêma	The wheeled platform which could be rolled out from backstage for *tableaux* or reveals.
Eleos	Pity (Aristotle).
Emmeleia	A sedate dance, or the music accompanying the dance.
Episkênion	The upper storey of the *skênê*.
Epôdos	Part of a lyric ode sung in a chorus following *strophê* and *antistrophê*.

Êthos	Character.
Exarchos	Leader of a chorus.
Exodos	The conclusion of a tragedy.
Exôstra	A reveal (Pollux).
Geranos	An alternative term in Pollux for the stage crane (*mêchanê*). Also the name of a dance.
Gymnastikê	Physical training.
Hêmikyklion	A piece of machinery (Pollux), thought to be a form of *ekkuklêma*.
Hêmistrophion or *Stropheion*	Another stage machine in Pollux used for 'translating heroes into heaven or for those who have died in war or at sea', whatever that may involve.
Hetaira	Courtesan, 'girl from the escort agency' (Green).
Hilarotragôdia	A tragic burlesque invented by Rhinthon.
Himation	A cloak.
Himatomisthês	Costume-hirer.
Hoplite	A heavily armed soldier. An athletic event at some Games involved races in armour.
Hubris	The act of getting above oneself; wanton violence; insolence.
Hypokritês	An 'answerer', the term for 'actor'.
Hyporchêma	A pantomimic dance to accompany a song.
Hyposkênion	A room beneath the stage.
Iambos	The speech rhythm of the iambic (short–long).
Ikria	The bleachers or benches in a theatre; also used as a term for 'stage'.
Isêgoria	Equal right of speech.
Katablêma	A drop-curtain in the theatre (Pollux).
Katharsis	A purging or cleansing (medical term used by Aristotle for the emotional impact of tragedy).
Keraunoskopeion	A lightning machine (Pollux).
Kerkides	Wedge-shaped blocks of seats in the *theatron*.
Kithara	Lyre.
Kommos	A formal lament in tragedy, sometimes involving more than one character as well as the Chorus.
Kômôdos	The actor in a comedy, sometimes the Chorus in a comedy.

Kômos	A revel, a band of revellers or the song sung by them.
Kordax	A rude comic dance.
Koruphaios	Leader of the Chorus.
Kothornos	A soft-soled knee-high boot worn by women and by stage characters, hence the emblem of Dionysus and of actors. Only in late Hellenistic times did it acquire a heightened sole.
Kratêr	An ornamental mixing bowl for wine.
Krotala	Clappers, castanets.
Leitourgia	A public service required of wealthy private citizens in Athens which might include meeting the expenses of dithyrambic or theatrical performance.
Logeion	The stage, possibly the 'raised' stage.
Lyra	A stringed instrument with a sounding-board made from a tortoise-shell.
Marmor Parium	The Parian Marble, an incomplete chronological record up to 263 BC which includes lists of prizewinners.
Mêchanê	The stage crane which was raised to show characters, usually gods, in mid-air.
Mêchanopoios	The operator of the *mêchanê*, probably located in one of the *parodoi*.
Melos	Choral song.
Mimêsis	A representation, impersonation or imitation.
Mimiamboi	Mimes written in iambics.
Mna	Greek coin of considerable value.
Monôdia	A solo song.
Mousikê	Training in music, dance and poetry.
Nomos	'Custom' or 'law'.
Obolos	Greek coin of small value.
Ôdeion	A roofed hall in the eastern side of the *theatron* in the Theatre of Dionysus in Athens.
Okribas	A platform in the *Odeion* where actors in the *proagôn* appeared.
Onkos	The high headdress used as a part of the mask in late Greek and Roman tragedy.
Opsis	The visual aspect of stage performance (Aristotle).

Orchêsis	Pantomimic dance.
Orchêstra	The 'dancing-place' in a Greek theatre, between the stage and the auditorium, used in later times for the seats of dignitaries.
Pallakê	A woman living with a man, not allowed by Athenian law to marry him.
Pantomimos	The dancer who is an 'imitator of everything'.
Parabasis	The sequence in Old Comedy where the playwright addressed the audience directly, through a speech of the Chorus or one of the characters.
Parachorêgêma	A subordinate role or secondary chorus.
Paraskênia	The projecting side-structures in Greek and Roman theatres which 'bounded' the performance space.
Parodos	The side-passage giving entry to the acting area from the sides; the first entry of a Chorus, usually, though not always, made along a side-passage.
Parrhêsia	Freedom of speech.
Peplos	A cloak worn by a man, or robe by a woman.
Periaktos	Prismatic scenic piece which could swivel to reveal a new setting on each facing surface: certainly used in Roman theatres, *periaktoi* are believed by some theatre historians to have been used in the theatre of classical Athens.
Peripeteia	'Reversal of expectation' in play construction (Aristotle).
Phallos	A representation of the penis, regularly worn as part of comic costume.
Phlyax	Farce which flourished in Greek cities in Sicily and southern Italy, many scenes from which survive on pottery.
Phobos	Fear (Aristotle).
Phora	Dance movement.
Phorminx	A type of lyre.
Phylê	A tribe or clan, one of the ten in Athens.
Pinakes	Panels set into the pillars of a stage-setting to indicate location.
Polis	The 'city' or 'city-state'.
Praxis	Stage action.

Proagôn	A preliminary to the dramatic festivals, held in the *Odeion*, when the competing playwrights presented their actors and the subject of their group of four plays.
Proedria	Stone seating in the *theatron*.
Proskênion	The acting-area in front of the *skênê*.
Prosôpon (prosôpeion)	The face (the word used for 'mask').
Prôtagonistês	The leading actor.
Prothuron	Porch.
Pyrrichê	A warlike dance.
Rhabdouchos	Rod-carrier responsible for keeping order.
Rhapsôdos	A reciter of epic poems.
Satyroi	Satyrs, animalistic supporters of Dionysus. Each group of tragedies at the City Dionysia concluded with a satyr play (named after the chorus of satyrs).
Schêma	A dance figure or 'pose'.
Scholia	Marginal comments by the transcriber found in manuscripts.
Sikinnis	A rude dance associated with satyrs.
Skênê	With a literal meaning of 'tent', *skênê* became the word used for the scenic facade from which actors entered and against which they played.
Skênographia	Scenic decoration: a disputed term used by Aristotle to denote stage decor and/or set-design.
Skeuê	Stage props.
Skeuopoios	A prop-maker.
Skopê	A lookout post in the stage setting (Pollux).
Skôps	An owl-dance.
Sophistês	A sophist or teacher of philosophy. Sometimes used satirically as a 'wise guy' in a comedy.
Stasimon	A choral song.
Stasis	Civil war.
Stegos	Stage roof.
Stichomuthia	Line-by-line balanced dialogue.
Stratêgos	An elected general in Athens, an office twice held by Sophocles.
Strophê and *antistrophê*	The circular, and complementary turning dance-movements in a choral sequence.

Stropheion	See *Hêmistrophion*.
Talanton	A large sum of money.
Technitai	Members of the acting guilds.
Teletê	An initiation ritual.
Theatês	Spectator.
Theatron	The 'seeing-place'. The auditorium for spectators.
Theatrônês, Theatropôlês	Theatre lessee.
Theologeion	A higher level of roof on which gods could appear.
Theôros	An ambassador (actors were sometimes used as such).
Thiasos	A band of Bacchic revellers.
Thrênos	A lament.
Thymelê	An altar in the centre of the *orchêstra*.
Thyrômata	Grooves in the side of the pillars of the *skênê* for the insertion of scenic panels (*pinakes*).
Thyrsos	The shaft with a pinecone on top carried by followers of Dionysus.
Tragôdos	A writer of tragedies; a player in tragedies; the Chorus in tragedy.
Tribôn	A threadbare cloak.
Trilogia	A group of three connected tragedies by the same playwright.
Tritagônistês	The third actor (sometimes used disparagingly to mean 'third-rate').
Tympanon	A drum.
Tyrannos	An absolute ruler by other than right of succession.
Tyrbasia	A riotous dithyramb.

Latin

Aediles	Roman magistrates responsible for, amongst other things, dramatic performances.
Angiportus	A passageway assumed to allow a character to move from one stage house to another by a backway.
Antiodermis	A mime-actress.
As	Roman coin of small value.

Atellana	Farce with stock characters, associated with the region of Atella, in which Plautus is believed to have acted in his early stage career.
Aulaeum	The stage front-curtain, or 'tab', which dropped into, or rose from, a shallow trough at the beginning/end of a performance.
Aureus	A large sum of money.
Caduceus	The Herald's staff carried by Mercury as a mark of his office as messenger of the gods.
Canticum	A song in Roman comedy.
Cantor	Musician or singer.
Cavea	The auditorium.
Centunculus	A patchwork tunic.
Choragus	The producer of a play who occasionally appears (Plautus' *The Persian Girl*) as the prologue.
Contaminatio	The process of amalgamating more than one Greek comedy to make a Roman one.
Controversia	A hypothetical legal case.
Cothurnus	The actor's boot in Roman tragedy with a raised sole.
Curator	Superintendent of theatrical productions.
Denarius	Roman coin of fairly high value.
Deus ex machina	Latin equivalent of *theos ex mêchanês*, 'god from the machine'.
Dissignator	Another name for an usher (*pedisequus*) or attendant.
Diverbium	The dialogue of comedy.
Dominus	Head of a theatrical company.
Fabula crepidata	Roman tragedy taken from the word *crepida*, an alternative word for *cothurnus*.
Fabula (comoedia) palliata	Comedy in Latin (Plautus and Terence) based on Greek originals.
Fabula praetexta/ praetextata	Play based on Roman history.
Fabula togata	Comedy based on Roman themes.
Fescennini (versus)	Fescennine verses, a performance form influential on early native Roman drama.
Galerum	A helmet-like head covering.
Grex	A company of actors (literally 'a flock of sheep').
Histrio	Actor.

Imperator	An honorary title bestowed on a successful Roman general, later to become the term used for 'Emperor'.
Imperator histricus	Theatre manager.
Imperium	The Roman Empire.
Instauratio	Repeated ritual because of a flaw.
Lectisternium	A banquet for the gods.
Lex talionis	Law of retribution in kind, 'an eye for an eye'.
Lucar	State support for the *Ludi*.
Ludi	The Games, Roman festivals.
Ludi (*scaenici*)	Games at which dramatic performances were staged.
Ludi circenses	Games for athletic competition.
Ludiones	Etruscan dances.
Mima	Mime actress.
Mimus	Mime actor; mime performance.
Munera	Gladiatorial games.
Naumachia	A staged sea-battle.
Odeum	Roman theatre, or Odeon, used for musical or dramatic performances.
Orchestra	See under (Greek) *orchêstra*.
Palliata	See *fabula palliata*.
Pantomimus	The masked Roman pantomime performer.
Pedisequui	Ushers.
Persona	Mask.
Planipes	'Flat-foot' or 'bare-foot'. Mime or dance performer.
Porticus	Porch.
Praeco	A herald in the Roman theatre.
Praetores	Senior Roman magistrates.
Prologus	Prologue in Roman comedy.
Proscenium	The acting area.
Pulpitum	The stage.
Recitatio	A public reading, perhaps the manner in which Seneca's plays were performed.
Sannio	Buffoon or *zanni*.
Satura	A 'mixture' (nothing to do with 'satyrs'), a possible influence on early Roman dramatic performance.
Scaena ductilis	Movable screen or painted stage flat.

Scaena versilis	Pivoting scenic unit, the equivalent of the Greek *periaktos*.
Scaenae frons	The facade of the scene-building.
Sestertius	A Roman coin.
Siparium	A stage-curtain, or drape, used to cover entrances.
Soccus	Soft shoe worn by comic actor.
Suasoria	A legal debate.
Tabernaria	Private-house comedy, same as the *fabula togata*.
Tibia/tibicen	Double-pipe, similar to the Greek *aulos*.
Tunica	A cloak.
Vela	The awning that could be used to cover the auditorium in some Roman theatres.
Venationes	Animal hunts included in the *Ludi*.
Virtus	Excellence.

SELECT BIBLIOGRAPHY

Primary sources

Much of what was written in the classical period is regarded as unreliable evidence for stage conditions of earlier times, but Plato and Aristotle offer serious analyses of the theatre within their society. More specialized works such as Vitruvius' *On Architecture* or Lucian's *On The Dance* are presumably reliable guides to certain aspects of the subjects they discuss *at the time when they were written*. Much of the rest is included to give some indication of the way in which the theatre functioned within society at various periods.

Sections of the following, together with a range of incidental material, can be found in Eric Csapo and William J. Slater (eds.), *The Context of Ancient Drama*, Ann Arbor: University of Michigan Press, 1994; A. M. Nagler, *A Source Book in Theatrical History*, New York: Dover, 1952; D. A. Russell and M. Winterbottom (eds.), *Classical Literary Criticism*, Oxford: Oxford University Press, 1972, 1989; Mary R. Lefkowitz, *The Lives of the Greek Poets*, London: Duckworth, 1981.

Apuleius (2nd C. AD)	*Metamorphoses* (*The Golden Ass*, Chapter XVII)
Aristotle (3rd C. BC)	*Poetics*
—	*Politics*, VIII, 7
—	*Rhetoric*
Athenaeus (3rd C. AD)	*Deipnosophists*, I, 21–2
Didaskaliai	Victory Lists
Donatus (4th C. AD)	*Commentary on Terence*
Homer (? *c.*9th C. BC)	*The Odyssey*
—	*The Iliad*
Horace (1st C. AD)	*Ars Poetica* (*Epistula ad Pisones*)
Inscriptiones Graecae	Greek inscriptions
Longinus (? 2nd C. AD)	*On the Sublime*
Lucian (2nd C. AD)	*On the Dance*
The *Marmor Parium*	A chronological table
Plato (4th C. BC)	*The Republic*, III, 394–8 and X, 605–6
Pollux (2nd C. AD)	*Onomasticon*, Book IV
Quintilian (1st C. AD)	*Institutes of Oratory*
Suidas (*c.*10th C. AD)	Greek Lexicon
Vitruvius (1st C. BC)	*De Architectura*, Book V

Other useful references can be found in various writers including Herodotus, Thucydides (5th C. BC); Plato *Ion*, *Laws* etc., Aristotle *Rhetoric* etc., Demosthenes, Aeschines, Theophrastus (4th C. BC); Cicero, Sallust (1st C. BC); Livy (1st C. BC–1st C. AD); Ovid (1st C. AD); Martial, Pliny the Elder, Aulus Gellius (1st C. AD); Tacitus, Suetonius, Tertullian, Plutarch (1st–2nd C. AD); Galen, Pausanias (2nd C. AD); Libanius (4th C. AD); Hesychius (5th C. AD). Also variously within the plays, especially those of Aristophanes and Terence, and in the *hypotheseis* (résumés) and *scholia* (manuscript notes).

Secondary sources

This is inevitably a selective bibliography, created from the recommendations of contributors and the wide range of accessible material about the Greek and Roman worlds and their cultures that has been published over the last forty years for the non-specialist. Though articles of immediate relevance to an argument have been included, most of the references are to books rather than to contributions in scholarly journals. It has not been possible to include everything mentioned within the chapters, though bibliographical details of the more specialized books are contained in the notes.

As so much involves overlap of genre, culture and period, no attempt has been made to pigeonhole sources under specific headings. Apart from their wider suggestions, the authors were invited to identify a small number of key works to be included at the end of their own chapter. These have also been included here in the select bibliography.

No translation is recommended over any other, if for no better reason than that as many as half of the contributors are involved in such work for different publishers. Most translations for study or stage date quickly. The capacity for the canon of Greek and Roman plays to be renewed and invigorated through performance ensures that much of the impact of production derives less from the text itself than from the director's approach to that text. Many directors prefer to commission a new translation for each new production; others opt for a variation or adaptation of the text in order to try to make the original seem less strange.

Some translations/'versions' are published as single editions, others form part of a major series involving various (and frequently contrasting) styles and priorities. Among the most reliable and effective representations of the original still readily available have been those published by (strictly in alphabetical order) Absolute Classics, Aris and Phillips, Cambridge University Press, Dent (Everyman), Faber and Faber, Hackett Publishing, Harvard University/Heinemann (Loeb editions with the original alongside the English), Methuen, Nick Hern Books, Oberon Books, Oxford University Press, Penguin, Princeton University Press, Signet Classics, Smith and Kraus, University of Chicago Press.

Alexiou, M., *The Ritual Lament in Greek Tradition*. Cambridge: Cambridge University Press, 1974.
Alföldy, G., *The Social History of Rome*, trans. D. Braund and F. Pollock, third ed. London: Croom Helm, 1985.
Arnott, P. D., *Greek Scenic Conventions in the Fifth Century BC*. 1962; rpt. Oxford: Clarendon Press, 1979.
— *An Introduction to the Greek World*. London: Macmillan, 1967.

— *An Introduction to the Roman World*. London: Macmillan, 1970.

— *The Ancient Greek and Roman Theater*. New York: Random House, 1971.

— *Public and Performance in the Greek Theatre*. London: Routledge, 1989.

Ashby, C., *Classical Greek Theatre: New Views of an Old Subject*. Iowa City: University of Iowa Press, 1999.

Aumont, J., Bergala, A., Marie, M., Vernet, M., *Aesthetics of Film*, trans. and rev. Richard Neupert. Austin: University of Texas Press, 1992.

Austin, M. M. and Vidal-Naquet, P., *Economic and Social History of Greece*. London, Batsford, 1972.

Aylen, L., *The Greek Theater*. Cranbury, NJ: Associated University Presses, 1985.

Bain, D., *Actors and Audience*. Oxford: Oxford University Press, 1977.

Baldry, H. C., *Ancient Greek Literature in its Living Context*. London: Thames and Hudson. 1968.

— *The Greek Tragic Theatre*. London: Chatto and Windus, 1971.

Barker, A. (ed.), *Greek Musical Writings, Vol. I: The Musician and his Art; Vol. II: Harmonic and Acoustic Theory*. Cambridge: Cambridge University Press, 1984/1989.

Bartsch, S., *Actors in the Audience: Theatricality and Doublespeak from Nero to Hadrian*. Cambridge, Mass.: Harvard University Press, 1994.

Bauman, R. (ed.), *Folklore, Cultural Performances, and Popular Entertainments: A Communications-Centered Handbook*. New York: Oxford University Press, 1994.

Beacham, R. C., *The Roman Theatre and its Audience*. London: Routledge, 1991.

— *Spectacle Entertainments of Early Imperial Rome*. New Haven: Yale University Press, 1999.

Beard, M., 'The Triumph of the Absurd: Roman Street Theatre', in C. Edwards and G. Woolf (eds.), *Rome in the Cosmopolis*. Cambridge: Cambridge University Press, 2003, pp. 21–43.

— with North, J. and Price, S., *Religions of Rome*. Cambridge: Cambridge University Press, 1998.

Beare, W., *The Roman Stage*. 1950; rev., London: Methuen, 1964.

Bennett, S., *Theatre Audiences: A Theory of Production and Reception*. London: Routledge, 1990.

Bergmann, B. and Kondoleon, C. (eds.), *The Art of Ancient Spectacle*. Washington, London: National Gallery of Art (*Studies in the History of Art*, 56), Yale University Press, 1990.

Bernal, M., *Black Athena: The Afroasiatic Roots of Classical Civilisation*. London: Vintage, 1987.

Betts, J. H., Hooker, J. T. and Green, J. R. (eds.), *Studies in Honour of T. B. L. Webster*. Bristol Classical Press: Bristol, 1986.

Bieber, M., *The History of the Greek and Roman Theater*. 1939; rev. Princeton: Princeton University Press, 1961.

Bignell, J., *An Introduction to Television Studies*. London and New York: Routledge, 2004.

Blumenthal, E. and Taymor, J., *Julie Taymor Playing with Fire: Theatre Opera Film*. 1995; rev. New York: Harry N. Abrams, 1999.

Boardman, J., *Greek Art*. 1964; rev. London: Thames and Hudson, 1985.

Boedeker, D. and Raaflaub, K. A. (eds.), *Democracy, Empire, and the Arts in Fifth-Century Athens*. Cambridge, Mass.: Harvard University Press, 1998.

Bowie, A. M., *Aristophanes: Myth, Ritual and Comedy*. Cambridge: Cambridge University Press, 1993.

Boyle, A., *Tragic Seneca: An Essay in the Theatrical Tradition*. London: Routledge, 1997.

— *Roman Tragedy*. London: Routledge, 2006.

Bradley, K., *Slavery and Society at Rome*. Cambridge: Cambridge University Press, 1994.

Bremmer, J. and Roodenburg, H. (eds.), *A Cultural History of Gesture from Antiquity to the Present Day*. Oxford: Oxford University Press, 1991.

Brooke, I., *Costume in Greek Classic Drama*. London: Methuen, 1962.

Bryant, J. H. and Cones, H. N., *The Zenith Trans-Oceanic: The Royalty of Radios*. Atglen, Pa.: Shiffer Publishing, 1995.

Burkert, W., *Greek Religion, Archaic and Classical*, trans. J. Raffan. 1977. Oxford: Oxford University Press, 1985.

Calame, C., *Choruses of Young Women in Ancient Greece*, trans. D Collins and J. Orion. Lanham: Rowman and Littlefield, 1997.

Calasso, R., *The Marriage of Cadmus and Harmony*, trans. T. Parks. London: Vintage, 1994.

Cameron, A., *Circus Factions: Blues and Greens at Rome and Byzantium*. Oxford: Clarendon Press, 1976.

Campbell, D. A. (ed.), *More Essays in Greek History and Literature*. Oxford: Blackwell, 1962.

— (ed.) *Greek Lyric*, Vols. I–III. Loeb Classical Library, Cambridge, Mass.: Harvard University Press, 1982–91.

Carcopino, J., *Daily Life in Ancient Rome*, trans. E. O. Lorimer. 1941; rpt. Harmondsworth: Penguin, 1956.

Cartledge, P., *Aristophanes and his Theatre of the Absurd*. Bristol: Bristol Classical Press, 1990.

— (ed.), *The Cambridge Illustrated History of Ancient Greece*. Cambridge: Cambridge University Press, 1998.

— with Cohen, E. E. and Foxhall, L. (eds.), *Money, Labour and Land: Approaches to the Economies of Ancient Greece*. London, Routledge, 2002.

Chaniotis, A., 'Theatricality Beyond the Theater: Staging Public Life in the Hellenistic World'. *Pallas* 47 (1997), 219–59.

Charitonides, S., Kahil, L. and Ginouves, R., *Les Mosaiques de la Maison du Ménandre à Mytilène*. Bern: Francke Verlag, 1970.

Cohen, E. E., *Athenian Economy and Society*. Princeton: Princeton University Press, 1992.

Coleman, K. M. 'Fatal Charades: Roman Executions Staged as Mythological Enactments'. *Journal of Roman Studies* 80 (1990), 44–73.

Comotti, G., *Music in Greek and Roman Culture*. Baltimore: Johns Hopkins University Press, 1989.

Connor, W. R., 'Tribes, Festivals and Processions; Civic Ceremonial and Political Manipulation in Archaic Greece'. *Journal of Hellenic Studies* 107 (1987), 40–50.

Conte, G. B., *Latin Literature: A History*, trans. J. B. Solodow, rev. D. Fowler and G. W. Most. Baltimore and London: Johns Hopkins University Press, 1994.

Cornford, F. M., *The Origin of Attic Comedy*. London: Edward Arnold, 1914; Cambridge: Cambridge University Press, 1934.

Crook, T., *Radio Drama, Theory and Practice*. London and New York: Routledge, 1999.

Csapo, E. and Slater, W. J., *The Context of Ancient Drama*. Ann Arbor: University of Michigan Press, 1994.

David, E., *Aristophanes and Athenian Society of the Early Fourth Century BC*. Leiden: Brill, 1984.

Dearden, C. W., *The Stage of Aristophanes*. London: Athlone Press, 1976.

— 'Plays for Export', *Phoenix* 53 (1999), 222–48.

Dickie, M. W., 'Mimes, Thaumaturgy, and the Theatre', *Classical Quarterly* 51.2 (2001), 599–603.

Dillon, M. and Garland, L., *Ancient Greece: Social and Historical Documents from Archaic Times to the Death of Socrates*. London and New York: Routledge 1994; rev. ed. 2000.

Dobrov, G. W. (ed.), *The City as Comedy: Society and Representation in Athenian Drama*. Chapel Hill: University of North Carolina Press, 1997.

Dorey, T. A. and Dudley, D. R. (eds.), *Roman Drama*. London: Routledge, 1965.

Dover, K. J., *Aristophanic Comedy*. London: Batsford, 1972.

— *Ancient Greek Literature*. Oxford: Oxford University Press, 1980.

Druskin, M., *Igor Stravinsky: His Personality, Works and Views*, trans. M. Cooper. Cambridge: Cambridge University Press, 1979.

Duckworth, G. E., *The Nature of Roman Comedy: A Study in Popular Entertainment*. Princeton: Princeton University Press, 1952.

Dudley, D. R., *The Civilization of Rome*. New York: Mentor, 1962.

Easterling, P. E., 'Tragedy and Ritual'. *Metis* 3 (1988), 87–109. Rpt. Ruth Scodel (ed.), *Theatre and Society in the Classical World*, pp. 7–24.

— 'The End of an Era? Tragedy in the Early Fourth Century', in A. H. Sommerstein, S. Halliwell, J. Henderson and B. Zimmerman (eds.), *Tragedy, Comedy and the Polis. Papers from the Greek Drama Conference, Nottingham, 18–20 July 1990*. Bari: Levante, 1993, pp. 559–69.

— (ed.), *The Cambridge Companion to Greek Tragedy*. Cambridge: Cambridge University Press, 1997.

— and Hall, E. (eds.), *Greek and Roman Actors: Aspects of an Ancient Profession*. Cambridge: Cambridge University Press, 2002.

Edmunds, L. and Wallace, R. W. (eds.), *Poet, Public, and Performance in Ancient Greece*. Baltimore: Johns Hopkins University Press, 1997.

Edwards, C., 'Unspeakable Professions: Public Performance and Prostitution in Ancient Rome', in J. P. Hallett and M. B. Skinner (eds.), *Roman Sexualities*. Princeton: Princeton University Press, 1997, pp. 66–95.

Else, G. F., *The Origin and Early Form of Greek Tragedy*. Cambridge, Mass.: Harvard University Press, 1965.

— *Plato and Aristotle*. Chapel Hill: University of North Carolina Press, 1986.

Emmanuel, M., *The Ancient Greek Dance*. New York and London: John Lane, 1916.

English, M. C., 'The Diminishing Role of Stage Properties in Aristophanic Comedy', *Helios* 27.2 (2000), 149–62.

Ephraim, D., *Aristophanes and Athenian Society of the Early Fourth Century BC*. Leiden: Brill, 1984.

Erasmo, M., *Roman Tragedy: Theatre to Theatricality*. Austin: University of Texas Press, 2004.

Ferguson, J. and Chisholm, K., *Political and Social Life in the Great Age of Athens*. London: Ward Lock Educational in association with the Open University, 1978.

Finley, M. I., *The Ancient Economy*. London: Chatto and Windus, 1973.

Fischer-Lichte, E., *The Show and the Gaze of Theatre: A European Perspective*. Studies in Theatre History & Culture. Iowa City: University of Iowa Press, 1997.

Fitton, J. W., 'Greek Dance', *Classical Quarterly* 23.2 (Nov. 1973), 254–74.

Flickinger, R. C., *The Greek Theater and its Drama*. 1918; fourth ed., Chicago: Chicago University Press, 1936.

Foley, H. P., *Ritual Irony: Poetry and Sacrifice in Euripides*. Ithaca: Cornell University Press, 1985.

— *Female Acts in Greek Tragedy*. Princeton: Princeton University Press, 2001.

Fowler, W. W., *The Roman Festivals of the Period of the Republic*. London: Macmillan, 1916.

Friedrich, R., 'Everything to Do with Dionysus?: Ritualism, the Dionysiac, and Tragedy', in M. S. Silk (ed.), *Tragedy and the Tragic: Greek Theatre and Beyond*. Oxford: Oxford University Press, 1996, 257–83.

Frost, K. B., *Exits and Entrances in Menander*. Oxford: Clarendon Press, 1988.

Gardiner, C. P., *The Sophoclean Chorus: A Study of Character and Function*. Iowa City: Iowa University Press, 1987.

Garton, C., *Personal Aspects of the Roman Theatre*. Toronto: Hakkert, 1972.

Gebhard, E. R., *The Theater at Isthmia*. Chicago: Chicago University Press, 1973.

Gentili, B., *Theatrical Performances in the Ancient World*. Amsterdam: Guiben, 1979.

Gott, B. (ed.), *History, Tragedy, Theory: Dialogues in Athenian Drama*. Austin: University of Texas Press, 1995.

Gold, B. K. (ed.), *Literary and Artistic Patronage in Ancient Rome*. Austin: University of Texas Press, 1982.

— *Literary Patronage in Greece and Rome*. London and Chapel Hill: University of North Carolina Press, 1987.

Goldberg, S. M., *The Making of Menander's Comedy*. London: Athlone Press; 1980.

— *Understanding Terence*. Princeton: Princeton University Press, 1986.

Goldhill, S., *Reading Greek Tragedy*. Cambridge: Cambridge University Press, 1988.

— 'The Great Dionysia and Civic Ideology', in Winkler and Zeitlin, 1990, pp. 97–130.

— 'Comic Inversion and Inverted Commas: Aristophanes and Parody', in *The Poet's Voice: Essays on Poetics and Greek Literature*. Cambridge: Cambridge University Press, 1991, p. 167.

— and Robin Osborne (eds.), *Performance Culture and Athenian Democracy*. Cambridge: Cambridge University Press, 1999.

Gomme, A. W., 'Aristophanes and Politics', in D. A. Campbell (ed.), *More Essays in Greek History and Literature*. Oxford: Blackwell, 1962, pp. 70–91.

Goodman, M., *The Roman World of 44 BC–AD 180*. London: Routledge, 1997.

Graf, F., *Greek Mythology: An Introduction*, trans. Thomas Marier. Baltimore: Johns Hopkins University Press, 1993.

— *Magic in the Ancient World*, trans. Franklin Philip. Cambridge, Mass.: Harvard University Press, 1997.

Grant, M., *Gladiators*. Harmondsworth: Penguin, 1967.

Green, J. R., '"Drunk Again": A Study in the Iconography of the Comic Theatre'. *American Journal of Archeology* 89 (1985), 465–72.

— 'A Representation of the *Birds* of Aristophanes', in *The J. Paul Getty Museum. Greek Vases* 2. Malibu: J. Paul Getty Trust, 1985, pp. 95–118.

— 'On Seeing and Depicting the Theatre in Classical Athens'. *Greek, Roman and Byzantine Studies* 32 (1991), pp. 15–50.

— *Theatre in Ancient Greek Society*. London: Routledge, 1994.

— and Handley, E., *Images of the Greek Theatre*. 1995; rpt. London: British Museum, 2001.

— Muecke, F., Sowada, K. N., Turner, M. and Bachmann, E., *Ancient Voices, Modern Echoes: Theatre in the Greek World*. Sydney: Nicholson Museum, University of Sydney, 2003.

Green, P., *A Concise History of Ancient Greece*. London: Thames and Hudson, 1974.

— *Alexander to Actium*. Berkeley: University of California Press, 1990.

Griffith, M., 'Contest and Contradiction in Early Greek Poetry', in M. Griffith and D. J. Mastronarde (eds.), *The Cabinet of the Muses*. Atlanta: Scholar's Press, 1990.

Gruen, E. S., *The Hellenistic World and the Coming of Rome*. Berkeley: University of California Press, 1984.

— *Studies in Greek Culture and Roman Policy*. Leiden: Brill, 1990.

— *Culture and National Identity in Republican Rome*. Ithaca: Cornell University Press, 1992.

Gunderson, E., *Staging Masculinity: The Rhetoric of Performance in the Roman World*. Ann Arbor: University of Michigan Press, 2000.

Hall, E., *Inventing the Barbarian: Greek Self-Definition Through Tragedy*. Oxford: Oxford University Press, 1989.

— 'Lawcourt Dramas: The Power of Performance in Greek Forensic Oratory'. *Bulletin of the Institute of Classical Studies* 40 (1999), 35–98.

— *The Theatrical Cast of Athens: Interactions between Ancient Greek Drama and Society*. Oxford: Oxford University Press, 2006.

— and Macintosh, F., *Greek Tragedy and the British Stage 1660–1914*. Oxford: Oxford University Press, 2005.

Halleran, M. R., *Stagecraft in Euripides*. London: Croom Helm; Totowa, NJ: Barnes & Noble, 1985.

Halliwell, S., *Aristotle's Poetics*. Bristol: Bristol Classical Press, 1998.

Hamilton, E., *The Greek Way to Western Civilization*. New York: Norton, 1930.

— *The Roman Way to Western Civilization*. New York: Norton, 1932.

Hanson, J. A., *Roman Theater-Temples*. Princeton: Princeton University Press, 1959.

Hardwick, L., *Translating Worlds, Translating Cultures*. London: Duckworth, 2000.

— Easterling, P. E., Ireland, S., Lowe, N. and Macintosh, F. (eds.), *Theatre Ancient and Modern*. Milton Keynes: Open University, 2000.

Harris, H. A., *Sport in Greece and Rome*. London: Thames & Hudson, 1976.

Harrison, W. M., *Seneca in Performance*. London: Duckworth, 2000.

Hathorn, R. Y., *Crowell's Handbook of Classical Drama*. New York: Crowell; as *The Handbook of Classical Drama*. London: Arthur Barker, 1967.

Heath, M., *Political Comedy in Aristophanes*. Göttingen: Vandenhoeck and Ruprecht, 1987.

Henderson, J. J., 'Women and the Athenian Dramatic Festivals', *Transactions of the American Philological Association* 121 (1991), 133–47.

Herington, C. J., *Poetry into Drama: Early Tragedy and the Greek Poetic Tradition*. Berkeley and Los Angeles: University of California Press, 1985.

Hesk, J. *Deception and Democracy in Classical Athens*. Cambridge: Cambridge University Press, 2000.

Hope, T., *Costumes of the Greeks and Romans*. New York: Dover, 1962; rpt. from *Costume of the Ancients*. London: H. G. Bohn, 1812.

Hourmouziades, N. C., *Production and Imagination in Euripides*. Athens: Greek Society for Humanistic Studies, 1965.

Hubbard, T. K., *The Mask of Comedy: Aristophanes and the Intertextual Parabasis*. Ithaca, NY: Cornell University Press, 1991.

Hughes, A., 'Comic Stages in Magna Graecia: the Evidence of the Vases', *Theatre Research International* 21.2 (1996), 95–107.

Hunningher, B., *The Origin of the Theater*. New York: Hill and Wang, 1961.

Hunter, R. L., *The New Comedy of Greece and Rome*. Cambridge: Cambridge University Press, 1985.

Izenour, G. C., *Roofed Theaters of Classical Antiquity*. New Haven: Yale University Press, 1992.

Janko, R., *Aristotle on Comedy: Towards a Reconstruction of Poetics 11*. London: Duckworth, 1984.

Jones, C. P., 'Dinner Theatre', in W. J. Slater (ed.), *Dining in a Classical Context*. Ann Arbor: University of Michigan Press, 1991.

Jones, J., *On Aristotle and Greek Tragedy*. London: Chatto & Windus, 1962.

Jory, E. J., 'Associations of Actors in Rome', *Hermes* 98 (1970), 224–51.

— 'Literary Evidence for the Beginnings of Imperial Pantomime', *Bulletin of the Institute of Classical Studies* 28 (1981), 147–61.

— 'The Drama of the Dance: Prolegomena to an Iconography of Imperial Pantomime', in W. J. Slater (ed.), *Roman Theater and Society*. Ann Arbor: University of Michigan Press, 1996, pp. 1–28.

Just, R., *Women in Athenian Law and Life*. London: Routledge, 1989.

Kelly, H. A., 'Tragedy and the Performance of Tragedy in Late Roman Antiquity', *Traditio* 35 (1979), 21–44.

Ketterer, R. C., 'Stage Properties in Plautine Comedy I', *Semiotica* 58.3/4 (1986), 193–216; 'Stage Properties in Plautine Comedy II', *Semiotica* 59.1/2 (1986), 93–135; 'Stage Properties in Plautine Comedy III', *Semiotica* 60.1/2 (1986), 29–72.

Kitto, H. D. F., *The Greeks*. Harmondsworth: Penguin, 1951.

Kurke, L., *Coins, Bodies, Games, and Gold: The Politics of Meaning in Archaic Greece*. Princeton: Princeton University Press, 1999.

Lape, S., *Reproducing Athens: Menander's Comedy, Democratic Culture, and the Hellenistic City*. Princeton: Princeton University Press, 2004.

Laver, J., *Costume in Antiquity*. London: Thames and Hudson, 1964.

Lawler, L. B., *The Dance in Ancient Greece*. London: A. and C. Black, 1964.

— *The Dance of the Ancient Greek Theatre*. Iowa: University of Iowa Press, 1964.

Lefkowitz, M. R., *The Lives of the Greek Poets*. London, Duckworth, 1981.

Le Guen, B. (ed.), *De la scène aux gradins: théâtre et représentations dramatiques après Alexandre le grand (Pallas, 47)*. Toulouse: Presses Universitaires du Mirail, 1997.

Lewis, S., *News and Society in the Greek Polis*. Chapel Hill: University of North Carolina Press; London: Duckworth, 1996.

Ley, G., *A Short Introduction to the Ancient Greek Theater*. Chicago: University of Chicago Press, 1991.

— 'The Nameless and the Named: *Techne* and Technology in Ancient Athenian Performance', *Performance Research*, 10.4 (2006), 97–104.

— *The Theatricality of Greek Tragedy: Playing Space and Choros*, Chicago: Chicago University Press, 2007.

Lloyd-Jones, H. (ed.), *The Greek World*. First published as *The Greeks*. London: Watts, 1962; Harmondsworth: Penguin, 1965.

Lonsdale, S. H., *Dance and Ritual Play in Greek Religion*. Baltimore: Johns Hopkins University Press, 1993.

McCarthy, K., *Slaves, Masters, and the Art of Authority in Plautine Comedy*. Princeton: Princeton University Press, 2000.

MacDowell, D. M., *Aristophanes and Athens: an Introduction to the Plays*. Oxford: Oxford University Press, 1995.

McDonald, M., *Euripides in Cinema: The Heart Made Visible*. Philadelphia: Centrum, 1983.

— *Ancient Sun, Modern Light: Greek Drama on the Modern Stage*. New York: Columbia University Press, 1992.

— *Sing Sorrow: Classics, History, and Heroines in Opera*. Westport: Greenwood, 2001.

— *The Living Art of Greek Tragedy*. 2003; rpt. Bloomington and Indianapolis: University of Indiana Press, 2004.

— and J. Michael Walton (eds.), *Amid Our Troubles: Irish Versions of Greek Tragedy*. London: Methuen, 2002.

McGlew, J. F., *Citizens on Stage: Comedy and Political Culture in the Athenian Democracy*. Ann Arbor: University of Michigan Press, 2002.

McLeish, K., *The Theatre of Aristophanes*. London: Thames and Hudson, 1980.

McLuhan, M., *Understanding Media: The Extension of Man*, intr. L. H. Lapham. Cambridge, Mass.: MIT Press, 1994.

Mannix, D., *Those About to Die*. London: Panther, 1960.

Marshall, C. W. and van Willigenburg, S., 'Judging Athenian Dramatic Competitions', *Journal of Hellenic Studies* 124 (2004), 90–107.

Martin, R. P., *The Language of Heroes: Speech and Performance in the Iliad*. Ithaca, NY: Cornell University Press, 1989.

— *Myths of the Ancient Greeks*. New York: New American Library, 2003.

Mastronarde, D. J., 'Actors on High: The *Skêne* Roof, the Crane and the Gods in Attic Drama', *Classical Antiquity*, 9.2 (1990), 247–94.

Mendelsohn, D., *Gender and the City in Euripides' Political Plays*. Oxford: Oxford University Press, 2002.

Mercouris, S., catalogue of the exhibition *A Stage for Dionysos: Theatrical Space and Ancient Drama*. Athens: Kapon, 1997.

Mikalson, J. D., *Honor Thy Gods: Popular Religion in Greek Tragedy.* Chapel Hill: University of North Carolina Press, 1991.

Modleski, T. (ed.), *Studies in Entertainment: Critical Approaches to Mass Culture.* Bloomington and Indianapolis: Indiana University Press, 1986.

Molloy, M. E., *Libanius and the Dancers.* Hildesheim, Zürich and New York: Olms-Weidmann, 1996.

Monaco, J., *How to Read a Film: Movies, Media, Multimedia.* 1977; third ed., New York and Oxford: Oxford University Press, 2000.

Moore, T. J., *The Theater of Plautus: Playing to the Audience.* Austin: University of Texas Press, 1998.

— 'Seats and Social Status in the Plautine Theatre', *Classical Journal* 90.2 (1994), 113–23.

Moretti, J.-C., *Théâtre et société dans la Grèce antique.* Paris: De Boccard, 2001.

Murphy, C. T., 'Popular Comedy in Aristophanes', *American Journal of Philology,* 93.369 (1972), 169–82.

Murray, G., *Aristophanes.* Oxford: Oxford University Press, 1993.

Murray, P. and Wilson, P. (eds.), *Music and the Muses: The Culture of Mousikê in the Classical Athenian City.* Oxford: Oxford University Press, 2004.

Naerebout, F. G., *Attractive Performances – Ancient Greek Dance: Three Preliminary Studies.* Amsterdam: Gieben, 1997.

Neils, J. (ed.), *Worshipping Athena: Panathenaia and Parthenon.* Madison, Wis.: University of Wisconsin Press, 1996.

Nicoll, A., *Masks, Mimes and Miracles: Studies in the Popular Theatre.* London: Harrap, 1931.

O'Connor, J. B., *Chapters in the History of Actors and Acting in Ancient Greece.* Chicago: University of Chicago Press, 1908.

Omitomoju, R., *Rape and the Politics of Consent in Classical Athens.* Cambridge: Cambridge University Press, 2002.

Osborne, R. and Hornblower, S. (eds.), *Ritual, Finance, Politics: Athenian Democratic Accounts Presented to David Lewis.* Oxford: Clarendon Press, 1994.

Parke, H. W., *Festivals of the Athenians.* London: Thames and Hudson, 1977.

Pasolini, P. P., *Pasolini on Pasolini: Interviews with Oswald Stack.* Bloomington and London: Indiana University Press, 1969.

— *Oedipus Rex, A Film by Pier Paolo Pasolini,* trans. J. Mathews. New York: Simon and Schuster; London: Lorrimer, 1971.

Patterson, C. B., *The Family in Greek History.* Cambridge, Mass.: Harvard University Press, 1998.

Phillips, D. and Pritchard, D., *Sport and Festival in the Ancient Greek World.* Swansea: Classical Press of Wales, 2003.

Pickard-Cambridge, A. W., *The Theatre of Dionysus in Athens.* Oxford: Clarendon Press, 1946.

— *Dithyramb, Tragedy and Comedy.* 1927; second ed. T. B. L. Webster (ed.), Oxford: Clarendon Press, 1970.

— *The Dramatic Festivals of Athens.* Oxford: Clarendon Press, 1953; second ed., J. Gould and D. M. Lewis (eds.), 1968.

Podlecki, A. 'Could Women Attend the Theatre in Ancient Athens? A Collection of Testimonia', *Ancient World* 21 (1990), 27–43.

Poe, J. P., 'Multiplicity, Discontinuity, and Visual Meaning in Aristophanic Comedy', *Rheinische Museum* 14.3 (2000), 256–95.

Pollitt, J. J., *Art and Experience in Classical Greece*. Cambridge: Cambridge University Press, 1972.

Rattigan, D., *Theatre of Sound: Radio and the Dramatic Imagination*. Dublin: Carysfort Press, 2002.

Rehm, R., *Greek Tragic Theatre*. London: Routledge, 1992.

— *The Play of Space: Spatial Transformation in Greek Tragedy*. Princeton: Princeton University Press, 2002.

— *Radical Theatre: Greek Tragedy and the Modern World*. London: Duckworth, 2003.

Reinhardt, K., *Aischylos als Regisseur und Theologe*. Berne: A. Francke, 1949.

Ridgeway, W., *The Dramas and Dramatic Dances of Non-European Races*. Cambridge: Cambridge University Press, 1915.

Rosand, E., *Opera in Seventeenth Century Venice: The Creation of a Genre*. Berkeley and Los Angeles: University of California Press, 1991.

Rossetto, P. and Sartorio, G., *Teatri Grecie e Romani*. Rome: Edizioni SEAT, 1996.

Russell, D. A. and Winterbottom, M., *Ancient Literary Criticism: The Principal Texts in New Translations*. Oxford: Oxford University Press, 1972.

Russo, C. F., *Aristophanes: An Author for the Stage*, trans. K. Wren. London: Routledge, 1994.

Sandbach, F. H., *The Comic Theatre of Greece and Rome*. London: Chatto and Windus, 1977.

Scafuro, A. C., *The Forensic Stage: Settling Disputes in Greco-Roman New Comedy*. Cambridge: Cambridge University Press, 1997.

Scheidel, W. and von Reden, S. (eds.), *The Ancient Economy*. Edinburgh: Edinburgh University Press, 2002.

Schwartz, B. D., *Pasolini Requiem*. New York: Pantheon, 1992.

Scodel, R. (ed.), *Theater and Society in the Ancient World*. Ann Arbor: University of Michigan Press, 1993.

Scolnicov, H. and Holland, P. (eds.), *The Play out of Context*. Cambridge: Cambridge University Press, 1989.

Scullard, H. H., *Festivals and Ceremonies of the Roman Republic*. Ithaca: Cornell University Press, 1981.

Scullion, S., '"Nothing to Do with Dionysus": Tragedy Misconceived as Ritual', *Classical Quarterly* 52 (2002), 102–37.

Seaford, R., *Reciprocity and Ritual: Homer and Tragedy in the Developing City State*. Oxford: Oxford University Press, 1994.

Seale, D., *Vision and Stagecraft in Sophocles*. London: Croom Helm, 1982.

Segal, E. (ed.), *Oxford Readings in Menander, Plautus, and Terence*. Oxford: Oxford University Press, 2001.

Shapiro, H. A., *Myth into Art*. London and New York: Routledge, 1994.

Shelton, J.-A., *As the Romans Did: A Source Book in Roman Social History*. Oxford: Oxford University Press, 1988.

Sifakis, G. M., *Studies in the History of Hellenistic Drama*. London: Athlone Press, 1967.

— *Parabasis and Animal Choruses*. London: Methuen, 1971.

Silk, M. S. (ed.), *Tragedy and the Tragic: Greek Theatre and Beyond*. Oxford: Oxford University Press, 1996.

— *Aristophanes and the Definition of Comedy*. Oxford: Oxford University Press, 2000.

Simon, E., *The Ancient Theatre*, trans. C. E. Vafopoulou-Richardson. London: Methuen, 1982.

Slater, N. W., *Plautus in Performance*. 1985; second ed., Amsterdam: Harwood, 2000.

— *Spectator Politics: Metatheatre and Performance in Aristophanes*. Philadelphia: University of Pennsylvania Press, 2002.

Slater, W. J. (ed.), *Roman Theater and Society*. E. Togo Salmon, Papers I. Ann Arbor: University of Michigan Press, 1996.

Sommerstein, A. H., *Tragedy and the Polis*. Bari: Levante, 1993.

—, Halliwell, S., Henderson, J. and Zimmermann, B. (eds.), *Tragedy, Comedy and the Polis. Papers from the Greek Drama Conference, Nottingham, 18–20 July 1990*. Bari: Levante, 1993.

Stam, R. and T. Miller (eds.), *Film and Theory: An Anthology*. Oxford: Blackwell, 2000.

Stehle, E., *Performance and Gender in Ancient Greece: Nondramatic Poetry in its Setting*. Princeton: Princeton University Press, 1997.

Stone, L. M., *Costume in Aristophanic Poetry*. New York: Ayer, 1981.

Storey, I. C. and Allan, A., *A Guide to Ancient Greek Drama*. Oxford: Blackwell, 2005.

Sutton, D. F., *Seneca on the Stage*. Leiden: Brill, 1986.

Taaffe, L. K., *Aristophanes and Women*. London: Routledge, 1993.

Taplin, O., *The Stagecraft of Aeschylus*. Oxford: Clarendon Press, 1977.

— *Greek Tragedy in Action*. London: Methuen, 1978.

— *Comic Angels and Other Approaches to Greek Drama through Vase-Painting*. Oxford: Clarendon Press, 1993.

Taylor, L. R., 'The Opportunities for Dramatic Performances in the Time of Plautus and Terence', *Transactions of the American Philological Association* 68 (1937), 284–304.

Tierno, M., *Aristotle's 'Poetics' for Screenwriters: Storytelling Secrets from the Greatest Mind in Western Civilization*. New York: Hyperion, 2002.

Townsend, R. F., 'The Fourth-Century Skene of the Theater of Dionysos at Athens', *Hesperia* 55 (1986), 421–38.

Treggiari, S., *Roman Social History*. London: Routledge, 2002.

Trendall, A. D., *Red Figure Vases of South Italy and Sicily*. London: Thames and Hudson, 1989.

— and Webster, T. B. L., *Illustrations of Greek Drama*. London: Phaidon, 1971.

Turner, U., *From Ritual to Theatre: The Human Seriousness of Play*. New York: Performing Arts Journal Publications, 1990.

Van Steen, G. A. H., 'Aspects of "Public Performance" in Aristophanes' *Acharnians*', *L'Antiquité Classique* 63 (1994), 211–24.

— *Venom in Verse: Aristophanes in Modern Greece*. Princeton: Princeton University Press, 2000.

Vernant, J.-P. and Vidal-Naquet, P., *Tragedy and Myth in Ancient Greece*. Brighton: Harvester Press, 1981.

Veyne, P., *Bread and Circuses*, trans. B. Pearce, abridged by O. Murray. Harmondsworth: Penguin, 1990.

Vickers, M., *Pericles on Stage: Political Comedy in Aristophanes' Early Plays*. Austin: University of Texas Press, 1997.

Vince, R. W., *Ancient and Medieval Theatre*. Westport: Greenwood Press, 1984.

Vitruvius, *Ten Books of Architecture*, trans. I. Rowland and T. Howe. Cambridge: Cambridge University Press, 1999.

Walcot, P., *Greek Drama in its Theatrical and Social Context*. Cardiff: University of Wales Press, 1976.

Wallace-Hadrill, A. (ed.), *Patronage in Ancient Society*. London: Routledge, 1989.

Walsh, S., *Stravinsky: Oedipus Rex* (Cambridge Music Handbooks). Cambridge: Cambridge University Press, 1993.

Walton, J. M., *Greek Theatre Practice*. 1980; rpt. London: Methuen, 1991.

— *The Greek Sense of Theatre: Tragedy Reviewed*. 1984; rev. ed. Amsterdam: Harwood, 1996.

— *Living Greek Theatre: A Handbook of Classical Performance and Modern Production*. Westport: Greenwood, 1987.

— *Found in Translation: Greek Drama in English*. Cambridge: Cambridge University Press, 2006.

— and Arnott, P. D., *Menander and the Making of Comedy*. Westport: Praeger, 1996.

Wardman, A., *Rome's Debt to Greece*. London: Paul Elek, 1976.

Warmington, E. H. (ed.), *Remains of Old Latin*, Vols. I–IV. Loeb Classical Library. Cambridge, Mass.: Harvard University Press, 1935.

Webster, T. B. L., *Athenian Culture and Society*. London: Batsford, 1973.

West, M. L., *Ancient Greek Music*. Oxford: Clarendon, 1992.

White, E. W., *Stravinsky: The Composer and his Work*. 1966; second ed., Berkeley: University of California Press, 1984.

Wiedemann, T., *Emperors and Gladiators*. London: Routledge, 1992.

Wiles, D., *The Masks of Menander: Sign and Meaning in Greek and Roman Performance*. Cambridge: Cambridge University Press, 1991.

— *Greek Theatre Performance: An Introduction*. Cambridge: Cambridge University Press, 2000.

— *Tragedy in Athens: Performance Space and Theatrical Writing*. Cambridge: Cambridge University Press, 1997.

— *Mask and Performance in Greek Tragedy: From Ancient Festival to Modern Experimentation*. Cambridge: Cambridge University Press, 2007.

Wilson, P., *The Athenian Institution of the Khoregia: The Chorus, the City and the Stage*. Cambridge, Cambridge University Press, 2000.

Winkler, J. and Zeitlin, F. (eds.), *Nothing To Do With Dionysos?: Athenian Drama in its Social Context*. Princeton: Princeton University Press, 1990.

Woodford, S., *Images of Myths in Classical Antiquity*. Cambridge: Cambridge University Press, 2003.

Wrigley, A., 'Stages of Imagination: Broadcasting Greek Plays 1920s–1970s'. E-seminar 2006 paper/discussion. Milton Keynes: The Open University, at http://www2open.ac.uk/ClassicalStudies/GreekPlays/e_archive/about.htm (forthcoming, 2007).

Zagagi, N., *The Comedy of Menander: Convention, Variation and Originality*. London: Duckworth, 1994.

INDEX

Cambridge Companions to...

AUTHORS

Shakespeare on Film *edited by Russell Jackson* (second edition)

Shakespearean Comedy *edited by Alexander Leggatt*

Shakespeare on Stage *edited by Stanley Wells and Sarah Stanton*

Shakespeare's History Plays *edited by Michael Hattaway*

Shakespearean Tragedy *edited by Claire McEachern*

Shakespeare's Poetry *edited by Patrick Cheney*

Shakespeare and Popular Culture *edited by Robert Shaughnessy*

George Bernard Shaw *edited by Christopher Innes*

Shelley *edited by Timothy Morton*

Mary Shelley *edited by Esther Schor*

Sam Shepard *edited by Matthew C. Roudané*

Spenser *edited by Andrew Hadfield*

Wallace Stevens *edited by John N. Serio*

Tom Stoppard *edited by Katherine E. Kelly*

Harriet Beecher Stowe *edited by Cindy Weinstein*

Jonathan Swift *edited by Christopher Fox*

Henry David Thoreau *edited by Joel Myerson*

Tolstoy *edited by Donna Tussing Orwin*

Mark Twain *edited by Forrest G. Robinson*

Virgil *edited by Charles Martindale*

Edith Wharton *edited by Millicent Bell*

Walt Whitman *edited by Ezra Greenspan*

Oscar Wilde *edited by Peter Raby*

Tennessee Williams *edited by Matthew C. Roudané*

Mary Wollstonecraft *edited by Claudia L. Johnson*

Virginia Woolf *edited by Sue Roe and Susan Sellers*

Wordsworth *edited by Stephen Gill*

W. B. Yeats *edited by Marjorie Howes and John Kelly*

Zola *edited by Brian Nelson*

TOPICS

The Actress *edited by Maggie B. Gale and John Stokes*

The African American Novel *edited by Maryemma Graham*

The African American Slave Narrative *edited by Audrey A. Fisch*

American Modernism *edited by Walter Kalaidjian*

American Realism and Naturalism *edited by Donald Pizer*

American Women Playwrights *edited by Brenda Murphy*

Australian Literature *edited by Elizabeth Webby*

British Romanticism *edited by Stuart Curran*

British Theatre, 1730–1830, *edited by Jane Moody and Daniel O'Quinn*

Canadian Literature *edited by Eva-Marie Kröller*

The Classic Russian Novel *edited by Malcolm V. Jones and Robin Feuer Miller*

Contemporary Irish Poetry *edited by Matthew Campbell*

Crime Fiction *edited by Martin Priestman*

The Eighteenth-Century Novel *edited by John Richetti*

Eighteenth-Century Poetry *edited by John Sitter*

English Literature, 1500–1600 *edited by Arthur F. Kinney*

English Literature, 1650–1740 *edited by Steven N. Zwicker*

English Literature, 1740–1830 *edited by Thomas Keymer and Jon Mee*

English Poetry, Donne to Marvell *edited by Thomas N. Corns*

English Renaissance Drama, second edition *edited by A. R. Braunmuller and Michael Hattaway*

English Restoration Theatre *edited by Deborah C. Payne Fisk*

Feminist Literary Theory *edited by Ellen Rooney*

Fiction in the Romantic Period *edited by Richard Maxwell and Katie Trumpener*

The Fin de Siècle *edited by Gail Marshall*

The French Novel: from 1800 to the Present *edited by Timothy Unwin*

Gothic Fiction *edited by Jerrold E. Hogle*

Greek and Roman Theatre *edited by Marianne McDonald and J. Michael Walton*

Greek Tragedy *edited by P. E. Easterling*

The Harlem Renaissance *edited by George Hutchinson*